Clashing Views in

Mass Media and Society

ELEVENTH EDITION

Selected, Edited, and with Introductions by

Alison Alexander
University of Georgia

and

Jarice Hanson
University of Massachusetts at Amherst

Mc
Graw
Hill

Connect
Learn
Succeed™

Connect
Learn
Succeed™

TAKING SIDES: MASS MEDIA AND SOCIETY, ELEVENTH EDITION

Published by McGraw-Hill, a business unit of The McGraw-Hill Companies, Inc., 1221 Avenue of the Americas, New York, NY 10020. Copyright © 2011 by The McGraw-Hill Companies, Inc. All rights reserved. Previous edition(s) 2009, 2007, 2005. No part of this publication may be reproduced or distributed in any form or by any means, or stored in a database or retrieval system, without the prior written consent of The McGraw-Hill Companies, Inc., including, but not limited to, in any network or other electronic storage or transmission, or broadcast for distance learning.

Some ancillaries, including electronic and print components, may not be available to customers outside the United States.

Taking Sides® is a registered trademark of the McGraw-Hill Companies, Inc.
Taking Sides is published by the **Contemporary Learning Series** group within the McGraw-Hill Higher Education division.

1 2 3 4 5 6 7 8 9 0 DOC/DOC 1 0 9 8 7 6 5 4 3 2 1 0

MHID: 0-07-804998-9
ISBN: 978-0-07-804998-9
ISSN: 94-31766

Managing Editor: *Larry Loeppke*
Director, Specialized Production: *Faye Schilling*
Senior Developmental Editor: *Jade Benedict*
Editorial Coordinator: *Mary Foust*
Editorial Assistant: *Cindy Hedley*
Production Service Assistant: *Rita Hingtgen*
Permissions Coordinator: *Lenny J. Behnke*
Senior Marketing Manager: *Julie Keck*
Senior Marketing Communications Specialist: *Mary Klein*
Marketing Coordinator: *Alice Link*
Senior Project Manager: *Jane Mohr*
Design Coordinator: *Brenda Rolwes*
Cover Graphics: *Rick D. Noel*

Compositor: MPS Limited, A Macmillan Company
Cover Image: © Jade Benedict

Library of Congress Cataloging-in-Publication Data

Main entry under title:
Taking sides: clashing views in mass media and society/selected, edited, and with introductions by Alison Alexander and Jarice Hanson.—11th ed.

Includes bibliographical references.
1. Mass media. 2. Information services. I. Alexander, Alison, *comp*. II. Hanson, Jarice, *comp*.
302.23

Editors/Academic Advisory Board

Members of the Academic Advisory Board are instrumental in the final selection of articles for each edition of TAKING SIDES. Their review of articles for content, level, and appropriateness provides critical direction to the editors and staff. We think that you will find their careful consideration well reflected in this volume.

TAKING SIDES: Clashing Views in MASS MEDIA AND SOCIETY
Eleventh Edition

EDITORS

Alison Alexander
University of Georgia
and
Jarice Hanson
University of Massachusetts at Amherst

ACADEMIC ADVISORY BOARD MEMBERS

Clifford Kobland
SUNY-Oswego

Gaylon E. Murray
Grambling State University

Michael Murray
Western Illinois University

R. Babatunde Oyinade
Fayetteville State University

Neil Goldstein
Montgomery County Community College

Ronald Thomas
Embry Riddle Aeronautical University-Daytona Beach

Douglas J. Glick
Binghamton University

James Harper
Lehigh University

Ray Merlock
University of South Carolina Upstate

Tom Proietti
Monroe Community College

Doug Spero
Meredith College

Kelley Crowley
West Virginia University-Morgantown

Mary Cassata
SUNY-Buffalo

Jeffrey McCall
DePauw University

Steven Miura
University of Hawaii-Hilo

Gerry McNulty
Marist College

Lisa Turowski
Towson University

Allan Stegeman
Drexel University

Machelle Palmer
Westwood College

Randye Spina
Manhattanville College

Jonathan Slater
SUNY College-Plattsburgh

Christopher Leigh
University of Charleston

Mark Bazil
Savannah College of Art & Design

Richard Boyd
Rogers State University

James Danowski
University of Illinois-Chicago

Gregory J. Gapsis
Indiana University-Southeast

Editors/Academic Advisory Board continued

Preface

Communication is one of the most popular college majors in the country, which perhaps reflects a belief in the importance of media, as well as students' desires to work in one of the communications industries. Increasingly, people have the capacity to become producers of mediated content that can be shared online, through blogs, Web sites, social networking sites, and podcasts. Never before have we had the capacity to consume mass media, as well as produce our own forms of media and have a platform for low-cost or free distribution over the Internet. This book, which contains 36 selections presented in a pro and con format, addresses 18 controversial issues in media and society. The purpose of the volume, and indeed of any course that deals with the social impact of media, is to create a literate consumer of media—someone who can walk the fine line between a naïve acceptance of all media and a cynical disregard for any positive benefits that they may offer.

When we began this series, we concentrated on mass media that produced content for mass distribution to a large, anonymous audience. Today, we live in a world in which mass media compete with user-generated content and media that are directed to niche audiences. Today's media reflect the evolution of industries that have spread their reach to multiple types of media and, indeed, to more nations of the world than ever before. In the United States we have seen the impact of entertainment media on many forms of public discourse—news, politics, education, and more. We have also seen communication technologies rapidly enter the home in a number of ways: through the Internet and personal devices such as iPods, PDAs, and cell phones. These many forms of media extend our capacities to communicate and to consume media content, as well as to become producers of media content.

The study of media and society is very much a part of the way in which we live our lives by blending technologies and services, public and private media uses, and public and private behaviors. In the near future, many of the technologies we use today may be subsumed by yet newer technologies, or greater use of those that we already use. Film, television, music, radio and print all come to us today over the Internet, and we expect that cell phones may soon replace laptop computers as the "all-in-one" portable technology.

Since many of the issues in this volume are often in the news (or even constitute the news), you may already have opinions about them. We encourage you to read the selections and discuss the issues with an open mind. Even if you do not initially agree with a position or do not even understand how it is possible to make an opposing argument, give it a try. Remember, these problems often are not restricted to only two views; there may be many, and we encourage you to discuss these topics as broadly as possible. We believe that thinking seriously about media is an important goal.

Plan of the Book

This book is primarily designed for students in an introductory course in mass communication (sometimes called introduction to mass media, or introduction to mass media and society). We know that various instructors have found this book useful for courses in writing about communication topics, ethics, and public speaking. The issues are such that they can be easily incorporated into any media course regardless of how it is organized—thematically, chronologically, or by media form. The 36 selections have been taken from a variety of sources and were chosen because of their usefulness in defending a position and for their accessibility to students.

Each issue in this volume has an *introduction,* which sets the stage for the debate as it is argued in the YES and NO selections. Each issue concludes with a *postscript* that makes some final observations about the selections and points the way to other questions related to the issue. We also offer suggestions for further reading on the issue. The introductions and the postscripts do not preempt the reader's task: to achieve a critical and informed view of the issues at stake. In reading an issue and forming your own opinion, you should not feel confined to adopt one or the other of the positions presented. Some readers may see important points on both sides of an issue and may construct for themselves a new and creative approach. Such an approach might incorporate the best of both sides, or it might provide an entirely new vantage point for understanding. Relevant Internet site addresses (URLs) that may prove useful as starting points for further research are provided on the *Internet References* page that accompanies each unit opener. At the back of the book is a listing of all of the *contributors* to this volume, which will give you additional information on the communication scholars, practitioners, policymakers, and media critics whose views are debated here.

Changes to This Edition

The eleventh edition represents a considerable revision, and the topics are perhaps more controversial than in past editions. This may be a reflection of the world in which we live, or perhaps it is the result of a greater awareness of media literacy and the ability of consumers of media now to become producers of content. We have expanded Unit 1, "Media and Social Issues," to include four issues, three of which are new to this edition. Unit 2, "A Question of Content," addresses three key pervasive issues about the impact of content in media, with one new issue and two popular issues from Edition 10. Unit 3, "News and Politics," addresses three issues (two of which are new to this edition) dealing with contemporary problems associated with politics and journalism. We have renamed Unit 4 to read "Law and Policy" to reflect issues that we formerly would have subsumed under the heading "Regulation" to better reflect today's discourse about legal and policy issues. Unit 5, "Media Businesses," now incorporates the viability of legacy industries adapting to online models, but also addresses two of the most rapidly changing industries, music and newspapers. We conclude with Unit 6, "Life in the Digital Age," with one new issue, and an update for Issue 18.

A Word to the Instructor

An Instructor's Resource Guide with Test Questions (multiple-choice and essay) is available through the publisher for the instructor using *Taking Sides* in the classroom. A general guidebook, *Using Taking Sides in the Classroom,* which discusses methods and techniques for integrating the pro-con approach to a classroom setting, is also available. An online version of *Using Taking Sides in the Classroom* and a correspondence service for *Taking Sides* adopters can be found at http://www.mhcls.com/takingsides.

Acknowledgments

We wish to acknowledge the encouragement, support, and detail given to this project. We are particularly grateful to Jade Benedict, who has thoughtfully, carefully, and painstakingly worked with us to produce the best edition possible. We would also like to extend our appreciation to the many professors who reviewed our previous edition, and we are grateful for the advice they have provided in the preparation of this edition.

We would also like to thank Alina Hogea at Temple University for valuable assistance. Jarice would like to thank the Verizon Corporation of Pennsylvania for funding the Endowed Chair at Temple University, where she is allowed to conduct research on topics that enhance our understanding of the impact of telecommunications, especially President Gale Given and Jim Reed, Director of Public Affairs. Jim has always been a great supporter of any project, and his pride in my accomplishments warms my heart. Finally, we would like to thank our families and friends (David, James, Katie, Jaime, and Torie, and Frank, Dewey and Xena) for their patience and understanding during the period in which we prepared this book. Being cats, Dewey and Xena particularly appreciated the number of pages that were generated for this book because they provided a comfortable place for a nap.

Alison Alexander
University of Georgia

Jarice Hanson
University of Massachusetts at Amherst

Contents in Brief

Contents

UNIT 1   MEDIA AND SOCIAL ISSUES   1

YES: **Herbert I. Schiller,** from *The Mind Managers* (Beacon Press, 1973)   *4*

NO: **James W. Carey,** from *Communication as Culture: Essays on Media and Society* (Unwin Hyman, 1989)   *13*

Critical scholar of modern mass media Professor Schiller argues that mass media institutions are key elements of the modern capitalistic world order. Media, he argues, produce economic profits and the ideology necessary to sustain a world system of exploitative divisions of social and financial resources. It is the job of the citizenry to understand the myths that act to sustain this existing state of power relationships. James Carey introduces the seminal ideas of ritual and transmission models of communication in this piece. Communication is not simply a process of sending messages as the transmission model would suggest. Communication is a symbolic process which is inherently linked to culture and our lives.

YES: **Rob Boston,** from "Witch Hunt: Why the Religious Right Is Crusading to Exorcise Harry Potter Books from Public Schools and Libraries," *Church & State* (March 1, 2002)   *29*

NO: **Lana A. Whited, with M. Katherine Grimes,** from *The Ivory Tower and Harry Potter: Perspectives on a Literary Phenomenon* (University of Missouri Press, 2002)   *36*

Though the popular *Harry Potter* series has received worldwide attention, the content remains questionable for some people. Writer Rob Boston examines the position of some members of the Christian Right, and identifies how and why some people think *Harry Potter* books endorse witchcraft and a belief in the occult. The controversy shows that children's books are often the subject of book banning and censorship, for a variety of reasons. Lana Whited and M. Katherine Grimes are English teachers who report that despite religious-based objections to *Harry Potter* books and films that are part of the fantasy genre in literature, children can be exposed to a number of situations and dilemmas that enhance children's moral reasoning abilities. Using a scheme developed by Professor Lawrence Kohlberg, they examine a number of situations in the *Harry Potter* series that they claim can help guide children's moral development.

Craig Anderson is an expert on the effect of violence in television and film. Based on extensive research, he holds the position that video games prompt young people toward even more aggression and violence than do other media content. Henry Jenkins tackles a broad array of misconceptions about the place and impact of video games on society. He argues that the primary audience is not children, that violence is not increasing in society, and that concerns about isolation, desensitization, and violence are overblown.

Issue 6. Do Copyright Laws Protect Ownership of Intellectual Property? 105

In this article, Siva Vaidhyanathan discusses how applications of copyright to music, film, publishing, and software companies all result in a complex system of trying to protect original ownership of intellectual property. The author gives several examples, including Google's efforts to digitize entire libraries, but reminds us that copyright also gives owners the right to say no. Independent researcher Stephanie Ardito examines how social networking sites have created problems for protecting copyright, because laws and enforcement of copyright law are so difficult. She believes big media companies and social networking sites will ultimately give up trying to enforce copyright, because it is too expensive and time consuming.

Issue 7. Is Advertising Good for Society? 129

John Calfee, a former U.S. Trade Commission economist, takes the position that advertising is very useful to people and that the information that advertising imparts helps consumers make better decisions. He maintains that the benefits of advertising far outweigh the negative criticisms. Dinyar Godrej makes the claim that advertising doesn't really tell us anything new about products, but instead, it acts upon our emotions to create anxiety if we don't buy products. The result, then, is a culture in which we consume more than we need to, and still feel bad about ourselves. This type of consumer culture then permeates our lifestyles.

UNIT 3 NEWS AND POLITICS 149

Issue 8. Can Media Regain Public Trust? 150

Michael Schudson argues that although news is essential for democracy, the behavior of journalists makes them unpopular. Journalists' conflict orientation, obsession with facts and events, and "in-your-face" interviewing are what make journalism effective and essential. And it is those behaviors that should restore faith in journalism. John Hockenberry is disillusioned about the ability of credible journalism to survive in the current corporate environment. Based on his experience at *Dateline NBC*, he explores the timidity of those in charge of newsrooms. Fear of corporate owners, of audience response, and of technology cripples authentic journalism.

Issue 9.   Does Fake News Mislead the Public?   173

This study examined political coverage of the first presidential debate and the political convention on *The Daily Show* and on network nightly newscasts. The study found the network coverage to be more hype than substance, and *The Daily Show* to be more humor than substance. The amount of substantive information between the two newscasts was about the same for both the story and for the entire half-hour program. Barry Hollander examined learning from comedy and late-night programs. National survey data were used to examine whether exposure to comedy and late-night programs actually inform viewers, focusing on recall and recognition. Some support is found for the prediction that the consumption of such programs is more associated with recognition of information than with actual recall.

Issue 10.   Will Evolving Forms of Journalism Be an Improvement?   204

Mark Deuze, Axel Bruns, and Christoph Neuberger conducted case studies of news organizations that developed extensive plans to incorporate participatory news practices. The case studies reveal the rewards and difficulties of these decisions. David Simon testified in May of 2009 to a Senate Committee examining the future of journalism. His conclusion was that high-end journalism was dying in America and could not be saved by the Internet and/or citizen journalists.

UNIT 4 LAW AND POLICY   227

Citizens' "right to know" in a democratic society is a foundation of freedom of the press. Jeffrey J. Maciejewski and David T. Ozar examine multiple meanings of the concept of right to know, asking what this implies about conduct at the personal and institutional level. Maciejewski and Ozar then situate the concept in natural law and applies that understanding to journalistic decisions. In contrast, the *State of the First Amendment: 2004* report reveals lackluster support for the First Amendment in general and its application to controversial cases in particular. Few know the freedoms guaranteed or care passionately about them—almost one-third feel the freedom granted under the First Amendment "goes too far." Moreover, Americans seem less supportive of freedom of the press than of any other freedoms guaranteed in our Bill of Rights.

In this essay, scholar Henry Giroux questions how and why our culture has become so mean spirited. By addressing media content in news and popular fare, he analyzes how the politics of a "pedagogy of hate" has become an exercise in power that ultimately has created a "culture of cruelty." As part of this imposed philosophy, citizens have begun to question and undermine our government's responsibility to protect their interests. Georgie Ann Weatherby and Brian Scoggins examine the content of the Web pages of four extremist groups on the Internet and discuss the persuasive techniques each uses. They find that the sites draw from traditional tactics that "soft-pedal" positions that emphasize recruiting, while downplaying the messages of hate.

Rhoda Rabkin strongly defends the industry system of self-censorship, and feels that any government intervention toward monitoring media content is doomed to failure. She examines a number of media forms and claims that any time there has been a question about content, the industry generally re-packages the products for different audiences and age groups. She advocates for voluntary codes of conduct over federal censorship of entertainment. Shortly after radio shock-jock Don Imus lost his job for comments considered to be inappropriate for the air, the House of Representatives held a hearing at which different individuals from industry, academe, and social interest groups commented on inappropriate content. Karen Dill commented on the psychological processes of media images and the way they influence girls and women. Lisa Fager Bediako, president of Industry Ears, a group dedicated to examining the images of persons of color, testified that degrading images of violence, sexism, racism, and hate are rampant in contemporary media.

UNIT 5   MEDIA BUSINESS   293

Chuck Salter looks at the way musical artists have had to become business people to control the branding of their "products." He examines the business model established by John Legend, and describes how today's musical artists must retain control of their brand to survive in the music industry today. Eric Boehlert describes why radio has become so bad, with regard to diversity of music, and how little opportunity there is for new artists to get their music on the air. He describes what has happened to the traditional music industry/radio alliance, and how independent record promoters have influenced both businesses.

Clay Shirkey argues that the old economies of newspapers are destroyed in the digital age. This is a revolution similar to that which occurred with the invention of the printing press. No one knows what the future will hold, but we can only hope that journalism is not lost with the demise of newspapers. All news media are facing challenges in these difficult economic times. Paul Farhi, a *Washington Post* staff writer, argues that newspapers have unique competitive advantages that should assure that the worst case won't happen.

UNIT 6   LIFE IN THE DIGITAL AGE   347

Linda Jackson et al. conducted a 16-month survey of Internet use by youth age 10 to 18 in low-income homes. They found that youth who used the Internet more had higher scores on standardized tests of reading achievement and higher GPAs. This work supports the optimism surrounding the Internet as a tool to level the educational playing field. Mark Bauerlein finds the hopes for better-educated youth in the digital age to be an empty promise. Youth spend much of their leisure time in front of computer and television screens, but the information age has failed to produce a well-informed, thoughtful public. Instead we have a nation of know-nothings who don't read, follow politics, or vote—and who can't compete internationally.

Correlation Guide

The *Taking Sides* series presents current issues in a debate-style format designed to stimulate student interest and develop critical thinking skills. Each issue is thoughtfully framed with an issue summary, an issue introduction, and a postscript. The pro and con essays—selected for their liveliness and substance—represent the arguments of leading scholars and commentators in their fields.

Taking Sides: Clashing Views in Mass Media and Society, 11/e is an easy-to-use reader that presents issues on important topics such as *the future of newspapers, video violence,* and *social media and bullying.* For more information on *Taking Sides* and other *McGraw-Hill Contemporary Learning Series* titles, visit www.mhhe.com/cls.

This convenient guide matches the issues in **Taking Sides: Mass Media and Society, 11/e** with the corresponding chapters in two of our best-selling McGraw-Hill Mass Media textbooks by Dominick and Baran.

Taking Sides: Mass Media and Society, 11/e	The Dynamics of Mass Communication: Media in Transition, 11/e by Dominick	Introduction to Mass Communication: Media Literacy and Culture, 6/e by Baran
Issue 1: Are American Values Shaped by the Mass Media?	**Chapter 3:** Historical and Cultural Context	**Chapter 1:** Mass Communication, Culture, and Media Literacy **Chapter 13:** Theories and Effects of Mass Communication
Issue 2: Are the *Harry Potter* Books Harmful for Children?	**Chapter 6:** Books	**Chapter 3:** Books **Chapter 13:** Theories and Effects of Mass Communication
Issue 3: Does Media Represent Realistic Images of Arabs?	**Chapter 3:** Historical and Cultural Context **Chapter 17:** Ethics and Other Informal Controls	**Chapter 1:** Mass Communication, Culture, and Media Literacy
Issue 4: Does Media Cause Individuals to Develop Negative Body Images?	**Chapter 15:** Advertising **Chapter 19:** Social Effects of Mass Communication	**Chapter 13:** Theories and Effects of Mass Communication
Issue 5: Do Video Games Encourage Violent Behavior?	**Chapter 12:** The Internet and the World Wide Web	**Chapter 9:** Video Games
Issue 6: Do Copyright Laws Protect Ownership of Intellectual Property?	**Chapter 16:** Formal Controls: Laws, Rules, Regulations	**Chapter 10:** The Internet and the World Wide Web **Chapter 14:** Media Freedom, Regulation, and Ethics
Issue 7: Is Advertising Good for Society?	**Chapter 15:** Advertising	**Chapter 12:** Advertising

(Continued)

Taking Sides: Mass Media and Society, 11/e	The Dynamics of Mass Communication: Media in Transition, 11/e by Dominick	Introduction to Mass Communication: Media Literacy and Culture, 6/e by Baran
Issue 8: Can Media Regain Public Trust?	**Chapter 14:** Public Relations	**Chapter 11:** Public Relations
Issue 9: Does Fake News Mislead the Public?	**Chapter 13:** News Gathering and Reporting	**Chapter 8:** Television, Cable, and Mobile Video
Issue 10: Will Evolving Forms of Journalism be an Improvement?	**Chapter 4:** Newspapers **Chapter 13:** News Gathering and Reporting	**Chapter 10:** The Internet and the World Wide Web
Issue 11: Should the Public Support Freedom of the Press?	**Chapter 13:** News Gathering and Reporting	**Chapter 14:** Media Freedom, Regulation, and Ethics
Issue 12: Is Hate Speech in the Media Directly Affecting our Culture?	**Chapter 17:** Ethics and Other Informal Controls	**Chapter 13:** Theories and Effects of Mass Communication **Chapter 14:** Media Freedom, Regulation, and Ethics
Issue 13: Has Industry Regulation Controlled Indecent Media Content?	**Chapter 16:** Formal Controls: Laws, Rules, Regulations	**Chapter 14:** Media Freedom, Regulation, and Ethics
Issue 14: Can the Independent Musical Artist Thrive in Today's Music Business?	**Chapter 8:** Sound Recording	**Chapter 7:** Radio, Recording, and Popular Music **Chapter 14:** Media Freedom, Regulation, and Ethics
Issue 15: Should Newspapers Shut Down Their Presses?	**Chapter 4:** Newspapers	**Chapter 4:** Newspapers
Issue 16: Do New Business Models Result in Greater Consumer Choice of Products and Ideas?	**Chapter 2:** Perspectives on Mass Communication	**Chapter 2:** The Evolving Mass Communication Process
Issue 17: Are Online Services Responsible for an Increase in Bullying and Harassment?	**Chapter 19:** Social Effects of Mass Communication	**Chapter 10:** The Internet and the World Wide Web **Chapter 13:** Theories and Effects of Mass Communication
Issue 18: Are People Better Informed in the Information Society?	**Chapter 13:** News Gathering and Reporting **Chapter 19:** Social Effects of Mass Communication	**Chapter 2:** The Evolving Mass Communication Process **Chapter 10:** The Internet and the World Wide Web **Chapter 13:** Theories and Effects of Mass Communication

Introduction

Ways of Thinking about Mass Media and Society

Alison Alexander and Jarice Hanson

Media are everywhere in the industrialized world today. It is likely that anyone reading this book has access to more forms of media than their grandparents could have ever dreamed of. Many readers are probably adept at multitasking—a term unheard of when this book series began in 1987. Many readers are probably adept at using so many technologies that deliver content over the Internet or cell phones that it almost seems strange to think that broadcast TV, cable TV, film, radio, newspapers, books and magazines, and the recording industry all once were thought of as different forms of media, all delivered in different ways, and all with different economic structures. The convergence of these media over wired and wireless distribution forms now presents us with words, sounds, and images that often blur former distinctions among media forms and industries.

Media are also often scapegoats for the problems of society. Sometimes the relationship of social issues and media seems too obvious *not* to have some connection. For example, violence in the media may be a reflection of society, or, as some critics claim, violence in the media makes it seem that violence in society is the norm. But in reality, one important reason that the media are so often blamed for social problems is that the media are so pervasive. Their very ubiquity gives them the status that makes them seem more influential than they actually are. If one were to look at the statistics on violence in the United States, it would be possible to see that there are fewer violent acts today than in recent history—but the presence of this violence in the media, through reportage or fictional representation, makes it appear more prevalent.

There are many approaches to investigating the relationships that are suggested by media and society. From an organizational perspective, the producers of media must find content and distribution forms that will be profitable, and therefore, they have a unique outlook on the audience as consumers. From the perspective of the creative artist, the profit motive may be important, but the exploration of the unique communicative power of the media may be paramount. The audience, too, has different use patterns, desires for information or entertainment, and demonstrates a variety of choices in content offered to them, as well as what they take from the media. Whether the media reflect society or shape society has a lot to do with the dynamic interaction of many of these different components.

To complicate matters, the "mass" media have changed in recent years. Not long ago, "mass" media referred to messages that were created by large organizations for broad, heterogeneous audiences. This concept no longer suffices for the contemporary media environments. While the "mass" media still exist in the forms of radio, television, film, and general interest newspapers and magazines, many media forms today are hybrids of "mass" and "personal" media technologies that open a new realm of understanding about how audiences process the meaning of the messages. Audiences may be smaller and more diverse, but the phenomenon of using media to form a picture of the world and our place in it is still the fundamental reason for studying the relationship of media and society.

As we look at U.S. history, we can see that almost every form of media was first subject to some type of regulation by the government or by the media industry itself. This has changed over the years so that we now have a media environment in which the responsibility for the content of media no longer rests entirely in the hands of the FCC or the major corporations. We, as consumers, are asked to be critical of that media which we consume. This requires that we become educated consumers, rather than relying on standards and practices of industry or government intervention into questionable content. While this may not seem like a big problem for adult consumers, the questions and answers become more difficult when we consider how children use the media to form judgments, form opinions, or seek information.

Our habits are changing as the media landscape grows. The average American still spends over three hours a day viewing television, which is on in the average home over seven hours a day, but recent statistics indicate that the "average" American actually spends about 10 hours a day facing a screen of some sort—whether that is a TV screen, computer screen, or cell phone screen. That interaction with media clearly warrants some understanding of what happens in the process of the person/media interaction and relationship.

Politics and political processes have changed, in part, due to the way politicians use the media to reach voters. A proliferation of television channels has resulted from the popularity of cable, but does cable offer anything different from broadcast television? Videocassettes deliver feature-length films to the home, changing the traditional practice of viewing film in a public place, and video distribution via the Internet is now a practical option for anyone with transmission lines large enough to download large files. The recording industry is still reeling over the impact of MP3 and free software that allows consumers to sample, buy, or steal music online. Communications is a multibillion-dollar industry and the third fastest-growing industry in America. From these and other simple examples, it is clear that the media have changed American society, but our understanding of how and why remains incomplete.

Dynamics of Interaction

In recent years, the proliferation and availability of new media forms have changed on a global scale. In the United States, 98 percent of the homes have at least one telephone, but in 2008 the number of cell phones outnumbered land phones. On a global scale, about half of the world's people now have access to a cell phone. In the United States, over 98 percent of the population has access to at least one television set, but in some parts of the world, televisions are still viewed communally or viewed only at certain hours of the day. The use of broadband connections continues to grow in the United States, while some other countries (usually smaller countries, with high GNP) are reaching saturation with broadband technologies, and other countries still have limited dial-up services for the Internet.

But apart from questions of access and available content, many fundamental questions about the power of media in any given society remain the same. How do audiences use the media available to them? How do message senders produce meaning? How much of the meaning of any message is produced by the audience? And increasingly important for discussion is, How do additional uses of media change our interpersonal environments and human interactions?

Progress in Media Research

Much of media research has been in search of theory. Theory is an organized, commonsense refinement of everyday thinking; it is an attempt to establish a systematic view of a phenomenon in order to better understand that phenomenon. Theory is tested against reality to establish whether or not it is a good explanation; so, for example, a researcher might notice that what is covered by news outlets is very similar to what citizens say are the important issues of the day. From such observations came agenda setting (the notion that the media confer importance on the topics they cover, directing public attention to what is considered important).

Much of the early media research was produced to answer questions of print media because print has long been regarded a permanent record of history and events. The ability of newspapers and books to shape and influence public opinion was regarded as a necessity to the founding of new forms of governments—including the U.S. government; and a good number of our laws and regulations were originally written to favor print (like copyright and freedom of the press). But the bias of the medium carried certain restrictions. Print media necessarily were limited to those individuals who could read. The principles that emerged from this relationship were addressed in an often-quoted statement attributed to Thomas Jefferson, who wrote, "Were it left to me to decide whether we should have a government without newspapers, or newspapers without a government, I should not hesitate a moment to prefer the latter." But the next sentence in Jefferson's statement is equally important and often omitted from quotations: "But I should mean that every man should receive those papers and be capable of reading them." Today, however, the newspaper is no longer the primary distribution form for information that is critical to living in a democracy.

Today, media research on the relationships of media senders, the channels of communication, and the receivers of messages is not enough. Consumers must realize that "media literacy" and maybe even "technological literacy" are important concepts too. People can no longer take for granted that the media exist primarily to provide news, information, and entertainment. They must be more attuned to what media content says about them as individuals and as members of a society, and they need to be aware of how the ability for almost everyone to create media (like blogging, or social networking) challenges traditional ownership and privacy laws and regulations. By integrating these various cultural components, the public can better criticize the regulation or lack of regulation that permits media industries to function the way they do.

The use of social science data to explore the effects of media on audiences strongly emphasized psychological and sociological schools of thought. It did not take long to move from the "magic bullet theory"—which proposed that media had a direct and immediate effect on the receivers of the message, and the same message intended by the senders was the same when it was "shot" into the receiver—to other ideas of limited, or even indirect, means of influencing the audience.

Media research has shifted from addressing specifically effects-oriented paradigms to exploring the nature of the institutions of media production themselves, as well as examining the unique characteristics of each form of media and the ability of the media user to also produce media products. What most researchers agree upon today is that the best way to understand the power and impact of media is to look at context-specific situations to better understand the dynamics involved in the use of media and the importance of the content.

Still, there are many approaches to media research from a variety of interdisciplinary fields: psychology, sociology, linguistics, art, comparative literature, economics, political science, and more. What these avenues of inquiry have in common is that they all tend to focus attention on individuals, families or other social groups, society in general, and culture in the broad sense. All of the interpretations frame meaning and investigate their subjects within institutional frameworks that are specific to any nation and/or culture.

Many of the questions for media researchers in the twenty-first century deal with the continued fragmentation of the audience, caused by greater choice of channels and technologies for traditional and new communication purposes. The power of some of these technologies to reach virtually any place on the globe within fractions of a second will continue to pose questions of access to media and the meaning of the messages transmitted. As individuals become more dependent upon the Internet for communication purposes, the sense of audience will further be changed as individual users choose what they want to receive, pay for, and keep. For all of these reasons, the field of media research is rich, growing, and challenging.

Questions for Consideration

In addressing the issues in this book, it is important to consider some recurring questions:

1. Are the media unifying or fragmenting? Does media content help the socialization process, or does it create anxiety or inaccurate portrayals of the world? Do people understand what they are doing when

they post personal information online or open themselves to immediate criticism and feedback?

2. How are our basic institutions changing as we use media in new and different ways? Do media support or undermine our political processes? Do they change what we think of when we claim to live in a "democracy"? Do media operate in the public interest, or do media serve the rich and powerful corporations' quest for profit? Can the media do both simultaneously?

3. Whose interests do the media represent? Do audiences actively work toward integrating media messages with their own experiences? How do new media technologies change our traditional ways of communicating? Are they leading us to a world in which interpersonal communication is radically altered because we rely on information systems to replace many traditional behaviors?

Summary

We live in a media-rich environment where almost everybody has access to some forms of media and some choices in content. As new technologies and services are developed, are they responding to the problems that previous media researchers and the public have detected? Over time, individuals have improved their ability to unravel the complex set of interactions that tie the media and society together, but they need to continue to question past results, new practices and technologies, and their own evaluative measures. When people critically examine the world around them—a world often presented by the media—they can more fully understand and enjoy the way they relate as individuals, as members of groups, and as members of a society.

Internet References . . .

Communication Studies: General Communication Resources

An encyclopedic resource related to a host of mass communication issues, this site is maintained by the University of Iowa's Department of Communication Studies. It provides excellent links covering advertising, cultural studies, digital media, film, gender, and media studies.

http://www.uiowa.edu/commstud/resources/general.html

About.com: Secondary Education

A useful article for understanding the process by which book complaints are brought to school systems, the variety of reasons why, and the possible outcomes. Extensive links to additional sources.

http://712educators.about.com/cs/bannedbooks/a/bookbanning.htm

Arab Media & Society

Arab Media & Society is an online journal about all forms of media and their interaction with society in the Muslim world. The site is multimedia and contains archival material as well as real-time excerpts of articles from the Arab media.

http://www.arabmediasociety.com/about_the_journal.php

Nielsen Media Glossary of Terms

A handy compendium of terms used within the media industries.

http://www.nielsenmedia.com/glossary/

Media Awareness Network

The Media Awareness Network is a Canadian site dedicated to promoting critical thinking in youth about the media. Media issues discussed include violence, stereotyping, online hate, and information privacy.

http://www.media-awareness.ca

Media and Social Issues

Do media reflect the social attitudes and concerns of our times, or are they also able to construct, legitimate, and reinforce the social realities, behaviors, attitudes, and images of others? Do they operate to maintain existing power structures, or are they symbolic communication central to our culture? The ways media help us to shape a sense of reality are complex. How much do media influence us, versus how we use media to fit our already preconceived ideas? Should concern be directed toward vulnerable populations like children? If we truly have a variety of information sources and content to choose from, perhaps we can assume that distorted images are balanced with realistic ones—but is this a likely scenario in our society? Questions about the place of media within society, and within what many people call the "information age," are important for us to understand, whether we use media, or whether media use us.

- Are American Values Shaped by the Mass Media?
- Are *Harry Potter* Books Harmful for Children?
- Do Media Represent Realistic Images of Arabs?
- Do Media Cause Individuals to Develop Negative Body Images?

ISSUE 1

Are American Values Shaped by the Mass Media?

YES: **Herbert I. Schiller,** from *The Mind Managers* (Beacon Press, 1973)

NO: **James W. Carey,** from *Communication as Culture: Essays on Media and Society* (Unwin Hyman, 1989)

ISSUE SUMMARY

YES: Critical scholar of modern mass media Professor Schiller argues that mass media institutions are key elements of the modern capitalistic world order. Media, he argues, produce economic profits and the ideology necessary to sustain a world system of exploitative divisions of social and financial resources. It is the job of the citizenry to understand the myths that act to sustain this existing state of power relationships.

NO: James Carey introduces the seminal ideas of ritual and transmission models of communication in this piece. Communication is not simply a process of sending messages as the transmission model would suggest. Communication is a symbolic process which is inherently linked to culture and our lives.

Can the media fundamentally reshape a culture? Americans are increasingly part of a culture in which information and ideas are electronically disseminated. Are media simply the conduit, the information channel, through which these ideas flow? Neither of the authors above would agree with that simplistic description. But they do disagree significantly on the way media influences society. Stop a moment and consider: what are the ways you feel media influence society? Groups within our society? And yourself? Currently in mass communication research, two vastly different perspectives on the impact of media on society exist. The critical/cultural perspective is advocated by Schiller, the ritual view of communication by Carey. These articles were chosen because they are classic statements of perspectives that still influence mass communication thought today.

Schiller outlines the five myths that structure media content and manipulate consciousness. These myths function to reproduce the status quo and maintain existing social power structures. Despite changes in technologies and practices, Schiller argues that the ideological core of media messages remains the same. He is not alone in his concern that electronic media are negatively influencing our society. There are a number of mass communication scholars from the critical and cultural perspectives who are concerned that the power of media to shape attitude and opinions, paired with the power of media organizations to craft messages, will inevitably result in a recreation of current power structures, which inequitably divide social resources.

James Carey introduced to mass communication theory the notion of a ritual versus a transmission model of media. He argues that the transmission view of communication in which the idea of communication is "a process of transmitting messages at a distance for the purpose of control. The archetypal case of communication then is persuasion, attitude change, behavior modification, socialization through transmission of information, influences, or conditioning." The ritual view looks at communication as central to culture, wherein communication is part of the culture and with its presentation and involvement is part of the structure of our life and time. He famously defines communication as a "symbolic process whereby reality is produced, maintained, repaired, and transformed." Whereas transmission has become associated with effects research, ritual models see communication as directed toward the maintenance of society in time and the representation of shared beliefs.

The media are so pervasive it is hard to believe they do not have important effects. Alternatively, many people do not believe that the media have personally influenced them to buy products or have harmed them, nor do they believe that the media hold a place of "prime importance" in shaping their lives. In everyday experience, many people do not consider the media as having an observable impact on them or on those around them. However, to understand how the media may shape the attitudes of individuals and of society, and how media may shape culture itself, requires that the reader stand back from his or her personal experiences in order to analyze the arguments presented on each side of this debate.

In the first selection, Schiller argues that U.S. media, through their "taken for granted" myths, help structure the practices and meanings around which society takes shape. Ideology is not imposed but is systematically preferred by certain features of television, whereas other oppositional ideas are ignored or domesticated. Schiller was a powerful proponent of the theory that media is structured by the economic conditions under which it operates.

In the second selection, Carey grounds his thinking in the philosophy of Dewey and his conception of society. He argues that commitment to the transmission model of communication has inevitably focused our attention on issues of power, administration, and control. The ritual view of communication reminds us that communication is more than an economic model, but one that turns our attention to aesthetics, religion, values, and intellect.

YES ↵

Herbert I. Schiller

The Mind Managers

Introduction

America's media managers create, process, refine, and preside over the circulation of images and information which determine our beliefs and attitudes and, ultimately, our behavior. When they deliberately produce messages that do not correspond to the realities of social existence, the media managers become mind managers. Messages that intentionally create a false sense of reality and produce a consciousness that cannot comprehend or willfully rejects the actual conditions of life, personal or social, are manipulative messages.

Manipulation of human minds, according to Paulo Freire, "is an instrument of conquest." It is one of the means by which "the dominant elites try to conform the masses to their objectives."[1] By using myths which explain, justify, and sometimes even glamorize the prevailing conditions of existence, manipulators secure popular support for a social order that is not in the majority's long-term real interest. When manipulation is successful, alternative social arrangements remain unconsidered. . . .

The permanent division of the society into two broad categories of "winners" and "losers" arises and persists as a result of the maintenance, recognition, and, indeed, sanctification of the system of private ownership of productive property and the extension of the ownership principle to all other aspects of human existence. The general acceptance of this arrangement for carrying on social activity makes it inevitable that some prosper, consolidate their success, and join the dominant shapers and molders of the community. The others, the majority, work on as mere conformists, the disadvantaged, and the manipulated; they are manipulated especially to continue to participate, if not wholeheartedly, at least positively, in the established routines. The system gives them a return adequate to achieve some marks of economic status, and manipulation leads them to hope that they might turn these routines to greater personal advantage for themselves or their children.

It is not surprising that manipulation, as an instrument of control, should reach its highest development in the United States. In America, more than anywhere else, the favorable conditions we have briefly noted permit a large fraction of the population to escape total suppression and thereby become potential actors in the historical process. Manipulation allows the appearance of active engagement while denying many of the material and *all* of the psychic benefits of genuine involvement. . . .

The means of manipulation are many, but, clearly, control of the infor-mational and ideational apparatus at all levels is essential. This is secured by the operation of a simple rule of the market economy. Ownership and control of the mass media, like all other forms of property, is available to those with capital. Inevitably, radio- and television-station ownership, news-paper and magazine proprietorship, movie-making, and book publishing are largely in the hands of corporate chains and media conglomerates. The appa-ratus is thus ready to assume an active and dominant role in the manipula-tive process.

My intention is to identify some of these conditioning forces and to reveal the means by which they conceal their presence, deny their influence, or exercise directional control under auspices plat superficially appear benign and/or natural. The search for these "hidden processes," along with their subtle mechanics, should not be mistaken for a more common kind of investigation—the exposé of clandestine activities. Conspiracy is neither invoked nor consid-ered in these pages. Though the idea of mind management lends itself easily to such an approach, the comprehensive conditioning carried on throughout American society today does not require, and actually cannot be understood in, such terms. . . .

Manipulation and the Packaged Consciousness
Five Myths That Structure Content

1. The Myth of Individualism and Personal Choice Manipulation's greatest tri-umph, most observable in the United States, is to have taken advantage of the special historical circumstances of Western development to perpetrate as truth a definition of freedom cast in individualistic terms. This enables the con-cept to serve a double function. It protects the ownership of productive private property while simultaneously offering itself as the guardian of the individual's well-being, suggesting, if not insisting, that the latter is unattainable without the existence of the former. Upon this central construct an entire scaffolding of manipulation is erected. What accounts for the strength of this powerful notion?

. . . The identification of personal choice with human freedom can be seen arising side-by-side with seventeenth-century individualism, both products of the emerging market economy.[2]

For several hundred years individual proprietorship, allied with techno-logical improvement, increased output and thereby bestowed great impor-tance on personal independence in the industrial and political processes. The view that freedom is a personal matter, and that the individual's rights supersede the group's and provide the basis for social organization, gained credibility with the rise of material rewards and leisure time. Note, however, that these conditions were not distributed evenly among all classes of Western society and that they did not begin to exist in the rest of the world. . . .

In the newly settled United States, few restraints impeded the imposition of an individualistic private entrepreneurial system and its accompanying myths of personal choice and individual freedom. Both enterprise and myth found a hospitable setting. The growth of the former and consolidation of the latter were inevitable. How far the process has been carried is evident today in the easy public acceptance of the giant multinational private corporation as an example of individual endeavor. . . .

Privatism in every sphere of life is considered normal. The American life style, from its most minor detail to its most deeply felt beliefs and practices, reflects an exclusively self-centered outlook, which is in turn an accurate image of the structure of the economy itself. The American dream includes a personal means of transportation, a single-family home, the proprietor-operated business. Such other institutions as a competitive health system are obvious, if not natural, features of the privately organized economy. . . .

Though individual freedom and personal choice are its most powerful mythic defenses, the system of private ownership and production requires and creates additional constructs, along with the techniques to transmit them. These notions either rationalize its existence and promise a great future, or divert attention from its searing inadequacies and conceal the possibilities of new departures for human development. Some of these constructs and techniques are not exclusive to the privatistic industrial order, and can be applied in any social system intent on maintaining its dominion. Other myths, and the means of circulating them, are closely associated with the specific characteristics of this social system.

2. The Myth of Neutrality   For manipulation to be most effective, evidence of its presence should be nonexistent. When the manipulated believe things are the way they are naturally and inevitably, manipulation is successful. In short, manipulation requires a false reality that is a continuous denial of its existence.

It is essential, therefore, that people who are manipulated believe in the neutrality of their key social institutions. They must believe that government, the media, education, and science are beyond the clash of conflicting social interests. Government, and the national government in particular, remains the centerpiece of the neutrality myth. This myth presupposes belief in the basic integrity and nonpartisanship of government in general and of its constituent parts—Congress, the judiciary, and the Presidency. Corruption, deceit, and knavery, when they occur from time to time, are seen to be the result of human weakness. The institutions themselves are beyond reproach. The fundamental soundness of the overall system is assured by the well-designed instrumentalities that comprise the whole.

The Presidency, for instance, is beyond the reach of special interests, according to this mythology. The first and most extreme manipulative use of the Presidency, therefore, is to claim the nonpartisanship of the office, and to seem to withdraw it from clamorous conflict. . . .

The chief executive, though the most important, is but one of many governmental departments that seek to present themselves as neutral agents, embracing no objectives but the general welfare, and serving everyone impartially and disinterestedly. For half a century all the media joined in propagating the myth of the FBI as a nonpolitical and highly effective agency of law enforcement. In fact, the Bureau has been used continuously to intimidate and coerce social critics.

The mass media, too, are supposed to be neutral. Departures from even-handedness in news reportage are admitted but, the press assure us, result from human error and cannot be interpreted as flaws in the basically sound institutions of information dissemination. That the media (press, periodicals, radio, and television) are almost without exception business enterprises, receiving their revenues from commercial sales of time or space, seems to create no problems for those who defend the objectivity and integrity of the informational services.[3] . . .

Science, which more than any other intellectual activity has been integrated into the corporate economy, continues also to insist on its value-free neutrality. Unwilling to consider the implications of the sources of its funding, the directions of its research, the applications of its theories, and the character of the paradigms it creates, science promotes the notion of its insulation from the social forces that affect all other ongoing activities in the nation.

The system of schooling, from the elementary through the university level, is also, according to the manipulators, devoid of deliberate ideological purpose. Still, the product must reflect the teaching: it is astonishing how large a proportion of the graduates at each stage continue, despite all the ballyhoo about the counterculture, to believe in and observe the competitive ethic of business enterprise.

Wherever one looks in the social sphere, neutrality and objectivity are invoked to describe the functioning of value-laden and purposeful activities which lend support to the prevailing institutional system. Essential to the everyday maintenance of the control system is the carefully nurtured myth that no special groups or views have a preponderant influence on the country's important decision-making processes. . . .

3. The Myth of Unchanging Human Nature   Human expectations can be the lubricant of social change. When human expectations are low, passivity prevails. There can, of course, be various kinds of images in anyone's mind concerning political, social, economic, and personal realities. The common denominator of all such imagery, however, is the view people have of human nature. What human nature is seen to be ultimately affects the way human beings behave, not because they must act as they do but because they believe they are expected to act that way. . . .

It is predictable that in the United States a theory that emphasizes the aggressive side of human behavior and the unchangeability of human nature would find approval, permeate most work and thought, and be circulated widely by the mass media. Certainly, an economy that is built on and rewards private ownership and individual acquisition, and is subject to the personal and social conflicts these arrangements impose, can be expected to be gratified with an explanation that legitimizes its operative principles. How reassuring to consider these conflictful relationships inherent in the human condition rather than imposed by social circumstance! This outlook fits nicely too with the antiideological stance the system projects. It induces a "scientific" and "objective" approach to the human condition rigorously measuring human microbehavior in all its depravities, and for the most part ignoring the broader and less measurable social parameters.

Daily TV programming, for example, with its quota of half a dozen murders per hour, is rationalized easily by media controllers as an effort to give the people what they want. Too bad, they shrug, if human nature demands eighteen hours daily of mayhem and slaughter. . . .

Fortune finds it cheering, for "example, that some American social scientists are again emphasizing "the intractability of human nature" in their explanations of social phenomena. "The orthodox view of environment as the all-important influence on people's behavior," it reports, "is yielding to a new awareness of the role of hereditary factors: enthusiasm for schemes to reform society by remolding men is giving way to a healthy appreciation of the basic intractability of human nature."[4]

The net social effects of the thesis that human nature is at fault are further disorientation, total inability to recognize the causes of malaise—much less to take any steps to overcome it—and, of most consequence, continued adherence to the *status quo*. . . .

It is to prevent social action (and it is immaterial whether the intent is articulated or not) that so much publicity and attention are devoted to every pessimistic appraisal of human potential. If we are doomed forever by our inheritance, there is not much to be done about it. But there is a good reason and a good market for undervaluing human capability. An entrenched social system depends on keeping the popular and, especially, the "enlightened" mind unsure and doubtful about its human prospects. . . .

This does not necessitate ignoring history. On the contrary, endless recitation of what happened in the past accompanies assertions about how much change is occurring under our very noses. But these are invariably *physical* changes—new means of transportation, air conditioning, space rockets, packaged foods. Mind managers dwell on these matters but carefully refrain from considering changes in social relationships or in the institutional structures that undergird the economy.

Every conceivable kind of futuristic device is canvassed and blueprinted. Yet those who will use these wonder items will apparently continue to be married, raise children in suburban homes, work for private companies, vote for a President in a two-party system and pay a large portion of their incomes for defense, law and order, and superhighways. The world, except for some glamorous surface redecorations, will remain as it is; basic relationships will not change, because they, like human nature, are allegedly unchangeable. As for those parts of the world that have undergone far-reaching social rearrangements, reports of these transformations, if there are any, emphasize the defects, problems, and crises, which are seized upon with relish by domestic consciousness manipulators. . . .

4. The Myth of the Absence of Social Conflict . . . Consciousness controllers, in their presentation of the domestic scene, deny absolutely the presence of social conflict. On the face of it, this seems an impossible task. After all violence is "as American as apple pie." Not only in fact but in fantasy: in films, on TV, and over the radio, the daily quota of violent scenarios offered the public is staggering. How is this carnival of conflict reconcilable with the media managers' intent to present an image of social harmony? The contradiction is easily resolved.

As presented by the national message-making apparatus, conflict is almost always an *individual* matter, in its manifestations and in its origin. The social roots of conflict just do not exist for the cultural-informational managers. True, there are "good guys" and "bad guys," but, except for such ritualized situations as westerns, which are recognized as scenarios of the past, role identification is divorced from significant social categories.

Black, brown, yellow, red, and other ethnic Americans have always fared poorly in the manufactured cultural imagery. Still, these are minorities which all segments of the white population have exploited in varying degrees. As for the great social division in the nation, between worker and owner, with rare exceptions it has been left unexamined. Attention is diverted elsewhere— generally toward the problems of the upward-striving middle segment of the population, that category with which everyone is supposed to identify. . . .

Elite control requires omission or distortion of social reality. Honest examination and discussion of social conflict can only deepen and intensify resistance to social inequity. Economically powerful groups and companies quickly get edgy when attention is called to exploitative practices in which they are engaged. *Variety*'s television editor, Les Brown, described such an incident. Coca-Cola Food Company and the Florida Fruit and Vegetable Association reacted sharply to a TV documentary, "Migrant," which centered on migrant fruit pickers in Florida. Brown wrote that "the miracle of *Migrant* was that it was televised at all." Warnings were sent to NBC not to show the program because it was "biased." Cuts in the film were demanded, and at least one was made. Finally, after the showing, "Coca-Cola shifted all its network billings to CBS and ABC."[5]

On a strictly commercial level, the presentation of social issues creates uneasiness in mass audiences, or so the audience researchers believe. To be safe, to hold onto as large a public as possible, sponsors are always eager to eliminate potentially "controversial" program material.

The entertainments and cultural products that have been most successful in the United States, those that have received the warmest support and publicity from the communications system, are invariably movies, TV programs, books, and mass entertainments (i.e., Disneyland) which may offer more than a fair quota of violence but never take up *social* conflict. . . .

5. *The Myth of Media Pluralism*   Personal choice exercised in an environment of cultural-information diversity is the image, circulated worldwide, of the condition of life in America. This view is also internalized in the belief structure of a large majority of Americans, which makes them particularly susceptible to thoroughgoing manipulation. It is, therefore, one of the central myths upon which mind management flourishes. Choice and diversity, though separate concepts, are in fact inseparable; choice is unattainable in any real sense without diversity. If real options are nonexistent, choosing is either meaningless or manipulative. It is manipulative when accompanied by the illusion that the choice is meaningful.

Though it cannot be verified, the odds are that the illusion of informational choice is more pervasive in the United States than anywhere else in the world. The illusion is sustained by a willingness, deliberately maintained by information controllers, to mistake *abundance of media for diversity of content.* . . .

The fact of the matter is that, except for a rather small and highly selective segment of the population who know what they are looking for and can therefore take advantage of the massive communications flow, most Americans are basically, though unconsciously, trapped in what amounts to a nochoice informational bind. Variety of opinion on foreign and domestic news or, for that matter, local community business, hardly exists in the media. This results essentially from the inherent identity of interests, material and ideological, of property-holders (in this case, the private owners of the communications media), and from the monopolistic character of the communications industry in general.

The limiting effects of monopoly are in need of no explanation, and communications monopolies restrict informational choice wherever they operate. They offer one version of reality—their own. In this category fall most of the nation's newspapers, magazines, and films, which are produced by national or regional communications conglomerates. The number of American cities in which competing newspapers circulate has shrunk to a handful.

While there is a competition of sorts for audiences among the three major TV networks, two conditions determine the limits of the variety presented. Though each network struggles gamely to attract as large an audience as possible, it imitates its two rivals in program format and content. If ABC is successful with a western serial, CBS and NBC will in all likelihood "compete" with "shoot-'em-ups" in the same time slot. Besides, each of the three national networks is part of, or is itself, an enormous communications business, with the drives and motivations of any other profit-seeking enterprise. This means that diversity in the informational-entertainment sector exists only in the sense that there are a number of superficially different versions of the main categories of program. For example, there are several talk shows on late-night TV; there may be half a dozen private-eye, western, or law-and-order TV serials to "choose from" in prime time; there are three network news commentators with different personalities who offer essentially identical information. One can switch the radio dial and get round-the-clock news from one or, at most, two news services; or one can hear Top 40 popular songs played by "competing" disc jockeys.

Though no single program, performer, commentator, or informational bit is necessarily identical to its competitors, *there is no significant qualitative difference.* Just as a supermarket offers six identical soaps in different colors and a drugstore sells a variety of brands of aspirin at different prices, disc jockeys play the same records between personalized advertisements for different commodities. . . .

Yet it is this condition of communicational pluralism, empty as it is of real diversity, which affords great strength to the prevailing system of consciousness-packaging. The multichannel communications flow creates confidence in, and lends credibility to, the notion of free informational choice. Meanwhile, its main effect is to provide continuous reinforcement of the *status quo*. Similar stimuli, emanating from apparently diverse sources, envelop the listener/viewer/reader in a message/image environment that ordinarily seems uncontrolled, relatively free, and quite natural. How could it be otherwise with such an abundance of programs and transmitters? Corporate profit-seeking, the main objective of conglomeratized communications, however real and ultimately determining, is an invisible abstraction to the consumers of the cultural images. And one thing is certain: the media do not call their audiences' attention to its existence or its mode of operation. . . .

The fundamental similarity of the informational material and cultural messages that each of the mass media independently transmits makes it necessary to view the communications system as a totality. The media are mutually and continuously reinforcing. Since they operate according to commercial rules, rely on advertising, and are tied tightly to the corporate economy, both in their own structure and in their relationships with sponsors, the media constitute an industry, not an aggregation of independent, freewheeling informational entrepreneurs, each offering a highly individualistic product. By need and by design, the images and messages they purvey are, with few exceptions, constructed to achieve similar objectives, which are, simply put, profitability and the affirmation and maintenance of the private-ownership consumer society.

Consequently, research directed at discovering the impact of a single TV program or movie, or even an entire category of stimuli, such as "violence on TV" can often be fruitless. Who can justifiably claim that TV violence is inducing delinquent juvenile behavior when violence is endemic to all mass communications channels? Who can suggest that any single category of programming is producing male chauvinist or racist behavior when stimuli and imagery carrying such sentiments flow unceasingly through all the channels of transmission?

It is generally agreed that television is the most powerful medium; certainly its influence as a purveyor of the system's values cannot be overstated. All the same, television, no matter how powerful, itself depends on the absence of dissonant stimuli in the other media. Each of the informational channels makes its unique contribution, but the result is the same—the consolidation of the *status quo*.

Notes

1. Paulo Freire, *Pedagogy of the Oppressed* (New York: Herder and Herder, 1971), p. 144.

2. C. B. MacPherson, *The Political Theory of Possessive Individualism* (Oxford: Clarendon Press, 1962).

3. Henry Luce, the founder of *Time, Life, Fortune, Sports Illustrated,* and other mass circulation magazines, knew otherwise. He told his staff at *Time:* "The alleged journalistic objectivity, a claim that a writer presents facts

without applying any value judgment to them [is] modem usage—and that is strictly a phony. It is that that I had to renounce and denounce. So when we say the hell with objectivity, that is what we are talking about." W. A. Swanberg, *Luce and His Empire* (New York: Charles Scribner's Sons, 1972), p. 331.

4. "The Social Engineers Retreat Under Fire," *Fortune,* October 1972, p. 3.

5. Les Brown, *Television: The Business Behind the Box* (New York: Harcourt, Brace Jovanovich, 1971), pp. 196–203.

James W. Carey   ➡ **NO**

A Cultural Approach to Communication

I

When I decided some years ago to read seriously the literature of communications, a wise man suggested I begin with John Dewey. . . .

Dewey opens an important chapter in *Experience and Nature* with the seemingly preposterous claim that "of all things communication is the most wonderful." What could he have meant by that? If we interpret the sentence literally, it must be either false or mundane. Surely most of the news and entertainment we receive through the mass media are of the order that Thoreau predicted for the international telegraph: "the intelligence that Princess Adelaide had the whooping cough." A daily visit with the New York *Times* is not quite so trivial, though it is an experience more depressing than wonderful. Moreover, most of one's encounters with others are wonderful only in moments of excessive masochism. Dewey's sentence, by any reasonable interpretation, is either false to everyday experience or simply mundane if he means only that on some occasions communication is satisfying and rewarding.

In another place Dewey offers an equally enigmatic comment on communication: "Society exists not only by transmission, by communication, but it may fairly be said to exist in transmission, in communication." What is the significance of the shift in prepositions? Is Dewey claiming that societies distribute information, to speak rather too anthropomorphically, and that by such transactions and the channels of communication peculiar to them society is made possible? That is certainly a reasonable claim, but we hardly need social scientists and philosophers to tell us so. It reminds me of Robert Nisbet's acid remark that if you need sociologists to inform you whether or not you have a ruling class, you surely don't. But if this transparent interpretation is rejected, are there any guarantees that after peeling away layers of semantic complexity anything more substantial will be revealed?

I think there are, for the body of Dewey's work reveals a substantial rather than a pedestrian intelligence. Rather than quoting him ritualistically (for the lines I have cited regularly appear without comment or interpretation in the literature of communications), we would be better advised to untangle this underlying complexity for the light it might cast upon contemporary studies. I think this complexity derives from Dewey's use of communication in two quite different

From *Communication as Culture: Essays on Media and Society* by James W. Carey (Unwin Hyman, 1989), pp. 13–35 (edited, notes omitted). Copyright © 1989 by Taylor & Francis Books, Inc. Reprinted by permission via Rightslink.

senses. He understood better than most of us that communication has had two contrasting definitions in the history of Western thought, and he used the conflict between these definitions as a source of creative tension in his work. . . .

Two alternative conceptions of communication have been alive in American culture since this term entered common discourse in the nineteenth century. Both definitions derive, as with much in secular culture, from religious origins, though they refer to somewhat different regions of religious experience. We might label these descriptions, if only to provide handy pegs upon which to hang our thought, a transmission view of communication and a ritual view of communication.

The transmission view of communication is the commonest in our culture—perhaps in all industrial cultures—and dominates contemporary dictionary entries under the term. It is defined by terms such as "imparting," "sending," "transmitting," or "giving information to others." It is formed from a metaphor of geography or transportation. In the nineteenth century but to a lesser extent today, the movement of goods or people and the movement of information were seen as essentially identical processes and both were described by the common noun "communication." The center of this idea of communication is the transmission of signals or messages over distance for the purpose of control. It is a view of communication that derives from one of the most ancient of human dreams: the desire to increase the speed and effect of messages as they travel in space. From the time upper and lower Egypt were unified under the First Dynasty down through the invention of the telegraph, transportation and communication were inseparably linked. Although messages might be centrally produced and controlled, through monopolization of writing or the rapid production of print, these messages, carried in the hands of a messenger or between the bindings of a book, still had to be distributed, if they were to have their desired effect, by rapid transportation. The telegraph ended the identity but did not destroy the metaphor. Our basic orientation to communication remains grounded, at the deepest roots of our thinking, in the idea of transmission: communication is a process whereby messages are transmitted and distributed in space for the control of distance and people. . . .

In its modern dress the transmission view of communication arises, as the *Oxford English Dictionary* will attest, at the onset of the age of exploration and discovery. We have been reminded rather too often that the motives behind this vast movement in space were political and mercantilistic. Certainly those motives were present, but their importance should not obscure the equally compelling fact that a major motive behind this movement in space, particularly as evidenced by the Dutch Reformed Church in South Africa or the Puritans in New England, was religious. The desire to escape the boundaries of Europe, to create a new life, to found new communities, to carve a New Jerusalem out of the woods of Massachusetts, were primary motives behind the unprecedented movement of white European civilization over virtually the entire globe. The vast and, for the first time, democratic migration in space was above all an attempt to trade an old world for a new and represented the profound belief that movement in space could be in itself a redemptive act. It is a belief Americans have never quite escaped. . . .

The moral meaning of transportation, then, was the establishment and extension of God's kingdom on earth. The moral meaning of communication was the same. By the middle of the nineteenth century the telegraph broke the identity of communication and transportation but also led a preacher of the era, Gardner Spring, to exclaim that we were on the "border of a spiritual harvest because thought now travels by steam and magnetic wires." Similarly, in 1848 "James L. Batchelder could declare that the Almighty himself had constructed the railroad for missionary purposes and, as Samuel Morse prophesied with the first telegraphic message, the purpose of the invention was not to spread the price of pork but to ask the question 'What Hath God Wrought?' " This new technology entered American discussions not as a mundane fact but as divinely inspired for the purposes of spreading the Christian message farther and faster, eclipsing time and transcending space, saving the heathen, bringing closer and making more probable the day of salvation. As the century wore on and religious thought was increasingly tied to applied science, the new technology of communication came to be seen as the ideal device for the conquest of space and populations. Our most distinguished student of these matters, Perry Miller, has commented:

> The unanimity (among Protestant sects), which might at first sight seem wholly supernatural, was wrought by the telegraph and the press. These conveyed and published "the thrill of Christian sympathy, with the tidings of abounding grace, from multitudes in every city simultaneously assembled, in effect almost bringing a nation together in one praying intercourse." Nor could it be only fortuitous that the movement should coincide with the Atlantic Cable, for both were harbingers "of that which is the forerunner of ultimate spiritual victory. . . ." The awakening of 1858 first made vital for the American imagination a realizable program of a Christianized technology.

Soon, as the forces of science and secularization gained ground, the obvious religious metaphors fell away and the technology of communication itself moved to the center of thought. Moreover, the superiority of communication over transportation was assured by the observation of one nineteenth century commentator that the telegraph was important because it involved not the mere "modification of matter but the transmission of thought." Communication was viewed as a process and a technology that would, sometimes for religious purposes, spread, transmit, and disseminate knowledge, ideas, and information farther and faster with the goal of controlling space and people.

There were dissenters, of course, and I have already quoted Thoreau's disenchanted remark on the telegraph. More pessimistically, John C. Calhoun saw the "subjugation of electricity to the mechanical necessities of man . . . (as) the last era in human civilization." But the dissenters were few, and the transmission view of communication, albeit in increasingly secularized and scientific form, has dominated our thought and culture since that time. Moreover, as can be seen in contemporary popular commentary and even in technical discussions of new communications technology, the historic religious undercurrent has never been eliminated from our thought. From the telegraph to the computer the same sense of profound possibility for moral improvement is present whenever these machines are invoked. And we need not be reminded of the regularity with which improved communication is invoked by an army of teachers, preachers, and columnists as the talisman of all our troubles. More controversially, the same root attitudes, as I can only assert here rather than demonstrate, are at work in most of our scientifically sophisticated views of communication.

The ritual view of communication, though a minor thread in our national thought, is by far the older of those views—old enough in fact for dictionaries to list it under "Archaic." In a ritual definition, communication is linked to terms such as "sharing," "participation," "association," "fellowship," and "the possession of a common faith." This definition exploits the ancient identity and common roots of the terms "commonness," "communion," "community," and "communication." A ritual view of communication is directed not toward the extension of messages in space but toward the maintenance of society in time; not the act of imparting information but the representation of shared beliefs.

If the archetypal case of communication under a transmission view is the extension of messages across geography for the purpose of control, the archetypal case under a ritual view is the sacred ceremony that draws persons together in fellowship and commonality.

The indebtedness of the ritual view of communication to religion is apparent in the name chosen to label it. Moreover, it derives from a view of religion that downplays the role of the sermon, the instruction and admonition, in order to highlight the role of the prayer, the chant, and the ceremony. It sees the original or highest manifestation of communication not in the transmission of intelligent information but in the construction and maintenance of an ordered, meaningful cultural world that can serve as a control and container for human action.

This view has also been shorn of its explicitly religious origins, but it has never completely escaped its metaphoric root. Writers in this tradition often trace their heritage, in part, to Durkheim's *Elementary Forms of Religious Life* and to the argument stated elsewhere that "society substitutes for the world revealed to our senses a different world that is a projection of the ideals created by the community." This projection of community ideals and their embodiment in material form—dance, plays, architecture, news stories, strings of speech—creates an artificial though nonetheless real symbolic order that operates to provide not information but confirmation, not to alter attitudes or change minds but to represent an underlying order of things, not to perform functions but to manifest an ongoing and fragile social process.

The ritual view of communication has not been a dominant motif in American scholarship. Our thought and work have been glued to a transmission view of communication because this view is congenial with the underlying well-springs of American culture, sources that feed into our scientific life as well as our common, public understandings. There is an irony in this. We have not explored the ritual view of communication because the concept of culture is such a weak and evanescent notion in American social thought. We understand that other people have culture in the anthropological sense and we regularly record it—often mischievously and patronizingly. But when we turn critical attention to American culture the concept dissolves into a residual category useful only when psychological and sociological data are exhausted. We realize that the underprivileged live in a culture of poverty, use the notion of middle-class culture as an epithet, and occasionally applaud our high and generally scientific culture. But the notion of culture is not a hard-edged term of intellectual discourse for domestic purposes. This intellectual aversion to the idea of culture derives in part from our obsessive individualism, which makes psychological life the paramount reality; from our Puritanism, which leads to disdain for the significance of human activity that is not practical and work oriented; and from our isolation of science from culture: science provides culture-free truth whereas culture provides ethnocentric error.

Consequently, when looking for scholarship that emphasizes the central role of culture and a ritual view of communication, one must rely heavily on European sources or upon Americans deeply influenced by European scholarship. As a result the opportunities for misunderstanding are great. Perhaps, then, some of the difference between a transmission and a ritual view of communication can be grasped by briefly looking at alternative conceptions of the role of the newspaper in social life.

If one examines a newspaper under a transmission view of communication, one sees the medium as an instrument for disseminating news and knowledge, sometimes *divertissement,* in larger and larger packages over greater distances. Questions arise as to the effects of this on audiences: news as enlightening or obscuring reality, as changing or hardening attitudes, as breeding credibility or doubt. Questions also are raised concerning the functions of news and the newspaper: Does it maintain the integration of society or its maladaptation? Does it function or misfunction to maintain stability or promote the instability of personalities? Some such mechanical analysis normally accompanies a "transmission" argument.

A ritual view of communication will focus on a different range of problems in examining a newspaper. It will, for example, view reading a newspaper less as sending or gaining information and more as attending a mass, a situation in which nothing new is learned but in which a particular view of the world is portrayed and confirmed. News reading, and writing, is a ritual act and moreover a dramatic one. What is arrayed before the reader is not pure information but a portrayal of the contending forces in the world. Moreover, as readers make their way through the paper, they engage in a continual shift of roles or of dramatic focus. . . . A story on the meeting of a women's political caucus casts them into the liberation movement as supporter or opponent; a tale of violence on the campus evokes their class antagonisms and resentments. The model here is not that of information acquisition, though such acquisition occurs, but of dramatic action in which the reader joins a world of contending forces as an observer at a play. We do not encounter questions about the effect or functions of messages as such, but the role of presentation and involvement in the structuring of the reader's life and time. We recognize, as with religious rituals, that news changes little and yet is intrinsically satisfying; it performs few functions yet is habitually consumed. Newspapers do not operate as a source of effects or functions but as dramatically satisfying, which is not to say pleasing, presentations of what the world at root is. And it is in this role—that of a text—that a newspaper is seen; like a Balinese cockfight, a Dickens novel, ah Elizabethan drama, a student rally, it is a presentation of reality that gives life an overall form, order, and tone.

Moreover, news is a historic reality. It is a form of culture invented by a particular class at a particular point of history—in this case by the middle class largely in the eighteenth century. Like any invented cultural form, news both forms and reflects a particular "hunger for experience," a desire to do away with the epic, heroic, and traditional in favor of the unique, original, novel, new—news. This "hunger" itself has a history grounded in the changing style and fortunes of the middle class and as such does not represent a universal taste or necessarily legitimate form of knowledge but an invention in historical time, that like most other human inventions, will dissolve when the class that sponsors it and its possibility of having significance for us evaporates.

Under a ritual view, then, news is not information but drama. It does not describe the world but portrays an arena of dramatic forces and action; it exists solely in historical time; and it invites our participation on the basis of our assuming, often vicariously, social roles within it.

Neither of these counterposed views of communication necessarily denies what the other affirms. A ritual view does not exclude the processes of information transmission or attitude change. It merely contends that one cannot understand these processes aright except insofar as they are cast within an essentially ritualistic view of communication and social order. Similarly, even writers indissolubly wedded to the transmission view of communication must include some notion to attest however tardily to the place of ritual action in social life. Nonetheless, in intellectual matters origins determine endings, and the exact point at which one attempts to unhinge the problem of communication largely determines the path the analysis can follow.

The power of Dewey's work derives from his working over these counterpoised views of communication. Communication is "the most wonderful" because it is the basis of human fellowship; it produces the social bonds, bogus or not, that tie men together and make associated life possible. Society is possible because of the binding forces of shared information circulating in an organic system. The following quotation reveals this tension and Dewey's final emphasis on a ritual view of communication:

> There is more than a verbal tie between the words common, community, and communication. Men live in a community in virtue of the things which they have in common; and communication is the way in which they come to possess things in common. What they must have in common . . . are aims, beliefs, aspirations, knowledge—a common understanding—likemindedness as sociologists say. Such things cannot be passed physically from one to another like bricks; they cannot be shared as persons would share a pie by dividing it into physical pieces. . . . Consensus demands communication.

Dewey was, like the rest of us, often untrue to his own thought. His hopes for the future often overwhelmed the impact of his analysis. Ah! "the wish is father to the thought." He came to overvalue scientific information and communication technology as a solvent to social problems and a source of social bonds. Nonetheless, the tension between these views can still open a range of significant problems in communication for they not only represent different conceptions of communication but correspond to particular historical periods, technologies, and forms of social order.

The transmission view of communication has dominated American thought since the 1920s. When I first came into this field I felt that this view of communication, expressed in behavioral and functional terms, was exhausted. . . .

II

From such sources one can draw a definition of communication of disarming simplicity yet, I think, of some intellectual power and scope: communication is a symbolic process whereby reality is produced, maintained, repaired, and transformed.

Let me attempt to unpack that long first clause emphasizing the symbolic production of reality.

One of the major problems one encounters in talking about communication is that the noun refers to the most common, mundane human experience. There is truth in Marshall McLuhan's assertion that the one thing of which the fish is unaware is water, the very medium that forms its ambience and supports its existence. Similarly, communication, through language and other symbolic forms, comprises the ambience of human existence. The activities we collectively call communication—having conversations, giving instructions, imparting knowledge, sharing significant ideas, seeking information, entertaining and being entertained—are so ordinary and mundane that it is difficult for them to arrest our attention. Moreover, when we intellectually visit this process, we often focus on the trivial and unproblematic, so inured are we to the mysterious and awesome in communication.

A wise man once defined the purpose of art as "making the phenomenon strange." Things can become so familiar that we no longer perceive them at all. Art, however, can take the sound of the sea, the intonation of a voice, the texture of a fabric, the design of a face, the play of light upon a landscape, and wrench these ordinary phenomena out of the backdrop of existence and force them into the foreground of consideration. When Scott Fitzgerald described Daisy Buchanan as having "a voice full of money" he moves us, if we are open to the experience, to hear again that ordinary thing, the sound of a voice, and to contemplate what it portends. He arrests our apprehension and focuses it on the mystery of character as revealed in sound.

The social sciences can take the most obvious yet background facts of social life and force them into the foreground of wonderment. They can make us contemplate the particular miracles of social life that have become for us just there, plain and unproblematic for the eye to see. When he comments that communication is the most wonderful among things, surely Dewey is trying just that: to induce in us a capacity for wonder and awe regarding this commonplace activity. Dewey knew that knowledge most effectively grew at the point when things became problematic, when we experience an "information gap" between what circumstances impelled us toward doing and what we needed to know in order to act at all. This information gap, this sense of the problematic, often can be induced only by divesting life of its mundane trappings and exposing our common sense or scientific assumptions to an ironic light that makes the phenomenon strange.

To a certain though inadequate degree, my first clause attempts just that. Both our common sense and scientific realism attest to the fact that there is, first, a real world of objects, events, and processes that we observe. Second, there is language or symbols that name these events in the real world and create more or less adequate descriptions of them. There is reality and then, after the fact, our accounts of it. We insist there is a distinction between reality and fantasy; we insist that our terms stand in relation to this world as shadow and substance. While language often distorts, obfuscates, and confuses our perception of this external world, we rarely dispute this matter-of-fact realism. We peel away semantic layers of terms and meanings to uncover this more substantial domain of existence. Language stands to reality as secondary stands to primary in the old Galilean paradigm from which this view derives.

By the first clause I mean to invert this relationship, . . . to render communication a far more problematic activity than it ordinarily seems.

I want to suggest . . . words are not the names for things but, to steal a line from Kenneth Burke, things are the signs of words. Reality is not given, not humanly existent, independent of language and toward which language stands as a pale refraction. Rather, reality is brought into existence, is produced, by communication—by, in short, the construction, apprehension, and utilization of symbolic forms. Reality, while not a mere function of symbolic forms, is produced by systems . . . that focus its existence in specific terms.

Under the sway of realism we ordinarily assume there is an order to existence that the human mind through some faculty may discover and describe. I am suggesting that reality is not there to discover in any significant detail. The world is entropic—that is, not strictly ordered—though its variety is constrained enough that the mind can grasp its outline and implant an order over and within the broad and elastic constraints of nature. To put it colloquially, there are no lines of latitude and longitude in nature, but by overlaying the globe with this particular, though not exclusively correct, symbolic organization, order is imposed on spatial organization and certain, limited human purposes served.

Whatever reality might be on the mind of Bishop Berkeley's God, whatever it might be for other animals, it is for us a vast production, a staged creation—something humanly produced and humanly maintained. Whatever order is in the world is not given in our genes or exclusively supplied by nature. As the biologist J. Z. Young puts it, "the brain of each one of us does literally create his or her own world"; the order of history is, as Eric Vogelin puts it, "the history of order"—the myriad forms in which people have endowed significance, order, and meaning in the world by the agency of their own intellectual processes.

Ernst Cassirer said it, and others have repeated it to the point of deadening its significance: man lives in a new dimension of reality, symbolic reality, and it is through the agency of this capacity that existence is produced. However, though it is often said, it is rarely investigated, More than repeat it, we have to take it seriously, follow it to the end of the line, to assess its capacity to vivify our studies. What Cassirer is contending is that one must examine communication, even scientific communication, even mathematical expression, as the primary phenomena of experience and not as something "softer" and derivative from a "realer" existent nature.

Lest someone think this obscure, allow me to illustrate with an example, an example at once so artless and transparent that the meaning will be clear even if engaging complexities are sacrificed. Let us suppose one had to teach a child of six or seven how to get from home to school. The child has been driven by the school, which is some six or seven blocks away, so he recognizes it, but he has no idea of the relation between his house and school. The space between these points might as well be, as the saving goes, a trackless desert. What does one do in such a situation?

There are a number of options. The ordinary method is simply to draw the child a map. By arranging lines, angles, names, squares denoting streets and buildings in a pattern on paper, one transforms vacant space into a featured environment. Although some environments are easier to feature than others—hence trackless deserts—space is understood and manageable when it is represented in symbolic form.

The map stands as a representation of an environment capable of clarifying a problematic situation. It is capable of guiding behavior and simultaneously transforming undifferentiated space into configured—that is, known, apprehended, understood—space.

Note also that an environment, any given space, can be mapped in a number of different modes. For example, we might map a particularly important space by producing a poetic or musical description. . . . A space can be mapped by a stream of poetic speech that expresses a spatial essence and that also ensures, by exploiting the mnemonic devices of song and poetry, that the "map" can be retained in memory. By recalling the poem at appropriate moments, space can be effectively configured.

A third means of mapping space is danced ritual. The movements of the dance can parallel appropriate movements through space. By learning the dance the child acquires a representation of the space that on another occasion can guide behavior.

Space can be mapped, then, in different modes—utilizing lines on a page, sounds in air, movements in a dance. All three are symbolic forms, though the symbols differ; visual, oral, and kinesthetic. Moreover, each of the symbolic forms possesses two distinguishing characteristics: displacement and productivity. Like ordinary language, each mode allows one to speak about or represent some thing when the thing in question is not present. This capacity of displacement, of producing a complicated act when the "real" stimulus is not physically present, is another often noted though not fully explored capacity. Second, each of these symbolic forms is productive, for a person in command of the symbols is capable of producing an infinite number of representations on the basis of a finite number of symbolic elements. As with language, so with other symbolic forms: a finite set of words or a finite set of phonemes can produce, through grammatical combination, an infinite set of sentences.

We often argue that a map represents a simplification of or an abstraction from an environment. Not all the features of an environment are modeled, for the purpose of the representation is to express not the possible complexity of things but their simplicity. Space is made manageable by the reduction of information. By doing this, however, different maps bring the same environment alive in different ways; they produce quite different realities. Therefore, to live within the purview of different maps is to live within different realities. Consequently, maps not only constitute the activity known as mapmaking; they constitute nature itself.

A further implication concerns the nature of thought. In our predominantly individualistic tradition, we are accustomed to think of thought as essentially private, an activity that occurs in the head—graphically represented by Rodin's "The Thinker." I wish to suggest, in contradistinction, that thought is predominantly public and social. It occurs primarily on blackboards, in dances, and in recited poems. The capacity of private thought is a derived and secondary talent, one that appears biographically later in the person and historically later in the species. Thought is public because it depends on a publicly available stock of symbols. It is public in a second and stronger sense. Thinking consists of building maps of environments. Thought involves constructing a model of an environment and then running the model faster than the environment to see if nature can be coerced to perform as the model does. In the earlier example, the map of the neighborhood and the path from home to school represent the environment; the finger one lays on the map and traces the path is a representation of the child, the walker. "Running" the map is faster than walking the route and constitutes the "experiment" or "test."

Thought is the construction and utilization of such maps, models, templates: football plays diagrammed on a blackboard, equations on paper, ritual dances charting the nature of ancestors, or streams of prose like this attempting, out in the bright-lit world in which we all live, to present the nature of communication.

This particular miracle we perform daily and hourly—the miracle of producing reality and then living within and under the fact of our own productions—rests upon a particular quality of symbols: their ability to be both representations "of" and "for" reality?

A blueprint of a house in one mode is a representation "for" reality: under its guidance and control a reality, a house, is produced that expresses the relations contained in reduced and simplified form in the blueprint. There is a second use of a blueprint, however. If someone asks for a description of a particular house, one can simply point to a blueprint and say, "That's the house." Here the blueprint stands as a representation or symbol of reality: it expresses or represents in an alternative medium a synoptic formulation of the nature of a particular reality. While these are merely two sides of the same coin, they point to the dual capacity of symbolic forms: as "symbols of" they present reality; as "symbols for" they create the very reality they present. . . .

It is no different with a religious ritual. In one mode it represents the nature of human life, its condition and meaning, and in another mode—its "for" mode—it induces the dispositions it pretends merely to portray.

All human activity is such an exercise (can one resist the word "ritual"?) in squaring the circle. We first produce the world by symbolic work and then take up residence in the world we have produced. Alas, there is magic in our self deceptions.

We not only produce reality but we must likewise maintain what we have produced, for there are always new generations coming along for whom our productions are incipiently problematic and for whom reality must be regenerated and made authoritative. Reality must be repaired for it consistently breaks down: people get lost physically and spiritually, experiments fail, evidence counter to the representation is produced, mental derangement sets in—all threats to our models of and for reality that lead to intense repair work. Finally, we must, often with fear and regret, toss away our authoritative representations of reality and begin to build the world anew. We go to bed, to choose an example not quite at random, convinced behaviorists who view language, under the influence of Skinner, as a matter of operant conditioning and wake up, for mysterious reasons, convinced rationalists, rebuilding our mode of language, under the influence of Chomsky, along the lines of deep structures, transformations, and surface appearances. These are two different intellectual worlds in which to live, and we may find that the anomalies of one lead us to transform it into another.

To study communication is to examine the actual social process wherein significant symbolic forms are created, apprehended, and used. When described this way some scholars would dismiss it as insufficiently empirical. My own view is the opposite, for I see it as an attempt to sweep away our existing notions concerning communication that serve only to devitalize our data. Our attempts to construct, maintain, repair, and transform reality are publicly observable activities that occur in historical time. We create, express, and convey our knowledge of and attitudes toward reality through the construction of a variety of symbol systems: art, science, journalism, religion, common sense, mythology. How do we do this? What are the differences between these forms? What art the historical and comparative variations in them? How do changes in communication technology influence what we can concretely create and apprehend? How do groups in society struggle over the definition of what is real? These are some of the questions, rather too simply put, that communication studies must answer.

Finally, let me emphasize an ironic aspect to the study of communication, a way in which our subject matter doubles back on itself and presents us with a host of ethical problems. One of the activities in which we characteristically engage, as in this essay, is communication about communication itself. However, communication is not some pure phenomenon we can discover; there is no such thing as communication to be revealed in nature through some objective method free from the corruption of culture. We understand communication insofar as we are able to build models or representations of this process. But our models of communication, like all models, have this dual aspect—an "of" aspect and a "for" aspect. In one mode communication models tell us what the process is; in their second mode they produce the behavior they have described. Communication can be modeled in several empirically adequate ways, but these several models have different ethical implications for they produce different forms of social relations.

Let us face this dilemma directly. There is nothing in our genes that tells us how to create and execute those activities we summarize under the term "communication." If we are to engage in this activity—writing an essay, making a film, entertaining an audience, imparting information and advice— we must discover models in our culture that tell us how this particular miracle is achieved. Such models are found in common sense, law, religious traditions, increasingly in scientific theories themselves. Traditionally, models of communication were found in religious thought. For example, in describing the roots of the transmission view of communication in nineteenth century American religious thought I meant to imply the following: religious thought not only described communication; it also presented a model for the appropriate uses of language, the permissible forms of human contact, the ends communication should serve, the motives it should manifest. It taught what it meant to display.

Today models of communication are found less in religion than in science, but their implications are the same. For example, American social science generally has represented communication, within an overarching transmission view, in terms of either a power or an anxiety model. These correspond roughly to what is found in information theory, learning theory, and influence theory (power) and dissonance, balance theory, and functionalism or uses and gratifications analysis (anxiety). . . . These views reduce the extraordinary phenomenological diversity of communication into an arena in which people alternatively pursue power or flee anxiety. And one need only monitor the behavior of modern institutions to see the degree to which these models create, through policy and program, the abstract motives and relations they portray.

Models of communication are, then, not merely representations of communication but representations *for* communication: templates that guide, unavailing or not, concrete processes of human interaction, mass and interpersonal. Therefore, to study communication involves examining the construction, apprehension, and use of models of communication themselves—their construction in common sense, art, and science, their historically specific creation and use: in encounters between parent and child, advertisers and consumer, welfare worker and supplicant, teacher and student. Behind and within these encounters lie models of human contact and interaction.

Our models of communication, consequently, create what we disingenuously pretend they merely describe. As a result our science is, to use a term of Alvin Gouldner's, a reflexive one. We not only describe behavior; we create a particular corner of culture—culture that determines, in part, the kind of communicative world we inhabit.

Raymond Williams, whose analysis I shall follow in conclusion, speaks to the point:

> Communication begins in the struggle to learn and to describe. To start this process in our minds and to pass on its results to others, we depend on certain communication models, certain rules or conventions through which we can make contact. We can change these models when they become inadequate or we can modify and extend them. Our efforts to do so, and to use the existing models successfully, take up a large part of our living energy. . . . Moreover, many of our communication models become, in themselves, social institutions. Certain attitudes to others, certain forms of address, certain tones and styles become embodied in institutions which are then very powerful in social effect. . . . These arguable assumptions are often embodied in solid, practical institutions which then teach the models from which they start.

This relation between science and society described by Williams has not been altogether missed by the public and accounts for some of the widespread interest in communication. I am not speaking merely of the contemporary habit of reducing all human problems to problems or failures in communication. Let us recognize the habit for what it is: an attempt to coat reality with cliches, to provide a semantic crucifix to ward off modern vampires. But our appropriate cynicism should not deflect us from discovering the kernel of truth in such phrases.

If we follow Dewey, it will occur to us that problems of communication are linked to problems of community, to problems surrounding the kinds of communities we create and in which we live. For the ordinary person communication consists merely of a set of daily activities: having conversations, conveying instructions, being entertained, sustaining debate and discussion, acquiring information. The felt quality of our lives is bound up with these activities and how they are carried out within communities.

Our minds and lives are shaped by our total experience—or, better, by representations of experience and a name for this experience is communication. If one tries to examine society as a form of communication, one sees it as a process whereby reality is created, shared, modified, and preserved. When this process becomes opaque, when we lack models of and for reality that make the world apprehensible, when we are unable to describe and share it; when because of a failure in our models of communication we are unable to connect with others, we encounter problems of communication in their most potent form. . . .

The object, then, of recasting our studies of communication in terms of a ritual model is not only to more firmly grasp the essence of this "wonderful" process but to give us a way in which to rebuild a model of and for communication of some restorative value in reshaping our common culture.

POSTSCRIPT

Are American Values Shaped by the Mass Media?

T elevision is pervasive in American life. Yet the influence of television on society is difficult to ascertain. Although these issues are as hotly debated today as they were when these articles were written, a number of things have changed since then. Carey stresses the view of communication as a process of negotiation for cultural ideas, images, and issues. With the proliferation of electronic and digital channels of information and entertainment, this symbolic process may be more complicated than ever, as audiences select from a variety of niche programming alternatives. Is the cultural negotiation lessened because choices are more diverse? Does this diversity threaten the foundations of community that underlie Carey's perspective?

Similarly, alterations in programming strategies, particularly the creation of niche programming, may strain the notion of an ideological core of myths that structure content as advanced by Schiller. Yet many argue that all this additional programming is simply "more of the same." Others disagree, arguing that specialized channels and additional electronic options like the Internet open up spaces for "contested meanings" that challenge the dominant hegemonic reality. For a different take on the ways in which production of media content is influenced by corporate ownership, see Issue 18 on news and public trust.

Yet some effects of television have been dramatically illustrated. The media were instrumental in bringing together the entire nation to mourn and to respond to the events of September 11, 2001. Television's ability to bring events to millions of viewers may mean that television itself is a factor in determining events. For example, television has reshaped American politics, but it may have little influence on how people actually vote. Television is now the primary source of news for most Americans. It has also altered the ways in which Americans spend their time, ranking third behind sleep and work.

Authors such as Neil Postman suggest that media shapes American values, by changing the nature of public discourse. Postman argues in *Amusing Ourselves to Death* (Viking Penguin, 1985) that television promotes triviality by speaking in only one voice—the voice of entertainment. Thus he maintains that television is transforming American culture into show business, to the detriment of rational public discourse.

ISSUE 2

Are *Harry Potter* Books Harmful for Children?

YES: Rob Boston, from "Witch Hunt: Why the Religious Right Is Crusading to Exorcise Harry Potter Books from Public Schools and Libraries," *Church & State* (March 1, 2002)

NO: Lana A. Whited, with M. Katherine Grimes, from *The Ivory Tower and Harry Potter: Perspectives on a Literary Phenomenon* (University of Missouri Press, 2002)

ISSUE SUMMARY

YES: Though the popular *Harry Potter* series has received worldwide attention, the content remains questionable for some people. Writer Rob Boston examines the position of some members of the Christian Right, and identifies how and why some people think *Harry Potter* books endorse witchcraft and a belief in the occult. The controversy shows that children's books are often the subject of book banning and censorship, for a variety of reasons.

NO: Lana Whited and M. Katherine Grimes are English teachers who report that despite religious-based objections to *Harry Potter* books and films that are part of the fantasy genre in literature, children can be exposed to a number of situations and dilemmas that enhance children's moral reasoning abilities. Using a scheme developed by Professor Lawrence Kohlberg, they examine a number of situations in the *Harry Potter* series that they claim can help guide children's moral development.

While the First Amendment to the Constitution guarantees "freedom of speech" and "freedom of the press," children have always been considered a special audience for whom some monitoring, or even censoring of media content, might be appropriate. Rob Boston, a writer for *Church & State,* examines a number of situations in which *Harry Potter* books and films have raised the ire of some religious and community leaders. In general, the objections by many, especially the Christian Right, deal with the fear of the normalizing of witchcraft and the alleged satanic overtones of the book and films. These fears, for the most part, deal with the possibility that children could become interested in the occult, through the *Harry Potter* series and identification with the characters.

The cry for censorship of the popular book series and films is nothing new. As Boston notes, there is a long history of classifying literature for children as unsuitable for one reason or another. In particular, fantasy fiction has always been among the most problematic for some groups of people who fear that children will not be able to tell fantasy from real life and, therefore, could become interested in the occult arts or lost in the fantasy world.

Lana Whited and M. Katherine Grimes acknowledge these concerns and take the position that the characters portrayed in *Harry Potter* media actually provide positive role models for children, especially in the area of moral development. They cite Harvard Professor Lawrence Kohlberg's work on developing a framework for evaluating moral reasoning, and find that the J. K. Rowling's characters in *Harry Potter* consistently provide valuable role models for children and adults. They discuss Kohlberg's multi-level schema that includes concepts of understanding moral conflict and their consequences, the need for role-playing to examine new perspectives and viewpoints, and the ability to understand issues of moral and social justice.

As you read these selections, you may want to think about the importance of social and moral values, and how they can be viewed differently by people of different faiths and belief systems, and the diversity of values represented in different communities and regions of the country. When we think about the impact of media content and the vulnerability of children, the controversy over appropriate values often becomes a battlefield of ideas and beliefs. While some teachers and librarians have heaped praise on the *Harry Potter* series for encouraging children to read, the problem of *what* children are willing to read will always stimulate discussion among parents, teachers, and cultural leaders.

The overwhelming popularity and success of J. K. Rowling's *Harry Potter* series, and the films, costumes, and products desired by Harry Potter fans, young and old, focus attention on the fantasy genre and the age-old question of whether children can tell the difference between fantasy and reality, and whether their ability to tell the difference really matters in the long run.

YES ↵

Rob Boston

Witch Hunt: Why the Religious Right Is Crusading to Exorcise Harry Potter Books from Public Schools and Libraries

Robert Fichthorn had decided to take a stand.

Fichthorn, captain of the Penryn, Pa., "fire police," a volunteer body that provides traffic control services during fires, auto accidents and civic events, declared in late January that his officers would not help cordon off streets during a YMCA-sponsored triathlon scheduled for this September.

Fichthorn's reason surprised many in the community. Despite its Christian roots, Fichthorn asserted, the YMCA is in fact supporting witchcraft by allowing students taking part in an after-school program to read the popular "Harry Potter" books. The fire police would do nothing, he insisted, to aid this nefarious behavior.

"I don't feel right taking our children's minds and teaching them [witch-craft]," Fichthorn hold the Lancaster New Era. "As long as we don't stand up, it won't stop."

Fichthorn's declaration hit the local papers and promptly sparked an uproar in the tiny central Pennsylvania community. But things really got interesting after the story was circulated nationally by the Associated Press and spread worldwide over the Internet. Irate residents squared off in letters to the editor. YMCA officials were swamped with messages from all over the country and even overseas as people offered to stand in for the fire police.

Newspaper columnists blasted Fichthorn and the rest of his department as narrow-minded and silly. *Sports Illustrated* cited the flap as "This Week's Sign of the Apocalypse." The *Denver Post* gave Fichthorn its "Doofus of the Month" award.

Many in the community and surrounding area were not pleased with the attention. "Yes, all across the country, people are reading about the Penryn Fire Police decision to spurn the triathlon because Harry Potter goes against their Christian morals," groused Gil Smart, a columnist with the Lancaster Sunday News. "And all across the country, people are thinking: What bumpkins."

But if the Penryn Fire Police are bumpkins for hating Harry Potter, they are not the only ones. All over the country, Religious Right groups and local activists have put the Potter series in their theological crosshairs. The Penryn incident captured national headlines, but it is in no way an aberration.

According to the American Library Association (ALA), the Potter series, authored by Scottish writer J.K. Rowling, now holds the dubious distinction of being the most censored books in America. Public schools and libraries in many communities are under siege as far-right forces demand that the books be removed outright or placed on restricted access.

At first glance, the books look like unlikely candidates for all this fuss. Designed for pre- and early teens, the series recounts the adventures of Harry Potter, an orphan growing up in London. Verbally abused and forced to live in a dingy space at his domineering uncle's house, Potter's fortunes take a dramatic turn for the better when he learns he is descended from a long line of wizards and is invited to attend Hogwarts, a private academy for wizards in training.

The series is phenomenally popular, and the four books so far have sold in the millions worldwide. Late last year, a movie based on the first book, *Harry Potter and the Sorcerer's Stone,* opened to long lines and generally favorable reviews.

But not everyone is wild about Harry. Religious Right forces, including TV preacher Pat Robertson's "700 Club," James Dobson's Focus on the Family, the Rev. Louis P. Sheldon's Traditional Values Coalition and a host of far-right lesser lights are convinced that the books promote evil and the occult—and they are spurring local activists to drive the books from public schools and libraries.

A sampling of recent incidents includes:

- York, Pa.: Led by a local pastor who is also an elementary school teacher, a handful of parents demanded that the Harry Potter books be removed from the Eastern York schools, asserting that the tomes promote witchcraft. "It's against my daughter's constitution, it's evil and it promotes witchcraft," parent Deb Eugenio told reporters. "I'm not paying taxes to teach my child witchcraft."

  The school board voted 7-2 in January to allow teachers to continue to use the Potter books provided that parents first sign permission slips. Sixth-grade teacher Ed Althouse had been using the first book, *Harry Potter and the Sorcerer's Stone,* during a unit on fantasy literature. The parents of four students declined to sign the permission slips, and their children were given an alternate assignment.

- Alamogordo, N.M.: In an incident that captured headlines worldwide, Pastor Jack Brock of the Christ Community Church led a mass burning of Harry Potter books Dec. 30. Brock told reporters that the books "encourage our youth to learn more about witches, warlocks and sorcerers, and those things are an abomination to God and to me." For good measure, Brock also tossed a copy of *The Collected Works of William Shakespeare* on the bonfire.

- Duvall County, Fla.: Parent Mendy Robinson challenged the Potter books at Thomas Jefferson Elementary School, insisting that they are "turning children to lies & falsehoods of this present world." A committee of teachers, parents and libraries in October spurned a request that the Potter books be removed from school library shelves. Students had to get parental permission to read the books while the committee deliberated the matter.

- Oskaloosa, Kan.: The board of directors of the local public library voted to cancel a Harry Potter-themed event after some fundamentalists complained. The library had planned a reading program in June for "aspiring young witches and wizards" featuring a storyteller who had appeared at other Kansas libraries. The board voted to cancel the program after a handful of residents complained that the program promoted witchcraft.

- Fargo, N.D.: Officials at Agassiz Middle School in November cancelled a planned field trip to the Harry Potter movie after a few parents, backed by a local right-wing radio talk-show host, denounced the outing. School officials took the action even though all of the students, aged between 12 and 15, had received parental permission.

    "It's a little bizarre," Fargo School Superintendent David Flowers said. "We believe that we were on firm ground in letting the kids go, but [the school] made the decision . . . that they would just as soon not be embroiled in controversy."

- Copley Township, Ohio: Library Coordinator Cathy Hall of the Copley-Fairlawn School District recommended in January that the district stop buying books in the Potter series. The system's library currently has two of the four Potter books, and Hall said she believes no more titles from the series should be added.

    Hall told the Akron *Beacon Journal* that she made the recommendation primarily on the basis of financial concerns but then went on to say she was "also keeping in mind those things that are being said about the book."

- Modesto, Calif.: The Rev. B. Joseph Mannion has called on "religious parents" to keep the Potter books out of local public schools. In a Dec. 29 letter to *The Modesto Bee, Mannion wrote,* "The Harry Potter books are evil. They are based on evil: witchcraft, wizardry and the occult."

- Lewiston, Maine: The Rev. Doug Taylor announced plans to hold a book burning of the Potter tomes in a community park in November. Taylor, head of a local organization called the Jesus Party, applied for a permit to hold a bonfire in the park but was turned down by the Lewiston Fire Department. Instead, he cut up a Potter book with a pair of scissors and tossed it into a trashcan.

    Maine newspapers reported that a minister from Portland who attended the event to support Taylor confronted members of a pro-Potter contingent mounting a counter-protest. "Some of you young people," the minister said, "should take a look at where you're going. Hell is a very bad place."

- Jacksonville, Fla.: Officials with the city's public library system dropped a plan to distribute "Hogwarts certificates" to encourage youngsters to read after a local resident, John Miesburg, complained that the books promoted "the evil of witchcraft." Librarians at the Regency Library did distribute some of the certificates in July of 2000 but stopped after attorneys with the Liberty Counsel, a Religious Right legal group affiliated with the Rev. Jerry Falwell, threatened to sue.

Mathew Staver, head of the Liberty Counsel, insisted that the library's plan violated church-state separation.

- Zeeland, Mich.: A long-running dispute over the Potter books has culminated in the resignation of a school board president. Tom Bock stepped down after repeatedly butting heads with Mary Dana, a middle school teacher who protested a 1999 vote by the board to ban the Potter books.

    The restrictions were later lifted, but Bock and Dana continued sparring over the matter. Bock resigned after school administrators turned down his demands that Dana be removed from her position as a mentor to new teachers, reported the *Grand Rapids Press*.

These incidents are just a few of the recent challenges to the Potter books. According to the ALA, which tracks incidents of censorship nationwide, Rowling's books have been the most challenged works in public school libraries and public libraries for three years running.

Beverly Becker, associate director of the ALA's Office of Intellectual Freedom, has noticed a common theme among the complaints. "It's always witchcraft," Becker told *Church & State*. "Occasionally they throw something else in, but ultimately these challenges are all about witchcraft."

Becker points out that the ALA noted a dramatic upswing in the challenges in October of 1999, when *Harry Potter and the Prisoner of Azkaban*, was published. Becker said this was probably due to increased media attention.

"When the third book came out," she said, "the publicity went crazy. I think that's when every adult heard about the books, not just the ones who had a 10- or 12-year-old at home." Becker notes that more public schools began using the books at that time as well.

As sales climbed, Religious Right groups went into a frenzy. Some of the charges they have lobbed against the books seem too fantastic to believe, but millions of Religious Right activists around the country are now apparently convinced that the Potter series is part of a plot to lure youngsters into Wiccan groups.

High-profile TV preacher Robertson launched a full-scale assault on the Potter books late last year. On the Dec. 5 "700 Club," cohost Terry Meeuwsen interviewed Caryl Matrisciana, identified as an "expert on the occult" and producer of a video titled "Harry Potter: Witchcraft Repackaged."

In fact, Matrisciana is the wife of Pat Matrisciana, a long-time far-right political operative who made his living during much of the 1990s peddling conspiracy-theory videos attacking President Bill Clinton, most notably "The Clinton Chronicles." During the CBN interview, Caryl Matrisciana asserted that Rowling based the books on "the religions of Celtic, druidic, Satanic, Wiccan and pagan roots and written them into her fiction books for children."

Asserted Matrisciana, "The harm is first of all that witchcraft is being normalized to our children. For the first time in the history of the world, witchcraft is being given to children in a children's format, and children are seeing other children practicing it and say it's all right."

Following the interview, Robertson felt moved to offer his own comments. Glaring sternly into the cameras, Robertson told the audience that God will turn his back on nations that tolerate witchcraft—with dire consequences.

"Now, ladies and gentlemen, we have been talking about God lifting his anointing and his mantle from the United States of America," Robertson said. "And if you read in Deuteronomy or Leviticus, actually, the eighteenth chapter, there's certain things that he says that is going to cause the Lord, or the land, to vomit you out. At the head of the list is witchcraft. . . . Now we're welcoming this and teaching our children. And what we're doing is asking for the wrath of God to come on this country. . . . And if there's ever a time we need God's blessing it's now. We don't need to be bringing in heathen, pagan practices to the United States of America."

(Strangely enough, a series of anti-Potter articles on the CBN website disappeared not long after Robertson's outburst. This may be due to the fact that ABC/Disney, which now owns the cable channel that carries the "700 Club," recently purchased the rights to broadcast the first Potter movie on television.)

Other Religious Right groups were quick to join the anti-Potter bandwagon.

"Is Harry Potter a Harmless Fantasy or a Wicca Training Program?" blared a recent press release issued by Sheldon's Traditional Values Coalition. Sheldon, one of the Religious Right's most vociferous gay bashers, even tried to link the Potter series to homosexuality, writing, "While the themes in Harry Potter books do not expressly advocate homosexuality or abortion, these are the philosophical beliefs deeply embedded in Wicca. The child who is seduced into Wicca witchcraft through Harry Potter books will eventually be introduced to these other concepts."

TV preacher D. James Kennedy of Coral Ridge Ministries is also promoting the alleged Potter-Wicca connection. In late October, Kennedy interviewed Richard Abanes, a self-proclaimed "expert on the occult" and author of the anti-Potter tome Harry Potter and the Bible.

Appearing on Kennedy's "Truths That Transform" radio show, Abanes asserted that as a result of the Potter books, Wiccan groups in England are flooded with new members. The leading Wiccan group in the United Kingdom, Abanes told Kennedy, has had to hire a youth minister.

Series author Rowling, Abanes asserted, "has had a fascination with the occult and witchcraft and wizardry every since she was a little girl. And so, her creativity, her talent, when she wrote something, that came out on the page—I'm not sure she actually meant to draw kids into the occult, but that's indeed what's already happening, especially in England."

The Rev. Donald Wildmon's American Family Association has also attacked Rowling's books and the film version of the first volume. In November the AFA's website (www.afa.net) posted an article by "contributing columnist" Berit Kjos, whose ministry has made attacking Potter into a cottage industry. The article, titled "Twelve Reasons Not to See the Harry Potter Movie," asserted that the film presents witchcraft as an appealing alternative lifestyle.

Wrote Kjos, "This pagan ideology comes complete with trading cards, computer and other wizardly games, clothes and decorations stamped with

[Harry Potter] symbols, action figures and cuddly dolls and audio cassettes that could keep the child's minds (sic) focused on the occult all day and into night. But in God's eyes, such paraphernalia become little more than lures and doorways to deeper involvement with the occult."

(Wildmon, whose AFA is based in Tupelo, Miss., is best known for attempting to censor television programs. Last month he joined 14 other groups in petitioning the Federal Communications Commission to demand the removal of an award-winning drama series, "Boston Public," from the Fox Network.)

Falwell has also recommended caution. Falwell's *National Liberty Journal* noted late last year "that there does appear to be a legitimate reason to be cautious in regard to Harry Potter" and asserted, "Even if the author's intent is anything but evil, the attractive presentation of witchcraft and wizardry—both ultimately godless pursuits—may desensitize children to important spiritual issues."

The unbylined piece, however, does note that some conservative Christians see no danger in the Potter books and adds, "Harry Potter is not worth causing a major schism within the church." (Falwell may have good reasons for not launching a full-scale assault on the Potter series. In 1999, he became the target of international ridicule after warning parents that a character named Tinky Winky from the PBS children's series "Teletubbies" is gay.)

Rowling, who wrote the first Potter book while struggling to keep her head above water as a single mom, has called the assertions that her books seek to lure youngsters into the occult "absurd." In one interview she observed, "I have met thousands of children now, and not even one time has a child come up to me and said, 'Ms. Rowling, I'm so glad I've read these books because now I want to be a witch.'"

Many experts on education and children's literature agree that the books are unlikely to draw children into the occult. They note that witches, fairies, dragons and other mythical beasts have a long lineage in stories aimed at young readers. Witches are a staple in *Grimm's Fairy Tales,* which date back to the Middle Ages and remain popular today. In the *Grimm Brothers' tales,* as in the Potter books today, good triumphs over evil in the end. Such stories usually end up teaching simple moral lessons that youngsters can readily understand.

None of this has slowed down the censors one iota. And, with three more books in the Potter series on the horizon—and more film adaptions on the way—anti-censorship activists expect to see more efforts to ban the Potter series and others. (According to the ALA, the most common targets of censorship in America for the period 1990–2000 include *The Adventures of Huckleberry Finn* by Mark Twain, John Steinbeck's *Of Mice and Men, The Catcher in the Rye* by J.D. Salinger, Harper Lee's *To Kill a Mockingbird, The Witches* by Roald Dahl and *A Wrinkle in Time* by Madeleine L'Engle.)

Officials at the ALA recommend that both public school libraries and public libraries have clear policies in place for dealing with censorship attempts. They advocate review committees that can examine challenged books and say it's essential that everyone involved in the committee and the larger effort actually read the book under challenge. These policies, ALA staffers say, can avoid a rush to judgment.

"That allows for a fair hearing, so everyone can cool down," says the ALA's Becker. "The decision is not made in such an emotional moment."

Given time, many censorship efforts collapse in the face of counter mobilization by concerned community members or just fail because the charges against a book are preposterous. This was often the case 100 years ago when efforts were made to censor another children's book featuring witches— L. Frank Baum's *The Wizard of Oz*. Outraged Oz fans stepped forward to defend the book, turning back some censorship efforts. (See "Lions And Tigers And Censors—Oh, My!")

An echo of that long-ago struggle was heard in central Pennsylvania recently during the incident in Penryn. Laura Montgomery Rutt, director of the Alliance for Tolerance and Freedom in Lancaster, which keeps tabs on the Religious Right locally, said community sentiment is running solidly against the fire police. Many people in the area, she said, think the fire police are being silly.

"People here are not supporting the decision of the fire police," she said. "And their actions have helped the YMCA. People are volunteering and saying they want to help. No one knew about the triathlon before this happened. Now they are volunteering to help run it—even people from other states."

Lancaster County is a conservative area, Rutt said, but that doesn't mean residents support censorship. "The community has seen and learned that extremism is not going to win," Rutt told *Church & State*. "This shows that even the guys in the fire police are going beyond what Lancaster County is willing to put up with. We've also seen that the community is willing to rally when an organization shows it is intolerant. So many have spoken out on behalf of the Potter books. A lot of people have a tendency to stay in their shells, but this was just too much. All in all, this was kind of a good thing. It really rallied the troops."

Lana A. Whited, with
M. Katherine Grimes

NO

What Would Harry Do?: J. K. Rowling and Lawrence Kohlberg's Theories of Moral Development

British writer J. K. Rowling's wildly famous character Harry Potter, star of four bestselling books so far, goes to school like any other child. However, the school he attends, Hogwarts School for Witchcraft and Wizardry, is unlike any real or "Muggle" school, for Harry and his classmates study subjects such as Transfiguration, Divination, Defense against the Dark Arts, Potions, History of Magic, and Care of Magical Creatures. Because of Harry's magical pursuits, the books have come under attack from the religious right, who fear that putting such notions as witchcraft into children's heads will lead youngsters away from the beliefs they are taught at home and in religious institutions, perhaps resulting in weakened morals and, consequently, inappropriate behavior. At the heart of conservative Christians' objections is what psychologists call "desensitization," the concern that exposure to something will lead to increased tolerance for it. Karen Jo Gounard of the Family Friendly Libraries group calls the Harry Potter series a "door-opener," implying that the books serve as a gateway into a taboo world that children might otherwise avoid or postpone encountering. Conservative Christians also object to the dichotomy Rowling establishes between the Muggle and magical worlds. Compare Harry to Dudley Dursley, Minerva McGonagall to Petunia Dursley, or Hagrid to Vernon Dursley, and it isn't hard to decide whose side Rowling is on. In general, nonmagical characters are ciphers at best and villains at worst, inhabitants of a black-and-white world that contrasts sharply with the colorful magical world. To what child would the idea of flying around on a broom during gym class or changing oneself into a cat not appeal, if only imaginatively?

It is easy to trivialize such religious-based objections to the Harry Potter books, and, in fact, many writers, amateur and professional, have done so. For example, writing for the *Times* of London, India Knight says that the ban of the books by St. Mary's Island Church of English Primary School in Kent "proves, yet again, that some people would not know a marvelous role model if it turned round and bit them on the behind." In an appearance on Cable

News Network's *Larry King Live*, Rowling spoke with less sarcasm but echoed the incredulity, as she said, "my feeling is that their objection is utterly unfounded." Some of those most vocal about kicking Harry Potter out of children's libraries and classrooms have not read the books, and those who would censor Rowling's books without reading them have a credibility problem that makes them an easy target, especially for intellectuals.

While reconciliation between the Potter-banners and the censor-censurers is unlikely, it is important to note that the positions of both camps are predicated on the same basic premise: that reading is a powerful influence on the moral development of children and adolescents. Whether a person argues that a child reading the Harry Potter series is likely to plot the triumph of evil, like Voldemort, or to launch a personal campaign to promote the welfare of the disenfranchised, like Hermione, the underlying implication is that our own attitudes and behaviors are influenced by the experiences of characters we encounter in books. Voldemort and Albus Dumbledore are, after all, contraries, not contradictions. One opinion that meets with universal agreement is that it is good to see more children becoming regular customers at libraries and bookstores (also like Hermione), and even those who object to Rowling's books on religious grounds or who feel the books lack real literary merit acknowledge that Harry has drawn children's noses into books.

Perhaps, then, a more valuable exercise than condemning or championing the Harry Potter books would be to examine them in light of the examples of moral and ethical decision-making Rowling provides for young readers. Probably the most influential research on children's moral reasoning is that conducted by psychologist Lawrence Kohlberg at Harvard University in the 1960s and 1970s. Applying Jean Piaget's approach to cognition to the development of moral reasoning, Kohlberg's work resulted in a six-stage model. Kohlberg would probably maintain that rather than mire in questions of what specific morals or values a child might derive from reading Harry Potter, we should consider what experiences of moral reasoning Rowling's books might offer young readers. Although Harry's dilemmas involve creatures and settings quite different from the "real" world, Rowling always puts him in the position of deciding between or among quite realistic alternatives, and Harry's saga ultimately provides an effective illustration of Kohlberg's theories.

Lawrence Kohlberg Meets Harry Potter

Educators and theorists in the field of education have debated since the time of Socrates the appropriateness of moral education in schools and the means of achieving it. Lawrence Kohlberg's doctoral research involved studying children's moral reasoning by confronting them with moral dilemmas, and he subsequently applied the theories he formulated from these and other studies to the school environment. Kohlberg conducted studies on moral reasoning with children and young adults, mostly boys. His general method was to present a child with a scenario involving a person facing a moral dilemma and then ask the child to discuss what the person should do and why. . . .

From this research, Kohlberg developed a scheme of moral maturation with three levels: Preconventional, Conventional, and Postconventional. In addition, each level has two stages; thus, there are six stages of development in all. The terms of the levels and stages are Kohlberg's.

Moral Development at the Preconventional Level

The first level, the Preconventional, contains two stages. During the first, Punishment and Obedience, young children learn to do what adults and older children want them to do in order to avoid punishment. They adopt an attitude of "might makes right" because it seems the safest. If they can figure out what grown-ups want and do it, they can avoid punishment. . . . Either way, avoiding negative consequences is the key motivation.

The character in Harry Potter's world who best exemplifies stage one morality appears early in *Harry Potter and the Sorcerer's Stone,* sticking his head in the door of Harry's train compartment on the first trip to Hogwarts. He is Draco Malfoy, son of a Hogwarts board member. In the four Harry Potter books published so far, Malfoy never acts out of any motive except "my daddy's an important person so I can get away with this." In book one, Malfoy steals perpetual underdog Neville Longbottom's "Remembrall," a gadget sent to him by his grandmother to keep him from forgetting important things. When a professor appears, Malfoy finally returns the remembrall, muttering that he was "Just looking" (*Sorcerer's Stone,* 145). When Neville subsequently breaks his wrist during his first broomstick practice, Malfoy makes fun of him, seizing the remembrall again and zooming off on his own broomstick. Harry finally intimidates Malfoy into dropping Neville's ball by threatening to knock him off his broomstick. Harry knows that the only tactic that will work with the bully is based on the reasoning that characterizes Kohlberg's stage one— "might makes right."

An adult character who illustrates the "might makes right" approach is Harry's uncle Vernon Dursley, in whose care Harry has been left after his parents' death. Dursley presumes that the strong-armed approach will work with Harry, at whom he roars, "I WARNED YOU! I WILL NOT TOLERATE MENTION OF YOUR ABNORMALITY!" (*Chamber of Secrets,* 2; emphasis Rowling's). The Dursleys lock Harry in a room under the stairs, thinking they will prevent him from practicing magic, and once, when Harry tries to leave, his uncle restrains him by grabbing his ankle. However, Dursley has misjudged Harry, for the young wizard is far beyond the "might makes right" stage, and he bides his time at the Dursleys', waiting out his tedious summer vacations broken only by occasional rescues by his magical friends. As an adult, Dursley is not actually in stage one himself, but he obviously thinks that Harry is and, therefore, that threatening his nephew will work.

Vernon Dursley's son Dudley, Harry's cousin, illustrates the second stage on Kohlberg's scale, Instrumental Exchange. During stage two, children do what they think they should in order to get what they want. A child learns to share his toys so that his playmate will share hers with him. The attitude is "You scratch my back; I'll scratch yours." . . .

At the second stage, children begin to understand the concept of fairness and can divide a treat such as candy equally among friends. Dudley Dursley, however, has no friends. Instead, he trades the behavior his parents want for their approval and favors, especially food. Not surprisingly, one of his first words is "Won't!" (*Sorcerer's Stone*, 6). In *Harry Potter and the Chamber of Secrets*, Dudley taunts Harry by asking him why he hasn't gotten birthday cards from his school friends. When Harry responds angrily, frightening Dudley with stereotypical magic words such as "hocus, pocus," Dudley runs to his mother to tattle and is rewarded with an ice cream cone. Dudley appears in only two chapters of *Harry Potter and the Goblet of Fire*, by which time his gluttony has made him obese. . . . Because he has outgrown the largest school uniform made, he is on a strict diet, allowed one quarter of a grapefruit for breakfast. Not surprisingly, he is usually out of sorts, and when the Weasleys arrive to collect Harry for the Quidditch World Cup and George and Fred drop toffees on the floor, Dudley sucks them up like a Hoover, unaware that they are charmed and will make his tongue swell. Even at age fourteen, Dudley's main interest is still what's in it for him.

Kohlberg found reasoning at the Preconventional level to be most common among children younger than nine. In *Sorcerer's Stone*, Harry and his classmates are eleven. Thus, even in the first book of the series, Draco Malfoy should be reasoning at the next level, the Conventional. However, even in *Harry Potter and the Prisoner of Azkaban* and *Harry Potter and the Goblet of Fire*, by which time students in Harry's year are thirteen and fourteen, respectively, Malfoy has achieved only stage two. . . .

A frightening example of adults still functioning at the stage two level comes in the Quidditch World Cup section of book four. As the Dark Mark, the sign of Voldemort, is conjured in the night sky, a group of "Death Eaters" (Voldemort's supporters) terrorize a group of Muggles by floating them along over the campsite and enjoying their terror and humiliation, even turning one woman upside down, so that her underwear is revealed to gawkers below. The prejudice that fuels the Death Eaters' harassment of anyone who isn't a "pureblood" is also a stage two concept: if they can belittle everyone who isn't 100 percent wizard, those who are "pureblood" (or who think they are) can think they belong to a more exclusive group. . . .

Moral Development at the Conventional Level

The second level in Kohlberg's scheme is the Conventional. At this level, children begin to be much more aware of abstract concepts of morality and social expectations and to conform their actions to the conventions they perceive around them. Again, there are two stages. The first is Interpersonal Conformity. During the third stage, children learn to do what earns them praise. Being told "You're such a nice girl!" or "What a good boy you are!" is sufficient at this stage to elicit desired behavior from children. It is at this stage that motivation begins to be important to children and they understand that accidents with bad consequences (knocking over a glass of milk unintentionally, for example) are not wrong in the same way as intentional bad acts, such as knocking over a glass of milk in a fit of pique. At this stage, a child begins to be able to put himself or herself into another person's place in the sense of the Golden Rule. . . . At this stage, adolescents and adults act in accordance with the expectations of others, as they perceive them.

Harry and his friends function comfortably at the stage three level. When he has just met Ron Weasley on the Hogwarts train, Harry buys a lot of candy to share with his new friend, whose family's modest means Harry has already perceived. In *Chamber of Secrets,* Harry, because of his celebrity, is given signed copies of a new professor's books, but he promptly gives them to Ginny Weasley, Ron's sister, perceiving that it will ease the family's burden of buying textbooks for five children. But Ginny and Ron are more privileged in another way: they share their large, loving family with Harry, and the Weasleys often provide Harry a hiatus from the drudgery of life at the Dursleys. In *Goblet of Fire,* when the school champions' families are invited to watch the third task, Harry is surprised when Molly and Bill Weasley (Ron's mother and brother) show up to serve as his surrogate relatives. In the same book, Harry clearly demonstrates a stage three motive, loyalty, when he regrets writing to his godfather, Sirius Black, about his scar hurting because he fears Black's return will put the fugitive in jeopardy. The only living person to whom Harry feels deeper loyalty than to Sirius Black is his headmaster, Albus Dumbledore. In fact, at the end of *Chamber of Secrets,* Harry is able to defeat a basilisk that has been terrorizing the school when Dumbledore's phoenix, Fawkes, arrives to assist him. Dumbledore tells Harry after the ordeal that only a demonstration of "real loyalty" could have summoned the bird. Dumbledore notes the fidelity associated with the phoenix on several occasions (*Chamber of Secrets . . .*).

However, while Harry usually functions at the stage three level (or higher), he at least once reverts to stage two thinking; when he is inside the maze attempting the third task in *Goblet of Fire,* he hears Fleur scream and briefly thinks, *"One champion down."* . . . Harry's reaction to Fleur's distress as something advantageous to him is a temporary regression, probably induced by stress.

In *Exploring Harry Potter,* Elizabeth D. Schafer argues that Hermione and Ron serve as Harry's Knights of the Round Table or Merry Men, and they "appear unremarkable . . . stereotypical of most children their age." It is clear by Halloween of their first year at Hogwarts that the three will be loyal to each other, when Harry and Ron battle a troll to rescue Hermione, and she lies— says she was stalking it because she'd read about trolls in books—to deflect blame from her friends. "[F]rom that moment on," Rowling writes, "Hermione Granger became their friend" (*Sorcerer's Stone,* 178–79).

Although one would have to take issue with Schafer's characterization of the intelligent, well-read Hermione as "unremarkable," Ron does seem "stereotypical," particularly where his moral reasoning is concerned. In fact, Ron is perhaps the best example of stage three reasoning in the Harry Potter series, as loyalty is his preeminent virtue. In *Sorcerer's Stone,* although he has known Harry only a few weeks, Ron is prepared to serve as Harry's second in a wizard's duel with Draco Malfoy, a role he has to explain: "A second's there to take over if you die." . . .

At the stage three level, much importance is placed on interpersonal relationships, as Ron demonstrates when Harry discovers his parents in the magical Mirror of Erised and Ron begs to look in the mirror, too. The value Ron places on loyalty to those he loves is often clearest when he perceives that others are disloyal. For example, in *Goblet of Fire,* Ron stops speaking to Harry for a few months after Harry's name is selected by the Goblet of Fire for the Triwizard Tournament. Ron refuses to believe that Harry didn't break the tournament rule about eligibility and enter himself, and, although Hermione explains away Ron's reaction as jealousy, Ron more likely feels that Harry made a decision which excluded him. Only after Ron watches Harry confront the dragon, when he realizes the real danger his best friend faces by virtue of being selected a champion, does he come around. In the same book, when Hermione shows interest in the Durmstrang champion Victor Krum, Ron lectures her that she is *"fraternizing with the enemy."* . . . When Hermione assures Ron that Harry is secure in her loyalty and that the point of the tournament is the opportunity to mingle with young people from other schools, Ron reverts to stage two: "No it isn't! It's about winning!". . .

Ron Weasley also illustrates conventional moral reasoning when it comes to social norms. He is hesitant to join Hermione's campaign for the house-elves' welfare, arguing a rationalization commonly used to defend slavery: that the elves not only accept but welcome their servitude and, furthermore, would be lost without their masters (*Goblet of Fire,* 224). Later, he explains to Harry the prejudice against half giants, an attitude he has clearly internalized: "they just like killing, everyone knows that" (*Goblet of Fire,* 430). Even at fourteen, in his fourth year at Hogwarts, Ron largely borrows his ethics from the society around him rather than forming them for himself.

As Hermione's attitude about the Triwizard Tournament makes clear, she also demonstrates the interpersonal emphasis of stage three. She values her friendships, and she shares her remarkable knowledge with Ron and Harry, because she is better at school than any of the other children in her year and because, as a lover of books and knowledge, she is eager to share them with others. Hermione's association with Victor Krum in *Goblet of Fire* effectively demonstrates the value she places on interpersonal relationships—to wit, that a friendship with someone she likes is more important to her than the inter-school competition Victor and Harry are engaged in.

But a more problematic aspect of Hermione's character has been pointed out by several writers. Often, in moments of real danger, Hermione becomes emotional, sometimes bursting into tears. As Harry and Ron fight off a troll early in their first year, Hermione, nearly faint, shrinks against a wall, then sinks to the floor in fright and remains there while the boys dispense with the troll. In the climax of *Sorcerer's Stone,* Harry urges Hermione to return to Ron as he moves on through passageways, anticipating a confrontation with Severus Snape and, possibly, Lord Voldemort, and Rowling describes a stereotypically feminine reaction, as, lip trembling, she embraces Harry and declares, "Harry—you're a great wizard, you know . . . oh Harry—be *careful!"*. . .

Hermione's emotional devotion to Harry touches on what has been the primary objection to Lawrence Kohlberg's work, a complaint described by his protégé and colleague Carol Gilligan, author of *In a Different Voice: Psychological*

Theory and Women's Development (1982). Gilligan criticized Kohlberg's methodology because the subjects of his interviews were all male and he generalized, from their responses, theories about the moral development of people in general. Gilligan felt, as Kohlberg himself explains, "that morality really includes two moral orientations: first, the morality of justice as stressed by Freud and Piaget and, second, an ethic of care and response which is more central to understanding female moral judgment and action than it is to the understanding of judgment and action in males." Gilligan and Kohlberg's disagreement is essentially over whether stage three reasoning, based on an "ethic of care," is inferior to stage four reasoning, based on an "ethic of justice." Gilligan's allegation, in other words, is that Kohlberg considered reasoning whose basis is the individual welfare of friends and loved ones as inferior to reasoning based on the concept of justice for all society. This disagreement is not likely to be resolved, as it touches on age-old stereotypes of the sexes and as subsequent theorists who got involved in trying to argue one position or the other, such as Lawrence Walker and Diana Baumrind, tend to line up along gender lines.

However, the application of Gilligan's objection is significant to the criticism of Hermione. One might well ask whether those who criticize her emotionalism, particularly her enthusiastic support of Harry, side with Kohlberg in the debate, viewing Harry's attempts to keep the dark forces in check as superior to, for example, Hermione's attention to the feelings of Neville Longbottom. In *Sorcerer's Stone,* when Hermione decides to petrify Neville rather than risk his following her, Harry, and Ron, she first apologizes to Neville (273). Hermione, in fact, often combines stage three motives with higher-order reasoning, as we shall see. She is also smart enough to know that different levels of reasoning work with different people. . . .

Kohlberg thought that, while most children move to the conventional level around the age of nine, some adults never move beyond it. Like the real world, the realm of Hogwarts and the Muggle world beyond provide plenty of examples of adults still in stage three. With the exceptions of when he is acting forcefully toward Harry (stage one) and when he orchestrates a dinner party for his boss in order to make the biggest deal of his career (stage two), Vernon Dursley generally functions at the level of Interpersonal Conformity. He is obsessed with what other people think of him, which explains why the owls continuously bringing Harry mail in book one concern him. In book four, he is anxious to know whether the Weasleys will be stopping by to pick up Harry in a car, fearing that they will employ some mode of wizard transportation that calls attention to them all. In fact, it is almost as though harboring a wizard in his home violates Mr. Dursley's concept of *himself,* as he forbids any mention of Harry's "abnormality." . . .

At the second stage of the Conventional level, adolescents and young adults believe in what our report cards once called "citizenship": obeying rules and laws in order to maintain harmony in society. This is called the Social System and Conscience Maintenance stage; a person in it has moved beyond doing good only in interpersonal relationships and desires to maintain a more abstract social order. . . . "Conscience," in stage four reasoning, becomes the internalization of society's dictates and precepts; this is the principle that Freud called the superego. Usually adherence to the social order results in good, but when citizens obey the law no matter what that law is, we have horrors such as the Holocaust.

By far, the character who best illustrates this level is Percy Weasley, a Hogwarts prefect and, later, employee of the Ministry of Magic. "Percy loves rules," says Ron in *Goblet of Fire,* and that is a perfect statement of stage four reasoning (534). . . .

Percy gets along with Hermione better than almost anyone else, as Rowling herself observes. . . . This is true because Hermione is, herself, quite rule-bound, fearing above all else that she, Harry, or Ron will be asked to leave the school. When Harry and Ron sneak out of the Gryffindor common room for a midnight duel with Draco Malfoy in *Sorcerer's Stone,* Hermione, clad in her bathrobe, invokes rules and authority, threatening to tell Percy, who is a prefect. . . . When Harry turns Malfoy into a ferret early in *Goblet of Fire,* Hermione cuts short Ron's enjoyment with her observation that Professor McGonagall was right to intervene, as Malfoy could have been injured. . . .

Because Harry understands the importance of order in his society, he obeys the rules of the magic world even when he is sorely tempted to break them. We see this at the beginning of *Chamber of Secrets* when the Dursleys have imprisoned his snowy owl, Hedwig, cutting off any hope of communication with his friends from Hogwarts. Despite his loneliness and his awareness of the owl's misery, he does not disobey the prohibition against using magic in the Muggle world. . . .

Harry and his friends also have the ability to prioritize rules. For example, in *Chamber of Secrets,* after Ron and Harry miss the Hogwarts Express at the beginning of the term, they decide to fly Mr. Weasley's car. Although Mr. Weasley has broken a Ministry of Magic rule in making the car flyable and could get in trouble with the Misuse of Muggle Artifacts Office if Ron and Harry are seen, Ron reasons that they must use the car in order to observe another rule: they are due at school, and even wizards-in-training can use magic to get out of a jam. . . . It is noteworthy that Ron's reasoning is a justification *not* for breaking a rule but for how their use of the car might not be perceived as a violation. As such, it is an example of stage four or rule-observant reasoning.

The importance of rules is underscored in the Harry Potter novels by the presence of a number of authorities, most notably the Hogwarts faculty and officials of the Ministry of Magic. With few exceptions, Harry's professors enforce rules and deduct points from the houses of students who break them. Even Severus Snape, whose behavior toward Harry is somewhat mysterious, is a strict guardian of rules where Harry is concerned, if only because of the delight he takes in penalizing Harry and his friends when they break them (Snape is less vigilant about the behavior of his Slytherin House charges). In fact, the more famous Harry becomes, the more Snape seems to delight in having leverage over him; in *Goblet of Fire,* Snape reminds Harry that no matter how much publicity the young wizard attracts, he is "nothing but a nasty little boy who considers rules to be beneath him." . . .

Moral Development at the Postconventional Level

Some adolescents and most adults reach a third level in their moral develop-ment, at which point they are willing to break rules if they feel a higher prin-ciple is at stake. Kohlberg called this level the Postconventional. Reasoning in this stage goes beyond what one is taught into a kind of morality that one discovers, even crafts, for oneself. Again, Kohlberg postulates two stages. Stage five is called Prior Rights and Social Contract. During this penulti-mate stage, people realize that rules and laws exist for mutual benefit and by mutual agreement—what Abraham Lincoln called "government of the people, by the people, and for the people." Thus, when the laws are unfair or when one side doesn't keep its bargain in an agreement, the contract no longer binds and the laws should be overthrown or even disobeyed. The atti-tude of a person in stage five is generally utilitarian. Henry David Thoreau explains this concept in "Civil Disobedience." So does Thomas Jefferson in "The Declaration of Independence." The Civil Rights movement was based entirely on this idea. . . .

Kohlberg asserts that a few people reach a final stage, Universal Ethical Principles, in which they realize that some moral truths are absolute, that there is a higher law that should be obeyed. Martin Luther King makes this argument in "Letter from Birmingham Jail" in his distinction between just and unjust laws: "A just law is a man-made code that squares with the moral law or the law of God. An unjust law is a code that is out of harmony with the moral law. . . . An unjust law is a human law that is not rooted in eternal law and natural law." The "Universal Declaration of Human Rights" also acknowl-edges this concept. However, some theorists believe that no one except Jesus and a few other important religious figures have ever reached this stage; other theorists think that Gandhi, Mother Teresa, and Martin Luther King also reached it. . . .

J. K. Rowling provides Harry with two models of behavior at the Postcon-ventional level, at least one of whom may be at Kohlberg's nebulous stage six: the falsely accused Sirius Black, who is Harry's godfather, and his remarkable headmaster, Albus Dumbledore.

Of course, Harry's most significant mentor is Dumbledore, a figure almost universally revered in the wizarding world. When Dumbledore is temporarily suspended and called to the Ministry of Magic at the height of the mysterious and terrible attacks in *Chamber of Secrets,* the reaction under-scores the esteem in which he is held. While he is away, an atmosphere of near hysteria pervades Hogwarts, and the minister himself, Cornelius Fudge, declares that if Dumbledore can't stop the attacks, the situation may be hope-less. . . . Part of Dumbledore's effectiveness with young people is that he, like Lawrence Kohlberg, is much more concerned with *why* students behave as they do than with the behavior itself. At the end of *Sorcerer's Stone,* Harry learns that Dumbledore does not subscribe to one of the most prevalent codes among magical folk, that Voldemort should be called "He-who-must-not-be-named." Instead, Dumbledore instructs Harry to "Call him Voldemort. . . .

Always use the proper name for things. Fear of a name increases fear of the thing itself." . . . The prohibition on Voldemort's name might seem a stage four concept—keeping the wizarding world intact by not invoking the name of its primary threat—but it is actually grounded in superstition, a stage one concept, having at its base the need for self-preservation. Nevertheless, it is a significant example for Harry of his headmaster's willingness to go against the grain. . . .

Moving Through the Maze

Lawrence Kohlberg believed that children between the ages of ten and eighteen progress through more moral stages than people at any other age because they are beginning to test their independence and have developed more formal reasoning abilities. For them, a black-and-white world is replaced by one in varying shades of gray. If Kohlberg and other psychologists are right that young people experience the bulk of their moral development between the ages of ten and eighteen, then what they read during those stages is vital, not only for them, but for the rest of us, who will eventually live in the world they run. Children who read J. K. Rowling's books are encouraged to elevate themselves above the bully Draco Malfoy, whose name calls to mind the draconian measures used by those in power to keep others oppressed. The dreaded Dursleys, too, are morally retarded; and, yes, Dudley is a dud. Young readers are encouraged to move with Harry Potter and his friends Ron Weasley and Hermione Granger into the Conventional level of Kohlberg's scheme, in which one treats one's friends kindly and tries to make the society—wizard, in this case—function smoothly and fairly. What a young person encounters in Harry Potter's world is a boy who is loyal to his friends, sensitive to outcasts and underdogs, respectful of his teachers—when they deserve his respect—aware of the moral dimensions of a decision, and capable of realizations that move him along toward adulthood. Finally, adolescents may be inspired to aim for the Postconventional or principled level, emulating such role models as Sirius Black, who teaches that black can, in fact, be white, and Albus Dumbledore, who, like the albumen, or egg white, suggested by his first name, nourishes the yolk of these young wizards and witches, preparing them to hatch into a world they know how to improve.

Readers such as William Safire, who finds the Harry Potter series insubstantial, and conservative Christian parents who object to the books on moral terms should reconsider Rowling's work in the light of Lawrence Kohlberg's work. Kohlberg maintained that there are three ways of provoking moral development in children and young people. First, they need the friction of cognitive-moral conflict, what Thomas Berendt calls "cognitive disequilibrium." It is important, at any stage, for children to have opportunities to discuss alternative resolutions to moral conflict and their consequences. It is helpful for them to hear the arguments of people reasoning in stages higher than theirs. The second method for helping children develop morally is to present them with opportunities for role-playing, particularly opportunities that challenge them to take different perspectives and explore new viewpoints. Finally, children who live in a community characterized by justice move through stages of moral development more rapidly than those who do not. This concept has been applied successfully to schools, with students being actively involved in formulating standards for community learning (and, in the case of college students, community living).

POSTSCRIPT

Are *Harry Potter* Books Harmful for Children?

In a country where we believe in freedom of expression, the idea of banning books seems almost arcane, and yet a group of organizations dedicates one week a year to identifying the most often cited controversial books in the American cultural sphere. Citing the importance of intellectual freedom to read material that challenges one's beliefs and ideas, Banned Books Week is sponsored by the American Booksellers Association, American Booksellers Foundation for Free Expression, the American Library Association, American Society of Journalists and Authors, Association of American Publishers, and the National Association of College Stores. It is also endorsed by the Center for the Book at the Library of Congress.

According to the Office for Intellectual Freedom, at least 42 of the top 100 novels of the twentieth century have been the target of attempts to ban or censor content. Among the list are some considered literary classics, including *The Great Gatsby, To Kill a Mockingbird, The Grapes of Wrath,* and *The Color Purple*. It is fascinating to read the reasons why some organizations have justified their censorship or banning of these books, and a rationale for such action can be viewed at: http://www.ala.org/ala/issuesadvocacy/banned/frequentlychallenged/challengedclassics/reasonsbanned/index.cfm.

There are a number of sources dealing with attempts to ban or censor literature for children, and useful sites include the University of Illinois' collection, http://www.library.illinois.edu/edx/challenged.htm and the National Council of English Teacher's Anti Censorship site, http://www.ncte.org/action/anti-censorship. In these cases, and in others, fundamental problems of freedom of expression are juxtaposed with the ability of children to discern the differences between the complex issues of storytelling and the creation of meaning.

For more studies on the impact of media and children, George A. Comstock and Ericka Scharrer's *Media and the American Child* (Elsevier, 2007) provides an excellent overview of literature in the field and the impact of media on a child's development of educational skills. Maria Nikolajeva's *Power, Voice and Subjectivity in Literature for Young Readers* (Routledge, 2010) examines a number of genres in children's literature, including the fantasy genre, and includes a chapter on *Harry Potter*.

For an overview of censorship in America, Robert Atkins and Svetlana Mintcheva's edited collection called *Censoring Culture: Contemporary Threats to Free Expression* (New Press, 2006) includes chapters on a variety of censored media, and a roundtable discussion with teens on censorship; and Paul S. Boyer's *Purity in Print: Book Censorship in America from the Gilded Age to the Computer Age* (University of Wisconsin Press, 2002) provides a history of social, moral, and cultural values in the United States since the Progressive era.

ISSUE 3

Do Media Represent Realistic Images of Arabs?

YES: Gal Beckerman, from "The New Arab Conversation," *Columbia Journalism Review* (January/February, 2007)

NO: Jack G. Shaheen, from "Prologue," *Guilty: Hollywood's Verdict on Arabs after 9/11* (Olive Branch Press, 2008)

ISSUE SUMMARY

YES: In this issue, journalist Gal Beckerman discusses how Arab bloggers from the Middle East are challenging popular stereotypes of Arab and Middle Eastern culture. Because these bloggers are writing about their lives, the global public can read about their situations and understand them as individuals, rather than racial or ethnic group members.

NO: Jack Shaheen, an expert on the image of the Arab in film and television, discusses how Arabs have been the most maligned stereotype in popular culture, and how the images, post 9/11, that conflate "Arab" and "Muslim," have fueled misperceptions about "the Other" and have influenced people's perceptions about victims and combatants while we are engaged in the war in Iraq. He discusses how Hollywood's images influence politicians and citizens and contribute to public opinion.

Stereotypes and distorted images of racial, ethnic, and gender groups abound in the media, but can these images distract the public so severely that they influence political ideology? Our history of understanding the impact of racial profiling, based on stereotypes that distort what is commonly called "the Other," indicates that these stereotypes can have multiple harmful effects. Throughout American popular culture, we have seen how different groups portrayed in the media contribute to public opinion of groups for whom we have little or no firsthand understanding.

It has been said that despite recent sensitivity to multiculturalism and a growing call for respect for people of other races and ethnicities, the image of the Arab still represents evil. No doubt our multiyear wars with people in

Iraq and Afghanistan have contributed to a misunderstanding of who or what our military troops are fighting, and for what purpose, but the conflation of the people of the Middle East with "the enemy" is an example of how powerful stereotypes can be. Reality does not support the images we see in fictional media. For example, Jack Shaheen shows that the Arab in American popular culture is often portrayed as a Muslim, even though Arabs represent a minority of Muslims, and that Muslims live on five continents and represent different languages and histories that defy "lumping" all of them together.

Shaheen's careful content analysis of portrayal of Arabs shows that these stereotypes have "mutated" over years, from the Arab riding a camel in the desert, to the "crazed Islamic fundamentalists bent on destruction." The result, Shaheen writes, is that the image of a people has been distorted for decades. What makes the situation even more problematic is the relationship between Hollywood and Washington—in the sense that popular culture, public opinion, and political policies are all interwoven.

Journalist Gal Beckerman focuses on the impact of bloggers and the ability of these individuals to get personal messages out to others beyond geographic borders. Despite the Arab world's limited Internet access, Beckerman finds blogs represent humane voices in a sea of confusion. The contrast of the individual bloggers' messages compared to the mainstream Arab media provides one point of departure for getting to know "the Other" in a more intimate way, but at the same time, as Beckerman writes, "the Middle East is a region where the historical and the personal slam up against each other daily in a way they do only once a decade or so in America." In the voices of bloggers, we get to know the daily beliefs, frustrations, and humanity of "the Other."

This issue brings up more than the question of the power of stereotyping in the media; it makes us ask whether the images in media really matter to us, and whether different types of media can communicate more effectively than others—depending upon the content. Anytime we are challenged to question our own beliefs, and how those beliefs may be influenced by media, we get one step closer to understanding the complexity of media images, media forms, and how we, individually and collectively, understand our place and role in society.

YES ⤶

Gal Beckerman

The New Arab Conversation

Bombs don't discriminate between combatants and children. This sad fact became an inconvenient one last summer [2006] for Israel, which had maintained that its bombing of Lebanon was solely an attack on Hezbollah, the Shiite militia that had kidnapped two Israeli soldiers and menaced the Jewish state's northern border. To an anxious Lebanese population who'd seen most of their country's south reduced to a parking lot, Israel's persistent message—We are doing this for your own good—rang increasingly hollow.

By the beginning of August, the French and American ambassadors to the United Nations had finally hammered out a cease-fire resolution. But as the Security Council prepared to vote, the Lebanese government and the Arab League declared that the agreement was too favorable to Israel. A tense and edgy delegation arrived in New York on August 8 to plead the Arab case.

Dan Gillerman, the Israeli ambassador to the UN, didn't have to do much at those deliberations—simply listen to the complaints, appear to be the least obstructionist in the room, and restate his country's position, as absurd as it may have sounded by that point, that Israel's bombs were in fact helping the Lebanese people to free themselves from the "cancer" of Hezbollah that had metastasized in their midst. In this last task, he had an unusual ally: "I believe that one courageous Lebanese youngster was speaking for many when he wrote in his Internet blog, and I quote, 'It is not only Israeli soldiers that the Hezbollah has taken hostage. It is us, the people of Lebanon.'"

This "Lebanese youngster" was, of course, a blogger, and maybe the first to have his words bounce off the solemn walls of the United Nations. And though he probably would not have appreciated being deployed as a weapon in Israel's public-relations war, the presence of his independent voice, a counterintuitive opinion not filtered through any official source, said a lot about the power of Middle Eastern Web logs to expose a hidden trove of multiple perspectives in a world that the West often imagines as having only one perspective—that of the "Arab Street," a place of conformity, of mass acquiescence to singular passions, be they blind support for a dictator or seething hatred of Israel.

Last summer was, in fact, a watershed moment for the Middle Eastern blogosphere. The conflict between Israel and Hezbollah not only brought attention to the many different Arab conversations that had taken place on homemade Web sites in the past two or three years, but also launched thousands more of them. And they were more than just a handful of aberrant

From *Columbia Journalism Review,* January/February 2007, pp. 17–19, 20, 21, 22–23 (excerpts). Copyright © 2007 by Columbia Journalism Review. Reprinted by permission.

voices. They reflected a new culture of openness, dialogue, and questioning. And unlike the neoconservative notion that these ideals can be dropped on a foreign population like so many bomblets, the push for change here is coming from within. Whether it is a Jordanian student discussing the taboo subject of the monarchy's viability or a Saudi woman writing about her sexual experiences or an Egyptian commenting with sadness at an Israeli blogger's description of a suicide bombing, each of these unprecedented acts is one small move toward opening up these societies.

The Arab blogosphere has been growing for a few years now, though not at a particularly quick pace. Only 10 percent of the Arab world has Internet access, yet that is a five-fold increase from 2000. Of course, not all Arab blogs are about liberalizing Arab society. Some use the technology as another front in the jihad against the West being waged by groups like Al Qaeda. One, Irhabi 007, who was recently profiled in *The Atlantic Monthly,* created Web sites to disseminate videos of beheadings and insurgent attacks on U.S. forces in Iraq. Most analysts and bloggers put the number of Arab bloggers at fewer than 25,000. Of those, a majority blog in Arabic. And though there are surely interesting discussions happening on those sites, Arab bloggers themselves say that a particularly interesting alternative space is being formed on the sites composed in English. Now aggregated on blogging portals like iToot.net and enhanced by the YouTube-like Web site Ikbis, it is in this community of people who are self-consciously half-turned toward the West that one can feel the breathing becoming easier.

Those bloggers are people like Roba Al-Assi, a twenty-one-year-old design student in Amman, Jordan, who recently wrote about her opposition to the death penalty for Saddam Hussein:

> It is the premeditated and cold-blooded killing of a human being by the state in the name of justice (I know he killed thousands, but it is in my moral fabric to be better than others. Throw him in jail for the rest of his life, that's a lot worse than death).

Or the Egyptian blogger who calls himself Big Pharaoh, a twenty-seven-year-old graduate of the American University in Cairo, who expressed his support for the Egyptian culture minister who was criticized for stating that he thought the hijab, the traditional woman's head covering worn by some Muslim women, was "regressive":

> There are numerous things that make me proud of this country. How the country descended into such stupidity, ignorance, and darkness is definitely not among them. I feel like vomiting every time I think about how this man was virulently attacked for merely stating his opinion on a thing as stupid as the hair cover.

Or Laila El-Haddad, who, on her blog, "Unplugged: Diary of a Palestinian Mother," describes herself as a "journalist, mom, occupied Palestinian—all packed into one," and posted this account of crossing at Rafah from Egypt back into Gaza, after waiting in limbo for weeks for the border to open:

Some wailed in exhaustion, others fainted; still others cracked dry humor, trying to pass the time. We stood, thousands of us, packed together elbow to elbow like cattle, penned in between steel barriers on one end, and riot-geared Egyptian security guards on the perimeter, who were given orders not to allow anyone through until they hear otherwise from the Israelis—and to respond with force if anyone dared.

In the American blogosphere, opinions and life tales blossom a million-fold every day. But against the background of a largely party-line mainstream local Arab media, and the absence of avenues for national conversation, these Arab bloggers, most of whom are anonymous for their own safety, commit small acts of bravery simply by speaking their minds. It should be said that most of the people maintaining blogs do come out of the highest strata of society, economically and educationally, so their opinions can seem at times to represent no wider a circle than the upper crust of any given country. But, as Ammar Abdulhamid, a Syrian blogger who was forced into exile in September 2005 for his democracy activism, which included blogging about his eight-month interrogation by Syrian security services, put it: "There is nothing wrong with admitting that we represent a certain elite. It's not exclusively an economic elite, though economics surely plays a large factor. These are people who are comfortable, who have more time to blog. But in itself this is not the problem. The importance of this technology at this stage is to connect the elites better, to network the elites, to make them able to share more ideas and organize." The power of the medium, Abdulhamid says, will come when those bloggers find a way to "cross the bridge between the elite and the grass roots"—a process that is already beginning, through a few organized demon-strations coordinated by bloggers, online campaigns, and the posting of infor-mation about police brutality or sexual harassment.

Blogs can serve two functions: they are diaries, where the minutiae of a life are spelled out in 500-word posts, and they are a personal op-ed page, in which a writer comments at will about news articles and daily political devel-opments, rambles in anger or appreciation, or promotes ideas. All of this hap-pens every day on American blogs. But the context in the Arab blogosphere is different. For one thing, it is so much smaller. In the U.S., political blogs tend to split off into separate spheres of left and right that rarely touch—call them Huffingtonville and Hewittland—each with its predictable response to any political event. But the small size of the Arab blogosphere forces people with contrary opinions, or even more mildly divergent viewpoints, to engage each other. As one Arab blogger said, "We're not big enough to preach to the choir yet. There is no choir."

But the more compelling reason for the singularity of the Arab blogo-sphere is that the Middle East is a region where the historical and the personal slam up against each other daily in a way they do only once a decade or so in America. This gives even mundane musings elevated significance. Bloggers are writing about their lives. But those lives are taking place in environments in which politics and history cannot be perceived as mere elements on the margins. For the twentysomething growing up in Riyadh, writing resentfully about the power of the religious authorities, the questions are fundamental ones about the state of her society. For the Egyptian blogger, the brutal suppression of a demonstration can make the difference in whether he chooses to stay in the country or leave. This urgency makes the commentary more complex and interesting than the us-versus-them combat of so many American blogs. "We see it's the whole country at stake," said a well-known Lebanese blogger who goes by the nom de blog Abu Kais. "For us, watching politics is not like watching a football game. It's existential."

⊷❀⊶

Salam Pax is widely acknowledged as the Adam of Middle East bloggers. The blogging revolution that first began to spread through America in the late 1990s (the first "online diary," as a blog was then known, was created by a Swarthmore student in January 1994) reached the Middle East three or four years ago, and it was only with Pax's quirky and insightful dispatches in 2003 from a prewar and then postwar Iraq that Americans were made aware that the phenomenon had arrived there, too.

His blog, "Where is Raed?" had all the hallmarks of those that would follow in its wake. A twenty-nine-year-old recently graduated architecture student who had spent time in the West, Pax wrote in fluent English, observing the chaos that was quickly accumulating around him. At first, he was writing for himself, using the blog as a diary, but then he became aware of the scarcity of Arab bloggers writing in English about anything other than religious matters. As he told *The Guardian* in 2003, "I was saying, 'Come on, look, the Arabs here: sex, alcohol, belly dancers, TV shows, where are they?' All you saw was people talking about God and Allah. There was nothing about what was happening here." Then the war began, and that impulse to expose the parts of his world that the West was not seeing took on an even greater urgency. By the time of the invasion, 20,000 people were reading Pax regularly. His posts captured an emotional, lived experience of the war, one that evaded most journalists covering the conflict. . . .

The dynamism of the blog posts, as well as the string of comments that usually follow each of them, can best be appreciated when viewed against a backdrop of the mainstream Arab media. With the exception of a few papers in Lebanon (notably, the English-language *Daily Star*) and a handful of publications in Egypt and Jordan, most local media in the Arab world are still either directly state-controlled or subject to such intimidation by the government that journalists and editors rarely challenge authority. Each country's media have their red lines that cannot be crossed. In Jordan, it is the monarchy. In Egypt, it's the Mubarak regime. Any criticism of fundamentalist Islam's growing role in Arab society is off limits to everyone. And in much of the Arab local media Israel is portrayed as the ultimate evil. Israel, in fact, can be a tool of state control in Arab media. A high level of anti-Israel rhetoric serves the purpose of directing anger and scrutiny away from the regimes in power.

That was mitigated somewhat by the advent in recent years of satellite channels like Al-Jazeera and Al-Arabiya, which offer at least the potential of a more independent analysis and criticism of Arab governments. But by some accounts, both channels, though AI-Jazeera more so, have taken on a tone and a content that plays, as one Syrian blogger put it, "to the largest common denominator, drawing on the same language of victimhood, the tired Arab nationalist line. It is Fox news. Many people compare it to CNN. I think it has to be compared to Fox." (The Israeli media, for their part, though certainly free and open to criticizing the government and not averse by any means to plastering the country's problems on the front page, also resort most often to simple narratives and well-known generalizations when it comes to depicting the Arab enemy, not giving serious attention to the aspiration of the Palestinians, for example.)

The bloggers have stood out against this background. Some of them have even used the Web for political action. Bloggers led an Arab movement to support products from Denmark in the aftermath of the Danish cartoon riots and the Arab boycott that followed. They have also organized demonstrations and, much like American bloggers, used their Web sites as forums to expose injustices. Egyptian bloggers recently circulated video of men wilding in the streets of Cairo, sexually assaulting women at random, eventually bringing the incident to the world's attention. Jordanian bloggers, angry that the government regulators had decided to block access to Skype, a phone service that allows users to communicate freely over the Internet, started a campaign that led to the decision's reversal. And then there was the war, in which bloggers organized donations for the displaced of Lebanon.

Still, there are good reasons why most of the Arab blogosphere remains anonymous. Just this past year, several bloggers were jailed in Egypt, including Abdel Karim Sulaiman Amer, who was arrested in November and charged with "spreading information disruptive of public order," "incitement to hate Muslims," and "defaming the President of the Republic." Earlier last year, another Egyptian blogger, Alaa Ahmed Seif al-Islam, was arrested and given three consecutive fifteen-day detentions in prison, largely for his blogging activity. Other countries, like Bahrain and Saudi Arabia, don't arrest bloggers, but they aggressively block blogs they find subversive.

The Committee to Protect Bloggers, a now defunct U.S. organization that monitored bloggers who found themselves in danger, kept track of the various forms of intimidation and suppression. Curt Hopkins, who was the group's director, says there are three basic methods that countries employ to suppress bloggers: technical filtering, the law, and direct intimidation. Though it is fairly easy to track down bloggers using IP addresses, bloggers have an easier time evading the authorities than do journalists working for a newspaper. "When it comes to shutting down a publication, it's pretty easy," says Hopkins. "You just send some goons with baseball bats and suddenly you don't have a publication. It's that simple. Also it's easier to find people because they are in the offices when you come to arrest them. And though it's true that if you have enough money and time, you can find almost anyone, you've got to remember that most governments don't have enough money and enough time." Abdulhamid, the Syrian blogger who continued to update his blog every day, even while the state police were interrogating him, also noticed such limitations. "During my interrogation, I saw that, one, most security apparatus really don't have access to the Internet; two, they don't know how to use that technology very well to begin with, even if they did have access." Still, enough bloggers have either been arrested or, as in Abdulhamid's case, had their lives threatened, for the fear to be well founded. . . .

Maybe the most dramatic way in which this blogosphere is affecting the Arab world is by breaking down that ultimate taboo. Even in a place like Lebanon, with a large portion of the population striving to create a liberal, modern society, Israel is the last barrier. That is rooted in Lebanon's history, including recent history. Yet there is so much investment in seeing Israel as the source of all its problems that it has become a mindless reflex for many.

There are, of course, plenty of bloggers who use the Internet as a way to disseminate more hate and misunderstanding, many of whom also gained attention last summer during the war. One case, infamous among Arab and Israeli bloggers, is Perpetual Refugee, a Lebanese businessman who had occasion to visit Israel a few times, socialized with Israelis . . . and subsequently wrote friendly posts about making peace. As soon as the war came, he made what was described as a "360-degree turn," becoming virulently hateful about Jews, about how Israel "massacred innocent souls to fulfill its biblical destiny." But Perpetual Refugee was something of a high-profile anomaly among the English-language bloggers.

"I always say there are two kinds of arguments," says Sandmonkey. "There are the arguments in which you hope to find the truth and the arguments in which you want to defend an established truth." It's the first type of argument that seems to be prevailing. Take this post by Charles Malik (also a pseudonym), a Lebanese blogger, who found himself exploring the Israeli blogosphere last April, by chance on Holocaust Remembrance Day. He asks questions that would seem almost blasphemous considering the climate in the Middle East:

> Think about what Israelis deal with on a daily basis: frequent suicide bombs, support for such attacks by the popularly elected Palestinian government, threats of annihilation from a country arming itself with nuclear weapons, constant words of hate from the Arabic speaking world, and remembrances of the Holocaust. . . . Not knowing about "them" is the worst crime we can commit. It invalidates them as humans, as if they don't even matter. They are Stalin's faceless enemy, the rabid dog, the evil bloodsuckers whom it is righteous to kill. Our papers definitely need to start covering more than major political events in Israel. We should remember their tragedies.

If the Arab bloggers tend to be those who have been exposed to the West, many of the Israelis interacting with them are recent immigrants like Lisa Goldman, who arrived six years ago, and Lirun Rabinowitz, who has been living in Israel for a year and a half. Rabinowitz shares his blog with a Lebanese woman and was recently invited to be a co-author on the United Arab Emirates community blog and, even more surprisingly, on an annual Ramadan blog, in which various bloggers write about how the Muslim holiday is celebrated in their countries. Recently, on the UAE blog, he was accused in the comments section of being needlessly provocative for putting the words "Tel Aviv" after his name at the end of his posts. To his surprise, a number of Arab readers rushed to his defense in the comments section.

Rabinowitz says that perusing the Arab blogosphere has deepened his understanding of what is happening inside Arab society. "When I go to them, I see what are they worrying about, what are they wondering, how they are feeling, what level of analysis they are putting on things, how keen they are to see my side, and when they are only prepared to see their own. Is there room for bridging? And I learn a lot about what their knee-jerk reaction looks like, what their analysis looks like, what their fears look like." And to him, that added layer of knowledge is a rebuke to the other forces in Israeli society that he feels are trying to define the "enemy" for him. "You want to tell me that these people are stupid? Well, they're not," says Rabinowitz. "You want to tell me that these people want to live in a dictatorship? Well, they don't. You want to tell me that they can't be Muslim and tolerant and friendly at the same time? Well, it's wrong. You want to tell me that they hate me just because they're Muslim and I'm Jewish? Well that's wrong, too. And they prove that to me every day. And I get this amazing opportunity to dispel every demonic myth and every stupid stereotype that I could have ever thought of, and that's amazingly liberating."

Is this hopeful? Yes, as long as one keeps in mind, once again, what a small segment of the population, both Arab and Israeli, is sitting in front of glowing screens and reaching out to the "other." The bloggers will say, universally, that revolutions almost always start with a tiny elite. But we are a long way from this revolution's doorstep. Instead, this blogosphere feels more like a small community of open-minded young people who have discovered pathways that were previously closed.

Still, seeds do grow. The grass-roots student wing of the civil rights movement, born at Shaw University in Raleigh, North Carolina, in 1960, in what evolved into the Student Nonviolent Coordinating Committee (or SNCC), was made up of young people, privileged enough to be attending college but not content with the pace of integration in America. They made themselves into a vanguard, tearing holes in walls so that others could then pass through after them. Someone had to take the first step, and who better than they—young, educated, and sensitive to the restrictions that were going to be placed on their personal and communal advancement.

The young insider-outsiders of the Middle East, blogging openly about their frustrations with the Arab world, about its persistent prejudices and limitations, as a way of liberalizing their societies, are doing what the front line of any social movement does—they say the unspeakable, they form the bonds that were previously unthinkable, they stand in the places that they are not supposed to stand. The Arab world will reform only when mindsets begin to change and a culture of dissent burgeons where it has never been allowed to exist openly before. If there is a way to kick-start this process, it is surely in the post of a twentysomething blogger wondering out loud why things can't be more open, more transparent—more different.

Jack G. Shaheen **NO**

Prologue

The Arab stereotype is the only vicious racial stereotype that's not only still permitted but actively endorsed by Hollywood.

—Godfrey Cheshire, film critic

At a time when the wounds of 9/11 remain raw, some of my colleagues asked about my motivation for writing a new book about Hollywood's portrayal of Arabs. Simple: Given the conflict in Iraq and Afghanistan, the al-Qaeda threat, and the repercussions of 9/11, it seems more important than ever to remain alert to prejudicial portraits, to test our own stereotypes, and our own sense of fairness. I decided to follow Robert Frost's wisdom— "more light, more light"— by offering fresh thoughts about reel Arabs, insights intended to stimulate thought and encourage discussion leading to a corrective. Seven years have passed since the July 2001 publication of my book *Reel Bad Arabs: How Hollywood Vilifies a People;* has anything—reel-wise—improved? Have Hollywood's powerful post–9/11 images smashed stereotypes or reinforced them? And if images have solidified viewers' perceptions of the Arab as the evil "other," as someone threateningly different, what steps should be taken to resolve the problem?

Arabs remain the most maligned group in the history of Hollywood. Malevolent stereotypes equating Islam and Arabs with violence have endured for more than a century; sweeping mischaracterizations and omissions continue to impact us all. One of the first lessons children learn about this evil "other" and one of the last lessons the elderly forget is: Arab = Muslim = Godless Enemy. And the context in which these images are viewed—against a montage of real-life images and reports of terror attacks (successful and thwarted) across the globe, of videotaped beheadings and messages from al-Qaeda, of the killing of American soldiers, journalists, and civilians in Iraq—has changed drastically. Today, the stereotype's power to inflict damage on innocent people is much greater than before 9/11. During times of armed conflict, stereotyping meets the least resistance; its mendacity most convincingly masquerades as truth, and it is most vigorously defended and justified as truth. Arabs have been so demonized that it has become impossible for some world citizens to believe they are real people; they are perceived only as the enemy, as terrorists, as the "other."

The demonic "other" is especially dangerous and seductive during conflicts. Be he Arab, Asian, black, Hispanic, Jew, or Indian, he has harmed us in the past and intends to harm us even more in the future. The "other" is always outside the circle of civilization, usually threateningly exotic or dark-looking. He speaks a different language, wears different clothing, and dwells in a primitive place such as Africa's jungles and Arabia's deserts—reel hostile environments with signposts. The "other" poses a threat—economic, religious, and sexual—to our way of life. He lusts after the fair-complexioned Western woman. Fortunately, he is inept in the bedroom and on the battlefield. Unlike our noble selves, the unkempt "other" is unethical and inferior, someone who plays dirty; he worships a strange, different deity and does not value human life as much as we do. Incapable of democracy, the "other" is projected as a violent primitive mass opposing world peace and religious tolerance. Only a brave white man and a light saber can save the "other" from himself. As settlers sing in Disney's *Pocahontas* (1995), "Savages, savages . . . not like you and me."

During times of war, government campaigns and media systems exert an especially strong influence in helping to create and shape public attitudes about the "other." Consider World War I. In this war, the "other" was white. So Anglo-Saxon Germans ceased being celebrated as torchbearers of civilization (forget Goethe, Schiller, Beethoven, and Mozart); instead, they became ugly "Huns" contaminating Americans with narcotics and determined to destroy civilization. US propaganda posters displayed steel-helmeted "Huns" threatening to murder women and children. Belgium's war films depicted the reel Hun horde torching villages and historical churches; Huns raped young girls, old ladies, and nuns and chopped off the hands of children. The Belgian films, points out film scholar Leen Engelen, were especially effective as propaganda, presenting Belgium as "a holy land that's been nailed to the cross by German devils." Sums up director Sally Potter, when governments and imagemakers collaborate to "reduce people to a single clichéd image of who they are—they become one homogenous thing." Thus, it's easy to despise and kill the evil 'other'—he's just not quite human.

Arab = Muslim

From cinema's beginning, Hollywood's fractured mirrors of popular imagination lumped together Muslims and Arabs as one homogenous blob. Yet, Arabs represent a minority of Muslims. Only one-fifth of the world's 1.3+ billion Muslims are Arabs. These distinctions are often blurred in American popular culture. For decades news reporters, editorial cartoonists, novelists, imagemakers, and other media professionals have vilified Arab Muslims.

This enduring mythology that "Muslim" is synonymous with "Arab" has two primary deficiencies. First, it glosses over the religious diversity of the Arabs themselves. Though faith plays an important role in the Arab world, just as it does here in the United States, it's also true that much of the Arab world is quite secular. When we think of the region does Christianity come to mind? After all, there are more than 20 million Arab Christians in the Arab world—ranging from Eastern Orthodox to Roman Catholic to Protestant—who have lived side by side with Muslims for centuries. The vast majority of Arab Americans (including me) are Christian. I've attended Mass in at least twelve Arab nations, praying at an Anglican cathedral in Bahrain, as well as lighting candles in memory of departed loved ones at a Coptic monastery in Egypt. Filmmakers, however, balk at projecting reel Christian Arabs, and their absence on silver screens misleads viewers into thinking all Arabs are Muslims. The exclusion also makes it much easier for directors to paint Arab Muslims as an alien "other," with no links to Western Christians.

Second, failure to present on movie screens Muslims of other ethnic extractions also makes it easier for producers to overlook Islam's universality, thereby simplifying its denigration of Arabs. If Hollywood demonized Turks, Indonesians, Asians, and Indians, the stereotype would lose some of its appearance of credibility. And, these ethnic groups and others would more readily mobilize against the stereotyping. Indonesia, for example, is the world's most populous Muslim country, but its residents are not projected as Hollywood's reel bad Indonesians; nor should they be.

The reality is that Muslims reside on five continents, speak dozens of different languages, and embrace diverse traditions and history. Like Christians, Jews, and others, "Muslims are as diverse as humanity itself," explains Vartan Gregorian, president of the Carnegie Corporation of New York and a specialist in Middle Eastern history. "Religious, cultural, and population centers for Muslims are not limited to far-off Asia and the Middle East," says Gregorian; "they also include Paris, Berlin, London, New York, Los Angeles, and Washington, DC. Muslims represent the majority population in more than fifty nations—one in five people in the world are Muslims."

Thankfully, most of Hollywood's more notorious portraits of other groups like Asians, blacks, Indians, and Hispanics are behind us. Lingering still, however, is the insidious Arab Muslim stereotype.

Post–9/11 Images

"Movies are part of the air we all breathe," reminds critic Michael Medved. While each of us watches films through the lenses of our own experience, my discussions here are based on decades of painstaking research and the reality of Hollywood's post–9/11's images, and not on my personal beliefs about real and/or reel Arabs.

The total number of films that defile Arabs now exceeds 1,150. In *Reel Bad Arabs* I discussed more than 950 pre–9/11 Hollywood features. Since then, I have viewed another 100+ pre–9/11 films defiling Arabs that were not included in *Reel Bad Arabs*. . . . In my detailed review of post–9/11 films I found that 22 movies (1 in 4) that otherwise have nothing whatsoever to do with Arabs or the Middle East contain gratuitous slurs and scenes that demean Arabs. Arab villains do dastardly things in 37 films (mostly gunning down or blowing up innocent people); ugly sheikhs pop up as dense, evil, over-sexed caricatures in 12 films; 3 of 5 films display unsavory Egyptian characters; 6 of 15 films project not-so-respectable images of maidens; and 6 out of 11 movies offer stereotypical portraits of Palestinians. Finally, Dream Works studios went out its way to distort folk tales and cinema history, seemingly depriving young viewers of not seeing reel images of traditional Arab heroes like Sinbad. Their animated Arabian adventure film, *Sinbad: Legend of the Seven Seas* (2003), displays no reel good Arabs. Not one, including Sinbad himself! Not even a burnoose or a chord of Arab music. The film was so anglicized it could have been billed *Homer: Legend of the Seven Seas.*

Refreshingly, about a third of the post–9/11 films discussed here, a total of 29, projected worthy Arabs and decent Arab Americans: Arab champions—men and women—are displayed in 19 movies; Arab Americans appear as decent folk in 10 of 11 films. Though the vast majority of films discussed here were released by major Hollywood studios, I also comment on some reel positive American and British independents, and several films from France, Israel, Italy, and Spain, such as *Only Human* (2004). And, I review three first-rate Arab-Israeli co-productions, including *Syrian Bride* (2005). I also comment on two 2005 dramas where Sikhs are tragically mistaken for Arabs (*Waterborne* and *The Gold Bracelet*).

Disturbingly, I found new, vicious, violent stereotypes polluting TV screens. I came across more than 50 post–9/11 TV shows that vilify Arab Americans and Muslim Americans. . . .

Reel Bad Omnipresent Arabs

Constant in their malevolency, reel Arabs have not been static, but have mutated over time, like a contaminated virus. In conjunction with current events, filmmakers have mixed and embellished new and polluted stereotypes with old, familiar ones. In the early 1900s, for example, movie-land's Arabs appeared as sex-crazed, savage, and exotic camel-riding nomads living in desert tents. When not fighting each other and Westerners, they bargained at slave markets, procuring blond women for their harems. In the late 1960s, the stereotyping of Arabs began to accelerate with the Israeli–Palestinian issue and by the 1970s—likely in connection with the 1973 Arab–Israeli war, the oil embargo, and the 1979–1981 Iranian hostage crisis—reel dark Palestinians appeared not as a real displaced people but as reel "terrorists." Other Arabs began surfacing as fanatic sheikhs: rich, vengeful, corrupt, sneaky, repulsive, and almost invariably fat.

Add to the reel mix the intersection of "news" programming—cable and network. It, too, had a profound impact on perceptions of "Arabs" and "Muslims," selectively framing them as Hollywood's evil "other"—violent ruthless people. Starting with the 1980s, especially since Israel's invasion of Lebanon (1982), Operation Desert Storm (January 1991), the military incursions into Afghanistan and Iraq (2001 and 2003), and the fighting between Hezbollah and Israel (2006), all those reel desert nomads and obese oily sheiks were suddenly dispatched to the dressing rooms to make room for the new head attraction: Arab as crazed Islamic fundamentalist bent on destruction.

Carried on the backs of the films that bear a single-minded vitriol, cinematic renderings of the Arab are infecting world viewers, from Bombay to Boston. "Cinema has been global since day one," says the noted Argentine critic Eduardo Antin, "and American studios have had distribution offices in every country since day two." In Cuba, for example, moviegoers watch more Hollywood films than movies from neighboring Latin America countries. Sums up *Variety*'s Peter Bart, "Hollywood's movies influence the way people see the world." Daily, American films become even more accessible. It works like this. Not long after films first appear in theaters they are released throughout the world to about 150 nations. Months later, world viewers purchase and/or rent the movies from discount outlets such as Wal-Mart and video stores such as Blockbuster; movie buffs go online to view movies, and they also rent or purchase them from sites such as Netflix, Amazon, Sinister Cinema, and eBay. Next, cable TV and commercial TV networks telecast the films—again and again and again. Even cable outlets in small towns regularly beam into our homes, by my estimate, more than two dozen anti-Arab films every week.

Large media companies such as Time Warner, CBS, Disney, and Sony take such popular brands as Batman, Spiderman, or Superman from comic books and turn them into movies, books, clothes, toys, and TV programs, with each of those outlets generating revenues worldwide. Movies are screened in airplanes, hospitals, schools, universities, bars, prisons, even in dentists' chairs. The more successful movies are pirated online, and cloned, leading to TV series, video games, records, CDs, games, trading cards in cereals, coloring books, theme-park rides, and magazines. Record companies release soundtracks, bookstores display glossy books about how-this-movie-was-made, and on and on.

Today, overseas box-office income overtakes domestic receipts, explains author Neal Gabler. At least "sixty percent of the studios' profits come from abroad." In France, Hollywood movies account "for nearly 70 percent of box office receipts." Muslim countries, says Gabler, make up "about ten percent" of the overseas box office. A former US ambassador to Algeria and Syria, Christopher Ross points out, "the electronic media are the premiere media in the Arab and Muslim worlds today." Thus, Arab viewers are regularly exposed to reel demeaning stereotypes of themselves and their culture. Arab teenagers, especially, he says, are impacted by reel stereotypes. Politics may be worlds apart, but young Arabs and Muslims are ardent movie buffs who regularly purchase and/or rent American films, old and new, for as little as fifty cents. Our movies, says Ross, "are the truly potent examples of our cultural imperialism."

A casual visitor abroad can see Hollywood's influence in little ways, every day, just walking down the street of capital cities across the globe: posters and billboards advertising the latest releases, eateries and bars named after famous film characters, and establishments emulating all things Hollywood. For example, in the heart of Berlin you can find the Hollywood Media Hotel; this luxury facility brims with movie memorabilia and all its ornate rooms are named after famous stars and directors.

As actor Leonardo DiCaprio said, "Film is forever"—and indeed movies seem to never die, no matter how bad, dull, or poorly done; the reel Arab in all its evolutions of ugliness lives on and on. I offer you *Ashanti*, a 1979 big-budget disaster that presents Arabs as vile slavers who abuse African boys and young women. Given this abominable film's age and its poor profit showing, I had hoped it would have been tossed onto a dump heap long ago, where its trashy images could rot in their own waste. Not so. On Christmas Eve, 2004, while I was with my family in Prague, happily preparing to attend midnight Mass, *Ashanti* resurfaced in the Czech Republic. My son turned on the TV and found a German TV station beaming the 25-year-old American film into our hotel room. Before I could turn off the TV, our granddaughters had already witnessed deranged desert Arabs raping and whipping chained African youths. After Mass, I lingered inside the church and mused about cinema's pervasive powers. Is there no safe place to take refuge from these images? The words of my supportive parish priest from Pittsburgh came to mind. "Movies are so powerful," he confided to me. "Some have more influence on my parishioners than church services."

Reel Political Implications

Filmmaking is political. Movies continuously transmit selected representations of reality to world citizens from Baghdad to Boston. Dehumanizing stereotypes emerging from the cinema, TV, and other media help support government policies, enabling producers to more easily advance and solidify stereotypes. "It has been a truism for a century that media stereotypes set the tone of many public events," writes Daniel Henninger in the *Wall Street Journal*. Policies enforce stereotypes; stereotypes impact policies. It's a continuous spiral, no matter which comes first. CNN's Peter Arnett describes the linkage best: "The media elite follow US policy," he says, "and those shaping policies are influenced in part by the stereotypical pictures in their heads."

Congress has never declared war on Iraq, not in March 2003, nor during Operation Desert Storm, January 1991. "For soldiers engaged in combat, there's probably not a difference—but in a legal and constitutional sense there is," explains my friend Professor Donald Bittner, who teaches at the Marine and Staff College. "The two US operations against Iraq," writes Bittner, "were authorized by Congressional resolutions that allowed the President to use whatever military force he saw fit, with minimal accountability and no limitations." Bittner characterizes the current conflict as "intervention, to repel aggression and to force regime change."

You, dear reader, should mull over this telling political-entertainment linkage: Long before the United States launched real expeditionary operations against Iraq in March 2003, Hollywood was already launching a reel war against reel Arabs. For years, numerous pre–9/11 Arab-as-Enemy movies helped fuel misperceptions and prejudices. Pre–9/11 action films showed Captain Kit Carson unloading bombs over Baghdad's "devil-worshippers" in *Adventure in Iraq* (1943); in *Deterrence* (1999) the US president dispatches a nuclear bomb over Baghdad. Viewers saw a marine captain blow up a Saddam look-alike and Iraqis in *The Human Shield* (1992); viewers also saw Meg Ryan and her troops gunning down Iraqis in *Courage under Fire* (1996). Kill-'em-all films like *Navy SEALs* (1990), *True Lies* (1994), *Executive Decision* (1996), and *Rules of Engagement* (2000) projected our GIs, civilians, secret agents, the American president, Israeli troops, even cowboys, terminating reel barbaric Arabs. These scenarios and others depicted us as perfectly good angels killing them perfectly evil infidels. They assured audiences that God was on our side, that we were good Clint "Make my day" Eastwood guys, sure to win easily over bad Arab guys. After seeing our reel Western heroes shoot those bad Arabs dead in their sandals, some viewers stood and applauded.

Our speedy 2003 military incursions into Iraq prompted *Los Angeles Times* critic Kenneth Turan to pose timely questions: Did pre–9/11 films help incite xenophobia and war fever? Did the Arab fiendish enemy "other" stereotype help "feed the unusual haste with which we became involved in Iraq?" Movies, explains Turan, are really "hard-wired into our psyches, shaping how we view the world." Regrettably, pre–9/11 features glossed over a needed view of Iraq—the suffering of civilians. As we may recall, the United States bears primary responsibility for the tough United Nations sanctions imposed against Iraq in 1990 following Iraq's invasion of Kuwait and continuing until the US-led 2003 invasion of Iraq. According to a UNICEF report, the UN sanctions resulted in the deaths of over a million Iraqis, most of whom were children. Turan notes this omission, writing that "It's when politics infiltrates entertainment that it is most subversive—and most effective. [Fiction films] change minds politically. . . . Artful entertainment easily beats full-on propaganda." To support his thesis, Turan reminds us that during the 1930s, just prior to the Holocaust, the average, cinema-going Germans were watching and "being influenced *not by documentaries, but by* Leni Riefenstahl's *entertainment movies* [emphasis added]." Riefenstahl's fantasy films "permeated German popular culture, forming a background on which the nation came to judge the emerging Nazi Party and its Aryan superiority."

Some critics have tried to bamboozle us into thinking reel images, public opinion, and politics are not linked, that movies do not impact viewers that much, here and abroad. They do. Carl Sagan calls "one of the saddest lessons of history" this: "If we've been bamboozled long enough, we tend to reject any evidence of the bamboozle; the bamboozle has captured us." Hollywood bamboozles us by placing influential stereotypes into the minds of viewers. One example: *300* (2007), a blockbuster hit celebrating, as Azadeh Moaveni wrote in *Time*, "war, militarism, and battlefield carnage." The movie follows other anti-Arab and anti-Islamic features, TV shows, and video games. In *300*, the evil, dark, uncivilized Persian "beast prepares to devour tiny Greece." The Persians represent tyranny, the barbaric Muslim East, while the heroic white Spartans represent liberty, the civilized Judeo-Christian West. When watching *300*, US Marines serving at Camp Pendleton cheered the outnumbered courageous Spartans as they brought down the Persian enemy horde. In Iran, however, nearly everyone was outraged—from dentists to taxi drivers—saying the film "was secretly funded by the US government to prepare Americans for going to war against Iran." One Tehran newscast declared: "Hollywood has opened a new front in the war against Iran." Though the film does not belittle Arabs, *300*'s dark-skinned "towel-headed" soldiers may be perceived as reel menacing Arabs, because many Americans think that like Iraq, Iran is also an Arab country, and that Iranians/Persians are Arabs.

"Of all the art forms," observes film historian Annette Insdorf, "film is the one that gives the greatest illusion of authenticity, of truth." Early on, astute political leaders recognized that motion pictures could be used to manipulate public policies and the social attitudes of mass audiences. In the 1920s, long before color, widescreens, DVDs, video outlets, and TV, Russia's Lenin declared, "For us, the cinema . . . is the most important of all the arts." Lenin and other political leaders began using black-and-white entertainment films as effective propaganda, advancing an agenda. Concurrently, in 1922, the Mexican government banned any US movie that was offensive to Mexicans. Mexico's actions prompted President Woodrow Wilson himself to intervene by asking Hollywood's leaders to: "Please be a little kinder to the Mexicans."

Advance ten years to the early 1930s, when Germany's Goebbels put into play the timeless blueprint for effective propaganda: "[Propaganda] must always be simple and repetitious . . . it confines itself to just a few points [and images] and repeats them over and over." Or, as the classic Arab proverb, has it: "By repetition, even the donkey learns." At about the same time, British filmmaker Alexander Korda was about to make a movie about T. E. Lawrence (decades before the release of David Lean's classic *Lawrence of Arabia* [1962]). But the British Foreign Office objected, arguing that because of political unrest in the Middle East it would be ill advised to depict Turks as villains. Pressure from the Foreign Office prompted Korda to acquiesce; he did not make the movie. Move ahead to the 1960s. One scene in *The 7th Dawn* (1964) shows British troops torching a Malaya village, displacing hundreds of men, women, and children. British officials refused to assist the producers, saying the scene was too violent. The filmmakers turned to the government of Australia for help, and found it. About 80 troops from the 2nd Battalion of the royal Australian regiment are in the film, portraying British soldiers.

Flash forward to France, 2006. Demonstrating anew the power of one motion picture to effect political change, in September French President Jacques Chirac decided to restore full pensions to the 80,000 Arab soldiers from North Africa who fought valiantly for the country against the Germans. What prompted President Chirac to decide to correct this long-standing and obvious injustice? He watched the superb film *Indigénes* (*Days of Glory*, 2006), which depicts heroic Arab soldiers in the French army fighting to liberate France during World War II. The scene in which the North Africans are not served the same food as the French troops, though they are fighting alongside them, against the same enemy, may have helped influence Chirac. A French sergeant who commands the regiment advises his captain to resolve the problem, telling him not to tag the Arabs "natives" nor to call them "Muslims—that's just as bad." Asks his officer: "What should I call them, then?" Says the sergeant, "The men, sir; the men."

Government strategies enforce stereotypes here at home, as well. In turn, the stereotypes influence policies. During times of conflict, especially, media systems function as common carriers for government policies. During World War II, for example, Washington turned to Hollywood to produce anti-Axis films that would inspire Americans on the front lines and their families back home. The government enlisted the services of talented filmmakers such as

Frank Capra (*Why We Fight*), John Huston, Alfred Hitchcock, and Walt Disney animators. Not surprisingly, as most of our major media outlets are now owned by corporations with "vested interests in Washington policy," points out Bill Moyers, "the symbiotic relationships between the political elites and the media elites have grown."

As early as 1987, Fox executives began screening their new motion pictures "in the nation's capital for Congressmen, their wives and staffers." Asked about the congressional screenings, Thomas R. Herwitz, Fox's vice president for corporate and legal affairs, said: "We make sure members of the Congress and other government officials know what we're doing; our discussions allow them to know what's on our minds and us to learn what's on theirs." According to reports from New York's International Action Center, weeks before *Black Hawk Down* (2002) was released, the Motion Picture Association of America (MPAA) held a private screening for senior White House advisors "and allowed them to make changes" in the film. Defense Secretary Donald Rumsfeld and Oliver North, along with 800 top officials and brass, attended the screening, applauding the premiere of *Black Hawk Down* in Washington.

US presidents, too, are linked with the industry. George W. Bush served from 1983 to 1992 on the board of Silver Screen Management, a company that has produced movies exclusively for TriStar, then Walt Disney. Following the August 2000 Hollywood Gala Salute to President Bill Clinton—the largest Hollywood tribute ever produced for a sitting president—the president and Mrs. Clinton attended a reception at Sony Pictures studios. In February 2007, the MPAA conducted a first one-day symposium in Washington, DC. On hand to discuss the role of entertainment in a digital age were Hollywood heavyweights such as Will Smith and Steven Soderbergh; they interacted with politicians Charles Rangel, Patrick Leahy, and Dianne Feinstein.

Best solidifying cinema's long-standing influence and linkage with American politics are these observations, made by former Republican senator, *Law & Order* actor, and 2008 presidential candidate Fred Thompson and Jack Valenti, ex-chair of the MPAA. Appearing on NBC-TV's *Tonight Show* Thompson confessed to host Jay Leno that he never intended to spend his life in Washington as a career politician, and that he had always "longed for the realism and sincerity of Hollywood." Several years before Thompson articulated his infatuation with Hollywood, Jack Valenti got it right when he emphatically remarked: "Washington and Hollywood spring from the same DNA."

No matter the country or its politics, the historical and ongoing connection between fiction film, public opinion, and public policies is real.

POSTSCRIPT

Do Media Represent Realistic Images of Arabs?

Whenever we deal with issues of stereotypes and whether they do or do not influence our perceptions of people in society, we broach the uncomfortable area of human biases and prejudices. We know that media do indeed shape our sense of self and how we "fit" our own culture, but what if you are a person who does not see images of people who look like you, or who share your traditions, heritage, race, ethnicity, gender, or religion in media? The people who are not portrayed and the images we don't see are just as important as the distorted images that we do see. Absence of accurate images can be as harmful as the presence of distorted images.

The most insidious thing about stereotypes is that we seldom question whether they are accurate or not, and yet questioning the images we see in media is one of the most important features of understanding media's relationship to society. There is evidence that U.S. media have improved in terms of portrayals of African Americans, Hispanics, and Asians, and images of gays and lesbians are starting to improve; but as these selections show, accurate representations of Arabs in the mainstream media still have a long way to go. Perhaps blogging or alternative media will lead the way.

There are several excellent resources to illuminate the problem of representation and misrepresentation of "the Other" in the media. Brigitte Lebens Nacos and Oscar Torres-Reyna have written *Fueling Our Fears: Stereotyping, Media Coverage, and Public Opinion of Muslim Americans* (Rowman & Littlefield, 2007), which also discusses the Arab/Muslim controversy, particularly for Muslims born in America, and considers how Americans look at Arabs and Muslims abroad. A number of excellent books have been written about other racial or ethnic groups maligned in the media. The *Journal of Arab and Muslim Media* is an online source that often focuses on content and images within media, and can be accessed through most academic libraries.

Edward Schiappa's *Beyond Representational Correctness: Rethinking Criticism of Popular Media* (State University of New York Press, 2008) addresses the role of stereotyping in general in the media, and discusses the parasocial relationships we have with people in the media. There are also a number of sources, too long to list here, that discuss different racial, ethnic, gender, and class representations in media; and many of these are readily available in academic libraries as well as in popular book stores.

ISSUE 4

Do Media Cause Individuals to Develop Negative Body Images?

YES: **Shari L. Dworkin and Faye Linda Wachs**, from "What Kinds of Subjects and Objects? Gender, Consumer Culture, and Convergence," in *Body Panic: Gender, Health, and the Selling of Fitness* (New York University, 2009)

NO: **Michael P. Levine and Sarah K. Murnen**, from "Everybody Knows That Mass Media Are/Are Not [*pick one*] a Cause of Eating Disorders: A Critical Review of Evidence for a Causal Link Between Media, Negative Body Image, and Disordered Eating in Females," *Journal of Social and Clinical Psychology* (2009)

ISSUE SUMMARY

YES: Shari Dworkin and Faye Wachs discuss the results of their content analysis of health magazine ads and find that the ads tell men and women that a healthy body is attainable if they buy the products and pamper themselves. Fat becomes something to be feared, and grooming practices and fashion are "sold" as imperatives for both men and women.

NO: Michael Levine and Sarah Murnen also investigate magazine ads, but find the assumption that media cause eating disorders to be too limited. Instead, they cite a wide range of social, behavioral, and cultural issues over time to understand the complex conditions under which girls begin to adopt negative body issues that result in eating disorders.

Often media are accused of representing images that result in people's negative behaviors. Sometimes, media are so present in our lives that it seems apparent that there is, or should be, a direct link between media images and real-life manifestations of those images. We know that media have *some* influence over the way *some* people construct their ideas of reality, but the most difficult considerations have to do with *who* is affected, and under *what* conditions. The authors of these two selections look specifically at magazines and how ideas of health and body image are constructed, with two different conclusions.

In their investigation, Professors Dworkin and Wachs find that men and women are increasingly being represented in similar ways in popular health and fitness magazine advertising. They discuss the way a healthy body image is constructed in ads, promising that if people consume these products, they can turn their negative body image around and be as fit, healthy, and happy as the people in the ads. They remark on how similar lifestyle ads are in targeting both men and women and representing a "healthy body" ideal. The result then is the consumers feeling that if they don't consume these products, they will feel worse about their bodies.

We also know that in extreme cases, some people develop eating disorders, based on the ideal body image as super thin, that are unhealthy and harmful to their bodies. Professors Levine and Murnen evaluate the literature on what causes girls to develop eating disorders, and find that media may play a limited role in contributing to one's negative body image, but that other cultural, social, and psychological issues play a much larger role in causing girls to actually harm themselves by extreme behaviors. Their perspective examines how behavior and self-image are formed over time, and in a world that has several competing causes for why someone psychologically succumbs to extreme eating behavior.

The complexities between media images and self-image are many indeed, and we know that not everyone is influenced by media in the same way. Socialization, family pressures and expectations, the type of media one consumes, and how peers talk about media images all have the potential to influence us in different ways, and, still, probably all of us at some time know that something we saw in media made us feel a certain way or think about something in a special way. When it comes to internalizing those images, our minds often register reactions in ways of which we may not be aware.

Advertisers often seek to understand the underlying motivations that cause us to respond—especially to buy products, but sometimes we look for support from other people to confirm what we want to believe. Celebrities also tend to project body images that are often significantly underweight, thereby providing role models that may influence conscious or unconscious desires to be "like them." American culture is rife with stories about the perils of obesity and unhealthy lifestyles. As a result, it is difficult to seek one particular cause that could be the definitive answer to why anyone develops the self-image he or she does. But the process of trying to understand the range of psychological processes that come part-and-parcel with media images is fascinating, and sometimes, frightening.

YES

Shari L. Dworkin and
Faye Linda Wachs

What Kinds of Subjects and Objects?: Gender, Consumer Culture, and Convergence

[Women] are said to be accounted for by these theories—and yet they barely make an appearance. On the other hand, if and when they do appear . . . they surface only as objects of various different agencies . . . which are seen to act upon them and force them into a particular range of roles. The question of how individuals make certain modes of behavior their own, how they learn to develop one particular set of needs as opposed to certain others, is never addressed.

Women are not only objects of male desire: they themselves play a part in their creation as such. To see femininity in this way is to identify a subjective aspect within being-as-object, and thus effectively to recognize the inadequacy of the subject-object metaphor.

Consumer culture had discovered and begun to develop the untapped resources of the male body.

How then is the idealized body constructed in consumer culture today? Examining mainstream health and fitness magazines provides insight into dominant cultural constructions of "health" and by extension allows researchers to examine what constitutes a privileged body. Given the importance of sex assignment in Western culture, this body is always already a gendered body. However, what the assignment of sex means for bodies is changing and evolving in consumer culture. Instead of reiterating long held subject/object dichotomies that tend to analyze the situation from the position that men are given the status of subjects while women are objects, we rely on Frigga Haug's concept of the "subjective-aspects-within-being-as-object" (defined below) and apply it to the case of women's fitness media texts. For an analysis of men's fitness media texts, we introduce a concept we term the "objective-aspects-within-being-as-subject" and therefore extend Haug's work to consider the case of men, bodies, and consumer culture. Indeed, looking at the two terms side by side suggests greater possibility for overlap between subjective and objective status than has typically been offered in previous analyses of gender and the body.

From *Body Panic: Gender, Health, and the Selling of Fitness* by Shari L. Dworkin and Faye Linda Wachs (New York University Press, 2009), pp. 29–48 (excerpts, notes omitted). Copyright © 2009 by New York University Press. Reprinted by permission.

Frigga Haug et al. coined and first used the phrase the "subjective-aspects-within-being-as-object" to refer to how women experience identity, subjecthood, and pleasure in the process of bodily objectification. In her book, *Female Sexualization: Questions for Feminism,* Haug described and analyzed cultural materials (newspaper articles, art, film) and women's own stories about what she calls "body projects"—for example, doing one's hair, shaving one's legs, choosing fashion trends, etc. Such an approach allowed Haug to structure an analysis of the relationship between subjectivity and objectivity in the process of female sexualization. A main part of her argument is that there is an extensive *process of subjectivity* (not necessarily harm and force) that goes unrecognized in the arguments on this topic. Previous arguments generally assumed that women were having something "done to them" by media images, texts, and larger cultural norms. Haug's work demonstrates the agency of the subject in the creation of objecthood. This does not diminish previous analysis, but adds a critical dimension to understanding relations of power and privilege.

Adding subjectivity to an analysis of gender and the body was a much needed corrective to feminists who had long noted that in Western culture, there is an imperative toward the sexual objectification of women—and this was conceived of as wholly negative. To a large degree, according to this position, women's power and experience of self is based on the ability to meet current cultural ideals. Women and girls come to experience themselves as if someone were looking at them (as an object) and evaluate themselves based on appearance and their successful presentation of self as an object. Some argue that this lack of subjecthood is not simply about the surface of the body but is linked to sexuality and the expression of desire. That is, the way in which subjecthood is constructed for young girls leads to a lack of female desire in heterosexuality, where girls and women are centrally concerned about making themselves into an attractive object of desire instead of "owning" or knowing desire for themselves. One might suspect that this more passive view of the body contrasts with what is found within sport coverage of female athletes, for example, that when female subjects are viewed as engaging in some type of action, the presentation of self is usually paramount to performance rather than some other standards.

Despite sport as a realm of action, researchers frequently note that women's performances are "offset" by depictions of feminine aesthetics and beauty standards. By contrast, male subjecthood has often been linked directly to status, societal position, or power, while male appearance historically has been considered far less important (until recently). Certainly, the history of fashion and its current state demonstrate that men too have taken great care in the presentation of self. However, the links between attractiveness, status, and bodily ideals have had a long and complicated racialized, classed, gendered history. Indeed, for men, it is generally the characteristics of the powerful that come to be imbued with attractiveness.

The subject/object distinction around gender and the body needs to be understood in the context of Western philosophy more generally. The choice between subject and object reflects traditional Western cultural dualisms, or the tendency to present people, domains, and/or groups as categorical opposites.

women was excluded from point of view...?

Feminist epistemology problematized traditional Western dualisms, such as nature/culture, male/female, and subject/object and how these dualisms have come into play in gender relations. This means that over time, femininity was associated with being an object and linked to emotion and nature. By contrast, masculinity was associated with subjecthood and was tied to Enlightenment principles such as knowledge and reason. Feminist theorists have long critiqued the exclusion of women's subjecthood, ways of knowing, and experiences from the production of knowledge and the limitations imposed on women as a result of these presumptions. Certainly, it could be argued that women have effectively been denied a philosophical experience of subjecthood that does not center on the self as object.

It is certain that both men and women have been objectified; however, male power and privilege have been maintained by partly limiting women's source of power to their ability to be the "right" kind of object. Specific researchers argue that women's consent to being a valued object seals the deal, as Connell notes in his 1987 work *Gender and Power*. Connell defines "emphasized femininity" as the most valued form of femininity, and contrasts it to hegemonic masculinity, the most privileged form of masculinity. In these definitions, there is a difference between male privilege and female value, indicating a patriarchal gender order. The subject/object dichotomy further underscores the difference between these two terms. . . .

As has been noted by Kimmel, at the turn of the millennium, men's and women's lives are becoming "more similar," at least for the most advantaged. For the privileged, most professions are gender-neutral, and women and men are routinely employed in the same professions, enjoy the same leisure activities, and engage in similar rituals of self-care. Women's increased earning power can also mean that some couples and single women are able to "buy off" the second shift of household labor and childcare. The growing importance of women as consumers has been linked to women's greater social power, especially in the world of sports and fitness. These tendencies combine with the objectifying propensities of consumer culture (for all bodies) to narrow the gap in how gender is defined, constructed in image, and practiced. This is revealed in the convergence of men's and women's bodily displays and practices in health and fitness magazines—the focus of this chapter.

Converging Bodies: Gender and Consumer Culture

Men's and women's bodily practices converge in several notable ways. First, fat is a powerfully feared cultural transgression for both women and men. Second, men and women are coming to be presented in a more similar manner, as objects (here, we analyze body positioning, smiles, head shots, and active/passive imagery). Third, what is marketed to male and female bodies is converging. Grooming practices and fashion expand, as it is framed as "imperative" for both women and men to be up to date in fashion. In addition, leisure practices are expanding as they converge for both women and men (manscaping, manicures, spa treatments, personal training, massages).

In the first case, fat is now a powerfully feared cultural transgression. For both men and women, any visible body fat is presented as problematic. "Are you fat?" asks *Men's Health* (January/February 1999). The article includes a test to determine this with certainty, followed by ratings of different diet and exercise plans. Given this trend, it may not be surprising that 38 percent of dieters in the United States are now male within a diet industry that is now worth $58.7 billion. The obesity crisis has been much touted in the mass media. Although we don't dispute the negative health consequences of being overweight, the link between (a relatively homogeneous) appearance and health is dubious at best. Moreover, there is an ongoing tendency to frame the overweight body as a threat to the self and to the general populace. Maintaining a fit body is no longer viewed as a personal choice, but as an obligation to the public good and a requirement for good citizenry. The once narcissistic body obsession has not only become a marker of individual health, but a form of social responsibility and civic participation. Over time, body weight has taken on the aura of a broader social problem related to public health. This obscures the relationship between social privilege and the development and maintenance of a fit body, and reinforces the stigmatization of "othered" bodies.

Despite evidence that suggests a totally fat-free form can be unrealistic and unhealthy, this form is idealized and venerated. Analyses of consumer culture suggest that this constructs a culture of "bodily lack" that requires constant maintenance. A key set of fundamental assumptions that shape the content and tone of the magazine center on the negative aspects of *any* body fat. Fat is unhealthy. Unaesthetic. Prevents you from being everything you can be. Leads to public ridicule, especially at the hands of the opposite sex. Is a sign of one's failure to demonstrate a proper "work ethic." The reification/deification of the fat-free form is visually reinforced almost continuously with the imagery in magazines. Idealized bodies with no body fat are featured on the covers and throughout the magazines.

It is not just imagery that offers this impression, but the tendency for magazines to blur the boundaries between the purpose of text, image, expert advice, and ads increases over time in our ten-year sample. In fact, the difference between advertising and content imagery can become largely irrelevant, and indeed, one cannot meaningfully separate magazine content from ads in many places. This is most notable when examining the ubiquitous short "snippet" that promotes new products, practices, or services, and the photo essay, usually a magazine-prepared advertisement. The images merge seamlessly in the magazine from article to ad and back again. They reinforce messages of idealized physical forms and undermine text that might speak in a bold or trite way of self-acceptance. An analysis of the covers demonstrates that only a few models, whose photographed bodies have been trimmed and touched up, meet these ideals. Mainstream newspaper articles that interview athletes, fitness experts, or trainers highlight that the athletes themselves are surprised at how their photographs have been altered in fitness imagery, underscoring that even professional athletes rarely measure up.

Advertisements also usually feature very slim or cut models, and similarly computer-altered, airbrushed, and trimmed photos of models. When taken together, they create the impression that the ideal body is *necessarily* fat-free. This is reinforced because more realistic but still presumably healthy bodies rarely appear. Heavier bodies appear only as "before" photos in "success stories." The paucity of a range of healthy fit images literally denies their existence, and refutes the possibility that a person can be larger and still be fit and healthy. The symbolic annihilation of the wide range of healthy bodies operates to conflate fat-free with "healthy" and undermines any textual references to the existence of this range. The assumptions that emerge in the text further vilify fat while extolling the moral virtue of the fat-free form. (Our own students exalt the value of the fat-free form as inherently right and healthy; we frequently compare notes about how to discuss the lack of a continuum of body fat in imagery—much of which could be conceived of as quite far from "fat," but also rather healthy and plenty attractive.) The obliteration of this continuum leaves the impression that the range of fit bodies is far narrower than it is in reality.

The preponderance of articles on diets, health, nutrition, and workouts included a discussion of cutting body fat for both men and women. While men were encouraged to "eat to grow," cutting body fat was the second most common diet proscription for men, and was frequently referenced in conjunction with gains in muscle size. *EMO* encourages men to "Torch Your Bodyfat! New Supplements Do the Trick." *Exercise & Health* offers "25 Ways to Shed Fat." Because historically, reducing body fat had feminine connotations, it is necessary to masculinize men's fat reduction. Cutting fat is masculinized by linking it to the revelation of manly striations and cuts. Abdominals are specifically noted as visible signs of masculinity that can only be revealed when body fat is exorcised. While *all* men should spend their time attempting to reveal a minimum of six-pack abdominals, the "eight-pack" is appearing with increasing frequency. The diet industry is attempting to further masculinize weight loss; even the weight-loss giant Nutrisystem recently hired its first male spokesperson, former quarterback Dan Marino.

For women, decreasing fat (without mention of the striations or cuts underneath) was the most common diet recommendation, coupled with recipes and hints. For women, fitness and dieting are critical to attaining a slim, toned, and cellulite-free form. *Shape* provide "7 Sneaky Reasons Dining Out Is Making You Fat." *Fitness* promises to "Speed Up Your Metabolism in Just 10 Minutes." The magazines do not present any obvious benefits to a faster metabolism, except weight loss.

The majority of workouts further highlighted a fat-free form, even when many explicitly acknowledged in the text that one cannot spot reduce, or that toning will not be visible without removing fat, and that the only way to reduce fat is to consume less. Workouts for women focused on toning and tightening muscles that could only be revealed with a modified and rather Spartan diet. *Fitness* exhorts women to "Lose Your Ab Flab" with a workout that combines aerobics and pilates that "Not only will you get your heart pumping and burn 420 calories per hour (about 17 percent more than in a traditional mat class), but you'll experience total-body conditioning through balance challenges and see the ab-sculpting benefits." Workouts like "The

No-Fat Back" promise a reduction in body fat with diet and exercise. Notice that despite textual references to the impossibility of spot reduction, the titles of workouts clearly suggest fat will be removed from a specific area of the body. For men, workouts also often emphasized lower fat intake to reveal cuts or to trim fat from the waist.

Success stories in women's magazines almost exclusively highlighted people who lost weight, with only a few that covered those who strove to gain weight or battled eating disorders. Weight loss was noted in pounds lost, inches lost, and accompanied by ab-baring before and after photos. *Shape* features "Success Stories: A Special Guide—How 5 Women Got in Shape! You can too with our sure-fire plan." This piece features a diet, followed by success stories of five women who followed the diet. For each woman, inches and pounds lost are the first statistics provided with their pictures. The focus on these types of measures sends a clear message about the primary meaning of success in fitness. Though many articles on being satisfied with oneself at a larger size appear, the almost complete exclusion of alternative imagery contradicts the messages of acceptance.

Control of the body remains a central organizing principle in postindustrial society. The need to control the unruly body emerges in the postindustrial world as a marker of the self. Linked to personal displays that demonstrate success or failure, the presentation of the body in the twenty-first century signifies a variety of meanings, not the least of which is one's moral worth. While the fat body remains stigmatized as lazy, undisciplined, or as a poor member of the social body, the fit body becomes a metaphor for success, morality, and good citizenship. Just as wealth marked morality for the Calvinists, the "fit" body marks a moral and disciplined self that demonstrates sufficient participation in the regimes of bodywork necessary to support consumer capitalism. As argued by Gimlin, "The body is fundamental to the self because it serves to indicate who an individual is internally, what habits the person has, and even what social value the individual merits." Hence, the fit body simultaneously validates the individual and legitimates the value of such a body.

Further, the normalization of the completely fat-free form operates to stigmatize bodies left out of the frame. Spitzack in 1990 and later on, Duncan, in 1994, employ Foucauldian thought to demonstrate how the confessional process centered on fitness and the body ultimately results in the disempowerment of the subject. While Duncan was studying the content of women's magazines and Spitzack studied women's narratives of "confessional excess" about their bodies, both of their arguments can be extended to men's experiences given trends of convergence. Here, we mean that all readers lose the ability to define the image of a healthy body as based on critical measures of health (cholesterol, pulse rate, blood pressure, cardiovascular fitness, pulmonary function, and so forth). Instead, an image of health becomes paramount and as Duncan suggests, "panoptic mechanisms" lead the reader to internalize self-surveillance of the surface of the body, conflating body image with morality, success, and good citizenship. The fat-free fit form also serves as a marker of class status to some degree, as the bodywork required to maintain this form requires a significant amount of time and money.

While body fat is one area where there is overlap across men's and women's magazines, there were other ways in which the presentation of male and female bodies converged. . . .

The results of the initial sample are consistent with Duncan's analysis of sports media texts which revealed that mainstream media construct men as active and women as inactive. In this view, women are often shown as "being visually perfect" and "passive, immobile, and unchanging." The initial sample reflects this tendency. Men are more often featured as active or with action implied. The presence of action implies subjecthood, that one is an active subject. In the initial sample, men are depicted actively engaging in sports or fitness with over 80 percent of the covers featuring them either directly engaged in action, or with action implied through the use of props. By contrast, women are far more often presented as objects, with just over 85 percent of covers featuring women engaging only in the act of posing, experiencing the subjective aspects of being as object. Further, the action-implied covers are almost exclusively from one publication, *Women's Sports & Fitness*. . . .

We coded covers according to models' facial expressions, gaze, and body positioning. These studies indicate that dominance and submission are transmitted through the body using nonverbal communication, reflective of one's status in society. Body language as expressed through body positioning, eye contact, head tilts, and facial expression (smiling, etc.) also provides culturally recognizable cues that media have used to produce and reflect gendered bodies. . . .

Duncan, in her examination of how sports photographers use corporeal cues to embody sexual difference, found that women were often portrayed with direct eye contact to the camera, accompanied by a sideways tilt of the head and/or slightly parted lips. Duncan labels these bodily cues as nonverbal heterosexual "come-ons" linked to those found in men's soft-core pornography. Head-on poses are generally less submissive than head-tilted shots. The tilt usually involves the model looking up at the camera, giving the viewer a "come hither gaze." Similarly, body positioning that is straight toward the camera is less submissive than bodies that are tilted up toward the camera. Hip thrusts further indicate a provocative pose designed to please and entice the viewer. Finally, facial expressions indicate status. Inviting smiles versus serious expression indicate one's status. . . .

While over 85 percent of the original men's sample featured shots that were taken head-on, only 50 percent of the second sample reveals the same tendency. For women, two-thirds of the original sample was shot head-on, while 37.9 percent of the new sample is shot this way. The shift to the "come hither look" for both men and women indicates a shift toward men as deploying self-presentation as object. As previously noted, the tilt usually indicates submission or enticement. This is further demonstrated in hand positioning. The hand on the self in the manner of most of these magazines connotes a "look at me" presentation, further enhancing the subjective aspects within being-as-object.

Trends toward bodily convergence by gender are evident in the models' facial expressions. The type of smile displayed reveals something about the status of the individual. An inviting smile is the most common facial expression in both codes. In the initial sample, 81.0 percent of women have full smiles, and the remaining 19 percent displayed partial smiles. In the full coding, 63.6 percent sport full smiles, 33.4 percent exhibit partial smiles, and 3.0 percent appear serious. Of the men's cover models in the original sample, 52.4 percent have a full smile, an additional 14.3 percent feature partial smiles, and 28.6 percent are serious. In the updated sample, 36.7 percent of men wear full smiles, but 21.7 percent present partial smiles, and almost the same percentage, 28.3 percent, have serious facial expressions. Though gender differences remain in terms of who can display a serious face and still be deemed desirable, Henley's work is particularly instructive, as she argues that women are often publicly responsible for a continuous display of pleasantness and amiability. We view the decrease in full smiles in favor of partial smiles for men and women as reflecting a shift. The partial smile also creates a more knowing look. We suggest the ironic presentation of the self as object is becoming more common. In other words, the model displays a realization of the self as object and the consciousness of display.

Researchers argue that women's smiles reify gender ideals of agreeableness or vulnerability, while men's smiles might be indicative of the fact that privileged and powerful men are allowed a wider range of emotional displays than subordinated men. In our original sample, there are only three men of color featured on the men's covers, and it is striking that all of these men had partial or full smiles. This seems consistent with researchers who argue that smiles are often used to represent men of color so as to undercut prevalent (racist) associations of potential threat or danger. In the original sample, boxer Oscar De La Hoya is shown boxing with his cocked fists aiming playfully at the reader. Boxing is a blood sport that has been widely contested as violent. Therefore, De La Hoya's smile might be employed to make him seem less threatening and aggressive. In the new sample, only two nonwhite men appear on the covers. Both are smiling. One is an NBA all-star, the other, an unknown model. We will return to more comments on the racialized dimensions of the findings at the end of the chapter. . . .

Third, what is advertised to men and women shows considerable overlap. For example, compare *Men's Health* from May 2004 with *Shape* from May 2004. *Men's Health* is 218 pages total (including front and back covers) and has 111 full pages devoted to advertising (though some ads were several pages, and others only half a page). Thus, 50.9 percent of the issue is devoted solely to advertising. (Additional ads sometimes shared pages with content, but in the interest of clarity, we focused on full-page ads only.) Twenty ads are for cars or motorcycles (18.0 percent), ten are for food or meal replacements (9.1 percent), nineteen are for clothing or accessories (17.1 percent), six are for grooming products of various types (5.4 percent), and four are for medications or pain killers (3.6 percent). *Shape* is 324 pages, of which 156 pages are devoted entirely to advertising (48.1 percent). Nine ads are for automobiles (5.8 percent), twenty-six are for food or meal replacements (16.7 percent), thirteen are for clothing or accessories (8.3 percent), thirty-three are for grooming products (21.2 percent), thirteen are for medications or pain killers (8.3 percent).

Increasingly, men and women are encouraged to use a wide range of hair, skin, hygiene, and grooming products. While *Men's Health* features more advertisements for automobiles than *Shape* (18.0 percent compared to 5.8 percent) and *Shape* features more advertisements for food than *Men's Health* (16.7 percent to 9.1 percent) and grooming products (21.2 percent to 5.4 percent), there is a great deal of overlap in what is being advertised to male and female consumers. Body products, such as skin care and hair care products, are increasingly being offered to both male and female consumers.

In addition to the direct ads, regular columns often provide coverage of products. These products are presented with the same excited aplomb as significant information regarding health, making a "new way to make hair shine" or a "new fragrance" appear to be as significant as a new way to combat breast or prostate cancer. While this may sound like a strange characterization, it is easier to explain with examples. For example, *Fit* mixed information about strokes, jump ropes, aquaphor healing ointment, osteoporosis, pony tails, growing longer nails, and new floral scents in snippets on different pages. *Men's Health* combined information on martial arts, Mr. Rogers, healthy meals, prostate cancer tests, pajamas, exercise bands, flashlights, sports drinks, digital voice recorders, airline tickets, how to shoot a basketball, microbrews, and more in just one "Malegrams" column. Mixing together different types of information, products, and expert advice creates the impression that all these topics should receive similar consideration.

The convergence of grooming products offered to both men and women is particularly noteworthy. Most of the men's magazines featured regular columns on grooming that cover such topics as alpha-hydroxy, hair care products, and potent scents. Though men and women may use products that smell different, are packaged in different colored bottles, and are described with different adjectives, the range of products offered overlapped considerably. Men's grooming products are expected to be a $10 billion market by 2008, compared to the $15 billion expected for women's grooming products in the same year. In 2006, the top-selling fragrance for 9 of 12 months was a man's fragrance. Not surprisingly, men's products were masculinized by linking them to sports stars and celebrities. For example, in 2006, Yankees' shortstop Derek Jeter began marketing a line of men's grooming products and a signature fragrance with Avon. Clive Owen, the ruggedly handsome Academy Award–nominated actor, is on the Lancôme payroll.

Additionally, leisure time activities were also de-gendered, having overlapped across women's and men's magazines. A key example is the repackaging of spa treatments and body services such as manicures and pedicures for male consumers. All of the magazines highlighted body treatments of various types for men. *EMO* included spa reports regularly, for example, in one issue they ranked body services such as the "Detoxifying Algae Wrap," "Holistic Back, Face and Scalp Session," and "Balneotherapy" (a combo tub soak, seaweed wrap, and massage) provided by Tethra Spa in Dublin, Ireland. *Prime* compared two spas and offered tips on finding a spa near you. One chain of spas reported that now, 15–20 percent of its clients are men, a new and growing trend. Manicures and pedicures are becoming regular recommendations for men in the magazines we studied and in popular culture in general.

Again, athletes and actors were used to market and masculinize such treatments. Just as men were encouraged to try services traditionally marketed exclusively to women, women were encouraged to try activities and experiences once thought of as more appropriate for men. For example, women were urged to try three North Spas that offer kayaking and other sport activities in addition to more traditional spa treatments. While privileged men have long been "pampered," modern conceptions of the hegemonic man have tended to exclude anything that carried the taint of femininity. By the same token, more adventurous activities tor women are also normalized as gender-appropriate for either men or women.

Michael P. Levine and
Sarah K. Murnen

 **NO**

"Everybody Knows That Mass Media Are/Are Not [*pick one*] a Cause of Eating Disorders": A Critical Review of Evidence for a Causal Link Between Media, Negative Body Image, and Disordered Eating in Females

Numerous professionals, parents, and adolescents find the media's status as a cause of body dissatisfaction, drive for thinness, and eating disorders to be self-evident: *"Of course,* mass media contribute to unhealthy beauty ideals, body dissatisfaction, and disordered eating—haven't you seen the magazine covers in the supermarket newsstands lately? No wonder so many girls have body image issues and eating disorders." On the contrary, a growing number of parents, biopsychiatric researchers, clinicians, and cynical adolescents find proclamations about media as a *cause* of any disorder to be an irritating distraction. Their contention is, in effect: *"Of course,* we know now that eating disorders, like mood disorders and schizophrenia, are severe, self-sustaining psychiatric illnesses with a genetic and biochemical basis. So, *of course,* no scientist seriously thinks that mass media and the escapades of actors, models, and celebrities have anything to do with causing them." . . .

The relationships between mass media, negative body image, and unhealthy behaviors (e.g., use and abuse of steroids and food supplements) in males are receiving increasing attention. The gender differences (conservatively, 6 to 8 females for each male) in the prevalence of anorexia nervosa, bulimia nervosa, and eating disorder not otherwise specified (EDNOS) other than Binge Eating Disorder are among the largest reported for mental disorders.

Although the matter of dimensions and/or categories is complex and unresolved, substantial evidence suggests that the serious and frequently chronic conditions recognized as the "Eating Disorders" are composite expressions of a set of dimensions, such as negative emotionality, binge eating, and

From *Journal of Social and Clinical Psychology,* vol. 28, no. 1, January 2009, pp. 9–16, 19–26, 30–34. Copyright © 2009 by Guilford Publications. Reprinted by permission via Copyright Clearance Center.

unhealthy forms of weight and shape management. The latter includes restrictive dieting, self-induced vomiting after eating, and abuse of laxatives, diuretics, diet pills, and exercise.

The adhesive drawing together and framing these intertwined continua is negative body image. In most media effects research the multidimensional construct of body image is represented by various measures of what are essentially perceptual-emotional conclusions (e.g., "I look too fat to myself and others" + "I am disgusted by and ashamed of this" = "I hate how fat I look and feel"). For females "body dissatisfaction" results from—and feeds—a schema that integrates three fundamental components: idealization of slenderness and leanness; an irrational fear of fat; and a conviction that weight and shape are central determinants of one's identity. . . .

Researchers in many fields have stopped thinking about "the" cause of a disorder as "the agent" that directly brings about the undesirable outcome. Instead, there is an emphasis on variables that are reliably and usefully associated with an increase over time in the probability of a subsequent outcome. Such variables are called risk factors.

Thinking in terms of risk factors has two major implications for investigating mass media as a "cause" of eating disorders. The first concerns the oft-heard "relative rarity" argument: How could mass media be a cause when the vast majority of girls and young women are exposed to ostensibly toxic influences, but only a small percentage develop eating disorders? This critique dissolves when one considers multiple risk factors as multiplicative probabilities. Assume, conservatively, that 35% of adolescent girls are engaged with those mass media containing various unhealthy messages. Assume also that three other risk factors—such as peer preoccupation with weight and shape; family history of overweight/obesity; and being socialized by parents and older siblings to believe firmly that a female's identity and worth are shaped primarily by appearance—each have a probability of .35 of occurring in the population. . . .

Second, if mass media constitute a *causal risk factor* for the spectrum of negative body image and disordered eating, then the following will be the case. *Cross-sectional studies* will show that the extent of exposure to mass media, or to various specific forms of mass media, is a correlate of that spectrum. *Longitudinal studies* will demonstrate that exposure to mass media precedes and predicts development of negative body image and disordered eating. *Laboratory experiments* should show that well-controlled manipulation of the media risk factor (independent variable) causes the hypothesized changes in "state" body satisfaction and other relevant dependent variables, while *controlled analog (laboratory) or field experiments* should demonstrate that prevention programs designed to combat known risk factors do indeed reduce or delay the onset of disordered eating.

These criteria are demanding in and of themselves. Nevertheless, it is also important to incorporate the contributions to knowledge of two further sources: common sense and people's "lived experience." Specifically, if mass media are a causal risk factor, then *content analyses* should document that media provide the raw material from which children and adolescents could *readily* extract and construct the information, affective valences, and behavioral cues necessary to develop the components of disordered eating. Similarly, *surveys and ecological analyses* will reveal that engagement with mass media is frequent and intensive enough to provide multiple opportunities for this type of social-cognitive learning. Finally, *surveys and qualitative studies* should find that, beginning at the age where they can think critically about themselves in relation to personal and outside influences, children and adolescents will report that mass media are sources of influence, and even pressure, on themselves, their peers, and others. . . .

Appearance, status, sexuality, and buying and consuming are, for many reasons (including the power of mass media), very important aspects of life throughout many countries. Consequently, the content of mass media provides daily, multiple, overlapping, and, all too often, unhealthy messages about gender, attractiveness, ideal body sizes and shapes, self-control, desire, food, and weight management. These messages sometimes intentionally, sometimes incidentally indoctrinate developing girls and boys with the following easily extracted themes: (a) being sexually attractive is of paramount importance; (b) the sources of ideals about attractiveness ("being 'hot'!"), style, and the best, most competitive practices for becoming and staying beautiful are obviously located outside the self; and (c) mass media are the most important and inherently enjoyable "external" source of the information, motivation, and products necessary to be attractive and fashionable.

Mass Media and the Thinness Schema

Thus, with respect to the cultural foundations of negative body image and disordered eating, even girls (and boys) as young as 4 or 5 have no trouble finding in mass media the raw materials for various maladaptive but *entirely normative* media-based *schemata* concerning gender and attractiveness. The *"thinness schema"* for females is a set of assumptions, "facts," and strong feelings that are organized so as to establish a readiness to think and respond in terms of, for example, the following themes: (1) Women are "naturally" invested in their beauty assets and thus beauty is a woman's principal project in life; (2) a slender, youthful attractive "image" is really something substantive, because it is pleasing to males and it demonstrates to females that one is in control of one's life; and (3) learning to perceive, monitor, and indeed experience yourself as the object of an essentially masculine gaze is an important part of being feminine and beautiful.

Transnational Idol: The Exaltation of Thinness and the Vilification of Fat

There is a wealth of evidence from content analyses that the ideal female body showcased on television, in movies, in magazines, and on the internet reflects, indeed embodies, the proposition that "thin is normative and attractive." While (because?) American girls and women are becoming heavier, the current body *ideal* (idol) for women has become and remains unrealistically thin.

In fact, mass media are one of many sociocultural sources for the normative prejudice that fat is "horrible and ugly," and that "getting fatter" is a sign of at least 4 of the classic "7 deadly sins"—extravagance, gluttony, greed, sloth, and, maybe, pride. . . .

The presence of a positive correlation between level of exposure to mass media, or to certain types of mass media, and the spectrum of disordered eating is a necessary but not sufficient condition for determination of causal agency. However, absence of a positive correlation negates the argument for causality. . . .

Longitudinal Correlates of Exposure to Mass Media

. . . Compared to cross-sectional studies, longitudinal research linking media exposure with body image is sparse. The few published studies do suggest that early exposure to thin-ideal television predicts a subsequent increase in body-image problems. For a sample of Australian girls aged 5 to 8, viewing of appearance-focused television programs (but not magazines) predicted a decrease in appearance satisfaction 1 year later. For European American and African American girls ages 7 through 12 greater overall television exposure predicted both a thinner ideal *adult* body shape and a higher level of disordered eating 1 year later. The results of both studies were valid regardless of whether the children were heavy, or perceived themselves to be thin or heavy, at the outset of the research. The thrust of these two studies is consistent with Sinton and Birch's finding that, among the 11-year-old American girls they studied, awareness of media messages about thinness was related to the strength of appearance schemas a year later.

The importance of a longitudinal design is revealed in recent studies of older children and young adolescents conducted by Tiggemann and by Field and colleagues. In a sample of 214 Australian high school girls (mean age = 14), Tiggemann found that the only measure of television exposure, including total hours of exposure, to produce meaningful cross-sectional and longitudinal correlations was the self-reported extent of watching soap operas. Cross-lagged correlational analyses showed that Time 1 exposure to soap operas predicted, to a small but significant degree, internalization of the slender ideal and level of appearance schema at 1-year follow up (Time 2). Time spent reading appearance-oriented magazines, but not other magazines, at Time 1 predicted, also to a small but significant degree, Time 2 levels of internalization, appearance schema, and drive for thinness. However, none of the media exposure variables was a significant longitudinal predictor of body dissatisfaction. Moreover, hierarchical regressions controlling for Time 1 level of each of the four criterion variables (e.g., internalization) found that none of the media exposure measures added significantly to prediction of the Time 2 criteria.

Although Field and colleagues used only single-variable measures of media exposure, their longitudinal research also casts doubt on exposure as a causal risk factor for older children and younger adolescents. Field et al. investigated a sample of over 6900 girls who were ages 9 through 15 at the 1996 baseline. Preliminary cross-sectional work did produce the expected positive linear association between frequency of reading women's fashion magazines and intensity of weight concerns. However, subsequent longitudinal research revealed that over a 1-year period the key predictor of the *development* of weight concerns and frequent dieting was "making a lot of effort to look like same-sex figures in the media." A 7-year follow-up showed that initiation of binge-eating, but not purging, in (now) adolescent and young adult females was predicted independently by frequent dieting and by Time 2 level of attempting to look like persons in the media.

The only longitudinal investigation of young adult women we could locate was Aubrey's 2-year panel study of college-age women. In support of Criterion 4, the extent of exposure to sexually objectifying media at Time 1 predicted level of self-objectification at Time 2, especially in women with low self-esteem. Measures of the tendency to self-objectify are positively correlated with eating disorder symptoms such as misperceptions of weight and shape, body shame, drive for thinness, and restrictive dieting.

Conclusion

Evidence from a very small number of longitudinal studies indicates that for children and very young adolescents, extent of media exposure does appear to predict increases in negative body image and disordered eating. Tiggemann's suggests that by early adolescence the causal risk factor is not media exposure, or even internalization of the slender beauty ideal, but rather the intensity and extent of "core beliefs and assumptions about the importance, meaning, and effect of appearance in an individual's life." . . .

Multimethod studies by Hargreaves and Tiggemann in Australia produced compelling evidence for the contention that mass media have negative and cumulative effects on body image in girls and young women. The adolescent girls whose body image was most negatively affected by experimental exposure to 20 television commercials featuring the thin ideal tended to have greater levels of body dissatisfaction and drive for thinness 2 years later, even when initial level of body dissatisfaction was controlled statistically.

The most vulnerable girls may well have a self-schema dominated by the core importance of physical appearance. In a study of girls ages 15 through 18 Hargreaves and Tiggemann found that appearance-focused TV commercials did activate an appearance-related self-schema, as reflected in several measures of cognitive set. Moreover, as predicted, appearance-focused commercials generated greater appearance dissatisfaction for those girls who began the study with a more extensive, emotionally charged, self-schema for appearance. Interestingly, the negative impact of the thin-beauty ideal in television commercials was, unlike previous findings with magazine images, unaffected by either the girls' initial level of body dissatisfaction or whether their viewing style was more personal (self-focused) or more detached (image-focused).

Positive (Assimilation) Effects. Durkin and Paxton found that 32% of the 7th grade girls and 22% of the 10th grade Australian girls who were exposed to images of attractive models from magazines exhibited an *increase* in state body satisfaction. Similarly, two studies of Canadian college students found that restrained eaters showed moderate to large increases in body satisfaction following exposure to similar magazine images, whereas unrestrained eaters had very large decreases in body satisfaction.

Two studies in the United States by Wilcox and Laird suggest that young women who focus on the slender models in magazines while defocusing attention on themselves are more likely to identify with the models and thus to feel better about their own bodies. Conversely, women who self-consciously divide their attention between the models and themselves are more likely to evaluate themselves and reach a conclusion that leaves them feeling inferior and worse. This finding is supported by research showing that self-evaluative processes, as opposed to self-improvement motives, are more likely to reflect and activate "upward" social comparison processes, which themselves tend to generate negative feelings about one's body.

Pro-Ana Web Sites. The internet offers many pro-anorexia (pro-ana) and pro-bulimia (pro-mia) web sites. Some of the most prominent pro-ana sites defiantly and zealously promote AN as a sacred lifestyle rather than a debilitating psychiatric disorder. Their "thinspirational" images of emaciation and their explicit behavioral instructions for attaining and sustaining the thin ideal are intended to reinforce the identity and practices of those already entrenched in AN or BN.

If concentrated exposure to typical images of slender models have negative experimental effects, then we might well expect the images and messages from pro-anorexia web sites to have even more negative effects. Two recent experiments by Bardone-Cone and Cass examined the effects of a web site that they constructed to feature the prototypical content of pro-ana sites. As predicted, exposure to this site had a large number of negative effects on young women, independent of their dispositional levels of thin ideal internalization and disordered eating. At present, we do not know what effects pro-ana and pro-mia sites have on the adolescent girls and young women who avidly seek them out because they already have a full-blown eating disorder. . . .

Media Literacy: Laboratory Investigations

. . . Media literacy (ML) is a set of knowledge, attitudes, and skills that enable people to work together to understand, appreciate, and critically analyze the nature of mass media and one's relationships with them. Systematic investigations of ML can be categorized into analog laboratory studies, brief interventions, and longer, more intensive programs.

. . . Several controlled experiments show that very brief written or video interventions can inoculate college-age women, including those who already have a negative body image, against the general tendency to feel worse about their bodies and themselves after viewing slides or video containing media-based images of the slender beauty ideal. The most effective ML "inoculation" highlights the clash between the artificial, constructed nature of the slender, flawless, "model look" versus two stark realities: (1) the actual shapes and weights of females (and males) naturally vary a great deal across a population; and (2) dieting to attain an "ideal" and "glamorous" weight/shape that is unnatural for a given individual has many negative effects, including risk for an eating disorder. . . .

Several programs for high-school and college-age females used slide presentations or Jean Kilbourne's video *Slim Hopes* (http://www.mediaed.org/videos/MediaAndHealth/SlimHopes) to help participants consider the history of changing, but consistently restrictive, beauty ideals and then to answer some fundamental questions: Do *real* women look like the models in advertising? Will buying the product being advertised make me look like this model? These programs emphasize how fashion models, working with the production staffs of magazines and movies, use "cosmetic" surgery, computer graphics, and other technologies to *construct* idealized *images*. Participants are encouraged to explore how these manipulations are carefully orchestrated to stir up the desire to purchase products, many of which will supposedly reduce the discrepancy between such unreal, "perfect" images versus the body shapes and weights of normal, healthy females.

These ML programs are brief, so positive effects are necessarily limited. Nevertheless, it is noteworthy that they tend to reduce, at least in the short run, one important risk factor for disordered eating: internalization of the slender beauty ideal.

Well-controlled studies of multi-lesson, multifaceted media literacy programs that unfold over 1 to 2 months have shown that media literacy training can help girls *and* boys ages 10 through 14 to reduce risk factors such as internalization of the slender or muscular ideal, while increasing the potentially protective factors of self-acceptance, self-confidence in friendships, and confidence in their ability to be activists and thus affect weight-related social norms. In addition to spending considerable time working on the same components as those in the analog and brief interventions, intensive ML programs address the process and costs of social comparison. They also get participants involved in working within their ML groups, their school, and their larger community to translate their increasing literacy into peer education, consumer activism, and creating and promoting new, healthier media.

Recent investigations with college students also show ML to be a promising form of prevention. For example, Watson and Vaughn developed a 4-week, 6-hour intervention consisting of psychoeducation about the nature and sources of body dissatisfaction; group-based content analysis of beauty ideals in popular women's magazines; discussion of media ideals and beauty enhancement techniques; and a brief cognitive intervention designed to help participants dispute negative beliefs and feelings activated by media images of the thin ideal. Compared to a 1-day, 90-min version of this intervention, a one-time viewing of a 34-min media literacy film, and a no-intervention control, the extended intervention was the most successful in reducing the following risk factors for disordered eating: unhealthy social attitudes, internalization of the slender ideal, and body dissatisfaction. . . .

Presumed Influences on Others

In thinking about the subjective experiences of media pressures and influences, it is worth examining more closely the construct of "awareness" of the thin ideal. The perception that peers and people in general (e.g., employers) are influenced by thin-ideal media can itself be a form of subjective pressure that motivates young people to diet in an attempt to meet that ideal. In fact, it appears that the mere presumption of media effects on others may exert its own effect, at least on older females. Park's path analytic study of over 400 undergraduates found that the more issues of beauty and fashion magazines a young woman reads per month, the greater the perceived prevalence of the thin ideal in those magazines. The greater this perceived prevalence, the greater the presumed influence of that ideal on *other women;* and in turn the greater the perceived influence on *self,* which predicted the desire to be thin. More research of this type with younger samples is needed to test this "cultivation of perceived social norms" hypothesis: Greater consumption of beauty and fashion magazines or of appearance-focused TV and internet content will foster stronger, more influential beliefs that the slender ideal is ubiquitous and normative for peers. This logic will, in turn, be a source of pressure and inspiration for the person's own desire to be thin(ner). . . .

And, yet, in light of the important research by Tiggemann and by Field et al. there remains a need to demonstrate more conclusively that either (1) direct engagement with mass media or (2) media effects that are mediated by parents and/or peers *precede* development of the more proximal risk factors such as negative body image. Similarly, despite the preliminary but encouraging evidence from media literacy interventions of varying intensities, to date no studies have tested the deceptively simple proposition that prevention programs can increase media literacy and thereby reduce or eliminate negative media influences—and in turn reduce or delay development of proximal risk factors (e.g., internalization of the thin ideal, social comparison tendencies) *and* attendant outcomes such as EDNOS.

What We Need to Know but Don't Know Yet

This review suggests five principal gaps in our knowledge about mass media as a potential causal risk factor for the spectrum of disordered eating. The first three are derived from the conclusion immediately above. First, there is a need for longitudinal research that examines the predictive validity of media exposure, motives for media use, and the subjective experience of media influences. Second, as noted by an anonymous reviewer of this manuscript, there remains a dearth of information about whether it is the thinness-depicting aspects of magazine, TV, and other media content that exert negative effects. Thus, survey-based longitudinal investigations of media exposure should strive to determine as precisely as possible not only frequency and intensity of consumption, but also the nature of the images, articles, programs, and such to which participants are exposed. Third, there is a need for prevention research that capitalizes on and extends the promising findings of extended media literacy interventions.

The fourth research direction concerns the relationship, particularly from a developmental perspective, between engagement with mass media and other causal risk factors. We need to learn much more about the ways in which body image disturbance and disordered eating are influenced by perceived social norms, by the confluence of media, family, and peer messages about weight and shape, and by *indirect* media exposure, such as acquisition of body ideals and eating behaviors via interactions with family, peers, and significant adults (e.g., coaches) who learned them directly from television and magazines. Direct media effects may be small to modest, but the combination of direct and indirect effects, that is, the cumulative media effect, may be substantial.

Finally, the transactions between the developing child (or adolescent) and media constitute another set of important research questions to address. A cross-sectional study by Gralen, Levine, Smolak, and Murnen (1990) indicated that the correlates of negative body image and disordered eating in young adolescents tended to be more concrete and behavioral (e.g., onset of dating, pubertal development, teasing about weight and shape), whereas the predictors in middle to later adolescence were more psychological, such as the experience of a discrepancy between perception of one's own shape versus an internalized ideal shape. More recently, a longitudinal study by Harrison found that the number of hours that children ages 6 through 8 watched television per week predicted an increase in disordered eating without predicting idealization of a slender body. This raises the interesting and testable proposition that exposure to various salient media messages, including those contained in the onslaught of advertisements for diet-, fitness-, and weight-related products, might have little effect on the "thinness beliefs" of young children, while leading them to vilify fat, glamorize dieting as a grown-up practice, and yet still think of fattening, non-nutritious foods as desirable in general and useful for assuaging negative feelings.

With respect to the transformation of relevant psychological processes over late childhood, early adolescence, and later adolescence, Thompson and colleagues have developed and validated various features of the Tripartite Model in which media, family, and peers influence directly internalization of the slender beauty ideal and social comparison processes. This valuable model reminds us that, after nearly 25 years of research on media and body image, we still know relatively little about the automatic, intentional, and motivational processes involved in the role of *social comparison* in media effects. Basic questions remain: What dispositional and situational factors determine when people will make upward social comparisons with highly dissimilar fashion models whose "image" has been constructed by cosmetic surgeons, photographers, and computer experts? And under what circumstances will such comparisons result in negative effects (contrast) or positive effects (assimilation)?

Multidimensional models such as Thompson's also emphasize the need to determine when and how in the developmental process a number of important mechanisms such as appearance schematicity, thin-ideal internalization, social comparison processes, and self-objectification begin to play key roles. Further experimental and longitudinal studies of these mediators will be a very positive step toward understanding the emergence, particularly around puberty, of attentiveness and vulnerability to thin-ideal media images *and* to the many other potentially negative influences that emanate from family, peers, and influential adults such as coaches.

POSTSCRIPT

Do Media Cause Individuals to Develop Negative Body Images?

The psychology of one's body image is a subject worthy of thought and contemplation. Many books and articles have been written to untangle the many possible threads that lead to self-image, and often these books become best sellers, indicating that the subject of self-reflection and self-understanding is important to many.

In 1991, Naomi Wolf published a very influential book, *The Beauty Myth: How Images of Beauty Are Used Against Women,* in which the author crafted a persuasive argument that the concept of beauty was a political issue that kept women stuck in a patriarchal system. By media and social issues preying on women's insecurities about their bodies, women's ability to fully participate in the labor force and in the social world was undermined. In 2002, Wolf published the second edition of the book with a new introduction, and in reviewing the new version, critic Emily Wilson, writing for *The Guardian* in the U.K., noted, "The world has changed—a bit—over the past decade and a half, but not enough."

Many critics have praised Dove soap's "Campaign for Real Beauty," which premiered in 2004 and featured girls and women who did not have the ideal media body type. The campaign used real people and identified them as beautiful for being who and what they are, but in 2008, Unilever (Dove's parent company) and Ogilvy and Mather, the product's advertising company, came under fire for retouching the pictures of the real people. In a May 12, 2008, article in *Advertising Age,* it was reported that the alleged retouching had created a "ruckus" that was one of the largest scandals in the history of advertising.

For more reading on images of ideal bodies in the media and the impact on consumers who may find their own bodies lacking, check out Vickie Rutledge Shields and Dawn Heinecken's *Measuring Up: How Advertising Affects Self-Image* (University of Pennsylvania Press, 2002), or Ellen Cole and Jessica Henderson Daniel, eds., *Featuring Females: Feminist Analyses of Media* (Washington, DC: American Psychological Association, 2005). For a study of body image from the male perspective, Arnold E. Andersen's *Making Weight: Men's Conflicts with Food, Weight, Shape & Appearance* (Gurze Books, 2000) is a helpful analysis of men's increasing sensitivity to issues of weight and appearance.

Internet References . . .

Advertising Age

The Web site of *Advertising Age* magazine provides access to articles and features about media advertising, such as the history of television advertising.

http://adage.com

Advertising World

This site is maintained by the Advertising Department of the University of Texas and contains links to material on a variety of advertising topics and issues.

http://advertising.utexas.edu/world/index.asp

Peabody Archives, University of Georgia

Since 1941, the University of Georgia Grady College has been home to the Peabody Awards, which recognize the best of broadcast programming. This archive of winners features news, entertainment, educational, children's, and documentary programming.

http://www.peabody.uga.edu

Television News Archive, Vanderbilt University

Since 1968, the Television News Archive has systematically recorded, abstracted, and indexed national television newscasts. This database is the guide to the Vanderbilt University collection of network television news programs.

http://tvnews.vanderbilt.edu

The Copyright Web Site

A commercial site with extensive copyright information. The URL listed below follows the current digital legal controversies in Internet, Web, and software. Specialized information for movie, television, and other outlets is available also on the site.

http://www.benedict.com/Digital/Digital.aspx

Entertainment Software Association

ESA serves the business and public affairs needs of video game publishers. Its sections on public policy and games in life provide extensive information about the benefits of video games.

www.theesa.com

A Question of Content

*W*e no longer live in a world in which all of our media are directed toward mass audiences. Today we have both mass media and personal media, like video games, iPods, and cell phones. Because people use media content in very different ways, and so much of how we make sense of media depends on our own ages and life experiences, the issue of media content that is appropriate for certain audiences takes on a new importance. In this section we deal with issues that often influence people from all ages, ethnic groups, and all walks of life—but the questions for discussion become more pointed when we consider that different audiences may perceive different things in the content of some forms of media. In this section we examine some specific aspects of using media for a sense of identity and belonging. We conclude with an issue that addresses some of the most fundamental questions about one industry and that is sure to spark debate.

- Do Video Games Encourage Violent Behavior?
- Do Copyright Laws Protect Ownership of Intellectual Property?
- Is Advertising Good for Society?

ISSUE 5

Do Video Games Encourage Violent Behavior?

YES: Craig A. Anderson, from "Violent Video Games: Myths, Facts, and Unanswered Questions," http://www.apa.org/science/psa/sb-anderson .html

NO: Henry Jenkins, from "Reality Bytes: Eight Myths about Video Games Debunked," http://www.pbs.org/kcts/videogamerevolution/impact/ myths.html

ISSUE SUMMARY

YES: Craig Anderson is an expert on the effect of violence in television and film. Based on extensive research, he holds the position that video games prompt young people toward even more aggression and violence than do other media content.

NO: Henry Jenkins tackles a broad array of misconceptions about the place and impact of video games on society. He argues that the primary audience is not children, that violence is not increasing in society, and that concerns about isolation, desensitization, and violence are overblown.

In recent years the subject of the effect of video games has joined television, film, and recorded music as a topic that provokes strong reactions among individuals who feel that some content may encourage violent, or at least aggressive behavior among young people. While there is less concern about how any type of content affects adults, most of the controversy deals with how children, adolescents, teens, and young adults use controversial media content. The underlying reason for this is that younger users are assumed to have a lesser sense of moral responsibility and judgment about the relationship of media content and reality.

Even though the video game industry voluntarily rates the content of video games (as do the motion picture, television, and recording industries), many parents and critics of media violence feel that video games are a unique form of entertainment that warrants special consideration. Since the games are often played alone, on personal devices, consoles, or computers, the video game user's interaction with the game is interactive and direct. The sophistication of computer graphics has produced images that look even more realistic than ever before. The controversy became especially heated during the summer of 2005 when "Grand Theft Auto" was released and found to contain some hidden sex scenes.

The selections chosen to represent controversial views for this issue both cite evidence of research studies that have different conclusions. This raises important problems for us, as readers. How do we decide which studies to believe? How do we weigh the evidence and the credibility of the authors of differing studies? How much of our own experience informs the way we think about some of these types of issues?

As you will see, both Dr. Anderson and Dr. Jenkins offer a list of myths about the effects of video games and purport to debunk them. In the process, they come to opposite conclusions. Dr. Anderson's list appears on the American Psychological Association Web site and evolves from his years of studying the relationship of media content and violence/aggression. He references decades of research that finds a link between violence and aggression, a conclusion that he has testified to before congressional committees. Less research has examined the concern about the violent content of video games, because the most violent games came to the market in the 1990s. Yet the amount of time spent with games and the high levels of engagement by players lead Anderson, program head of psychology at Iowa State University, to fear that the relationship between violent content and aggressive/violent behavior may be enhanced.

Dr. Jenkins, professor at the University of Southern California and previously head of the comparative media studies program at MIT, offers eight myths about video games. On his MIT Web site (www.mit.edu/cms), Professor Jenkins describes his desire to "challenge the dominant media effects paradigm and call for a more complex understanding of teens' relationship to popular culture." Whether speaking and writing about Columbine or about video games and violence, Dr. Jenkins argues—somewhat in the terms that James Carey used to explain ritual models of communication (Issue 1)—that the fantasies of children's culture are an important arena to understand how we as a culture are constructing our future.

As you consider the evidence provided by the two positions on this issue, how do you formulate your own position? If you were a parent, would you see things differently? Are video games different from any other form of traditional media content?

YES 🢰   Craig A. Anderson

Violent Video Games: Myths, Facts, and Unanswered Questions

After 40+ years of research, one might think that debate about media violence effects would be over. A historical examination of the research reveals that debate concerning whether such exposure is a significant risk factor for aggressive and violent behavior should have been over years ago. Four types of media violence studies provide converging evidence of such effects: laboratory experiments, field experiments, cross-sectional correlation studies, and longitudinal studies. But the development of a new genre—electronic video games—reinvigorated the debate.

Two features of video games fuel renewed interest by researchers, public policy makers, and the general public. First, the active role required by video games is a double-edged sword. It helps educational video games be excellent teaching tools for motivational and learning process reasons. But it also may make violent video games even more hazardous than violent television or cinema. Second, the arrival of a new generation of ultraviolent video games beginning in the early 1990s and continuing unabated to the present resulted in large numbers of children and youths actively participating in entertainment violence that went way beyond anything available to them on television or in movies. Recent video games reward players for killing innocent bystanders, police, and prostitutes, using a wide range of weapons including guns, knives, flame throwers, swords, baseball bats, cars, hands, and feet. Some include cut scenes (i.e., brief movie clips supposedly designed to move the story forward) of strippers. In some, the player assumes the role of hero, whereas in others the player is a criminal.

The new debate frequently generates more heat than light. Many criticisms are simply recycled myths from earlier media violence debates, myths that have been repeatedly debunked on theoretical and empirical grounds. Valid weaknesses have also been identified (and often corrected) by media violence researchers themselves. Although the violent video game literature is still relatively new and small, we have learned a lot about their effects and have successfully answered several key questions. So what is myth and what do we know?

From *Psychological Science Agenda,* vol. 16, no. 5, October 2003. Copyright © 2003 by Craig A. Anderson. Reprinted by permission of the author. http://www.apa.org/science/psa/sb-anderson.html.

Myths and Facts

Myth 1. Violent video game research has yielded very mixed results.

Facts: Some studies have yielded nonsignificant video game effects, just as some smoking studies failed to find a significant link to lung cancer. But when one combines all relevant empirical studies using meta-analytic techniques, five separate effects emerge with considerable consistency. Violent video games are significantly associated with: increased aggressive behavior, thoughts, and affect; increased physiological arousal; and decreased prosocial (helping) behavior. Average effect sizes for experimental studies (which help establish causality) and correlational studies (which allow examination of serious violent behavior) appear comparable.

Myth 2. The studies that find significant effects are the weakest methodologically.

Facts: Methodologically stronger studies have yielded the largest effects. Thus, earlier effect size estimates—based on all video game studies—probably underestimate the actual effect sizes.

Myth 3. Laboratory experiments are irrelevant (trivial measures, demand characteristics, lack external validity).

Facts: Arguments against laboratory experiments in behavioral sciences have been successfully debunked many times by numerous researchers over the years. Specific examinations of such issues in the aggression domain have consistently found evidence of high external validity. For example, variables known to influence real world aggression and violence have the same effects on laboratory measures of aggression.

Myth 4. Field experiments are irrelevant (aggression measures based either on direct imitation of video game behaviors, e.g., karate kicks) or are normal play behaviors.

Facts: Some field experiments have used behaviors such as biting, pinching, hitting, pushing, and pulling hair, behaviors that were not modeled in the game. The fact that these aggressive behaviors occur in natural environments does not make them "normal" play behavior, but it does increase the face validity (and some would argue the external validity) of the measures.

Myth 5. Correlational studies are irrelevant.

Facts: The overly simplistic mantra, "Correlation is not causation," is useful when teaching introductory students the risks in too-readily drawing causal conclusions from a simple empirical correlation between two measured variables. However, correlational studies are routinely used in modern science to test theories that are inherently causal. Whole scientific fields are based on correlational data (e.g., astronomy). Well conducted correlational studies provide opportunities for theory falsification. They allow examination of serious acts of aggression that would be unethical to study in experimental contexts. They allow for statistical controls of plausible alternative explanations.

Myth 6. There are no studies linking violent video game play to serious aggression.

Facts: High levels of violent video game exposure have been linked to delinquency, fighting at school and during free play periods, and violent criminal behavior (e.g., self-reported assault, robbery).

Myth 7.   Violent video games affect only a small fraction of players.
Facts: Though there are good theoretical reasons to expect some populations to be more susceptible to violent video game effects than others, the research literature has not yet substantiated this. That is, there is not consistent evidence for the claim that younger children are more negatively affected than adolescents or young adults or that males are more affected than females. There is some evidence that highly aggressive individuals are more affected than nonaggressive individuals, but this finding does not consistently occur. Even nonaggressive individuals are consistently affected by brief exposures. Further research will likely find some significant moderators of violent video game effects, because the much larger research literature on television violence has found such effects and the underlying processes are the same. However, even that larger literature has not identified a sizeable population that is totally immune to negative effects of media violence.

Myth 8.   Unrealistic video game violence is completely safe for adolescents and older youths.
Facts: Cartoonish and fantasy violence is often perceived (incorrectly) by parents and public policy makers as safe even for children. However, experimental studies with college students have consistently found increased aggression after exposure to clearly unrealistic and fantasy violent video games. Indeed, at least one recent study found significant increases in aggression by college students after playing E-rated (suitable for everyone) violent video games.

Myth 9.   The effects of violent video games are trivially small.
Facts: Meta-analyses reveal that violent video game effect sizes are larger than the effect of second hand tobacco smoke on lung cancer, the effect of lead exposure to I.Q. scores in children, and calcium intake on bone mass. Furthermore, the fact that so many youths are exposed to such high levels of video game violence further increases the societal costs of this risk factor.

Myth 10.   Arousal, not violent content, accounts for video game induced increases in aggression.
Facts: Arousal cannot explain the results of most correlational studies because the measured aggression did not occur immediately after the violent video games were played. Furthermore, several experimental studies have controlled potential arousal effects, and still yielded more aggression by those who played the violent game.

Myth 11.   If violent video games cause increases in aggression, violent crime rates in the U.S. would be increasing instead of decreasing.
Facts: Three assumptions must all be true for this myth to be valid: (a) exposure to violent media (including video games) is increasing; (b) youth violent crime rates are decreasing; (c) video game violence is the only (or the primary) factor contributing to societal violence. The first assumption is

probably true. The second is not true, as reported by the 2001 Report of the Surgeon General on Youth Violence. The third is clearly untrue. Media violence is only one of many factors that contribute to societal violence and is certainly not the most important one. Media violence researchers have repeatedly noted this.

Theory

One frequently overlooked factor in this debate is the role of scientific theory. Pure empirical facts often have relatively little meaning and are seldom convincing. When those same facts fit a broader theory, especially one that has been tested in other contexts, those facts become more understandable and convincing. Recent years have seen considerable progress in basic theoretical models of human aggression.

Most such models take a social cognitive view of human aggression, integrating social learning theory, advances in cognitive psychology, script theory, developmental theories, and biological influences. Using such general models, media violence scholars now have a clear picture of how media violence increases aggression in short and long term contexts. Immediately after exposure to media violence, there is an increase in aggressive behavior tendencies because of several factors. 1. Aggressive thoughts increase, which in turn increase the likelihood that a mild or ambiguous provocation will be interpreted in a hostile fashion. 2. Aggressive affect increases. 3. General arousal (e.g., heart rate) increases, which tends to increase the dominant behavioral tendency. 4. Direct imitation of recently observed aggressive behaviors sometimes occurs.

Repeated media violence exposure increases aggression across the lifespan because of several related factors. 1. It creates more positive attitudes, beliefs, and expectations regarding use of aggressive solutions. 2. It creates aggressive behavioral scripts and makes them more cognitively accessible. 3. It decreases the accessibility of nonviolent scripts. 4. It decreases the normal negative emotional reactions to conflict, aggression, and violence.

Unanswered Questions

Several major gaps remain in the violent video game literature. One especially large gap is the lack of longitudinal studies testing the link between habitual violent video game exposure and later aggression, while controlling for earlier levels of aggression and other risk factors. Indeed, of the four major types of empirical studies mentioned earlier, this is the only type missing. There are such studies focusing on television violence but none on video games.

Another gap concerns potential differences in effect sizes of television versus video game violence. There are theoretical reasons to believe that violent video game effects may prove larger, primarily because of the active and repetitive learning aspects of video games. However, this is a very difficult question to investigate, especially with experimental designs. How does one select violent video game and television stimuli that are matched on other dimensions? On what dimensions should they be equivalent? Number of bodies? Amount of blood and gore? Realism of the images? There are a couple of unpublished correlational studies that have compared the effects of television and video game violence on aggression, using comparable measures of violence exposure. Both yielded results suggesting a larger effect of video game violence. But the issue is not settled.

Finally, more research is needed to: (a) refine emerging general models of human aggression; (b) delineate the processes underlying short and long term media violence effects; (c) broaden these models to encompass aggression at the level of subcultures and nations. Several different research groups around the world are working on these various issues.

Henry Jenkins   ➜ **NO**

Reality Bytes: Eight Myths about Video Games Debunked

$\mathbf{A}$ large gap exists between the public's perception of video games and what the research actually shows. The following is an attempt to separate fact from fiction.

1. The Availability of Video Games Has Led to an Epidemic of Youth Violence.

According to federal crime statistics, the rate of juvenile violent crime in the United States is at a 30-year low. Researchers find that people serving time for violent crimes typically consume less media before committing their crimes than the average person in the general population. It's true that young offenders who have committed school shootings in America have also been game players. But young people in general are more likely to be gamers—90 percent of boys and 40 percent of girls play. The overwhelming majority of kids who play do NOT commit antisocial acts. According to a 2001 U.S. Surgeon General's report, the strongest risk factors for school shootings centered on mental stability and the quality of home life, not media exposure. The moral panic over violent video games is doubly harmful. It has led adult authorities to be more suspicious and hostile to many kids who already feel cut off from the system. It also misdirects energy away from eliminating the actual causes of youth violence and allows problems to continue to fester.

2. Scientific Evidence Links Violent Game Play with Youth Aggression.

Claims like this are based on the work of researchers who represent one relatively narrow school of research, "media effects." This research includes some 300 studies of media violence. But most of those studies are inconclusive and many have been criticized on methodological grounds. In these studies, media images are removed from any narrative context. Subjects are asked to engage with content that they would not normally consume and may not understand. Finally, the laboratory context is radically different from the environments where games would normally be played. Most studies found a correlation, not

From *The Video Game Revolution* (KCTS-TV) seen at www.pbs.org. Copyright © 2009 by Henry Jenkins. Reprinted by permission of the author.

a causal relationship, which means the research could simply show that aggressive people like aggressive entertainment. That's why the vague term "links" is used here. If there is a consensus emerging around this research, it is that violent video games may be one risk factor—when coupled with other more immediate, real-world influences—which can contribute to anti-social behavior. But no research has found that video games are a primary factor or that violent video game play could turn an otherwise normal person into a killer.

3. Children Are the Primary Market for Video Games.

While most American kids do play video games, the center of the video game market has shifted older as the first generation of gamers continues to play into adulthood. Already 62 percent of the console market and 66 percent of the PC market is age 18 or older. The game industry caters to adult tastes. Meanwhile, a sizable number of parents ignore game ratings because they assume that games are for kids. One quarter of children ages 11 to 16 identify an M-Rated (Mature Content) game as among their favorites. Clearly, more should be done to restrict advertising and marketing that targets young consumers with mature content, and to educate parents about the media choices they are facing. But parents need to share some of the responsibility for making decisions about what is appropriate for their children. The news on this front is not all bad. The Federal Trade Commission has found that 83 percent of game purchases for underage consumers are made by parents or by parents and children together.

4. Almost No Girls Play Computer Games.

Historically, the video game market has been predominantly male. However, the percentage of women playing games has steadily increased over the past decade. Women now slightly outnumber men playing Web-based games. Spurred by the belief that games were an important gateway into other kinds of digital literacy, efforts were made in the mid-90s to build games that appealed to girls. More recent games such as *The Sims* were huge crossover successes that attracted many women who had never played games before. Given the historic imbalance in the game market (and among people working inside the game industry), the presence of sexist stereotyping in games is hardly surprising. Yet it's also important to note that female game characters are often portrayed as powerful and independent. In his book *Killing Monsters,* Gerard Jones argues that young girls often build upon these representations of strong women warriors as a means of building up their self confidence in confronting challenges in their everyday lives.

5. Because Games Are Used to Train Soldiers to Kill, They Have the Same Impact on the Kids Who Play Them.

Former military psychologist and moral reformer David Grossman argues that because the military uses games in training (including, he claims, training soldiers to shoot and kill), the generation of young people who play such games are similarly being brutalized and conditioned to be aggressive in their everyday social interactions.

Grossman's model only works if:

- we remove training and education from a meaningful cultural context.
- we assume learners have no conscious goals and that they show no resistance to what they are being taught.
- we assume that they unwittingly apply what they learn in a fantasy environment to real world spaces.

The military uses games as part of a specific curriculum, with clearly defined goals, in a context where students actively want to learn and have a need for the information being transmitted. There are consequences for not mastering those skills. That being said, a growing body of research does suggest that games can enhance learning. In his recent book, *What Video Games Have to Teach Us about Learning and Literacy*, James Gee describes game players as active problem solvers who do not see mistakes as errors, but as opportunities for improvement. Players search for newer, better solutions to problems and challenges, he says. And they are encouraged to constantly form and test hypotheses. This research points to a fundamentally different model of how and what players learn from games.

6. Video Games Are Not a Meaningful Form of Expression.

On April 19, 2002, U.S. District Judge Stephen N. Limbaugh Sr. ruled that video games do not convey ideas and thus enjoy no constitutional protection. As evidence, Saint Louis County presented the judge with videotaped excerpts from four games, all within a narrow range of genres, and all the subject of previous controversy. Overturning a similar decision in Indianapolis, federal Court of Appeals Judge Richard Posner noted: "Violence has always been and remains a central interest of humankind and a recurrent, even obsessive theme of culture both high and low. It engages the interest of children from an early age, as anyone familiar with the classic fairy tales collected by Grimm, Andersen, and Perrault are aware." Posner adds, "To shield children right up to the age of 18 from exposure to violent descriptions and images would not only be quixotic, but deforming; it would leave them unequipped to cope with the world as we know it." Many early games were little more than shooting galleries where players were encouraged to blast everything that moved. Many current games are designed to be ethical testing grounds. They allow players to navigate an expansive and open-ended world, make their own choices and witness their consequences. *The Sims* designer Will Wright argues that games are perhaps the only medium that allows us to experience guilt over the actions of fictional characters. In a movie, one can always pull back and condemn the character or the artist when they cross certain social boundaries. But in playing a game, we choose what happens to the characters. In the right circumstances, we can be encouraged to examine our own values by seeing how we behave within virtual space.

7. Video Game Play Is Socially Isolating.

Much video game play is social. Almost 60 percent of frequent gamers play with friends. Thirty-three percent play with siblings and 25 percent play with spouses or parents. Even games designed for single players are often played socially, with one person giving advice to another holding a joystick. A growing number of games are designed for multiple players—for either cooperative play in the same space or online play with distributed players. Sociologist Talmadge Wright has logged many hours observing online communities interact with and react to violent video games, concluding that meta-gaming (conversation about game content) provides a context for thinking about rules and rule-breaking. In this way there are really two games taking place simultaneously: one, the explicit conflict and combat on the screen; the other, the implicit cooperation and comradeship between the players. Two players may be fighting to death on screen and growing closer as friends off screen. Social expectations are reaffirmed through the social contract governing play, even as they are symbolically cast aside within the transgressive fantasies represented onscreen.

8. Video Game Play Is Desensitizing.

Classic studies of play behavior among primates suggest that apes make basic distinctions between play fighting and actual combat. In some circumstances, they seem to take pleasure wrestling and tousling with each other. In others, they might rip each other apart in mortal combat. Game designer and play theorist Eric Zimmerman describes the ways we understand play as distinctive from reality as entering the "magic circle." The same action—say, sweeping a floor—may take on different meanings in play (as in playing house) than in reality (housework). Play allows kids to express feelings and impulses that have to be carefully held in check in their real-world interactions. Media reformers argue that playing violent video games can cause a lack of empathy for real-world victims. Yet, a child who responds to a video game the same way he or she responds to a real-world tragedy could be showing symptoms of being severely emotionally disturbed. Here's where the media effects research, which often uses punching rubber dolls as a marker of real-world aggression, becomes problematic. The kid who is punching a toy designed for this purpose is still within the "magic circle" of play and understands her actions on those terms. Such research shows us only that violent play leads to more violent play.

POSTSCRIPT

Do Video Games Encourage Violent Behavior?

It may be true that there are few long-term studies of the effect of playing video games now, but this will change in time. There are many longitudinal studies of the way violence and aggression are portrayed in other forms of media. In all of these cases, it is important to consider who sponsors the research and what agenda the sponsoring agency may have. In this edition of *Taking Sides*, you will see several cases for which the attitudes or biases of the authors of certain studies should suggest a critical framework for evaluating their position.

This type of controversy also takes into consideration whether a media industry can adequately control access to questionable material through ratings systems. While ratings on the packages of many games and other content may be somewhat effective as a measure of who may have access to media content, how are those ratings enforced? Is it possible for an industry to monitor use when the bottom line is selling their product? How much regulation should be exercised from outside? Should the government take a stronger role in creating guidelines, or should the bulk of the responsibility be placed on the shoulders of parents and guardians?

As mentioned in the preface to this book, the distribution and appearance of media content has changed dramatically over the years. As mediated images become more realistic through computer enhancement or computer generation, studies of perception will undoubtedly change too. And, as individuals continue to use interactive media, we can expect to see more sophistication in future studies about the effects of media content on audiences of different ages, and in different circumstances.

If you would like to focus on additional studies of understanding how to evaluate important questions such as these, you may consider *Violent Video Game Effects on Children and Adolescents: Theory, Research, and Public Policy* by Craig A. Anderson, Douglas A. Gentile, and Katherine E. Buckley (2007). See also an edited volume about the issue of violence and other uses and consequences of video games, *Playing Video Games: Motives, Responses, and Consequences* (2006), by Peter Vorderer and Jennings Bryant. And for a cultural approach similar to that advocated by Jenkins, see *The Video Game Theory Reader 2* (2008), edited by Bernard Perron and Mark J. P. Wolf.

If you are concerned about the way the entertainment industry targets young audiences, you may want to read an article by Thomas A. Hemphill, "The Entertainment Industry, Marketing Practices, and Violent Content: Who's Minding the Children?" in *Business and Society Review* (2003, vol. 108, pp. 263–277).

Finally, as more researchers apply new methods to studying the impact of video games, you might find an interesting approach toward balancing older research with newer media use (among other topics) in the popular book by Steven Johnson, *Everything Bad Is Good for You* (London: Penguin Press, 2005).

ISSUE 6

Do Copyright Laws Protect Ownership of Intellectual Property?

YES: **Siva Vaidhyanathan**, from "Copyright Jungle," *Columbia Journalism Review* (September–October 2006)

NO: **Stephanie C. Ardito**, from "MySpace and YouTube Meet the Copyright Cops," *Searcher* (May 2007)

ISSUE SUMMARY

YES: In this article, Siva Vaidhyanathan discusses how applications of copyright to music, film, publishing, and software companies all result in a complex system of trying to protect original ownership of intellectual property. The author gives several examples, including Google's efforts to digitize entire libraries, but reminds us that copyright also gives owners the right to say no.

NO: Independent researcher Stephanie Ardito examines how social networking sites have created problems for protecting copyright, because laws and enforcement of copyright law are so difficult. She believes big media companies and social networking sites will ultimately give up trying to enforce copyright, because it is too expensive and time consuming.

Copyright, or the legal protection of ownership of original materials in a tangible, fixed medium, has a long history. U.S. copyright law was established in 1790, and was based on the British Licensing Act of 1662, created not long after the invention of the printing press and the distribution of printed materials to the masses. In 1886, the Berne Convention resulted in copyright principles for most nations of the globe, and established principles for fair and equitable treatment for original authors of artifacts resulting from scientific and creative endeavors.

Once digital technology began to make it easy and cheap to duplicate media content with virtually no signal degradation, the foundation of the old copyright law began to crumble. Now, when it is possible for someone to record, edit, and rearrange material into a new form, like that often posted on

MySpace or YouTube, it becomes increasingly difficult to police the ownership of the original material.

The authors of these selections provide a number of examples to show how copyright law is being challenged in a number of ways. Siva Vaidhyanathan focuses on the adaptation of traditional print media to electronic form, discusses how copyright, file sharing, plagiarism, and fair use have all become muddled in the world of digital forms of media. Stephanie Ardito focuses more on social networking sites on which anyone can post creative works of their own—often using material from other sources. She discusses how various companies have attempted to create service agreements that place the responsibility for copyright clearance on the person posting information, not the company distributing the message—but how the legal agreements are complicated, difficult to enforce, and probably doomed to extinction. She also discusses digital rights management and attempts to protect copyright, which have not served their purpose as well as one might hope.

The positions taken for this issue raise many more questions as well. If it does become increasingly difficult to protect one's creative products, will there be a chilling effect on innovation, or will different structures of payment or control of the product have to be considered? Who does copyright violation actually hurt? Can the definition of fair use be extended to a greater number of media forms, or uses of content?

At this time in history, newer technologies, like digital forms, are challenging older laws and practices that had been created to protect earlier forms of media. How might industries change in the future, if the economic base of copyright is eroded? What other laws, regulations, and practices could also be challenged by the growth of user-friendly, low-cost digital technologies? The answers to these questions are put into perspective by Professor Vaidhyanathan, who reminds us that "the copyright system will help determine the richness and strength of democracy in the twenty-first century."

YES ⤶

Siva Vaidhyanathan

Copyright Jungle

Last May [2005], Kevin Kelly, *Wired* magazine's "senior maverick," published in *The New York Times Magazine* his predictive account of flux within the book-publishing world. Kelly outlined what he claimed will happen (not might or could—*will*) to the practices of writing and reading under a new regime fostered by Google's plan to scan millions of books and offer searchable texts to Internet users.

"So what happens when all the books in the world become a single liquid fabric of interconnected words and ideas?" Kelly wrote. "First, works on the margins of popularity will find a small audience larger than the near-zero audience they usually have now. . . . Second, the universal library will deepen our grasp of history, as every original document in the course of civilization is scanned and cross-linked. Third, the universal library of all books will cultivate a new sense of authority. . . ."

Kelly saw the linkage of text to text, book to book, as the answer to the information gaps that have made the progress of knowledge such a hard climb. "If you can truly incorporate all texts—past and present, multilingual—on a particular subject," Kelly wrote, "then you can have a clearer sense of what we as a civilization, a species, do know and don't know. The white spaces of our collective ignorance are highlighted, while the golden peaks of our knowledge are drawn with completeness. This degree of authority is only rarely achieved in scholarship today, but it will become routine."

Such heady predictions of technological revolution have become so common, so accepted in our techno-fundamentalist culture, that even when John Updike criticized Kelly's vision in an essay published a month later in *The New York Times Book Review*, he did not so much doubt Kelly's vision of a universal digital library as lament it.

As it turns out, the move toward universal knowledge is not so easy. Google's project, if it survives court challenges, would probably have modest effects on writing, reading, and publishing. For one thing, Kelly's predictions depend on a part of the system he slights in his article: the copyright system. Copyright is not Kelly's friend. He mentions it as a nuisance on the edge of his dream. To acknowledge that a lawyer-built system might trump an engineer-built system would have run counter to Kelly's sermon.

Much of the press coverage of the Google project has missed some key facts: most libraries that are allowing Google to scan books are, so far, providing

From *Columbia Journalism Review,* September/October 2006, pp. 42–48. Copyright © 2006 by Columbia Journalism Review. Reprinted by permission.

only books published before 1923 and thus already in the public domain, essentially missing most of the relevant and important books that scholars and researchers—not to mention casual readers—might want. Meanwhile, the current American copyright system will probably kill Google's plan to scan the collections of the University of Michigan and the University of California system—the only libraries willing to offer Google works currently covered by copyright. In his article, Kelly breezed past the fact that the copyrighted works will be presented in a useless format—"snippets" that allow readers only glimpses into how a term is used in the text. Google users will not be able to read, copy, or print copyrighted works via Google. Google accepted that arrangement to limit its copyright liability. But the more "copyright friendly" the Google system is, the less user-friendly, and useful, it is. And even so it still may not fly in court.

Google is exploiting the instability of the copyright system in a digital age. The company's struggle with publishers over its legal ability to pursue its project is the most interesting and perhaps most transformative conflict in the copyright wars. But there are many other battles—and many other significant stories—out in the copyright jungle. Yet reporters seem lost.

Copyright in recent years has certainly become too strong for its own good. It protects more content and outlaws more acts than ever before. It stifles individual creativity and hampers the discovery and sharing of culture and knowledge. To convey all this to readers, journalists need to understand the principles, paradoxes, licenses, and limits of the increasingly troubled copyright system. Copyright is not just an interesting story. As the most pervasive regulation of speech and culture, the copyright system will help determine the richness and strength of democracy in the twenty-first century.

The Copyright Wars

It's not that the press has ignored copyright. Recent fights have generated a remarkable amount of press. Since Napster broke into the news in 2000, journalists have been scrambling to keep up with the fast-moving and complicated stories of content protection, distribution, and revision that make up the wide array of copyright conflicts.

During this time of rapid change it's been all too easy for reporters to fall into the trap of false dichotomies: hackers versus movie studios; kids versus music companies; librarians versus publishers. The peer-to-peer and music-file-sharing story, for instance, has consistently been covered as a business story with the tone of the sports page: winners and losers, scores and stats. In fact, peer-to-peer file sharing was more about technological innovation and the ways we use music in our lives than any sort of threat to the commercial music industry. As it stands today, after dozens of court cases and congressional hearings, peer-to-peer file-sharing remains strong. So does the music industry. The sky did not fall, our expectations did.

The most recent headline-grabbing copyright battle involved *The Da Vinci Code*. Did Dan Brown recycle elements of a 1982 nonfiction book for his best-selling novel? The authors of the earlier book sued Brown's publisher, Random

House U.K., in a London court in the spring of 2006 in an effort to prove that Brown lifted protected elements of their book, what they called "the architecture" of a speculative conspiracy theory about the life of Jesus. In the coverage of the trial, some reporters—even in publications like *The New York Times*, *The Washington Post*, and *The San Diego Union-Tribune*—used the word "plagiarism" as if it were a legal concept or cause of action. It isn't. Copyright infringement and plagiarism are different acts with some potential overlap. One may infringe upon a copyright without plagiarizing and one may plagiarize—use ideas without attribution—without breaking the law. Plagiarism is an ethical concept. Copyright is a legal one.

Perhaps most troubling, though, was the way in which the *Da Vinci Code* story was so often covered without a clear statement of the operative principle of copyright: one cannot protect facts and ideas, only specific expressions of ideas. Dan Brown and Random House U.K. prevailed in the London court because the judge clearly saw that the earlier authors were trying to protect ideas. Most people don't understand that important distinction. So it's no surprise that most reporters don't either.

Reporters often fail to see the big picture in copyright stories: that what is at stake is the long-term health of our culture. If the copyright system fails, huge industries could crumble. If it gets too strong, it could strangle future creativity and research. It is complex, and complexity can be a hard thing to render in journalistic prose.

The work situation of most reporters may also impede a thorough understanding of how copyright affects us all. Reporters labor for content companies, after all, and tend to view their role in the copyright system as one-dimensional. They are creators who get paid by copyright holders. So it's understandable for journalists to express a certain amount of anxiety about the ways digital technologies have allowed expensive content to flow around the world cheaply.

Yet reporters can't gather the raw material for their craft without a rich library of information in accessible form. When I was a reporter in the 1980s and 1990s, I could not write a good story without scouring the library and newspaper archives for other stories that added context. And like every reporter, I was constantly aware that my work was just one element in a cacophony of texts seeking readers and contributing to the aggregate understanding of our world. I was as much a copyright user as I was a copyright producer. Now that I write books, I am even more aware of my role as a taker and a giver. It takes a library, after all, to write a book.

The Right to Say No

We are constantly reminded that copyright law, as the Supreme Court once declared, is an "engine of free expression." But more often these days, it's instead an engine of corporate censorship.

Copyright is the right to say no. Copyright holders get to tell the rest of us that we can't build on, revise, copy, or distribute their work. That's a fair bargain most of the time. Copyright provides the incentive to bring work to market. It's impossible to imagine anyone anteing up $300 million for *Spider-Man 3* if we did not have a reasonable belief that copyright laws would limit its distribution to mostly legitimate and moneymaking channels.

Yet copyright has the potential of locking up knowledge, insight, information, and wisdom from the rest of the world. So it is also fundamentally a *conditional* restriction on speech and print. Copyright and the First Amendment are in constant and necessary tension. The law has for most of American history limited copyright—allowing it to fill its role as an incentive-maker for new creators yet curbing its censorious powers. For most of its 300-year history, the system has served us well, protecting the integrity of creative work while allowing the next generation of creators to build on the cultural foundations around them. These rights have helped fill our libraries with books, our walls with art, and our lives with song.

But something has gone terribly wrong. In recent years, large multinational media companies have captured the global copyright system and twisted it toward their own short-term interests. The people who are supposed to benefit most from a system that makes ideas available—readers, students, and citizens—have been excluded. No one in Congress wants to hear from college students or librarians.

More than ever, the law restricts what individuals can do with elements of their own culture. Generally the exercise of copyright protection is so extreme these days that even the most innocent use of images or song lyrics in scholarly work can generate a legal threat. Last year one of the brightest students in my department got an article accepted in the leading journal in the field. It was about advertising in the 1930s. The journal's lawyers and editors refused to let her use images from the ads in question without permission, even though it is impossible to find out who owns the ads or if they were ever covered by copyright in the first place. The chilling effect trumped any claim of scholarly "fair use" or even common sense.

What Has Changed

For most of the history of copyright in Europe and the United States, copying was hard and expensive, and the law punished those who made whole copies of others' material for profit. The principle was simple: legitimate publishers would make no money after investing so much in authors, editors, and printing presses if the same products were available on the street. The price in such a hypercompetitive market would drop to close to zero. So copyright created artificial scarcity.

But we live in an age of abundance. Millions of people have in their homes and offices powerful copying machines and communication devices: their personal computers. It's almost impossible to keep digital materials scarce once they are released to the public.

The industries that live by copyright—music, film, publishing, and software companies—continue to try. They encrypt video discs and compact discs so that consumers can't play them on computers or make personal copies. They monitor and sue consumers who allow others to share digital materials over the Internet. But none of these tactics seem to be working. In fact, they have been counterproductive. The bullying attitude has alienated consumers. That does not mean that copyright has failed or that it has no future. It just has a more complicated and nuanced existence.

Here is the fundamental paradox: media companies keep expanding across the globe. They produce more software, books, music, video games, and films every year. They charge more for those products every year. And those industries repeatedly tell us that they are in crisis. If we do not radically alter our laws, technologies, and habits, the media companies argue, the industries that copyright protects will wither and die.

Yet they are not dying. Strangely, the global copyright industries are still rich and powerful. Many of them are adapting, changing their containers and their content, but they keep growing, expanding across the globe. Revenues in the music business did drop steadily from 2000 to 2003—some years by up to 6.8 percent. Millions of people in Europe and North America use their high-speed Internet connections to download music files free. From Moscow to Mexico City to Manila, film and video piracy is rampant. For much of the world, teeming pirate bazaars serve as the chief (often only) source of those products. Yet the music industry has recovered from its early-decade lull rather well. Revenues for the major commercial labels in 2004 were 3.3 percent above 2003. Unit sales were up 4.4 percent. Revenues in 2004 were higher than in 1997 and comparable to those of 1998—then considered very healthy years for the recording industry. This while illegal downloading continued all over the world.

Yet despite their ability to thrive in a new global/digital environment, the companies push for ever more restrictive laws—laws that fail to recognize the realities of the global flows of people, culture, and technology.

Recent changes to copyright in North America, Europe, and Australia threaten to chill creativity at the ground level—among noncorporate, individual, and communal artists. As a result, the risk and price of reusing elements of copyrighted culture are higher than ever before. If you wanted to make a scholarly documentary film about the history of country music, for example, you might end up with one that slights the contribution of Hank Williams and Elvis Presley because their estates would deny you permission to use the archival material. Other archives and estates would charge you prohibitive fees. We are losing much of the history of the twentieth century because the copyright industries are more litigious than ever.

Yet copyright, like culture itself, is not zero-sum. In its first weekend of theatrical release, *Star Wars Episode III: Revenge of the Sith* made a record $158.5 million at the box office. At the same time, thousands of people downloaded high-quality pirated digital copies from the Internet. Just days after the blockbuster release of the movie, attorneys for 20th Century Fox sent thousands of "cease-and-desist" letters to those sharing copies of the film over the Internet. The practice continued unabated.

How could a film make so much money when it was competing against its free version? The key to understanding that seeming paradox—less control, more revenue—is to realize that every download does not equal a lost sale. As the Stanford law professor Lawrence Lessig has argued, during the time when music downloads were 2.6 times those of legitimate music sales, revenues dropped less than 7 percent. If every download replaced a sale, there would be no commercial music industry left. The relationship between the free version and the legitimate version is rather complex, like the relationship between a public library and a book publisher. Sometimes free stuff sells stuff.

Checks and Unbalances

Here's a primer for reporters who find themselves lost in the copyright jungle: American copyright law offers four basic democratic safeguards to the censorious power of copyright, a sort of bargain with the people. Each of these safeguards is currently at risk:

1. First and foremost, copyrights eventually expire, thus placing works into the public domain for all to buy cheaply and use freely. That is the most important part of the copyright bargain: We the people grant copyright as a temporary monopoly over the reproduction and distribution of specific works, and eventually we get the material back for the sake of our common heritage and collective knowledge. The works of Melville and Twain once benefited their authors exclusively. Now they belong to all of us. But as Congress continues to extend the term of copyright protection for works created decades ago (as it did in 1998 by adding twenty years to all active copyrights) it robs the people of their legacy.

2. Second, copyright restricts what consumers can do with the text of a book, but not the book itself; it governs the content, not the container. Thus people may sell and buy used books, and libraries may lend books freely, without permission from publishers. In the digital realm, however, copyright holders may install digital-rights-management schemes that limit the transportation of both the container and the content. So libraries may not lend out major portions of their materials if they are in digital form. As more works are digitized, libraries are shifting to the lighter, space-saving formats. As a result, libraries of the future could be less useful to citizens.

3. Third, as we have seen, copyright governs specific expressions, but not the facts or ideas upon which the expressions are based. Copyright does not protect ideas. But that is one of the most widely misunderstood aspects of copyright. And even that basic principle is under attack in the new digital environment. In 1997, the National Basketball Association tried to get pager and Internet companies to refrain from distributing game scores without permission. And more recently, Major League Baseball has tried, but so far has failed, to license the use of player statistics to limit "free riding" firms that make money facilitating fantasy baseball leagues. Every Congressional session, database companies try to create a new form of intellectual property that protects facts and data, thus evading the basic democratic right that lets facts flow freely.

4. Fourth, and not least, the copyright system has built into it an exception to the power of copyright: fair use. This significant loophole, too, is widely misunderstood, and deserves further discussion.

Generally, one may copy portions of another's copyrighted work (and sometimes the entire work) for private, noncommercial uses, for education, criticism, journalism, or parody. Fair use operates as a defense against an accusation of infringement and grants confidence to users that they most likely will not be sued for using works in a reasonable way.

On paper, fair use seems pretty healthy. In recent years, for example, courts have definitively stated that making a parody of a copyrighted work is considered "transformative" and thus fair. Another example: a major ruling in 2002 enabled image search engines such as Google to thrive and expand beyond simple Web text searching into images and video because "thumbnails" of digital photographs are considered to be fair uses. Thumbnails, the court ruled, do not replace the original in the marketplace.

But two factors have put fair use beyond the reach of many users, especially artists and authors. First and foremost, fair use does not help you if your publisher or distributor does not believe in it. Many publishers demand that every quote—no matter how short or for what purpose—be cleared with specific permission, which is extremely cumbersome and often costly.

And fair use is somewhat confusing. There is widespread misunderstanding about it. In public forums I have heard claims such as "you can take 20 percent" of a work before the use becomes unfair, or, "there is a forty-word rule" for long quotes of text. Neither rule exists. Fair use is intentionally vague. It is meant for judges to apply, case by case. Meanwhile, copyright holders are more aggressive than ever and publishers and distributors are more concerned about suits. So in the real world, fair use is less fair and less useful.

The Biggest Copy Machine

Fair use is designed for small ball. It's supposed to create some breathing room for individual critics or creators to do what they do. Under current law it's not appropriate for large-scale endeavors—like the Google library project. Fair use may be too rickety a structure to support both free speech and the vast dreams of Google.

Reporters need to understand the company's copyright ambitions. Google announced in December 2004 that it would begin scanning in millions of copyrighted books from the University of Michigan library, and in August 2006 the University of California system signed on. Predictably, some prominent publishers and authors have filed suit against the search-engine company.

The company's plan was to include those works in its "Google Book Search" service. Books from the library would supplement both the copyrighted books that Google has contracted to offer via its "partner" program with publishers and the uncopyrighted works scanned from other libraries, including libraries of Harvard, Oxford, and New York City. While it would offer readers full-text access to older works out of copyright, it would provide only "snippets" of the copyrighted works that it scans without the authors' permission from Michigan and California.

Google says that because users will only experience "snippets" of copyrighted text, their use of such material should be considered a fair use. That argument will be tested in court. But whether those snippets constitute fair use is just one part of the issue. To generate the "snippets," Google is scanning the entire works and storing them on its servers. The plaintiffs argue that the initial scanning of the books itself—done to create the snippets from a vast database—constitutes copyright infringement, the very core of copyright. Courts will have to weigh whether the public is better served by a strict and clear conception of copyright law—that only the copyright holder has the right to give permission for any copy, regardless of the ultimate use or effect on the market—or a more flexible and pragmatic one in which the user experience matters more.

One of the least understood concepts of Google's business is that it copies everything. When we post our words and images on the Web, we are implicitly licensing Google, Yahoo, and other search engines to make copies of our content to store in their huge farms of servers. Without such "cache" copies, search engines could not read and link to Web pages. In the Web world, massive copying is just business as usual.

But through the library project, Google is imposing the norms of the Web on authors and publishers who have not willingly digitized their works and thus have not licensed search engines to make cache copies. Publishers, at first, worried that the Google project would threaten book sales, but it soon became clear that project offers no risk to publishers' core markets and projects. If anything, it could serve as a marketing boon. Now publishers are most offended by the prospect of a wealthy upstart corporation's "free-riding" on their content to offer a commercial and potentially lucrative service without any regard for compensation or quality control. The publishers, in short, would like a piece of the revenue, and some say about the manner of display and search results.

Copyright has rarely been used as leverage to govern ancillary markets for goods that enhance the value or utility of the copyrighted works. Publishers have never, for instance, sued the makers of library catalogs, eyeglasses, or bookcases. But these are extreme times.

The mood of U.S. courts in recent years, especially the Supreme Court, has been to side with the copyright holder in this time of great technological flux. Google is an upstart facing off against some of the most powerful media companies in the world, including Viacom, News Corporation, and Disney—all of which have publishing wings. Courts will probably see this case as the existential showdown over the nature and future of copyright and rule to defend the status quo. Journalists should follow the case closely. The footnotes of any court decision could shape the future of journalism, publishing, libraries, and democracy.

Out of the Jungle

Google aside, in recent years—thanks to the ferocious mania to protect everything and the astounding political power of media companies—the basic, democratic checks and balances that ensured that copyright would not operate as an instrument of private censorship have been seriously eroded. The most endangered principle is fair use: the right to use others' copyrighted works in a reasonable way to promote important public functions such as criticism or education. And if fair use is in danger then good journalism is also threatened. Every journalist relies on fair use every day. So journalists have a self-interest in the copyright story.

And so does our society. Copyright was designed, as the Constitution declares, to "promote the progress" of knowledge and creativity. In the last thirty years we have seen this brilliant system corrupted and captured by the very industries that the old laws fostered. Yet the complexity and nuanced nature of copyright battles make it hard for nonexperts to grasp what's at stake.

So it's up to journalists to push deeper into stories in which copyright plays a part. Then the real challenge begins: explaining this messy system in clear language to a curious but confused audience.

Stephanie C. Ardito

NO

MySpace and YouTube Meet the Copyright Cops

Since the dawn of the Internet, many of us have marveled at the ground-breaking novelty of Internet sites that seem to appear from nowhere, gain rapid popularity, and become staples on everyone's set of bookmarks. The founders of these sites do not usually come from traditional content providers, so the phenomenon of Web-based services such as Yahoo!, Amazon, Travelocity, MapQuest, and Google continue to amaze us.

And just when we think there can't possibly be any more innovation, along come social networking and video-sharing sites such as MySpace and YouTube and their hundreds of imitators.

As these companies take off and continue to soar, inevitably, it seems, the copyright infringement lawsuits begin, often initiated by the traditional media powerhouses which feel threatened by the upstarts' popularity. The truly groundbreaking Internet companies manage to survive. Negotiations and settlements are worked out, conglomerates with bottomless financial pockets come to the rescue, or deep-rooted media companies finally accept the need to change their business paradigms or lose their considerable customer base.

The latest round of battles is occurring within the music and movie industries. The background and conflicts are no different than what we've seen before. Ten years ago, the scientific, technical, and medical (STM) publishers resisted placing full-text articles on the Internet. These publishers worried about losing expensive annual subscriptions if individual articles were easily accessible for purchase, as well as about how to collect royalties on multiple copies of articles circulating on the Web. Although struggling with customer demand for replication of Web services inspired by Internet technology, publishers finally figured out how to make their content widely and instantly available. Now publishers struggle with open access and end users (both authors and readers) going directly to the Web. The music and movie industries are bound to do the same.

The New Reality

A former employee of mine will graduate from music school this year. His dream is to earn a living as a jazz drummer. Recently, he created a MySpace page, listing upcoming band engagements, announcing his availability as a private instructor, and providing videos and audio clips of his live performances. There are no copyright notices on the page, but Matt shared his opinion that the original purpose of MySpace was to make budding artists known. If his videos and music show up somewhere else on the Internet or if users download the clips, Matt doesn't care. Copyright won't become an issue for him until he's famous. His major concern now is to get his name known.

As for school policies and educational efforts informing kids about copyright, teachers at my nephews' and niece's high schools and colleges do not discuss the ramifications of downloading content from the Internet. English and computer science teachers who require electronic copies of papers talk to their students about plagiarism and warn students that their compositions are being run against the Turnitin . . . to verify originality.

However, colleges and universities may soon intensify instructional efforts to enlighten students about copyright, including possible litigation initiated around the illegal downloading and storing of videos and music. On Feb. 28, 2007, the Recording Industry Association of America (RIAA) announced another round of lawsuits against college students for copyright infringements. . . .

Regarding my own personal experience with the social networking sites, I will admit that I'm a frequent user of YouTube. A while back, I saw a VH1 documentary on Meat Loaf, in which the television show played clips from Meat Loaf's *Bat Out of Hell* video. Being a fan, after the program ended, I immediately went to YouTube and looked for the full videos of a couple of songs from the album—"You Took the Words Right Out of My Mouth" and "Paradise by the Dashboard Light" (a particular favorite of mine). I was tempted to download the videos to my computer so I could view them whenever the mood struck, but my niece told me that the videos remain on YouTube "forever," so I wouldn't have a problem finding them whenever I wanted. Since I still worry that someday the copyright police will knock on my door, take my computer, and lock me up in copyright jail, I listened to my niece's advice and did not download the videos.

However, my niece's assertion that videos stay on YouTube into infinity isn't true. I'm also a celebrity news junkie. Earlier this year, I was intrigued about the scuttlebutt surrounding the Justin Timberlake/Scarlett Johannsson video, "What Goes Around . . . Comes Around." I had seen clips of a steamy swimming pool scene from the video and immediately went to YouTube to find it. And there it was. In fact, there were several uploads of the video from a number of the site's users. I watched the entire video to see what the fuss was about and told my neighbor about it. Of course she asked me for the URL, but when I went back to look for the video on YouTube, it had vanished. Since Sony, the legal distributor, allows "sharing" of the video directly from its Musicbox Web site, I emailed the URL to my neighbor. . . . I suspect that Sony must have warned YouTube to take the illegal copies off its site.

So, what prompts my nephews, niece, colleagues, and me to go to MySpace and YouTube to view grainy, unprofessional, uploaded videos and audios recorded on camera phones and camcorders versus searching the music label or movie studio Web sites for the originals? The answer lies in the ease and convenience of MySpace and YouTube. Without much fuss and no required registration, you can quickly identify videos of interest, see which ones are the most popular with others (both sites rank videos by the number of hits received, similar to Amazon's "Top Sellers"), click on the videos you want to watch, and, within a matter of seconds, have them appear on your screen. In comparison, the traditional media companies often require users to download special software to view videos and click through several pages of terms and conditions before gaining access. Even when that access is finally granted, you may sit for several minutes waiting for the videos to download to your screen. Since consumers want instant gratification, the established players need to learn some lessons from MySpace and YouTube. So, let's review the genesis and appeal of these two Web sites.

YouTube

Founded in February 2005, YouTube is typical of many startup Internet companies. It originated in a garage, followed quickly by significant funding from a venture capital company, in this case, Sequoia Capital. At first, users shared personal videos, but as the Web site's popularity grew rapidly, YouTube contracted with traditional content providers (television and movie studios and record labels) to load commercial clips. In less than a year, the video and user statistics were staggering. The company claims that 65,000 videos are uploaded daily, with consumers watching more than 100 million videos a day. Twenty million unique users, mainly in the 18–49 age range, view the Web site monthly.

In October 2006, Google, also initially funded by Sequoia Capital, bought YouTube for $1.65 billion. YouTube has struggled to find advertising revenue, so it should benefit from Google's ownership and experience in generating revenue. Although YouTube faced some copyright legal challenges from the music industry prior to Google's purchase, lawsuits seemed to have multiplied since the takeover. Some industry analysts speculate this litigiousness stems from the arrival of Google's deep financial pockets. For now, Google doesn't seem deterred by the legal wrangling.

YouTube's Boilerplate

Let's take a look at YouTube's copyright notices. Within the Terms of Use document . . . section 4 deals with Intellectual Property Rights. The section's statements are typical of the notices we see on the Web sites of publishers, database producers, and other content providers:

> The content on the YouTube Website, except all User Submissions (as defined below), including without limitation, the text, software, scripts, graphics, photos, sounds, music, videos, interactive features and the like ("Content") and the trademarks, service marks and logos contained therein ("Marks"), are owned by or licensed to YouTube, subject to copyright and other intellectual property rights under United States and foreign laws and international conventions. Content on the Website is provided to you AS IS for your information and personal use only and may not be used, copied, reproduced, distributed, transmitted,

broadcast, displayed, sold, licensed, or otherwise exploited for any other purposes whatsoever without the prior written consent of the respective owners. YouTube reserves all rights not expressly granted in and to the Website and the Content. You agree to not engage in the use, copying, or distribution of any of the Content other than expressly permitted herein, including any use, copying, or distribution of User Submissions of third parties obtained through the Website for any commercial purposes. If you download or print a copy of the Content for personal use, you must retain all copyright and other proprietary notices contained therein. You agree not to circumvent, disable or otherwise interfere with security related features of the YouTube Website or features that prevent or restrict use or copying of any Content or enforce limitations on use of the YouTube Website or the Content therein.

As with traditional content providers who negotiate author contracts, those who upload original videos "grant YouTube a worldwide, non-exclusive, royalty-free, sublicenseable and transferable license to use, reproduce, distribute, prepare derivative works of, display, and perform the User Submissions in connection with the YouTube Website and YouTube's (and its successor's) business, including without limitation for promoting and redistributing part or all of the YouTube Website (and derivative works thereof) in any media formats and through any media channels."

But YouTube goes one step further than traditional publishers and database producers by granting "each user of the YouTube Website a non-exclusive license to access your User Submissions through the Website, and to use, reproduce, distribute, prepare derivative works of, display and perform such User Submissions as permitted through the functionality of the Website and under these Terms of Service." In other words, as I interpret this clause, those who upload videos they have created own the rights to their works. In the publishing world of newspapers, journals, and books, authors generally turn over their rights to the publishers, who then own the authors' works into perpetuity.

By clicking on the Terms of Use, YouTube's registered users also agree they will not submit any copyrighted material, with YouTube reserving the right to remove content if it detects infringement. YouTube cites the Digital Millennium Copyright Act (DMCA) of 1998 as the company's guideline for dealing with potential copyright violations, requiring written communication if copyright holders find their intellectual property has been illegally uploaded to the YouTube Web site. . . . DMCA seems to protect YouTube and Google from lawsuits if the infringing works are removed when copyright holders notify them, but actual litigation that would give us precedent has yet to be established.

In a separate document, "Copyright Tips," . . . . YouTube admits: "The most common reason we take down videos for copyright infringement is that they are direct copies of copyrighted content and the owners of the copyrighted content have alerted us that their content is being used without their permission." YouTube mentions "fair use," providing links to four Web sites that outline the factors considered to establish fair use status: U.S. Copyright Office; . . . Stanford University Libraries and Academic Information Resources; . . . Copyright Web site LLC; . . . and the Chilling Effects Clearinghouse. . . .

MySpace

MySpace . . . was founded in 2003 as a social networking Web site. In 2005, Rupert Murdoch's News Corporation acquired MySpace as part of a $580 million acquisition, with the "lifestyle portal" now a unit of Fox Interactive Media Inc. Users must be at least 14 to join MySpace (one must be 13 to access YouTube), but I'm not sure how this is enforced on either site.

The MySpace Terms of Use Agreement is similar to YouTube's and applies to users who are Visitors (those who browse the Web site) or Members (those who register). . . . Under the section titled Proprietary Rights in Content on MySpace.com, when members display, publish, or post any content on the Web site, MySpace acknowledges that ownership rights belong to members, but members grant MySpace "a limited license to use, modify, publicly perform, publicly display, reproduce, and distribute such Content solely on and through the MySpace Services." The license is "non-exclusive . . . fully-paid and royalty-free (meaning that MySpace.com is not required to pay you for the use on the MySpace Services of the Content that you post), sublicenseable (so that MySpace.com is able to use its affiliates and subcontractors such as Internet content delivery networks to provide the MySpace Services), and worldwide (because the Internet and the MySpace Services are global in reach)." Members must "warrant" that the posted content "does not violate the privacy rights, publicity rights, copyrights, contract rights or any other rights of any person" and agree "to pay for all royalties, fees, and any other monies owing any person by reason of any Content posted . . . through the MySpace Services."

The Agreement includes a "partial" list of 27 prohibitive content activities. Illicit activities include promoting an "illegal or unauthorized copy of another person's copyrighted work, such as providing pirated computer programs or links to them, providing information to circumvent manufacture-installed copy-protect devices, or providing pirated music or links to pirated music files." Advertising and paid commercial activity is also prohibited. As with YouTube, MySpace includes several paragraphs on liabilities and disclaimers.

The Agreement is dated Oct. 25, 2006, coinciding with MySpace's announcement that the company had implemented a filtering system to identify copyrighted materials posted by its users. The audio fingerprinting technology came from Gracenote . . . , a California-based company specializing in the organization of digital music. Music files uploaded by MySpace users are run against Gracenote's MusicID software and Global Media Database to detect copyright infringements.

In February 2007, MySpace announced the implementation of a second program to block videos containing copyrighted content posted by its users. In this case, digital fingerprinting technology licensed from Audible Magic . . . is used to screen and block videos.

YouTube seems to lag behind MySpace in applying filtering technology. The company hoped to introduce a new mechanism to filter out unauthorized videos by the end of 2006. On Feb. 22, 2007, the *Mercury News* reported that Google had signed a deal with Audible Magic to provide its filtering technology on the YouTube Web site. However, YouTube and Audible Magic had not directly issued an "official" statement about such a deal as of that date, nor would either company comment.

Storms of Litigation

On Oct. 11, 2006, *The Wall Street Journal* interviewed two copyright experts about the Google purchase of YouTube: John Palfrey, a Harvard University law professor and director of the Berkman Center for Internet & Society . . . , and Stan Liebowitz, an economics professor at the University of Texas at Dallas and director of the Center for the Analysis of Property Rights and Innovation. . . . Mr. Palfrey said, "Google is no stranger to copyright risk. Much to their credit, Google has not let a lack of precision in the copyright context stop them from taking on major projects. The YouTube deal is no exception. As with Google News and the Libraries Project, the YouTube technology and service is going to make some people—competitors and people elsewhere in the value chain alike—somewhat unhappy."

Mr. Liebowitz agreed with Palfrey: "Google is no stranger to these issues. Its attempt (the library project) to copy all the books in existence without getting copyright permission in advance has led to a lawsuit against it by copyright owners. Perhaps there are economies of scale in fighting such lawsuits. I also agree that YouTube is no Napster. Nevertheless, whether there will be copyright litigation depends on several issues. Although the purpose of YouTube might be to encourage home-grown creative endeavors, some portion of YouTube files have been pure copyrighted files with no home-grown component, although it appears that YouTube has taken them down when requested."

Palfrey expressed his opinion that if users agree to YouTube's Terms of Service agreement—"not to post anything that violates anyone else's copyright," and YouTube removes copyrighted works immediately that come to the company's attention—then YouTube and Google should be protected by the DMCA if lawsuits are filed. If the companies ignore or don't respond to claims of infringement, he considered litigation inevitable.

In fairness to YouTube, the company has quickly responded when notified about copyrighted materials, not only from media conglomerates, but also from individual directors and writers. For example, in July 2006, journalist Robert Tur sued YouTube for posting a video he had shot of a white truck driver named Reginald Denny being dragged out of his truck and beaten during the Los Angeles riots in 1992. When YouTube learned of the lawsuit, the video was immediately removed. Shortly before Google's purchase of YouTube, the Japanese Society for Rights of Authors, Composers and Publishers notified the company of nearly 30,000 illegal clips floating around the YouTube Web site. Again, when alerted, YouTube removed the offending clips.

Preceding the sale of YouTube to Google, a flurry of announcements appeared regarding potential content deals with Sony, Bertelsmann, Universal Music, and CBS. While the CBS talks ultimately broke down, YouTube brokered a deal with the British Broadcasting Company to load selective BBC news and entertainment content on the company Web site. Analysts forecast that

Google's significant financial resources would prompt an immediate upsurge in copyright litigation after the company's takeover of YouTube. In fact, as this issue of *Searcher* went to press, lawsuits were being announced on a daily basis, so many, that it was difficult for me to keep up. For example, on Jan. 18, 2007, competitor News Corp. subpoenaed YouTube for the identity of users who uploaded full episodes of Fox's TV show *24* before the episodes debuted. Apparently, YouTube gave in to Fox's pressure and identified the users.

In addition, Viacom Inc.—which owns MTV, Nickelodeon, Comedy Central, and Paramount, not to mention, the immortal *I Love Lucy* and *Perry Mason* TV series—ordered YouTube to remove more than 100,000 video clips. Viacom had been in discussions with YouTube to keep the videos on the Web site. Some critics speculated that Viacom may have demanded the removal of the videos to force YouTube into a quicker royalty arrangement, rather than let negotiations drag on indefinitely. Since Comedy Central's *The Daily Show with Jon Stewart* is among the most heavily viewed videos on the YouTube Web site, industry analysts thought Viacom's strategy would compel YouTube to immediately agree on terms favorable to Viacom. As of this writing, YouTube and Google had not budged.

Shortly after the breakdown in talks, on March 13, 2007, Viacom filed a lawsuit against Google and YouTube, seeking more than $1 billion in damages for "160,000 unauthorized clips of Viacom's programming . . . viewed more than 1.5 billion times" on the YouTube Web site. Some critics commented that Viacom not only wants control over its media programs, but doesn't like its materials displayed along side the work of amateurs on YouTube, mainly because the unprofessional videos turn off advertisers. However, the real truth may lie in the threat Viacom is experiencing over YouTube's popularity and the significant Google resources supporting the Web site. Interestingly, in the month prior to the lawsuit announcement, Viacom signed a licensing deal with Joost . . . , a company whose technology will be used to load videos from Viacom's television networks onto the Internet. One has to wonder if Viacom entered into the Joost deal knowing that the lawsuit against Google and YouTube would follow. The Viacom lawsuit will be the one to watch, as the company will argue that YouTube had direct knowledge of the illegal videos and profited from the postings (i.e., most likely citing Section 512 from the DMCA safe harbor clause).

In an ironic twist, on March 22, 2007, the Electronic Frontier Foundation (EFF) sued Viacom on behalf of MoveOn.org and Brave New Films. In August 2006, the two companies had created and uploaded a video, *Stop the Falsiness,* to YouTube. The video parodied *The Colbert Report,* another popular Comedy Central program owned by Viacom, and included clips from the show as well as original interviews. EFF argues that Viacom unlawfully asked YouTube to remove the video parody, which EFF claims was protected by free speech and fair use. Google and YouTube are not named in the lawsuit.

Another conglomerate, Vivendi (and its subsidiary, Universal Music Group), has received frequent press coverage for its aggressive tactics in filing copyright infringement lawsuits against social networking and video Web sites. The company continues to pressure MySpace and YouTube to pay royalties, either by forcing users to "pay-per-play" or by sharing ad revenues. These tactics are being blasted by critics, who write that customers are alienated when media companies fail to adopt to new technology.

As an aside, in early February 2007, a privately held video-sharing company called Veoh Networks, Inc. was formed by media giants Time Warner and Michael Eisner (former Disney Chairman and CEO) and various investment firms. In a bit of irony, considering the corporate backgrounds of the founders, Veoh found itself facing copyright infringement lawsuits less than a week after its video Web site debuted.

Watching and Waiting

Some media giants are choosing to stay out of the copyright fray but continue to cautiously watch legal developments at their competitors. For example, late in 2006, Warner Music chose not to sue YouTube for uploading songs and videos, but rather, negotiated a deal to share revenue from ads placed next to Warner material. Warner's strategy differed sharply from the approach employed against Napster nearly 6 years ago. In that case, a class action suit from a number of music companies shut down Napster.

Commenting on the Viacom lawsuit against YouTube, Paul Cappuccio, Time Warner's general counsel, expressed his opinion that "companies should reach a compromise . . . We are still of the opinion that we can negotiate a business solution with YouTube that will efficiently identify and filter out unauthorized copyrighted works while also allowing us to license copyright works to them for a share of revenue."

Some conglomerates decide to sit back because they have found themselves between a rock and a hard place. Illegal videos and music give them exposure and may help to generate sales. Sound familiar? Years ago, information professionals pleaded with traditional publishers to allow access to individual articles and to consider alternative forms of electronic advertising to generate revenue, foreseeing that money (and profits) could be made without paying for annual subscriptions. Back then, we called the publishers dinosaurs. Now, the media conglomerates are being labeled with the same term.

Personally, I think the media giants will eventually calm down and learn to work with social networking and video Web sites. Otherwise, these outlets risk losing their substantial customer base, not to mention access to revolutionary marketing strategies and technologies that only upstart Internet companies can seem to initiate. For example, YouTube is piloting some innovative advertising programs that may allay the fears of the conglomerates, while at the same time, rewarding them with revenue. One program, called "participatory video ads," is being embraced by companies such as General Motors, Adidas, and Coca-Cola. These firms have purchased YouTube video space to spotlight their brands. As with personal videos placed on the Web site, users can rate and comment on the commercially made videos.

In a separate marketing development, on Feb. 22, 2007, Fox Interactive Media (owner of MySpace) announced that it had acquired Strategic Data Corporation. Like DoubleClick . . . Strategic Data is a digital advertising company.

Fox hopes to use Strategic Data's systems to persuade more users to click on ads placed on the MySpace Web site.

Until the media giants simmer down, however, MySpace and YouTube will face legal battles over copyrighted music and movie clips for some time to come. The confrontations will be fierce, but Google and News Corp. have significant financial resources and large legal staffs to handle the lawsuits. In fact, after its takeover of YouTube, Google set aside more than $200 million (funded through stock held in escrow) to cover future litigation costs.

As we went to press, News Corp. and NBC Universal announced plans to launch a legally pure, video distribution network some view as a potential competitor to YouTube. Scheduled to launch this summer, the new service will stock an online video site with masses of TV shows and videos, plus clips that users will be allowed to modify and share. Partners in the project already include the usual Google competitors—AOL, MSN, and Yahoo!. Television library content will be advertiser-supported and free to users. Some outlets will support mashups and online communities. Downloading movies will require user payments.

Digital Rights Management and the Steve Jobs Controversy

Like the digital object identifier (DOI) technology developed by publishers to tag and track electronic copyrighted works, media companies have created features in digital rights management (DRM) technology to make it difficult for users to copy or transfer audio and video files. Generally, technologies to thwart file sharing have failed, with media companies relying on their own personnel to scan the Internet for unauthorized copies. Even after threatening the offending parties, content providers continue to struggle in tracking down the same illegal copies likely to appear elsewhere on the Web.

On Feb. 6, 2007, Apple's Steve Jobs posted an essay on his company's Web site . . . entitled "Thoughts on Music." Jobs proposed that digital rights management (DRM) software preventing music reproduction and piracy be eliminated, so that songs could be played on any device. Apple licenses music rights from the "big four" music companies: Universal, Sony BMG, Warner, and EMI. According to Jobs, these companies "control the distribution of over 70% of the world's music." When Apple started its iTunes service, the company "was able to negotiate landmark usage rights at the time, which include allowing users to play their DRM protected music on up to 5 computers and on an unlimited number of iPods. Obtaining such rights from the music companies was unprecedented at the time, and even today is unmatched by most other digital music services. However, a key provision of our agreements with the music companies is that if our DRM system is compromised and their music becomes playable on unauthorized devices, we have only a small number of weeks to fix the problem or they can withdraw their entire music catalog from our iTunes store. . . . So far we have met our commitments to the music companies to protect their music, and we have given users the most liberal usage rights available in the industry for legally downloaded music."

The controversy with Jobs' posting comes with his proposal to completely abolish blocking DRM protections. He wrote: "Imagine a world where every online store sells DRM-free music encoded in open licensable formats. In such a world, any player can play music purchased from any store, and any store can sell music which is playable on all players." Jobs justifies such an open source solution because he believes that DRM systems have never worked to prevent music piracy. He claims that music CDs are completely unprotected, so that "all the music distributed on CDs can be easily uploaded to the Internet, then (illegally) downloaded and played on any computer or player. In 2006, under 2 billion DRM-protected songs were sold worldwide by online stores, while over 20 billion songs were sold completely DRM-free and unprotected on CDs by the music companies themselves. The music companies sell the vast majority of their music DRM-free, and show no signs of changing this behavior, since the overwhelming majority of their revenues depend on selling CDs which must play in CD players that support no DRM system. . . . Convincing [the big four] to license their music to Apple and others DRM-free will create a truly interoperable music marketplace."

Many music industry analysts agree with Jobs—that nothing will prevent piracy. Those who buy iPods are not purchasing many DRM-protected recordings. Rather, consumers purchase music on CDs and download individual tracks into the format of their choice on the iPods. Jobs justified his position on DRMs by providing statistics on what the iTunes store sells: "Today's most popular iPod holds 1000 songs, and research tells us that the average iPod is nearly full. This means that only 22 out of 1000 songs, or under 3% of the music on the average iPod, is purchased from the iTunes store and protected with a DRM. The remaining 97% of the music is unprotected and playable on any player that can play the open formats. It's hard to believe that just 3% of the music on the average iPod is enough to lock users into buying only iPods in the future. And since 97% of the music on the average iPod was not purchased from the iTunes store, iPod users are clearly not locked into the iTunes store to acquire their music."

On the flip side, those opposed to Jobs' proposal to eliminate DRM protections point out the pressure Jobs faces from European fair trade laws that will soon mandate making iTunes music available to non-Apple devices. If an unrestricted MP3 format is adopted across the music industry, any digital device could download music from any source. Looking to the future, Jobs may envision expanding the iTunes concept to movies, TV programs, electronic books, and other media. With DRM blocking eliminated, content from a wide range of formats could be downloaded to any digital device.

On Feb. 15, 2007, Rob Pegoraro, a reporter with *The Washington Post*, succinctly summarized all the fuss whirling in the entertainment industry:

> The [DRM] technology can still serve a role in online music or movie rental services, which have drawn far fewer customers than stores like iTunes, but for purchases it does too little to justify its costs. In practice, it only stops copying by the unmotivated, the over-scheduled or the inexperienced—the people most likely to buy a song or movie

online as long as they can do so quickly, easily and cheaply. In the music industry, a growing number of outlets beyond the big-name companies, from tiny indie-rock operations to the Philadelphia Orchestra and the Smithsonian Institution's Folkways label, have realized the futility of copy-restriction software and now sell digital downloads in open, unrestricted formats. At this point, this all amounts to little more than expensive psychotherapy for Hollywood executives. It's the height of arrogance for them to keep sending us the bill.

My thoughts exactly! . . .

POSTSCRIPT

Do Copyright Laws Protect Ownership of Intellectual Property?

One of the most difficult aspects about copyright is that depending on how the law is enforced, the result can be a form of censorship. The challenge, then, is to find the balance of protecting original work that truly belongs to an author who justifiably can claim credit for the work it took to produce something, versus creating an atmosphere that either does not recompense an author, or shifts all work into public domain.

As courts have tried to sort out problems with traditional copyright legislation and newer technologies, several attempts have been made to narrow the focus of the application of the law. The court case that resulted in a consumer's right to record film and television programs off of the television came from *Universal City Studios, Inc. v. Sony Corp. of America, 659 F.2d 963* (9th Cir. 1981), but stipulated that the copy was to be for personal use only. The current Copyright Act allows consumers to duplicate CDs and computer software for backup purposes, and to modify them as necessary, but all of these court cases favored the consumer with clear stipulation that duplicated material cannot and should not be sold to anyone else.

Problems with copyright become much more difficult when people post things on the Internet, digitally manipulate images, or link to other Web sites. Does the content copied from one form take on a new identity as "creative, original work" when an artist (or home consumer) manipulates images and puts them into a new form—such as taking still pictures and animating them, then posting them on the Web? How might a wiki, like wikipedia, inadvertently violate copyright? It may come as no surprise that copyright law is one of the fastest growing topics and areas of specializations in law schools around the country.

In addition to the way a home consumer might harmlessly use someone else's copyrighted work, organizations that deal with fairness legal issues are concerned about their involvement in abuses of copyright, and their liability. James G. Neal writes in "Copyright Is Dead . . . Long Live Copyright," *American Libraries* (December 2002, pp. 48–51) of the problems public institutions have with trying to police the Internet and duplication technologies in their organizations. Heather Green's article, "Whose Video Is It, Anyway? YouTube's Runaway Success Has Opened a Pandora's Box of Copyright Issues," *Business-Week* (August 7, 2006, p. 38), explains how businesses should be aware of copyright violations. Rob Pegorano, the technology writer for the *Washington Post*, has written a series of articles on copyright infringements, including "Time to Face the Music on File Sharing" (February 15, 2007, p. D1).

As you consider the many sides of the debate on copyright and digital technology, it might be useful to think of how different persons might respond to the issues. For example, how might a screenwriter think about file sharing of his or her film, downloaded from the Internet? How would the author of a book feel about electronic distribution of the book she or he wrote, if no royalties, or lesser royalties were paid for the copies of the work? How do those people who work in the important—yet often less visible fields—such as CD package design, feel about digital duplication? And of course, what would the position of an independent retailer be on the elimination of copyrighted works for sale? How would you feel if a paper you wrote over a long period of time were posted to the Internet and other people used your work without attributing credit to you?

ISSUE 7

Is Advertising Good for Society?

YES: John E. Calfee, from "How Advertising Informs to Our Benefit," *Consumers' Research* (April 1998)

NO: Dinyar Godrej, from "How the Ad Industry Pins Us Down," *New Internationalist* (September 2006)

ISSUE SUMMARY

YES: John Calfee, a former U.S. Trade Commission economist, takes the position that advertising is very useful to people and that the information that advertising imparts helps consumers make better decisions. He maintains that the benefits of advertising far outweigh the negative criticisms.

NO: Dinyar Godrej makes the claim that advertising doesn't really tell us anything new about products, but instead, it acts upon our emotions to create anxiety if we don't buy products. The result, then, is a culture in which we consume more than we need to, and still feel bad about ourselves. This type of consumer culture then permeates our lifestyles.

P rofessor Dallas Smythe first described commercial media as a system for delivering audiences to advertisers. This perception of the viewing public as a "market" for products as well as an audience for advertising—a main source of media revenue—reflects the economic orientation of the current media system in America. The unplanned side effects of advertising, however, concern many critics. The creation of a consumer society, materialism, and high expectations are one set of concerns, but these issues also conflict with many cultural expectations, histories, and social systems in many countries where advertising is considered a Western, capitalist construct.

John Calfee addresses many of these issues, but also focuses on how the information in ads benefits consumers. He takes the position that advertising functions in the public's interest, and that even the controversies about ads can be beneficial because they can result in competitive pricing for consumers. Citing some specific cases, he states that individuals can learn about important issues (such as health) through ads. He even considers what he calls "less bad" ads, which give consumers important negative information that can be useful to their well-being.

In the second selection, Dinyar Godrej takes the perspective that advertising creates an assault on our senses, that advertising can act as a "compulsive liar," and that the clutter that advertising creates bombards us with images and ideas that result in a subtle cultural shift that creates desires that only the wealthy can actually attain. This author takes the point of view that there is really nothing positive that advertising contributes to a society, and that just about everything about advertising is negative.

These views illustrate the extreme polarities in positions that people often take when it comes to the topic of advertising. There are also other, more neutral views, such as those held by people who don't mind advertising, and see it as an economic engine to deliver "free" programs to people, or the idea that advertising is an art form in itself, that, if viewed critically, can make a social comment on the styles, consumer culture, and artifacts of different social groups. Yet others focus on the creative aspects of advertising and revere the way it can stimulate, motivate, or resonate with viewers. Whatever the perspective, one thing is true: advertising can have both manifest and latent impact. It can be defended on solid ground, and criticized on solid ground.

Many students today don't seem to mind advertising. A typical comment is that they just don't let the messages "get" to them, but it is important to think about one's own critical faculties, and those of others. Do you think of advertising as one of today's most persuasive forms of communication, or just a by-product of something else? It might be interesting to try to think about how a person's environment would be different if there were no ads.

A thorough understanding of how advertising functions in society, and as an industry that is responsible for billions of dollars annually, helps form a person's views on the impact of advertising in their lives, and in the lives of others. It also helps to think about what products are advertised and to whom: Should tobacco and alcohol ads be targeted to children and teens? Do advertising costs actually raise the price of goods, rather than stimulate the circulation of goods in society? Is advertising the engine that runs a consumer society, or does capitalism create industries, like advertising, to continue to support its operation within a society? Furthermore, as Godrej points out, what impact does advertising (particularly from Western societies) have on traditional cultures?

It should also be noted that there are many forms of advertising. We often first think of product advertising, but what of corporate sponsorship, or indirect advertising through product placement (referred to in the industry as "product enhancement")? Dinyar Godrej does an excellent job of reminding us that there are many subtle styles of influence that go beyond the initial knee-jerk reaction to advertising as a harmless by-product of industry in the twenty-first century.

How Advertising Informs to Our Benefit

A great truth about advertising is that it is a tool for communicating information and shaping markets. It is one of the forces that compel sellers to cater to the desires of consumers. Almost everyone knows this because consumers use advertising every day, and they miss advertising when they cannot get it. This fact does not keep politicians and opinion leaders from routinely dismissing the value of advertising. But the truth is that people find advertising very useful indeed.

Of course, advertising primarily seeks to persuade and everyone knows this, too. The typical ad tries to induce a consumer to do one particular thing—usually, buy a product—instead of a thousand other things. There is nothing obscure about this purpose or what it means for buyers. Decades of data and centuries of intuition reveal that all consumers everywhere are deeply suspicious of what advertisers say and why they say it. This skepticism is in fact the driving force that makes advertising so effective. The persuasive purpose of advertising and the skepticism with which it is met are two sides of a single process. Persuasion and skepticism work in tandem so advertising can do its job in competitive markets. Hence, ads represent the seller's self interest, consumers know this, and sellers know that consumers know it.

By understanding this process more fully, we can sort out much of the popular confusion surrounding advertising and how it benefits consumers.

How useful is advertising?   Just how useful is the connection between advertising and information? At first blush, the process sounds rather limited. Volvo ads tell consumers that Volvos have side-impact air bags, people learn a little about the importance of air bags, and Volvo sells a few more cars. This seems to help hardly anyone except Volvo and its customers.

But advertising does much more. It routinely provides immense amounts of information that benefits primarily parties other than the advertiser. This may sound odd, but it is a logical result of market forces and the nature of information itself.

The ability to use information to sell products is an incentive to create new information through research. Whether the topic is nutrition, safety, or more mundane matters like how to measure amplifier power, the necessity of achieving credibility with consumers and critics requires much of this research to be placed in the public domain, and that it rest upon some academic credentials. That kind of research typically produces results that apply to more than just the brands sold by the firm sponsoring the research. The lack of property rights to such "pure" information ensures that this extra information is available at no charge. Both consumers and competitors may borrow the new information for their own purposes.

Advertising also elicits additional information from other sources. Claims that are striking, original, forceful or even merely obnoxious will generate news stories about the claims, the controversies they cause, the reactions of competitors (A price war? A splurge of comparison ads?), the reactions of consumers and the remarks of governments and independent authorities.

Probably the most concrete, pervasive, and persistent example of competitive advertising that works for the public good is price advertising. Its effect is invariably to heighten competition and reduce prices, even the prices of firms that assiduously avoid mentioning prices in their own advertising.

There is another area where the public benefits of advertising are less obvious but equally important. The unremitting nature of consumer interest in health, and the eagerness of sellers to cater to consumer desires, guarantee that advertising related to health will provide a storehouse of telling observations on the ways in which the benefits of advertising extend beyond the interests of advertisers to include the interests of the public at large.

A cascade of information   Here is probably the best documented example of why advertising is necessary for consumer welfare. In the 1970s, public health experts described compelling evidence that people who eat more fiber are less likely to get cancer, especially cancer of the colon, which happens to be the second leading cause of deaths from cancer in the United States. By 1979, the U.S. Surgeon General was recommending that people eat more fiber in order to prevent cancer.

Consumers appeared to take little notice of these recommendations, however. The National Cancer Institute decided that more action was needed. NCI's cancer prevention division undertook to communicate the new information about fiber and cancer to the general public. Their goal was to change consumer diets and reduce the risk of cancer, but they had little hope of success given the tiny advertising budgets of federal agencies like NCI.

Their prospects unexpectedly brightened in 1984. NCI received a call from the Kellogg Corporation, whose All-Bran cereal held a commanding market share of the high-fiber segment. Kellogg proposed to use All-Bran advertising as a vehicle for NCI's public service messages. NCI thought that was an excellent idea. Soon, an agreement was reached in which NCI would review Kellogg's ads and labels for accuracy and value before Kellogg began running their fiber-cancer ads.

The new Kellogg All-Bran campaign opened in October 1984. A typical ad began with the headline, "At last some news about cancer you can live with." The ad continued: "The National Cancer Institute believes a high fiber, low fat diet may reduce your risk of some kinds of cancer. The National Cancer

Institute reports some very good health news. There is growing evidence that may link a high fiber, low fat diet to lower incidence of some kinds of cancer. That's why one of their strongest recommendations is to eat high-fiber foods. If you compare, you'll find Kellogg's All-Bran has nine grams of fiber per serving. No other cereal has more. So start your day with a bowl of Kellogg's All-Bran or mix it with your regular cereal."

The campaign quickly achieved two things. One was to create a regulatory crisis between two agencies. The Food and Drug Administration thought that if a food was advertised as a way to prevent cancer, it was being marketed as a drug. Then the FDA's regulations for drug labeling would kick in. The food would be reclassified as a drug and would be removed from the market until the seller either stopped making the health claims or put the product through the clinical testing necessary to obtain formal approval as a drug.

But food advertising is regulated by the Federal Trade Commission, not the FDA. The FTC thought Kellogg's ads were non-deceptive and were therefore perfectly legal. In fact, it thought the ads should be encouraged. The Director of the FTC's Bureau of Consumer Protection declared that "the [Kellogg] ad has presented important public health recommendations in an accurate, useful, and substantiated way. It informs the members of the public that there is a body of data suggesting certain relationships between cancer and diet that they may find important." The FTC won this political battle, and the ads continued.

The second instant effect of the All-Bran campaign was to unleash a flood of health claims. Vegetable oil manufacturers advertised that cholesterol was associated with coronary heart disease, and that vegetable oil does not contain cholesterol. Margarine ads did the same, and added that vitamin A is essential for good vision. Ads for calcium products (such as certain antacids) provided vivid demonstrations of the effects of osteoporosis (which weakens bones in old age), and recounted the advice of experts to increase dietary calcium as a way to prevent osteoporosis. Kellogg's competitors joined in citing the National Cancer Institute dietary recommendations.

Nor did things stop there. In the face of consumer demand for better and fuller information, health claims quickly evolved from a blunt tool to a surprisingly refined mechanism. Cereals were advertised as high in fiber and low in sugar or fat or sodium. Ads for an upscale brand of bread noted: "Well, most high-fiber bran cereals may be high in fiber, but often only one kind: insoluble. It's this kind of fiber that helps promote regularity. But there's also a kind of fiber known as soluble, which most high-fiber bran cereals have in very small amounts, if at all. Yet diets high in this kind of fiber may actually lower your serum cholesterol, a risk factor for some heart diseases." Cereal boxes became convenient sources for a summary of what made for a good diet.

Increased independent information   The ads also brought powerful secondary effects. These may have been even more useful than the information that actually appeared in the ads themselves.

One effect was an increase in media coverage of diet and health. *Consumer Reports*, a venerable and hugely influential magazine that carries no advertising, revamped its reports on cereals to emphasize fiber and other ingredients (rather than testing the foods to see how well they did at providing a complete diet for laboratory rats). The health-claims phenomenon generated its own press coverage, with articles like "What Has All-Bran Wrought?" and "The Fiber Furor." These stories recounted the ads and scientific information that prompted the ads; and articles on food and health proliferated. Anyone who lived through these years in the United States can probably remember the unending media attention to health claims and to diet and health generally.

Much of the information on diet and health was new. This was no coincidence. Firms were sponsoring research on their products in the hope of finding results that could provide a basis for persuasive advertising claims. Oat bran manufacturers, for example, funded research on the impact of soluble fiber on blood cholesterol. When the results came out "wrong," as they did in a 1990 study published with great fanfare in *The New England Journal of Medicine*, the headline in *Advertising Age* was "Oat Bran Popularity Hitting the Skids," and it did indeed tumble. The manufacturers kept at the research, however, and eventually the best research supported the efficacy of oat bran in reducing cholesterol (even to the satisfaction of the FDA). Thus did pure advertising claims spill over to benefit the information environment at large.

The shift to higher fiber cereals encompassed brands that had never undertaken the effort necessary to construct believable ads about fiber and disease. Two consumer researchers at the FDA reviewed these data and concluded they were "consistent with the successful educational impact of the Kellogg diet and health campaign: consumers seemed to be making an apparently thoughtful discrimination between high- and low-fiber cereals," and that the increased market shares for high-fiber non-advertised products represented "the clearest evidence of a successful consumer education campaign."

Perhaps most dramatic were the changes in consumer awareness of diet and health. An FTC analysis of government surveys showed that when consumers were asked about how they could prevent cancer through their diet, the percentage who mentioned fiber increased from 4% before the 1979 Surgeon General's report to 8.5% in 1984 (after the report but before the All-Bran campaign) to 32% in 1986 after a year and a half or so of health claims (the figure in 1988 was 28%). By far the greatest increases in awareness were among women (who do most of the grocery shopping) and the less educated: up from 0% for women without a high school education in 1984 to 31% for the same group in 1986. For women with incomes of less than $15,000, the increase was from 6% to 28%.

The health-claims advertising phenomenon achieved what years of effort by government agencies had failed to achieve. With its mastery of the art of brevity, its ability to command attention, and its use of television, brand advertising touched precisely the people the public health community was most desperate to reach. The health claims expanded consumer information along a broad front. The benefits clearly extended far beyond the interests of the relatively few manufacturers who made vigorous use of health claims in advertising.

A pervasive phenomenon   Health claims for foods are only one example, however, of a pervasive phenomenon—the use of advertising to provide essential health information with benefits extending beyond the interests of the advertisers themselves.

Advertising for soap and detergents, for example, once improved private hygiene and therefore, public health (hygiene being one of the underappreciated triumphs in twentieth century public health). Toothpaste advertising helped to do the same for teeth. When mass advertising for toothpaste and tooth powder began early in this century, tooth brushing was rare. It was common by the 1930s, after which toothpaste sales leveled off even though the advertising, of course, continued. When fluoride toothpastes became available, advertising generated interest in better teeth and professional dental care. Later, a "plaque reduction war" (which first involved mouthwashes, and later toothpastes) brought a new awareness of gum disease and how to prevent it. The financial gains to the toothpaste industry were surely dwarfed by the benefits to consumers in the form of fewer cavities and fewer lost teeth.

Health claims induced changes in foods, in non-foods such as toothpaste, in publications ranging from university health letters to mainstream newspapers and magazines, and of course, consumer knowledge of diet and health.

These rippling effects from health claims in ads demonstrated the most basic propositions in the economics of information. Useful information initially failed to reach people who needed it because information producers could not charge a price to cover the costs of creating and disseminating pure information. And this problem was alleviated by advertising, sometimes in a most vivid manner.

Other examples of spillover benefits from advertising are far more common than most people realize. Even the much-maligned promotion of expensive new drugs can bring profound health benefits to patients and families, far exceeding what is actually charged for the products themselves.

The market processes that produce these benefits bear all the classic features of competitive advertising. We are not analyzing public service announcements here, but old-fashioned profit-seeking brand advertising. Sellers focused on the information that favored their own products. They advertised it in ways that provided a close link with their own brand. It was a purely competitive enterprise, and the benefits to consumers arose from the imperatives of the competitive process.

One might see all this as simply an extended example of the economics of information and greed. And indeed it is, if by greed one means the effort to earn a profit by providing what people are willing to pay for, even if what they want most is information rather than a tangible product. The point is that there is overwhelming evidence that unregulated economic forces dictate that much useful information will be provided by brand advertising, and *only* by brand advertising.

Of course, there is much more to the story. There is the question of how competition does the good I have described without doing even more harm elsewhere. After all, firms want to tell people only what is good about their brands, and people often want to know what is wrong with the brands. It turns out that competition takes care of this problem, too.

Advertising and context   It is often said that most advertising does not contain very much information. In a way, this is true. Research on the contents of advertising typically finds just a few pieces of concrete information per ad. That's an average, of course. Some ads obviously contain a great deal of information. Still, a lot of ads are mainly images and pleasant talk, with little in the way of what most people would consider hard information. On the whole, information in advertising comes in tiny bits and pieces.

Cost is only one reason. To be sure, cramming more information into ads is expensive. But more to the point is the fact that advertising plays off the information available from outside sources. Hardly anything about advertising is more important than the interplay between what the ad contains and what surrounds it. Sometimes this interplay is a burden for the advertiser because it is beyond his control. But the interchange between advertising and environment is also an invaluable tool for sellers. Ads that work in collaboration with outside information can communicate far more than they ever could on their own.

The upshot is advertising's astonishing ability to communicate a great deal of information in a few words. Economy and vividness of expression almost always rely upon what is in the information environment. The famously concise "Think Small" and "Lemon" ads for the VW "Beetle" in the 1960s and 1970s were highly effective with buyers concerned about fuel economy, repair costs, and extravagant styling in American cars. This was a case where the less said, the better. The ads were more powerful when consumers were free to bring their own ideas about the issues to bear.

The same process is repeated over again for all sorts of products. Ads for computer modems once explained what they could be used for. Now a simple reference to the Internet is sufficient to conjure an elaborate mix of equipment and applications. These matters are better left vague so each potential customer can bring to the ad his own idea of what the Internet is really for.

Leaning on information from other sources is also a way to enhance credibility, without which advertising must fail. Much of the most important information in advertising—think of cholesterol and heart disease, antilock brakes and automobile safety—acquires its force from highly credible sources *other* than the advertiser. To build up this kind of credibility through material actually contained in ads would be cumbersome and inefficient. Far more effective, and far more economical, is the technique of making challenges, raising questions and otherwise making it perfectly clear to the audience that the seller invites comparisons and welcomes the tough questions. Hence the classic slogan, "If you can find a better whisky, buy it."

Finally, there is the most important point of all. Informational sparseness facilitates competition. It is easier to challenge a competitor through pungent slogans—"Where's the beef?", "Where's the big saving?"—than through a step-by-step recapitulation of what has gone on before. The bits-and-pieces approach makes for quick, unerring attacks and equally quick responses, all under the watchful eye of the consumer over whom the battle is being fought. This is an ideal recipe for competition.

It also brings the competitive market's fabled self-correcting forces into play. Sellers are less likely to stretch the truth, whether it involves prices or subtleties about safety and performance, when they know they may arouse a merciless response from injured competitors. That is one reason the FTC once worked to get comparative ads on television, and has sought for decades to dismantle government or voluntary bans on comparative ads.

"Less-bad" advertising There is a troubling possibility, however. Is it not possible that in their selective and carefully calculated use of outside information, advertisers have the power to focus consumer attention exclusively on the positive, i.e., on what is good about the brand or even the entire product class? Won't automobile ads talk up style, comfort, and extra safety, while food ads do taste and convenience, cigarette ads do flavor and lifestyle, and airlines do comfort and frequency of departure, all the while leaving consumers to search through other sources to find all the things that are wrong with products?

In fact, this is not at all what happens. Here is why: Everything for sale has something wrong with it, if only the fact that you have to pay for it. Some products, of course, are notable for their faults. The most obvious examples involve tobacco and health, but there are also food and heart disease, drugs and side effects, vacations and bad weather, automobiles and accidents, airlines and delay, among others.

Products and their problems bring into play one of the most important ways in which the competitive market induces sellers to serve the interests of buyers. No matter what the product, there are usually a few brands that are "less bad" than the others. The natural impulse is to advertise that advantage—"less cholesterol," "less fat," "less dangerous," and so on. Such provocative claims tend to have an immediate impact. The targets often retaliate; maybe their brands are less bad in a different respect (less salt?). The ensuing struggle brings better information, more informed choices, and improved products.

Perhaps the most riveting episode of "less-bad" advertising ever seen occurred, amazingly enough, in the industry that most people assume is the master of avoiding saying anything bad about its product.

Less-bad cigarette ads Cigarette advertising was once very different from what it is today. Cigarettes first became popular around the time of World War I, and they came to dominate the tobacco market in the 1920s. Steady and often dramatic sales increases continued into the 1950s, always with vigorous support from advertising. Tobacco advertising was duly celebrated as an outstanding example of the power and creativity of advertising. Yet amazingly, much of the advertising focused on what was wrong with smoking, rather than what people liked about smoking.

The very first ad for the very first mass-marketed American cigarette brand (Camel, the same brand recently under attack for its use of a cartoon character) said, "Camel Cigarettes will not sting the tongue and will not parch the throat." When Old Gold broke into the market in the mid-1920s, it did so with an ad campaign about coughs and throats and harsh cigarette smoke. It settled on the slogan, "Not a cough in a carload."

Competitors responded in kind. Soon, advertising left no doubt about what was wrong with smoking. Lucky Strike ads said, "No Throat Irritation— No Cough . . . we . . . removed . . . harmful corrosive acids," and later on, "Do you inhale? What's there to be afraid of? . . . famous purifying process removes certain impurities." Camel's famous tag line, "more doctors smoke Camels than any other brand," carried a punch precisely because many authorities thought smoking was unhealthy (cigarettes were called "coffin nails" back then), and smokers were eager for reassurance in the form of smoking by doctors themselves. This particular ad, which was based on surveys of physicians, ran in one form or another from 1933 to 1955. It achieved prominence partly because physicians practically never endorsed non-therapeutic products.

Things really got interesting in the early 1950s, when the first persuasive medical reports on smoking and lung cancer reached the public. These reports created a phenomenal stir among smokers and the public generally. People who do not understand how advertising works would probably assume that cigarette manufacturers used advertising to divert attention away from the cancer reports. In fact, they did the opposite.

Small brands could not resist the temptation to use advertising to scare smokers into switching brands. They inaugurated several spectacular years of "fear advertising" that sought to gain competitive advantage by exploiting smokers' new fear of cancer. Lorillard, the beleaguered seller of Old Gold, introduced Kent, a new filter brand supported by ad claims like these: "Sensitive smokers get real health protection with new Kent," "Do you love a good smoke but not what the smoke does to you?" and "Takes out more nicotine and tars than any other leading cigarette—*the difference in protection is priceless*," illustrated by television ads showing the black tar trapped by Kent's filters.

Other manufacturers came out with their own filter brands, and raised the stakes with claims like, "Nose, throat, and accessory organs not adversely affected by smoking Chesterfields. First such report ever published about any cigarette," "Takes the fear out of smoking," and "Stop worrying . . . Philip Morris and only Philip Morris is entirely free of irritation used [sic] in all other leading cigarettes."

These ads threatened to demolish the industry. Cigarette sales plummeted by 3% in 1953 and a remarkable 6% in 1954. Never again, not even in the face of the most impassioned anti-smoking publicity by the Surgeon General or the FDA, would cigarette consumption decline as rapidly as it did during these years of entirely market-driven anti-smoking ad claims by the cigarette industry itself.

Thus advertising traveled full circle. Devised to bolster brands, it denigrated the product so much that overall market demand actually declined. Everyone understood what was happening, but the fear ads continued because they helped the brands that used them. The new filter brands (all from smaller manufacturers) gained a foothold even as their ads amplified the medical reports on the dangers of smoking. It was only after the FTC stopped the fear ads in 1955 (on the grounds that the implied health claims had no proof) that sales resumed their customary annual increases.

Fear advertising has never quite left the tobacco market despite the regulatory straight jacket that governs cigarette advertising. In 1957, when leading cancer experts advised smokers to ingest less tar, the industry responded by cutting tar and citing tar content figures compiled by independent sources. A stunning "tar derby" reduced the tar and nicotine content of cigarettes by 40% in four years, a far more rapid decline than would be achieved by years of government urging in later decades. This episode, too, was halted by the FTC. In February 1960 the FTC engineered a "voluntary" ban on tar and nicotine claims.

Further episodes continue to this day. In 1993, for example, Liggett planned an advertising campaign to emphasize that its Chesterfield brand did not use the stems and less desirable parts of the tobacco plant. This continuing saga, extending through eight decades, is perhaps the best documented case of how "less-bad" advertising completely offsets any desires by sellers to accentuate the positive while ignoring the negative. *Consumer Reports* magazine's 1955 assessment of the new fear of smoking still rings true:

> ". . . companies themselves are largely to blame. Long before the current medical attacks, the companies were building up suspicion in the consumer by the discredited 'health claims' in their ads. . . . Such medicine-show claims may have given the smoker temporary confidence in one brand, but they also implied that cigarettes in general were distasteful, probably harmful, and certainly a 'problem.' When the scientists came along with their charges against cigarettes, the smoker was ready to accept them."

And that is how information works in competitive advertising.

Less-bad can be found wherever competitive advertising is allowed. I already described the health-claims-for-foods saga, which featured fat and cholesterol and the dangers of cancer and heart disease. Price advertising is another example. Prices are the most stubbornly negative product feature of all, because they represent the simple fact that the buyer must give up something else. There is no riper target for comparative advertising. When sellers advertise lower prices, competitors reduce their prices and advertise that, and soon a price war is in the works. This process so strongly favors consumers over the industry that one of the first things competitors do when they form a trade group is to propose an agreement to restrict or ban price advertising (if not ban all advertising). When that fails, they try to get advertising regulators to stop price ads, an attempt that unfortunately often succeeds.

Someone is always trying to scare customers into switching brands out of fear of the product itself. The usual effect is to impress upon consumers what they do not like about the product. In 1991, when Americans were worried about insurance companies going broke, a few insurance firms advertised that they were more solvent than their competitors. In May 1997, United Airlines began a new ad campaign that started out by reminding fliers of all the inconveniences that seem to crop up during air travel.

Health information is a fixture in "less-bad" advertising. Ads for sleeping aids sometimes focus on the issue of whether they are habit-forming. In March

1996, a medical journal reported that the pain reliever acetaminophen, the active ingredient in Tylenol, can cause liver damage in heavy drinkers. This fact immediately became the focus of ads for Advil, a competing product. A public debate ensued, conducted through advertising, talk shows, news reports and pronouncements from medical authorities. The result: consumers learned a lot more than they had known before about the fact that all drugs have side effects. The press noted that this dispute may have helped consumers, but it hurt the pain reliever industry. Similar examples abound.

We have, then, a general rule: sellers will use comparative advertising when permitted to do so, even if it means spreading bad information about a product instead of favorable information. The mechanism usually takes the form of less-bad claims. One can hardly imagine a strategy more likely to give consumers the upper hand in the give and take of the marketplace. Less-bad claims are a primary means by which advertising serves markets and consumers rather than sellers. They completely refute the naive idea that competitive advertising will emphasize only the sellers' virtues while obscuring their problems.

Dinyar Godrej

How the Ad Industry Pins Us Down

Buddhism and Hinduism recommend it. A retreat from clamour, a wondrous detachment that allows the material world to float up, like a sloughed-off skin, for one's dispassionate consideration. Whether they offer useful advice on re-engaging after this revelation, I don't know. The first astronauts saw a floating world, too. It provoked suitably joined-up thoughts about its (and our) fragility and essential unity.

But there are other worlds. And the one that elbows itself to the front of our attention's queue painstakingly creates surface and whips up froth. It's the one that the 125 residents of Clark, Texas, signed up to in 2005 when they changed the name of their township to Dish in return for a decade's free cable TV from the DISH Network. Hey, what's in a name except a wacky corporate PR opportunity, right?

The bubbly, dazzling world of which Dish has become an emblem shows little sign of floating up for our inspection. If we inspect it nonetheless, it reveals itself to be firmly riveted down by that old culprit—disproportionate corporate power.

Advertising is a bit of a compulsive liar. In the early days it was quite barefaced—the beverage giant, Dewar's, claiming in the 1930s that their Scotch whiskey repelled colds and flu; cigarette brands claiming that they soothed the throat and helped asthma. Some of this still goes on. Quack cures are advertised in numerous Majority World countries. The half of all Mexican citizens who are overweight are pummelled daily on TV by products that promise to melt 10 centimetres off the waistline in two hours.

Repeat After Me

Nowadays, regulatory bodies will see off many of the more obviously fraudulent claims.

But advertising is involved in soul fraud instead. If that sounds a bit deep, just stay with me a while.

Advertising today has little to do with introducing a new product or describing an existing one's virtues. It has everything to do with images, dreams and emotions; stuff we are evolutionarily programmed to engage with but which is, almost without exception in the ad biz, fake. Imagine how much attention you would pay if there were just text and no images. When ads for Sprite (owned by Coca-Cola) proclaimed: 'Image is nothing, thirst is everything', they were reassuring people that they were right to be distrustful, while building up images of honesty and straight talk, using professional basketball players to push the product: Sprite jumped several notches up the soft-drink rankings; moolah was minted. Image was everything, even if it was purporting to be an anti-image.

Amid the visual clutter, advertising—the chief agent of the mess—has to jump out at us. It must trigger off associations, however tangential, that will keep our attention. Endless repetition through media channels should build up a handy cloud of associations. According to one industry executive: 'In the context of most advertising, particularly passively consumed media like television and cinema, learning is incidental, not deliberate. This is why people tell you they are not influenced by advertising. They are not actively trying to take anything away from the experience, and therefore are not influenced at that time; but the effects will show up later, long after a particular viewing experience is forgotten.

Much effort is expended upon trying to sink boreholes into the vast iceberg of the subconscious mind, probably because the products being flogged are in reality just variations on the same old same old. A recent buzzword is 'neuromarketing'. Neuroscientists and psychiatrists are searching for the buy-button in the brain. This involves putting subjects into brain-scanning machinery and pitching concepts and images at them to see which ones make the lights flash. In one experiment, subjects were made to blind-taste Pepsi and Coke. Pepsi scored higher in terms of response in the ventral putamen, the part of the brain associated with feelings of reward—ie, most thought Pepsi tasted better. But when the subjects were informed which drink was Coke before they tried it, their medial prefrontal cortexes lit up. This is an area of the brain believed to control cognition. Most now said they preferred Coke. So just the name had prompted memories and brand nostalgia which influenced the taste of the stuff. One might question the validity of using expensive hospital equipment and highly trained medical professionals to explain choices of fizzy drinks with no nutritional value whatsoever—but that would be to get a bit real.

The good news is that all this dubious effort is just as likely to fail as it is to succeed. If an ad can latch on to the emotion of a winning goal in a football match or the tears and triumphs of Pop Idol, then there's a good chance it will do the trick. Much else is trial and error. Focus groups assembled to pretest the vibe are notoriously unreliable as they can be suggestible and become dominated by loudmouths.

Anxieties of Influence

One might well ask: so what? So what if silly money . . . pushes the usual goods/junk, if I can still make an informed choice about what I buy?

Well, maybe. . . . But how would you react if all this were seeping into the very pores of the culture you're part of—and changing it? Mass advertising is about brands with the most money behind them pushing to the top. Smaller companies with less of this fluff-muscle don't always survive.

More perniciously, corporate giants try every trick in the book to control our media channels. Much of the mainstream media exists to sell audiences to advertisers. Newspapers aren't profitable based on sales alone. The missing factor is ad money. It's their lifeblood. Teen magazines (especially those aimed at girls) are little more than catalogues for products—and that's the content. The profile of the chubby hero who saved a life is usually tucked away at the end.

Here's what an agency representing Coca-Cola demanded in a letter to magazines: 'We believe that positive and upbeat editorial provides a compatible environment in which to communicate the brand's message. . . . We consider the following subjects to be inappropriate and require that our ads are not placed adjacent to articles discussing the following issues: Hard News; Sex related issues; Drugs (Prescription or Illegal); Medicine (eg chronic illnesses such as cancer, diabetes, AIDS, etc); Health (eg mental or physical conditions); Negative Diet Information (eg bulimia, anorexia, quick weight loss, etc); Food; Political issues; Environmental issues; Articles containing vulgar language; Religion'. So, not much chance of a mention of the intimidation of union workers in Coke's Colombian plant, or of the charges of water pollution in India, then (read more at www.killercoke.org).

If anyone still thought they were watching 'the news' on CNN, anchor Jack Cafferty's on-air views might disabuse them: 'We are not here as a public service. We're here to make money. We sell advertising, and we do it on the premise that people are going to watch. If you don't cover the miners because you want to do a story about a debt crisis in Brazil at the time everybody else is covering the miners, then Citibank calls up and says, "You know what? We're not renewing the commercial contract." I mean, it's a business'. In the US, one study found that 40 per cent of the 'news' content of a typical newspaper originated in press releases, story memos and suggestions from PR companies.

Hungry for Cool

More subtle is the cultural shift wrought in the media—light, non-political television programming that contributes to a 'buying mood'; magazines filled with little nuggets of 'instant gratification'; serious newspapers that insert lengthy travel and fashion sections for no obvious reason. So much happiness, so unbearable.

Advertising consistently portrays 'lifestyles' that are beyond the reach of all but the wealthy. This is somehow viewed as 'apolitical'. Yet charities' ads calling for dropping Southern debt or opposing cruelty to animals often fall foul of regulators or media ad-sales teams for being 'too political'.

As a child I loved the ads before the movie. They were zippy and bright. I found the varied angles they took before the 'Ta-dahhh!' moment when the product was plugged ingenious. I still find the creative energy that goes into them intriguing, but feel tired by their consistently conservative values and know better about the social, economic and environmental issues behind the products they push. I also feel fed up by the sheer volume of the glitzy deluge. Corporate advertisers know this fed up feeling all too well and have responded with marketing moves that look less like traditional advertising but seep more than ever into our lives. The upshot is that everything gets branded, logoed or sponsored. Supermarkets that shaft farmers sponsor children's play areas and school computers. Children are employed to hand out freebies to other kids and talk them up ('peer marketing'). Conspicuous charity abounds, trying to make the brand look more benign—for example, Ronald McDonald House offers accommodation to families with sick children. Product placement sneaks into movies, TV shows, computer games and even novels. Our email and cell phones are bombarded. Most websites would collapse without revenue from ads that get ever more lively and mysterious.

With traditional advertising showing diminishing returns, corporations get into all sorts of contortions. The apparel company Diesel ran a multimillion-dollar campaign contrasting clothing ads with scenes of hardship in North Korea; Benetton notoriously used the image of a man dying of AIDS to push its duds. Wow, just feel that edge!

A certain amount of advertising is probably unavoidable—indeed, countries that curb it often flood mental spaces with political propaganda instead. But the worldview the ad biz pushes is so out of touch with real life that it can mess up our heads. Ever wondered where that urge to shop when you're feeling a bit down comes from? Or how our desire for social change or rebellion gets transformed into speed, sex, indulgence and living for the moment? Why is so much of our culture about dictating taste (the tyrannies of 'cool') and transforming it into want? Why are disadvantaged groups (be they dark-skinned, sexual minorities, people with disabilities, you name it) so absent from this trendy world, unless they are being fetishized by niche marketing?

With the deluge comes avoidance. Ungrateful wretches that we are, we try to block out as much as we can. TV advertising is in crisis. Ad guru Lord Saatchi thinks young people nowadays have 'continual partial attention—the kind of brain that's constantly sifting but records little. His answer is for companies to strive for 'one-word equity' to fit this goldfish attention span—Be™, Live™, Buy™, anyone?

This dizziness is reflected in the philosophical musings of Maurice Levy, top honcho of advertising giant Publicis: 'Consumers do not want only to be given an astonishingly wide-ranging choice. They want that choice to be renewed at intervals that are always shorter. This is the reason why we have to redefine our very notion of time. What we have to deal with is not only change, but an acceleration of change itself. Not only transformations, but the transformation of transformations: it will be a real challenge to make fidelity out of inconstancy.'

He doesn't stop to ponder how his work is all about creating this blur of inconstancy. Advertising's influence is being implicated in eating, compulsive and attention-deficit disorders. In the Majority World the big brand steamroller is intent on creating Westernized aspirational cultures often at odds with local cultures.

If we are to free identity from consumerism, reality checks are our strongest weapon. If struck by an ad, it's useful to measure how much of it is actually telling you something about the product and how much is image. Brands are eager that you identify with them, make them a part of your lives—deny them that privilege. Independent media (like the NI and, yes, this is a shameless plug) can give us all the dirt we need to chuck at corporate ad lies. Thinking before we buy, and buying nothing—especially when irrational urges prompt us to do otherwise—are bound to punch a few holes. The idea of our world and its public spaces as shared commons is becoming increasingly visible. Streets are being reclaimed by 'citizen artists' redrawing ads to reveal their subterfuges, and by social movements gathering to protest government by corporations.

There's quite a bit of ad-industry nervousness as brands come under attack and marketing tactics backfire. Could the industry one day start to tell us things we actually want to know? The distorting mirror will need to shatter first before a floating world comes into view.

POSTSCRIPT

Is Advertising Good for Society?

Since the development of the advertising industry, the question of advertising ethics has periodically resurfaced. Advertising was once considered a way to keep the cost of newspapers down, to help deliver "free" TV and radio to the public, and to help consumers understand what issues were important in society. Many defenses of advertising relied on helping consumers make more informed decisions about how to spend their money. But over the years, the real impact of advertising has been more critically considered. Today, issues of corporate power, mind-control, deceptive advertising, and cultivating desires in children and people who can't afford to buy products are considered to be more pressing social problems.

The ad industry has responded to criticism in many ways. Traditional defenses of tobacco and alcohol advertising have resulted in the creation of industry-supported projects to "prevent" misuse, but the purpose of these projects must also be carefully considered. Do industries attempt to fight regulation by doing "something" about a problem—like establishing programs to prevent underage drinking, or placing warning labels on cigarettes—or do they exercise "good neighbor" practices because they feel that they have a moral obligation to do so? In most cases, the real reason is that the industries would prefer to demonstrate that they can police their own industries, rather than accept regulation from outside.

Since the growth of technologies that are more individually used, like the Internet, the advertising industry has responded with a far more complicated structure to attract attention, and a far more complicated system of appealing to audiences they consider are most easily persuaded. Use of pop-up ads, banners, and promises of easy consumption permeate Internet sites. Advertisers don't seem to mind spam, or links that lead to new products or services, or cookies that unobtrusively collect consumer data about computer users.

Digital video recorders have the technological capability of screening out commercials, but advertisers have created ways to insert ads into programs so that the eye catches them, even if the conscious brain does not. Even some television programming has become a substitute for ads, when products used in shows like *Extreme Make-Over* and *Queer Eye for the Straight Guy* are mentioned and highlighted.

Ultimately, as the authors of these two selections indicate, advertising does infiltrate society on a number of levels. Fortunately, we have many wonderful sources to consider to help us understand advertising's social impact. Jean Kilbourne's *Can't Buy My Love* (Touchstone, 1999), provides a social critique of what advertising does to our feelings. Arthur Asa Berger's *Ads, Fads, and Consumer Culture: Advertising's Impact on American Character and Society*, now in its third edition (Rowman and Littlefield, 2007), has a number of contemporary examples, and covers critical analysis methods, sexuality in advertising, global advertising, and neuromarketing. Finally, Alissa Quart's *Branded: The Buying and Selling of Teenagers* (Basic Books, 2003) reflects on the impact advertising has had on today's typical college student.

Students are also encouraged to examine some of the academic journals that deal with issues of advertising in a number of venues, such as *The Journal of Advertising Ethics, Ethics and Society*, and the *Journal of Mass Media Ethics*, and to become familiar with Web sites that call attention to examples of blurring ads and ethical practices. The Center for Media and Democracy (http://www.prwatch.org/) regularly posts interesting items on the interface between politics and advertising, and Project Censored (http://www.projectcensored.org/) often reports on attempts by the ad industry to control information.

Internet References . . .

Center for Media and Public Affairs

This site offers information about ongoing debates concerning media fairness and impact, with particular attention to political campaigns and political journalism.

http://www.cmpa.com

Poynter Online: Resource Center

The Poynter Institute for Media Studies provides extensive links to information and resources on all aspects of media, including political journalism. Find this resource center in the "About Poynter" section.

http://www.poynter.org/

Pew Research Center for People and the Press

The purpose of the Pew Research Center for People and the Press is to serve as a forum for ideas on the media and public policy through public opinion research.

http://people-press.org

Society of Professional Journalists

The Web site for *The Electronic Journalist,* the online service for the Society of Professional Journalists (SPJ), will lead you to a number of articles on media ethics, accuracy, media leaders, and other topics.

http://www.spj.org

NewsSources

The *American Journalism Review*'s NewsSources section of their Web site provides links to newspapers around the country. Links to organizations that are concerned with the ethics and quality of media coverage may be found on this site, as well.

http://www.ajr.org

The Project for Excellence in Journalism

The Project for Excellence in Journalism is a research organization that studies the performance of the press. Their goal is to help both journalists and citizens understand what the press is delivering.

http://www.journalism.org

The Annenberg Public Policy Center

FactCheck.org within the political communication research section aims to reduce the level of deception and confusion in U.S. politics. FactCheck monitors the accuracy of what is said by major U.S. political players in the form of TV ads, debates, speeches, interviews, and news.

http://www.annenbergpublicpolicycenter.org

News and Politics

*A*t one time, one of the most hotly debated questions about media was whether media content demonstrated a liberal or conservative bias. In recent years, this question has receded, while other, more important issues have risen to the fore. Since the FCC began to revise ownership restrictions for media outlets, and since the Bush administration's attention to information control has grown throughout the Iraq War, news and politics have begun to be viewed through a slightly different social lens. Issues about news control are now far more complicated than in the days when Walter Lippmann wrote about the ideal of objectivity. While many cities and regions once had many newspapers, now they may have one. Broadcast news dominated the airwaves by powerful networks. Today, a person is as likely to start the day with checking the news on the Internet as they are to pick up a newspaper or watch TV sometime through the day. One of the most popular "news" programs for college-aged students is on Comedy Central. The issues in this section address three important, contemporary topics, and lead us toward discussions of how much, and what type of information we actually use.

- Can Media Regain Public Trust?
- Does Fake News Mislead the Public?
- Will Evolving Forms of Journalism Be an Improvement?

ISSUE 8

Can Media Regain Public Trust?

YES: Michael Schudson, from *Why Democracies Need an Unlovable Press* (Polity Press, 2008)

NO: John Hockenberry, from "'You Don't Understand Our Audience': What I Learned about Network Television at *Dateline NBC*," *Technology Review* (January/February 2008)

ISSUE SUMMARY

YES: Michael Schudson argues that although news is essential for democracy, the behavior of journalists makes them unpopular. Journalists' conflict orientation, obsession with facts and events, and "in-your-face" interviewing are what make journalism effective and essential. And it is those behaviors that should restore faith in journalism.

NO: John Hockenberry is disillusioned about the ability of credible journalism to survive in the current corporate environment. Based on his experience at *Dateline NBC*, he explores the timidity of those in charge of newsrooms. Fear of corporate owners, of audience response, and of technology cripples authentic journalism.

A 2009 survey highlights the diminishing credibility of journalism. The Pew Research Center for People and the Press found that only 29 percent of people surveyed believed that the news generally gets the facts straight, and only 18 percent believe that the press deals fairly with all sides of an issue. Yet, despite their disillusionment with the press, 71 percent of people see the press as a necessary watchdog on the government.

There is an irony in this downward spiral. In mid-twentieth century America, daily newspapers, nightly news on the big three networks, and a handful of news magazines dominated the news landscape. Many objected to the concentration of voices, reflected in the Walter Cronkite sign-off tag, "And that's the way it is." Yet as voices multiplied with cable and the Internet, as the objectivity of dominant media was attacked, as viewers fractured into niche consumers and independent content creators, the prestige and credibility of journalism have diminished. At the same time, television remains the dominant source of national and local news, with the Internet now in second place before newspapers. What have we gained through these changes? What have we lost?

In his book, Schudson lists seven things that news can do for democracy, including information, investigation, analysis, creating social empathy, facilitating a public forum, mobilization, and publicizing a representative democracy. He argues that journalistic obsession with facts and events is the unlovely side of this goal, but is the job of journalists who "get in the face of power." In so doing, they keep democracy from grave danger. In this selection, Schudson contends that some of the behaviors that have made journalists so unpopular are exactly what is needed to make it effective. He explains how story selection is kept unpredictable by an event orientation toward reporting, journalists' inherent skepticism about politicians, and how they relish confrontation and their outsider status. Yet these are the foundations that must be retained if journalism is again to be trusted.

John Hockenberry is disillusioned about the potential of contemporary journalists to achieve these goals. He describes a process of deciding which stories would air that was influenced by corporate ownership and timid management. With the focus clearly on audience size, Hockenberry argues that television news has "lost its most basic journalistic instincts in its search for the audience-driven sweet spot, the 'emotional center' of the American people." His pessimistic conclusion is that television news has lost its center in its search for numbers. Technology is freeing communication, and that may be good news for the news.

What do you think are the reasons that the press is held in such low esteem? Most studies ask about "the press" as if it were monolithic. Are these perceptions coming from only a few bad examples? Or is it a broader social perception that overall the press is not what it should be? Ask yourself about your perception of the credibility of the press and current journalism. Then try to decide why you hold that opinion.

Schudson calls the press "unlovable." But his work urges the public to realize that it is exactly these unlovable behaviors that enable the press to be effective. Do you agree? Is it possible that so many dislike media because of their confrontational manner, their constant "stirring up" of issues, or their overly critical stance?

Hockenberry thinks the media pander to audiences. They search for "feel good" stories that will keep audiences listening. Is this true in media other than television? How can you be a profit-centered organization, encourage viewership, and provide audiences with what they need to know? How many times have we cringed at yet another statehouse or corporate scandal, and turned instead to the news celebrity scandal? How often have we forgone the extended story on a important bill making its way through Congress because it was too complex? Yet, in so doing, do we get what we deserve and make it impossible for hard news to thrive?

Perhaps your answers about why media have lost the public trust are different from either of the positions in the selctions. In Issue 10 on evolving forms of journalism, we will discuss the difference between news and opinion. That may provide additional reasons as to why journalism is so poorly rated. In debating this thorny issue, keep in mind three interrelated questions: (1) Have media lost the public trust? (2) Why? and (3) What can they do to regain it?

Michael Schudson

Why Democracies Need an Unlovable Press

Alexis de Tocqueville, widely cited for his view that the American press is a necessary and vital institution for American democracy, did not actually have much affection for it. He objected to its violence and vulgarity. He saw it as a virtue of the American system that newspapers were widely dispersed around the country rather than concentrated in a capital city—they could do less harm this way. He confessed, "I admit that I do not feel toward freedom of the press that complete and instantaneous love which one accords to things by their nature supremely good. I love it more from considering the evils it prevents than on account of the good it does."

. . . Taking a leaf from Tocqueville . . . I want to propose here that most critics of journalism, in and outside journalism itself, have attacked just those features of the press that, for all their defects, best protect robust public discussion and promote democracy. The focus of the news media on events, rather than trends and structures; the fixation of the press on conflict whenever and wherever it erupts; the cynicism of journalists with respect to politics and politicians; and the alienation of journalists from the communities they cover make the media hard for people to love but hard for democracies to do without. These are precisely the features that most regularly enable the press to maintain a capacity for subverting established power.

This is not to suggest that there is anything wrong with in-depth reporting of the sort that Pulitzer juries and media critics applaud and I greatly admire. Nor do I mean to suggest that the dialogue of democracy should jettison editorial writers, Op-Ed columnists, investigative reporters, expert analysts who can produce gems of explanatory journalism. That would be absurd. But I do mean to suggest that the power of the press to afflict the comfortable derives more often than not from the journalistic equivalent of ambulance-chasing. Just as the ambulance-chasing trial lawyer sees another person's tragedy as a million-dollar opportunity, the newshound reporter sees it as an attention-grabbing, career-advancing front-page sensation. I want to explore here the ways the most narrow and unlovable features of news may make the most vital of contributions to democracy.

The Press as an Establishment Institution

The press is presumably the bastion of free expression in a democracy, but too often it has been one of the institutions that limits the range of expression, especially expression that is critical of leading centers of power in society. Almost all social scientific study of news shows that journalists themselves, of their own volition, limit the range of opinion present in the news. There are at least three significant ways this happens. First, there is source-dependence. Reporters rely on and reproduce the views of their primary sources and these tend to be high government officials. Second, reporters and editors operate according to a set of professional norms that are themselves constraints on expression. Third, journalists operate within conventional bounds of opinion, opinions common among a largely secular, college-educated upper middle class. All of this has been abundantly documented. . . . I will quickly summarize the research conclusions but only as a preface to arguing that accounts of the press as unable or unwilling to resist the demands of established political power have been exaggerated.

Dependence on Official Sources

Media scholars have consistently found that official sources dominate the news. This is invariably presented as a criticism of the media. If the media were to fulfill their democratic role, they would offer a wide variety of opinions and perspectives and would encourage citizens to choose among them in considering public policies. If the media allow politicians to set the public agenda, they may unduly narrow public discussion and so diminish democracy. This is the argument made . . . by W. Lance Bennett, who states the media "tend to 'index' the range of voices and viewpoints in both news and editorials according to the range of views expressed in mainstream government debate about a given topic." Bennett argues that this helps perpetuate a "world in which governments are able to define their own publics and where 'democracy' becomes whatever the government ends up doing."

Sociologist Herbert Gans makes an argument about official sources related to Bennett's. For him, the routines of daily journalism undermine democracy. If supporting democracy means encouraging citizens to be active, informed, and critical, then the standard operating procedures of mainstream journalism subvert their own best intentions. Since most news is "top down," relaying the views of high government officials over lower government officials, all government officials over unofficial groups and oppositional groups, and groups of any sort over unorganized citizens, it diminishes the standing and efficacy of individual citizens.

Whether the normative implications of journalism's favoring high government officials are as dire as Gans fears may be doubted, but it is indisputable that news media coverage emphasizes the views and actions of leading politicians and other top government officials. It is likewise indisputable that this limits the range of opinion to which the general public is exposed.

The Constraints of Professional Culture

Journalists favor high government officials—but why? The answer is that they work within a professional culture or a set of professional values that holds that a journalist's obligation is to report government affairs to serve the informational functions that make democracy work. One might still ask why that general function should lead to such a strong emphasis on government officials. The answer seems to be that newspapers, once divorced from direct service to political parties (the leading nineteenth-century model) and once aspiring to neutral or objective professionalism, developed occupational routines and a professional culture that reinforce what media scholar Janet Steele calls an "operational bias" in news reporting. That is, in the work of political reporting, journalists emphasize "players, policies, and predictions of what will happen next." So even when the press goes to outside experts rather than inside government officials, they seek people with experience in government, access to and knowledge of the chief players in government, and a ready willingness to speak in the terms of government officials, interpreting and predicting unfolding events. In television reporting and to a large degree in the print media, too, historians or area experts on the Middle East, for instance, are unlikely to be asked to comment on developments there to set contemporary events in a broader historical and cultural context. It is rare almost to the vanishing point for the press to seek out people even further from the policy-making community to comment on daily political affairs—for instance, religious leaders. The use of religious leaders to discuss key foreign policy matters is essentially non-existent. Why? No publisher dictates that religious opinion is irrelevant. There is no force anywhere dictating anything about this except the well-learned habits and patterns of journalists.

The Constraints of Conventional Wisdom

Journalists seem to be paragons of conventional wisdom. They are wrapped up in daily events, and it would be disconcerting for them and for their readers if they took a long view. It might also be disconcerting for them to take a comparative (non-American) view. It would certainly be disconcerting for them to spend too much time with academics or others removed from the daily fray of political life. It is in relation to the conventional wisdom that journalists know how to identify "a story." Individual journalists may take issue with convention. Some journalists who work for publications with non-conventional audiences may write with unconventional assumptions and unusual points of departure. But the mainstream journalist writing for a standard news institution is likely to be ignorant of, or, if informed, dismissive of opinions outside the fold.

In Washington, in state capitals, and even more in smaller countries, journalists pick up conventional wisdom through lives intertwined with the lives of politicians. In France, for instance, Thomas Ferenczi, associate editor of *Le Monde,* complains that journalists and politicians—and it does not matter if they are left-wing or right-wing—belong to the same "microcosm": . . . Ferenczi warns, "There is real danger for democracy here: namely, that journalists and politicians, because they are so closely linked, have their own, narrow, idea of what the media should cover . . . and ignore the interests of the people." This is less of a problem in the more pluralistic United States. . . . However, the same general phenomenon occurs.

Other factors also limit the range of opinion in the American media, vitally important factors, although they lie outside the news media as such. For instance, the American political system generally offers a narrower political spectrum, and one less accommodating of minorities, than most other democratic systems. Ralph Nader complained bitterly after the 2000 election that he had not been well covered in the press. Why, he asked, when he had been raising real issues did he get no coverage, while Al Gore and George W. Bush, the Tweedle-dum and Tweedle-dee of American politics, got coverage every time they blew their noses? The answer seemed pretty straightforward: Ralph Nader was not going to be elected president of the United States in 2000. Either Al Gore or George W. Bush would. The press—part of its conventional wisdom—believed its job was to follow what the American political system had tossed up for it. It was not the job of the press to offer the public a wide range of issues but to cover, analyze, and discuss the issues the two viable candidates were presenting. Imagine, however, if Ralph Nader had been running for chancellor in Germany. Would the German press have shown greater interest in his ideas? Yes, but not because the German press is better or more democratic, but because Germany has a parliamentary political system. If Ralph Nader's party received 5 percent of the vote in Germany, it would receive 5 percent of the seats in Parliament and Nader would be a force, potentially a decisive force, in forming a government. If Ralph Nader received 5 percent of the vote in the United States, he would get no seats in Congress and would remain an outsider to the legislative process.

So there are many reasons why the media discourse in the United States fails to approximate an ideal of robust and wide open discussion. Even so, journalism as it functions today is still a practice that offends powerful groups, speaks truth to power, and provides access for a diversity of opinion. How and why does this happen despite all that constrains it? The standard sociological analysis of news places it in so airless a box that exceptional journalistic forays are not readily explained. They are the exceptions that prove the rule. They are the ones that got away from the powers of constraint and cooptation and routine. But these "exceptions" happen every year, every week, and at some level every day. How can we explain that?

Strategic Opportunities for Free Expression
Eventfulness

There is a fundamental truth about journalism recognized by all journalists but almost no social scientists: things happen. Not only do things happen but, as the bumper sticker says, shit happens. That is what provides a supply of occurrences for journalists to work with. Shit even happens to the rich and powerful and it makes for a great story when it does.

Because shit happens, journalists gain some freedom from official opinion, professional routines, and conventional wisdom. Journalism is an event-centered discourse, more responsive to accidents and explosions in the external world than to fashions in ideas among cultural elites. The journalists' sense of themselves as street-smart, nose to the ground, adventurers in places where people don't want them has an element of truth to it and it is very much linked to event-centeredness.

News, like bread or sausage, is something people make. Scholars emphasize the manufacturing process. Journalists emphasize the raw material their work brings them to; they insist that their jobs recurrently place them before novel, unprecedented, and unanticipated events. While sociologists observe how this world of surprises is tamed, journalists typically emphasize that the effort at domestication falls short.

The journalists have a point. Sometimes something happens that is not accounted for in any sociology or media studies. Take President Bill Clinton's efforts to create a system of national service. This was part of his 1992 campaign and he mentioned it as one of the priorities of his administration. . . . He appointed a friend, Eli Segal, to run a new Office of National Service, and Segal set to work. . . . The administration's efforts led to passage of the National and Community Service Trust Act . . . in . . . 1993. One year later, "AmeriCorps" would be officially launched. Segal took charge of orchestrating a major public relations event which would feature President Clinton swearing in 9,000 AmeriCorps volunteers at sixteen sites around the country by satellite hook-up. . . . Segal looked forward to a triumphant day on the South Lawn of the White House followed by extensive, favorable news coverage. At 4.30 a.m. on the morning of the ceremony, Segal's phone rang. The event as planned would have to be scrapped. Why? Because at that hour a deranged pilot crashed his Cessna aircraft into the back of the White House precisely on the spot where the ceremony was to be staged. The news media predictably went gaga over this bizarre and unprecedented event and could scarcely be bothered by the launching of AmeriCorps—no doubt more important than the plane crash, but infinitely more routine.

Social scientists insist that most news is produced by Eli Segals, not deranged pilots. Quantitatively, they are right; the vast majority of daily news items on television or in print come from planned, intentional events, press releases, press conferences, and scheduled interviews. Even so, journalists find their joy and their identity in the adrenalin rush that comes only from deranged pilots, hurricanes, upset victories in baseball or politics, triumphs against all odds, tragedy or reversal in the lap of luxury, and other unplanned and unanticipated scandals, accidents, mishaps, gaffes, embarrassments, and wonders. The scholars delight in revealing how much of the news is produced by the best-laid plans of government officials who maneuver news to their own purposes; the journalists enjoy being first to the scene when the best-laid plans go awry. . . .

Journalists make their own stories but not from materials they have personally selected. Materials are thrust upon them. It can even be argued, as Regina Lawrence has, that in recent years news has become more event-driven and less institution-driven. Moreover, the news media take events not as ends in themselves but as "jumping-off points for thematic exploration of social issues." Content analysis of news over the past 100 years indicates journalists pay increasing attention to context, to reporting events in detail especially when they serve as "invitations for the news media to grapple, however gracefully or clumsily, with political and social issues." This preoccupation with unpredictable events keeps something uncontrollable at the forefront of journalism. The archetypal news story, the kind that makes a career, the sort every reporter longs for, is one that is unroutinized and unrehearsed. It gives journalism its recurrent anarchic potential. And it is built into the very bloodstream of news organizations, it is the circulatory system that keeps the enterprise oxygenated.

The AmeriCorps incident does not show that journalism's passion for events aids democracy; in fact, the story displaced was probably more vital to informing a self-governing public than the story that captured the journalists' attention. But the case still shows that official efforts to play the media can be decisively trumped by startling, unprecedented events. All the media consultants and handlers in the world cannot prevent this—and *that* is what serves democracy, the irresistible drive of journalists to focus on events, including those that powerful forces cannot anticipate and often cannot manage.

Conflict

Almost all journalists relish conflict. Almost all media criticism attacks journalists for emphasizing conflict. But conflict, like events, provides a recurrent resource for embarrassing the powerful.

Consider a story by Randal C. Archibold that appeared in the *New York Times* on January 11, 2003 with the headline: "Nuclear Plant Disaster Plan Is Inadequate, Report Says." To summarize, New York Governor George Pataki had commissioned a report on safety at the Indian Point nuclear power plant just 35 miles away from midtown Manhattan. The report was produced by a consulting group the governor hired, Witt Associates. James Lee Witt, its chief executive, was formerly the director of the Federal Emergency Management Agency. So journalists knew the report was being written, knew its chief author was a high-ranking former federal official, knew roughly when it would appear. This sounds like the kind of government-centered "official" news story critics complain about.

But is it? Why did Governor Pataki commission the report? Clearly, he commissioned it after the September 11 terrorist attack made more urgent the concerns that citizens and citizens' groups had already expressed about the safety of the Indian Point nuclear reactor. The plant's safety became a major local political issue in 2000 when a small leak forced the plant to shut down for nearly a year. So an event—a leak at the plant—spawned political mobilization; lively political mobilization plus September 11, another event, made it necessary for the governor to at least make a show of doing something. September 11 further mobilized opposition to the plant, particularly because one of the hijacked jets flew very close to it en route to the World Trade Center. Governor Pataki finally commissioned the report in August 2002 "in response to the rising outcry over safety at the plant." The Witt Report . . . declared that the disaster preparedness plan was inadequate for protecting people from unacceptable levels of radiation in case of a release at the plant. . . .

The Witt Report became news not because the governor's office generated it, but because the governor acted in the face of raging controversy. The continuing controversy made the story news and made the news story interesting. In the end, the report obviously gives legitimacy to the environmentalists and others who had urged that Indian Point be shut down. The news story helped keep opponents of government policy alert, encouraged, and legitimated.

Skepticism about Politicians

Political reporters have increasingly made it a point not only to report the statements and actions of leading public officials but to report on the motives behind the actions as well as they can. They report not only the show and the dazzle that the politician wants foregrounded, but the efforts that go into the show and the calculations behind them. They do not intend to under-cut the politicians, but they do intend not to be manipulated. The result is a portrait of politicians as self-interested, cynically manipulative, and contemp-tuous of the general public.

Take, for instance, the *New York Times'* April 16, 2003, front-page story on the proposed Bush tax cut, "In a Concession, Bush Lowers Goal of Tax Cut Plan." The story began curtly observing that President Bush lowered his target for a tax cut in a tacit admission that his original package was "dead." Then reporter Elisabeth Bumiller cites White House advisers who said "that they were now on a war footing with Capitol Hill" to pass the biggest tax cut they could. They, along with other Republican strategists, said "it was imperative for Mr. Bush to be seen as fighting hard for the economy to avoid the fate of his father, who lost the White House after his victory in the 1991 Persian Gulf war in large part because voters viewed him as disengaged from domes-tic concerns." The orientation of the story was to the timing and style of the president's speech on the economy, not to its substance. The background—strategy and image—is the foreground. This kind of a story, once exceptional, has become standard.

At the end of September 2003, Laura Bush went to Paris as part of the cer-emonies signaling the American re-entry to UNESCO after a boycott of nearly two decades. The First Lady's trip was, of course, a well-planned public rela-tions gesture. Would anyone have suspected otherwise? But Elaine Sciolino, the *Times'* veteran foreign correspondent and chief Paris correspondent, made a point of it, noting that Mrs. Bush did not face the American flag as the American national anthem was sung: "Instead, she stood perpendicular to it, enabling photographers to capture her in profile, with the flag and the Eiffel Tower behind. The scene was carefully planned for days by a White House advance team, much to the amusement of longtime UNESCO employees.

Reporting of this sort—showing the president or in this case his wife as performers putting on their makeup—is a sign of a free press. A particularly dramatic example was the decision of *Time* magazine to run, as its October 6, 2003, cover, the carefully staged and widely celebrated photograph of Presi-dent Bush, attired in a flight jacket and standing on the deck of an aircraft carrier in early May. Behind the president was the much-discussed banner that boldly proclaimed, "Mission Accomplished," signaling the victorious end of the Iraq war. But the prematurely declared end of the war unraveled in the next months and now the magazine provided its own emphatic headline: "MISSION NOT ACCOMPLISHED."

This kind of reporting may not be a sign of a press that motivates or mobilizes or turns people into good citizens. It may do more to reinforce political apathy than to refurbish political will. But it may be just what democracy requires.

Outsider News

Why was Trent Lott forced out of his post as majority leader of the US Senate? The answer is that, on December 5, 2002, he made remarks at Senator Strom Thurmond's 100th birthday party that suggested Americans would all be better off if Senator Thurmond, running on a segregationist platform for the presidency in 1948, had won the election. The room apparently was full of politicians and journalists, none of whom immediately caught the significance of the remark. It was all part of the general celebration of the extraordinary event of a 100th birthday party for the man who had served in the Senate longer than any other person in American history. No one objected to or even noticed the over-the-top encomium that could at best have been interpreted as thoughtless but, if it was judged to have any real content at all, would have to have been viewed as racist.

But if no one noticed, how did it become news and force Lott's resignation from his leadership post?

The first part of the answer is that several practitioners of then still novel "blogs" . . . took note of Lott's remarks, including several prominent and widely read bloggers. These included Joshua Marshall (at talkingpointsmemo.com), Timothy Noah (at slate.com), and Andrew Sullivan (at AndrewSullivan.com)—all three of them journalists. Noah and Sullivan were once employed by (and in Sullivan's case served as editor of) the *New Republic*. Marshall had worked for the *American Prospect*. Although mainstream press outlets, both print and broadcast, noted the remarks (and C-SPAN had aired them), the bloggers pressed the fact that Thurmond ran as a segregationist and that Lott had taken many conservative stands through the years, including speaking before white supremacist groups and voting against the Civil Rights Act of 1990. Matt Drudge, in his on-line report, even found that Senator Lott had made an almost identical statement in praise of Thurmond in 1980.

Thanks to the "blogosphere," the party that Senator Lott and nearly everyone else present regarded as an insider event was available for outsider news. Moreover, as Heather Gorgura argues, the bloggers succeeded in getting the "dump Lott" bandwagon moving not simply by pointing out an indiscreet remark but, in documenting Senator Lott's long and consistent history of association with organizations and policies offensive to African-Americans, by persuading mainstream journalists that Lott's remarks were not casual and thoughtless but representative of a racism Lott had repeatedly expressed and acted upon. . . .

The cyber-pamphleteers today can attract broad attention, including the attention of the old media. They do so, I might point out, by name-calling sensationalism. The most prominent and most consequential cases are those of Matt Drudge breaking the Monica Lewinsky story—"The President is an adulterer"—and the bloggers who cried, "The Senator is a racist." An unlovable press, indeed, but perhaps just what democracy requires.

Outsiders are always troublemakers. The news media are supposed to be institutionalized outsiders even though they have in fact become institutionalized insiders. There is much more that might be done to keep journalists at arm's length from their sources. This is something that journalism education could orient itself to more conscientiously—for instance, insisting that journalism students take a course in comparative politics or . . . serious US history course. . . . The idea would be to disorient rather than orient the prospective journalist. Disorientation—and ultimately alienation of journalists—helps the press to be free.

Social scientists regularly observe how much reporters have become insiders, socializing with their sources, flattered by their intimacy with the rich and powerful, dependent on intimacy for the leaks and leads officialdom can provide. All of this is true, but it is all the more reason to observe carefully and nurture those ways in which journalists remain outsiders. Bloggers, in the Trent Lott case, although journalists, took up outposts on journalism's frontier, outside conventional news organizations. But even standard-issue journalists are outsiders to the conventional opinions of government officials in several respects. For one, they advance the journalistic agenda of finding something novel that will set tongues a-flutter across a million living rooms, breakfast tables, bars, lunch rooms, and lines at Starbucks. Second, journalists have access to and professional interest in non-official sources of news. Most important of these non-official sources is public opinion as measured by polls or by informal journalistic "taking of the pulse" of public opinion. The American press in particular has a populist streak that inclines it toward a sampling of civilian views. A front page story in the April 24, 2003, *Chicago Tribune,* for instance, by Jill Zuckman, the *Tribune*'s chief Congressional correspondent, and datelined Northfield, Wisconsin, was based on both national opinion polls and local interviewing of people who objected to the USA Patriot Act. . . . Feingold, not incidentally, was the only Senator to have voted against the Patriot Act.

Zuckman wanted, as she says, "to take the pulse of the voters," especially on the war in Iraq, and she thought that she would be able to sample the widest range of opinions if she traveled with a Democratic Senator during the spring recess. She ended up with Senator Feingold when she learned that he holds town meetings almost every recess and weekend in fulfillment of a campaign pledge to visit every county in the state. As it happened, the Iraq war was declared over before the town meetings began, and people had little to say about the war—but they had a surprising amount to say about their fears for domestic civil liberties. So the topic Zuckman wrote about was not what she intended to cover, but her populist instinct made it possible to report on a phenomenon that elites did not anticipate and that the administration could not have found comforting.

Conclusion

Journalists are not free agents. They are constrained by a set of complex institutional relations that lead them to reproduce day after day the opinions and views of establishment figures, especially high government officials. They are constrained by broad conventional wisdom that they are not well placed to buck and they are powerfully constrained by the conventions and routines of their own professionalism. At the same time, they are not without some resources for expanding the range of expression in the news. What are the structures that can preserve their capacity to speak freely themselves and to expand the range of voices and views they represent in their reporting? What journalistic predispositions can enable them to take advantage of their limited but real autonomy to fulfill the potential of a free press for vigorous, robust discussion of public issues? I am defending, somewhat to my surprise, what are usually attacked as the worst features of the American press—a preoccupation with events, a morbid sports-minded fascination with gladiatorial combat, a deep, anti-political cynicism, and a strong alienation of journalists from the communities they cover.

I hasten to add that the journalists I most admire get behind and beneath events, illuminate trends and structures and moods and not just conflicts, believe in the virtues and values of political life and the hopes it inspires, and feel connected and committed to their communities—global, national, or local. The journalists of greatest imagination discover the non-events that conceal their drama so well. They recognize the story in conflicts that never arose because of strong leadership or a stroke of luck, or the conflict that was resolved peacefully over a painstakingly long time without sparking a front-page "event." But I propose, nonetheless, that some of the greatest service the media provide for democracy lies in characteristics that few people regard as very nice or ennobling about the press. These features of journalism—and perhaps these features more than others—make news a valuable force in a democratic society, and this means that—if all goes well—we are saddled with a necessary institution we are not likely ever to love.

John Hockenberry

➡ **NO**

"You Don't Understand Our Audience": What I Learned About Network Television at *Dateline NBC*

T he most memorable reporting I've encountered on the conflict in Iraq was delivered in the form of confetti exploding out of a cardboard tube. I had just begun working at the MIT Media Lab in March 2006 when Alyssa Wright, a lab student, got me to participate in a project called "Cherry Blossoms." I strapped on a backpack with a pair of vertical tubes sticking out of the top; they were connected to a detonation device linked to a Global Positioning System receiver. A microprocessor in the backpack contained a program that mapped the coördinates of the city of Baghdad onto those for the city of Cambridge; it also held a database of the locations of all the civilian deaths of 2005. If I went into a part of Cambridge that corresponded to a place in Iraq where civilians had died in a bombing, the detonator was triggered.

When the backpack exploded on a clear, crisp afternoon at the Media Lab, handfuls of confetti shot out of the cardboard tubes into the air, then fell slowly to earth. On each streamer of paper was written the name of an Iraqi civilian casualty. I had reported on the war (although not from Baghdad) since 2003 and was aware of persistent controversy over the numbers of Iraqi civilian dead as reported by the U.S. government and by other sources. But it wasn't until the moment of this fake explosion that the scale and horrible suddenness of the slaughter in Baghdad became vivid and tangible to me. Alyssa described her project as an upgrade to traditional journalism. "The upgrade is empathy," she said, with the severe humility that comes when you suspect you are on to something but are still uncertain you aren't being ridiculous in some way.

The falling confetti transported me back three years to the early days of the war in Iraq, when the bombs intended to evoke "shock and awe" were descending on Baghdad. Most of the Western press had evacuated, but a small contingent remained to report on the crumbling Iraqi regime. In the New York offices of NBC News, one of my video stories was being screened. If it made it through the screening, it would be available for broadcast later that evening. Producer Geoff Stephens and I had done a phone interview with a reporter in Baghdad who was experiencing the bombing firsthand. We also had a series of still photos of life in the city. The only communication with Baghdad in those early days was by satellite phone. Still pictures were sent back over the few operating data links.

Our story arranged pictures of people coping with the bombing into a slide show, accompanied by the voice of Melinda Liu, a *Newsweek* reporter describing, over the phone, the harrowing experience of remaining in Baghdad. The outcome of the invasion was still in doubt. There was fear in the reporter's voice and on the faces of the people in the pictures. The four-minute piece was meant to be the kind of package that would run at the end of an hour of war coverage. Such montages were often used as "enders," to break up the segments of anchors talking live to field reporters at the White House or the Pentagon, or retired generals who were paid to stand on in-studio maps and provide analysis of what was happening. It was also understood that without commercials there would need to be taped pieces on standby in case an anchor needed to use the bathroom. Four minutes was just about right.

At the conclusion of the screening, there were a few suggestions for tightening here and clarification there. Finally, an NBC/GE executive responsible for "standards" shook his head and wondered about the tone in the reporter's voice. "Doesn't it seem like she has a point of view here?" he asked.

There was silence in the screening room. It made me want to twitch, until I spoke up. I was on to something but uncertain I wasn't about to be handed my own head. "Point of view? What exactly do you mean by *point of view*?" I asked. "That war is bad? Is that the *point of view* that you are detecting here?"

The story never aired. Maybe it was overtaken by breaking news, or maybe some pundit-general went long, or maybe an anchor was able to control his or her bladder. On the other hand, perhaps it was never aired because it contradicted the story NBC was telling. At NBC that night, war was, in fact, not bad. My remark actually seemed to have made the point for the "standards" person. Empathy for the civilians did not fit into the narrative of shock and awe. The lesson stayed with me, exploding in memory along with the confetti of Alyssa Wright's "Cherry Blossoms." Alyssa was right. Empathy was the upgrade. But in the early days of the war, NBC wasn't looking for any upgrades.

"This Is London"

When Edward R. Murrow calmly said those words into a broadcast microphone during the London Blitz at the beginning of World War II, he generated an analog signal that was amplified, sent through a transatlantic cable, and relayed to transmitters that delivered his voice into millions of homes. Broadcast technology itself delivered a world-changing cultural message to a nation well convinced by George Washington's injunction to resist foreign "entanglements." Hearing Murrow's voice made Americans understand that Europe was close by, and so were its wars. Two years later, the United States entered World War II, and for a generation, broadcast technology would take Americans ever deeper into the battlefield, and even onto the surface of the moon. Communication technologies transformed America's view of itself, its politics, and its culture.

One might have thought that the television industry, with its history of rapid adaptation to technological change, would have become a center of innovation for the next radical transformation in communication. It did not. Nor did the ability to transmit pictures, voices, and stories from around the world to living rooms in the U.S. heartland produce a nation that is more sophisticated about global affairs. Instead, the United States is arguably more isolated and less educated about the world than it was a half-century ago. In a time of such broad technological change, how can this possibly be the case?

In the spring of 2005, after working in television news for 12 years, I was jettisoned from NBC News in one of the company's downsizings. The work that I and others at *Dateline NBC* had done—to explore how the Internet might create new opportunities for storytelling, new audiences, and exciting new mechanisms for the creation of journalism—had come to naught. After years of timid experiments, NBC News tacitly declared that it wasn't interested. The culmination of *Dateline*'s Internet journalism strategy was the highly rated pile of programming debris called *To Catch a Predator.* The *TCAP* formula is to post offers of sex with minors on the Internet and see whether anybody responds. *Dateline*'s notion of New Media was the technological equivalent of etching "For a good time call Sally" on a men's room stall and waiting with cameras to see if anybody copied down the number.

Networks are built on the assumption that audience size is what matters most. Content is secondary; it exists to attract passive viewers who will sit still for advertisements. For a while, that assumption served the industry well. But the TV news business has been blind to the revolution that made the viewer blink: the digital organization of communities that are anything but passive. Traditional market-driven media always attempt to treat devices, audiences, and content as bulk commodities, while users instead view all three as ways of creating and maintaining smaller-scale communities. As users acquire the means of producing and distributing content, the authority and profit potential of large traditional networks are directly challenged.

In the years since my departure from network television, I have acquired a certain detachment about how an institution so central to American culture could shift so quickly to the margins. Going from being a correspondent at *Dateline*—a rich source of material for *The Daily Show*—to working at the MIT Media Lab, where most students have no interest in or even knowledge of traditional networks, was a shock. It has given me some hard-won wisdom about the future of journalism, but it is still a mystery to me why television news remains so dissatisfying, so superficial, and so irrelevant. Disappointed veterans like Walter Cronkite and Dan Rather blame the moral failure of ratings-obsessed executives, but it's not that simple. I can say with confidence that Murrow would be outraged not so much by the networks' greed (Murrow was one of the first news personalities to hire a talent agent) as by the missed opportunity to use technology to help create a nation of engaged citizens bent on preserving their freedom and their connections to the broader world.

I knew it was pretty much over for television news when I discovered in 2003 that the heads of NBC's news division and entertainment division, the president of the network, and the chairman all owned TiVos, which enabled them to zap past the commercials that paid their salaries. "It's such a great gadget. It changed my life," one of them said at a corporate affair in the *Saturday Night Live* studio. It was neither the first nor the last time that a television executive mistook a fundamental technological change for a new gadget.

Setting the Table for *Law and Order*

On the first Sunday after the attacks of September 11, pictures of the eventual head of NBC littered the streets and stuffed the garbage cans of New York City; Jeff Zucker was profiled that week in the *New York Times Magazine.* The piles of newspapers from the weekend were everywhere at 30 Rockefeller Center. Normally, employee talk would have been about how well or badly Zucker had made out in the *Times.* But the breezy profile was plainly irrelevant that week.

The next morning I was in the office of David Corvo, the newly installed executive producer of *Dateline,* when Zucker entered to announce that the network was going to resume the prime-time schedule for the first time since the attacks. The long stretch of commercial-free programming was expensive, and Zucker was certain about one thing: "We can't sell ads around pictures of Ground Zero." At the same time, he proceeded to explain that the restoration of the prime-time shows *Friends, Will and Grace,* and *Frasier* was a part of America's return to normalcy, not a cash-flow decision. He instructed Corvo that a series of news specials would be scattered through the next few days, but as it was impossible to sell ads for them, scheduling would be a "day to day" proposition. . . .

At the moment Zucker blew in and interrupted, I had been in Corvo's office to propose a series of stories about al-Qaeda, which was just emerging as a suspect in the attacks. While well known in security circles and among journalists who tried to cover international Islamist movements, al-Qaeda as a terrorist organization and a story line was still obscure in the early days after September 11. It had occurred to me and a number of other journalists that a core mission of NBC News would now be to explain, even belatedly, the origins and significance of these organizations. But Zucker insisted that *Dateline* stay focused on the firefighters. The story of firefighters trapped in the crumbling towers, Zucker said, was the emotional center of this whole event. Corvo enthusiastically agreed. "Maybe," said Zucker, "we ought to do a series of specials on firehouses where we just ride along with our cameras. Like the show *Cops,* only with firefighters." He told Corvo he could make room in the prime-time lineup for firefighters, but then smiled at me and said, in effect, that he had no time for any subtitled interviews with jihadists raging about Palestine. . . .

This was one in a series of lessons I learned about how television news had lost its most basic journalistic instincts in its search for the audience-driven sweet spot, the "emotional center" of the American people. Gone was the mission of using technology to veer out onto the edge of American understanding in order to introduce something fundamentally new into the national debate. The informational edge was perilous, it was unpredictable, and it required the news audience to be willing to learn something it did not already know. Stories from the edge were not typically reassuring about the future. In this sense they were like actual news, unpredictable flashes from the unknown. On the other hand, the coveted emotional center was reliable, it was predictable, and its story lines could be duplicated over and over. It reassured the audience by telling it what it already knew rather than challenging it to learn. This explains why TV news voices all use similar cadences, why all anchors seem to sound alike, why reporters in the field all use the identical tone of urgency no matter whether the story is about the devastating aftermath of an earthquake or someone's lost kitty.

It also explains why TV news seems so archaic next to the advertising and entertainment content on the same networks. Among the greatest frustrations of working in TV news over the past decade was to see that while advertisers and entertainment producers were permitted to do wildly risky things in pursuit of audiences, news producers rarely ventured out of a safety zone of crime, celebrity, and character-driven tragedy yarns.

Advertisers were aggressive in their use of new technologies long before network news divisions went anywhere near them. This is exactly the opposite of the trend in the 1960s and '70s, when the news divisions were first adopters of breakthroughs in live satellite and video technology. But in the 1990s, advertisers were quick to use the Internet to seek information about consumers, exploiting the potential of communities that formed around products and brands. Throughout the time I was at the network, GE ads were all over NBC programs like *Meet the Press* and CNBC's business shows, but they seemed never to appear on *Dateline*. (They also had far higher production values than the news programs and even some entertainment shows.) Pearl Jam, Nirvana, and N.W.A. were already major cultural icons; grunge and hip-hop were the soundtrack for commercials at the moment networks were passing on stories about Kurt Cobain's suicide and Tupac Shakur's murder.

Meanwhile, on *60 Minutes,* Andy Rooney famously declared his own irrelevance by being disgusted that a spoiled Cobain could find so little to love about being a rock star that he would kill himself. Humor in commercials was hip—subtle, even, in its use of obscure pop-cultural references—but if there were any jokes at all in news stories, they were telegraphed, blunt visual gags, usually involving weathermen. That disjunction remains: at the precise moment that Apple cast John Hodgman and Justin Long as dead-on avatars of the PC and the Mac, news anchors on networks that ran those ads were introducing people to multibillion-dollar phenomena like MySpace and Facebook with the cringingly naïve attitude of "What will those nerds think of next?"

Entertainment programs often took on issues that would never fly on *Dateline*. On a Thursday night, *ER* could do a story line on the medically uninsured, but a night later, such a "downer policy story" was a much harder sell. In the time I was at NBC, you were more likely to hear federal agriculture policy discussed on *The West Wing*, or even on Jon Stewart, than you were to see it reported in any depth on *Dateline*.

Sometimes entertainment actually drove selection of news stories. Since *Dateline* was the lead-in to the hit series *Law & Order* on Friday nights, it was understood that on Fridays we did crime. Sunday was a little looser but still a hard sell for news that wasn't obvious or close to the all-important emotional center. In 2003, I was told that a story on the emergence from prison of a former member of the Weather Underground, whose son had graduated from Yale University and won a Rhodes Scholarship, would not fly unless it dovetailed with a storyline on a then-struggling, soon-to-be-cancelled, and now-forgotten Sunday-night drama called *American Dreams,* which was set in the 1960s. I was told that the Weather Underground story might be viable if *American Dreams* did an episode on "protesters or something." At the time, *Dateline's* priority was another series of specials about the late Princess Diana. This blockbuster was going to blow the lid off the Diana affair and deliver the shocking revelation that the poor princess was in fact even more miserable being married to Prince Charles than we all suspected. Diana's emotional center was coveted in prime time even though its relevance to anything going on in 2003 was surely out on some voyeuristic fringe.

To get airtime, not only did serious news have to audition against the travails of Diana or a new book by Dr. Phil, but it also had to satisfy bizarre conditions. In 2003, one of our producers obtained from a trial lawyer in Connecticut video footage of guards subduing a mentally ill prisoner. Guards themselves took the footage as part of a safety program to ensure that deadly force was avoided and abuses were documented for official review. We saw guards haul the prisoner down a greenish corridor, then heard hysterical screaming as the guard shooting the video dispassionately announced, "The prisoner is resisting." For 90 seconds several guards pressed the inmate into a bunk. All that could be seen of him was his feet. By the end of the video the inmate was motionless. Asphyxiation would be the official cause of death.

This kind of gruesome video was rare. We also had footage of raw and moving interviews with this and another victim's relatives. The story had the added relevance that one of the state prison officials had been hired as a consultant to the prison authority in Iraq as the Abu Ghraib debacle was unfolding. There didn't seem to be much doubt about either the newsworthiness or the topicality of the story. Yet at the conclusion of the screening, the senior producer shook his head as though the story had missed the mark widely. "These inmates aren't necessarily sympathetic to our audience," he said. The fact that they had been diagnosed with schizophrenia was unimportant. Worse, he said that as he watched the video of the dying inmate, it didn't seem as if anything was wrong.

"Except that the inmate died," I offered.

"But that's not what it looks like. All you can see is his feet."

"With all those guards on top of him."

"Sure, but he just looks like he's being restrained."

"But," I pleaded, "the man died. That's just a fact. The prison guards shot this footage, and I don't think their idea was to get it on *Dateline.*"

"Look," the producer said sharply, "in an era when most of our audience has seen the Rodney King video, where you can clearly see someone being beaten, this just doesn't hold up."

"Rodney King wasn't a prisoner," I appealed. "He didn't die, and this mentally ill inmate is not auditioning to be the next Rodney King. These are the actual pictures of his death."

"You don't understand our audience."

"I'm not trying to understand our audience," I said. I was getting pretty heated at this point—always a bad idea. "I'm doing a story on the abuse of mentally ill inmates in Connecticut."

"You don't get it," he said, shaking his head.

The story aired many months later, at less than its original length, between stories that apparently reflected a better understanding of the audience. During my time at *Dateline,* I did plenty of stories that led the broadcast and many full hours that were heavily promoted on the network. But few if any of my stories were more tragic, or more significant in news value, than this investigation into the Connecticut prison system.

Networks have so completely abandoned the mission of reporting the news that someone like entrepreneur Charles Ferguson, who sold an Internet software company to Microsoft in 1996 . . . can spend $2 million of his own money to make an utterly unadorned documentary about Iraq and see it become an indie hit. Ferguson's *No End in Sight* simply lays out, without any emotional digressions or narrative froth, how the U.S. military missed the growing insurgency. The straightforward questions and answers posed by this film are so rare in network news today that they seem like an exotic, innovative form of cinema, although they're techniques that belong to the Murrow era. In its way, Ferguson's film is as devastating an indictment of network television as it is of the Bush administration. . . .

Six Sigma in the Newsroom

Perhaps the biggest change to the practice of journalism in the time I was at NBC was the absorption of the news division into the pervasive and all-consuming corporate culture of GE. GE had acquired NBC back in 1986, when it bought RCA. By 2003, GE's managers and strategists were getting around to seeing whether the same tactics that made the production of turbine generators more efficient could improve the production of television news. This had some truly bizarre consequences. To say that this *Dateline* correspondent with the messy corner office greeted these internal corporate changes with self-destructive skepticism is probably an understatement.

Six Sigma—the methodology for the improvement of business processes that strives for 3.4 defects or fewer per million opportunities—was a somewhat mysterious symbol of management authority at every GE division. Six Sigma messages popped up on the screens of computers or in e-mail in-boxes every day. Six Sigma was out there, coming, unstoppable, like a comet or rural electrification. . . .

While Six Sigma's goal-oriented blather and obsession with measuring everything was jarring, it was also weirdly familiar, inasmuch as it was strikingly reminiscent of my college Maoism I class. Mao seemed to be a good model for Jack Welch and his Six Sigma foot soldiers; Six Sigma's "Champions" and "Black Belts" were Mao's "Cadres" and "Squad Leaders."

Finding such comparisons was how I kept from slipping into a coma during dozens of NBC employee training sessions where we were told not to march in political demonstrations of any kind, not to take gifts from anyone, and not to give gifts to anyone. At mandatory, hours-long "ethics training" meetings we would watch in-house videos that brought all the drama and depth of a driver's-education film to stories of smiling, swaggering employees (bad) who bought cases of wine for business associates on their expense accounts, while the thoughtful, cautious employees (good) never picked up a check, but volunteered to stay at the Red Roof Inn in pursuit of "shareholder value."

To me, the term "shareholder value" sounded like Mao's "right path," although this was not something I shared at the employee reëducation meetings. As funny as it seemed to me, the idea that GE was a multinational corporate front for Maoism was not a very widespread or popular view around NBC. It was best if any theory that didn't come straight from the NBC employee manual (a Talmudic tome that largely contained rules for using the GE credit card, most of which boiled down to "Don't") remained private.

I did, however, point out to the corporate-integrity people unhelpful details about how NBC News was covering wars in Iraq and Afghanistan that our GE parent company stood to benefit from as a major defense contractor. I wondered aloud, in the presence of an integrity "team leader," how we were to reconcile this larger-scale conflict with the admonitions about free dinners. "You make an interesting point I had not thought of before," he told me. "But I don't know how GE being a defense contractor is really relevant to the way we do our jobs here at NBC news." Integrity, I guess, doesn't scale.

Other members of the "GE family" had similar doubts about their relevance to the news division. In early 2002, our team was in Saudi Arabia covering regional reaction to September 11. We spent time on the streets and found considerable sympathy for Osama bin Laden among common citizens at the same time that the Saudi government expressed frustration that Americans seemed not to consider it an ally in the war on terror. We tracked down relatives of the September 11 hijackers, some of whom were deeply shocked and upset to learn what their family members had done. We wanted to speak with members of Osama bin Laden's family about their errant son's mission to bring down the Saudi government and attack the infidel West. We couldn't reach the bin Ladens using ordinary means, and the royal family claimed that it had no real clout with the multibillion-dollar bin Laden construction giant that built mosques, roads, and other infrastructure all over the world.

But GE had long done business with the bin Ladens. In a misguided attempt at corporate synergy, I called GE headquarters in Fairfield, CT, from my hotel room in Riyadh. . . . Within a few hours I received a call in my hotel room from a senior corporate communications officer who would only read a statement over the phone. It said something to the effect that GE had an important, long-standing, and valuable business relationship with the Bin Laden Group and saw no connection between that relationship and what *Dateline* was trying to do in Saudi Arabia. He wished us well. We spoke with no bin Laden family member on that trip.

In the end, perhaps the work that I was most proud of at NBC marginalized me within the organization and was my undoing. I had done some of the first live Internet audio and video webcasts on MSNBC. I anchored live Web broadcasts from the political conventions in 2000 when such coverage was just beginning. I helped produce live interactive stories for *Dateline* where the audience could vote during commercial breaks on how a crime mystery or a hostage situation would turn out. I loved what we could do through the fusion of TV and the Internet. During one interactive broadcast, I reported the instant returns from audience surveys live in the studio, with different results for each time zone as *Dateline* was broadcast across the country. . . .

When I got the word that I'd been axed, I was in the middle of two projects that employed new media technology. In the first, we went virtually undercover to investigate the so-called Nigerian scammers who troll for the gullible with (often grammatically questionable) hard-luck stories and bogus promises of hidden millions. We descended into the scammers' world as a way of chasing them down and also illustrating how the Internet economy works. With search techniques and tracing strategies that reveal how Internet traffic is numerically coded, we chased a team of con artists to a hotel in Montreal, where we nailed them on hidden camera. With me playing the patsy, the story showed, in a very entertaining and interesting way, how the mechanics of the Internet worked to assist criminals. The second story unearthed someone who spammed people with porn e-mails. It was a form of direct-mail advertising that paid decent money if you had the right e-mail lists. The spammers didn't get involved with the porn itself; they just traded in e-mail lists and hid behind their digital anonymity. We exposed one of these spammers and had him apologize on camera, without spectacle, to a Dallas housewife to whom he had sent hard-core e-mails. The story wasn't merely about porn and spammers; it showed how electronic media gave rise to offshore shadow companies that traded e-mail lists on a small but very effective scale. The drama in the story was in seeing how we could penetrate spammers' anonymity with savvy and tenacity while educating people about technology at the same time. It was admittedly a timid effort that suggested the barest glimpse of new media's potential, but it was something.

Dateline started out interested but in the end concluded that "it looks like you are having too much fun here." David Corvo asked us to go shoot interviews of random people morally outraged by pornographic e-mails to "make it clear who the bad guys are." As might have been predicted, he was sending us back to find the emotional center after journalistic reality, once again, had botched the audition. I had long since cleaned out my office when the stories finally aired. *Dateline* eventually found the emotional center with *To Catch a Predator,* which had very little to do with Internet technology beyond 1990s-era chat rooms. What it did have was a supercharged sense of who the bad guys were (the upgrade for my spammer's simple apology was having the exposed predators hauled off to jail on camera) and a superhero in the form of grim reaper Chris Hansen, who was now a star.

I moved on. My story for *Wired* on bloggers from the Iraq War landed me an appearance on *The Daily Show.* Jon Stewart bluntly asked me what it's like to be at *Dateline* for nine years: "Does it begin to rot you from the inside?" The audience seemed not entirely convinced that this was a joke. They were actually interested in my answer, as though I were announcing the results of a medical study with wide implications for human health. I had to think about this rotting-from-the-inside business. I dodged the question, possibly because it was the one I had been asking myself for most of those nine years. But the answer is that I managed not to rot.

Life at the Media Lab has reminded me once again that technology is most exciting when it upsets the status quo. Big-screen TVs and downloadable episodes of *Late Night with Conan O'Brien* are merely more attempts to control the means of distribution, something GE has been doing since the invention of the light bulb. But exploding GPS backpacks represent an alien mind-set; they are part of the growing media insurgency that is redefining news, journalism, and civic life. This technological insurgency shouldn't surprise us: after all, it's wrapped up in language itself, which has long defied any attempt to commodify it. Technology, as it has done through the ages, is freeing communication, and this is good news for the news. A little empathy couldn't hurt.

POSTSCRIPT

Can Media Regain Public Trust?

With the proliferation of media "news" voices, the issue of public trust becomes more difficult to understand. Part of the problem is the burgeoning diversity of voices that could claim to be part of "the press." What outlets are people referencing when they say that the press does not deal fairly with all sides of an issue? Do they mean network news, their local newspaper, the variety of cable news channels, Rush Limbaugh, *The Onion*? With the advent of partisan press outlets, of course, the "news" doesn't deal fairly with all sides. Some outlets are known for their particular point of view and make no claim of balanced coverage.

An international group prepared a statement "In Defense of Journalism as a Public Trust" (search Poynter.org under that title for the full announcement). The group concluded that market pressures are undermining journalism to the detriment of the public interest. They conclude with the strong statement that "It is this fundamental role of the press to inform and empower citizens that is being endangered."

Questions of this sort are studied within normative theories of mass communication. Normative theory asks about ideal ways to structure and operate news systems. We talk about freedom of the press in Issue 11. A group called the Hutchins Commission on Freedom of the Press released a report in 1947 that has become known as the introduction of the social responsibility theory of the press. A few of the principles of that report were that media (1) had certain obligations to society, (2) which obligations were to be met by setting high professional standards of informativeness, truth, accuracy, objectivity, and balance, and that (3) journalists should be accountable to society as well as to their employers. This general perspective is sometimes communicated by the brief phrase, "with rights come obligations." How does the current media system do at fulfilling these goals?

One of the most prominent current answers to the question of public trust is user content. The Internet is a massive social experiment in grassroots communication. Whether information is provided by users to professional outlets or whether individuals develop their own blog or post their political and social commentary on YouTube, the public has greater access to media than ever before. Some feel that this has opened up the process of "news" perhaps even to the point that professional news media outlets are no longer needed. Others worry that opinion and rumor have taken the place of considered analysis.

There are a number of organizations that monitor the performance of the media. Two that you might find interesting are www.fair.org and www.cjr.org. For two classic books on press performance theory, explore Bennett's 1988 *News: The Politics of Illusion* and Tuchman's 1978 *Making News: A Study in the Construction of Reality.*

ds with second-hand information that is central to
reality (Ball-Rokeach, 1998). Such media effects on
as well as behaviors, are more likely when media serve
unction (Ball-Rokeach, 1998; DeFleur & Ball-Rokeach,
t or necessity, we incorporate the media system as a
erstanding, then the media system takes on a certain
ow we think, feel, and act" (DeFleur & Ball-Rokeach,

rmation, in particular, most people have very little direct
ns and get most of their political information from the
ency theory suggests, then, that it is critically important
ent of mediated political communication as such infor-
used as the basis for political knowledge, attitudes, and
minations should, of course, include traditional sources
people have relied for decades for political information,
t television networks' nightly newscasts. But media depen-
sts it is also critical to examine emerging and increasingly
d sources of political information, as media dependencies
e a function of expectations about the potential utility of
(DeFleur & Ball-Rokeach, 1989). Given the growing number
ho say they expect *The Daily Show with Jon Stewart* to fulfill
ormation needs, it begs the question as to whether those
sfied with that show as well as they can be with more tradi-
news coverage of political information.

Show with Jon Stewart as a Source
gn Information

million under-30 voters cast their ballots in the 2004 presiden-
arking the highest voter turnout for that age group in more
(Fleischer, 2004; "Under-30," 2004). As voter turnout among
increased, news sources of political information for these vot-
ay from the broadcast television networks and toward comedy
h as *The Daily Show with Jon Stewart*. Specifically, a Pew Research
a) nationwide survey found the percentage of under-30 respon-
who said they relied regularly upon comedy shows such as *The
with Jon Stewart* for campaign information was the same as the
f under-30 respondents (23%) who said they regularly relied upon
n networks' evening news for campaign information. The percent-
r-30 respondents who said they relied on comedy shows for cam-
mation is more than double the percentage found in a similar Pew
000 (9%), while the percentage of under-30 voters who regularly
roadcast network news declined to almost half of what was found in
) (Pew Research Center, 2004a). Furthermore, television ratings dur-
wa Caucus, New Hampshire primary, and State of the Union address
re male viewers in the 18- to 34-year-old demographic watched *The
w with Jon Stewart* than network news ("Young America's," 2004).

ISSUE 9

Does Fake News Mislead the Public?

YES: Julia R. Fox, Glory Koloen, and Volkan Sahin, from "No Joke: A Comparison of Substance in *The Daily Show with Jon Stewart* and Broadcast Network Television Coverage of the 2004 Presidential Election Campaign," *Journal of Broadcasting & Electronic Media* (June 2007)

NO: Barry A. Hollander, from "Late-Night Learning: Do Entertainment Programs Increase Political Campaign Knowledge for Young Viewers?" *Journal of Broadcasting & Electronic Media* (December 2005)

ISSUE SUMMARY

YES: This study examined political coverage of the first presidential debate and the political convention on *The Daily Show* and on network nightly newscasts. The study found the network coverage to be more hype than substance, and *The Daily Show* to be more humor than substance. The amount of substantive information between the two newscasts was about the same for both the story and for the entire half-hour program.

NO: Barry Hollander examined learning from comedy and late-night programs. National survey data were used to examine whether exposure to comedy and late-night programs actually inform viewers, focusing on recall and recognition. Some support is found for the prediction that the consumption of such programs is more associated with recognition of information than with actual recall.

T raditionally journalism has been defined as what appears in newspapers, newsmagazines, and electronic media news programming. In the age of the Internet, simple "medium-based" descriptions of news are no longer accurate. Shifting trends in media usage see young voters turning to comedic sources for information, rather than traditional media. Programs such as *The Daily Show with Jon Stewart* are cited by youth as among the most important sources of political information.

If an enlightened citizenry is one of the foundations of a successful democracy, what are the consequences of this shift for an informed electorate? In *Tuned Out: Why Americans Under 40 Don't Follow the News,* David Mindich notes that fewer than 20 per cent of youth read a newspaper daily. While television news has an average viewer age near 60, the Pew Center for the People and the Press report on the fragmented political universe of 2004, noting that television is still the public's—including youth's—main source of campaign news. Nontraditional and Internet sources are on the rise, but are still not the major news source for youth. Within the age group 18–29, 27 per cent reported that they got *no* news yesterday.

This generational shift in declining audience is matched with a decline in average political awareness according to Mindich. Younger citizens have lower rates of news and current affairs awareness. In addition to knowing less, this group cares less, votes less, and follows the news less than their elders. Additionally, youth are less likely to trust political systems, or believe that they can have an influence. If it is true as believed by many in the media industries, that in their adult years individuals will follow the media patterns of their youth, the decline in newspapers and traditional television newscasts will certainly continue. The 2004 Pew Report finds, however, that the most knowledgeable Americans were those who use the Internet (primarily using Web-based versions of traditional media sites), listeners of National Public Radio, and readers of newsmagazines. By comparison, the least knowledgeable Americans got their news from comedy and late-night TV shows, more often viewed by youth. The effects of advocacy journalism on television are being felt in that about 40 per cent of the public believe that news is biased in favor of one of the two parties. This is matched by the 40 per cent who say there is no bias.

These confusing trends should not obscure the improved youth voter turnout of 2004. In "No Joke," Fox, Koloen, and Sahin compare the substantive information in network newscasts with substantive information in *The Daily Show with Jon Stewart*. Their surprising conclusion is that level of substance is remarkably similar across the shows. Perhaps the shift to comedic news will begin to engage viewers who would not be involved without the humor and skepticism of fake news.

Hollander wonders what we learn from fake news. His question is simple: Does late-night and comedic news exposure actually inform viewers? He distinguishes between recall and recognition memory. Recognition memory is the less demanding measure, asking to recognize some fact or person from a list. Recall would ask the respondent to simply know the answer. Hollander found the consumption of comedic viewers to be more related to recognition than to recall.

Journalism functions to maintain the level of knowledge and involvement necessary for a democracy. In this increasingly diverse world of media forms, what is the implication of fake news for journalism and for democracy?

YES ⬅

The 2004 elections saw
than a decade ("Election *T*
important in the political p
particular, young voters are t
tion, rather than more traditi
What are the implications of t
presumption that a successful
(Williams & Edy, 1999)? Can a
informative as traditional politi
requires multiple studies address
date there has been little scholar
tion of how comedic television m
sion news messages as sources of su
begins to address the questions raise
paring *The Daily Show with Jon Stewa*
casts as sources of political campaign
compare the quality and quantity of
provided by *The Daily Show with Jon Stew*

Media Dependency Theor

Communication scholars have long cons
the world to be a central function of
Lippmann, 1921; Price & Roberts, 1987;
writings in this area, Lippmann (1921) not
of the world outside are based on informati
larly for the world beyond one's direct experie
Ball-Rokeach (1989) define this relationship w
based on goals and resources. According to t
media control information resources that are imp
as goals of social understanding (Ball-Rokeach,
1989). For issues and events outside of direct expe
needed to create social meaning, which creates a

Media can fill those vo
constructions of social
knowledge and beliefs,
a central information f
1989). "If, out of habi
major vehicle for und
power to influence h
1989, p. 316).

For political info
contact with politicia
media. Media depend
to examine the cont
mation may well be
behaviors. Such exa
of news on which
such as the broadca
dency theory sugge
important mediate
are considered to
the media content
of young voters w
their political in
needs can be sati
tional television

The Daily
of Campa

More than 20
tial election, n
than 12 years
this age grou
ers shifted aw
programs suc
Center (2004
dents (21%)
Daily Show
percentage o
the televisio
age of und
paign infor
study in 2
relied on t
2000 (39%
ing the Io
found m
Daily Sho

Despite the growing reliance in recent years among young voters on comedy programs for campaign information, there has been precious little systematic examination of this information source, and no published systematic comparison of substantive political coverage in *The Daily Show with Jon Stewart* with traditional television newscasts. In discussing whether or not *The Daily Show with Jon Stewart* should be considered real "news," McKain (2005) describes how the format and formal structural features (e.g. "live" reports) of *The Daily Show with Jon Stewart* mimic those of traditional television newscasts. He also discusses how much of *The Daily Show with Jon Stewart* focuses on skewering broadcast and cable network television news coverage of politics as well as politicians' efforts to spin that coverage. McKain goes so far as to consider whether those who only get their news from *The Daily Show with Jon Stewart* will "get" the jokes without benefit of learning factual information first from traditional news sources. And, he points out that, occasionally, content first presented on *The Daily Show with Jon Stewart*, notably John Edwards announcing his candidacy on the show, is later covered as legitimate news by traditional news outlets. But McKain never makes a direct comparison between the substantive political content presented on *The Daily Show with Jon Stewart* and on more traditional television newscasts.

What would such a comparison find? First, the sources must be considered separately in terms of their substantive political content. Concerning the relative amount of substantive political information presented on *The Daily Show with Jon Stewart*, it seems somewhat obvious that a systematic analysis is likely to find considerably more humorous content than substantive political information on the show. While *The Daily Show with Jon Stewart* was nominated for a Television Critics Association award for "Outstanding Achievement in News and Information" in 2003 and in 2005 and won the award in 2004 ("Comedy Central's," 2003; "The Daily Show's," 2005), Stewart insists that he is a comedian, not a journalist, and that his program is a comedy show, not a newscast (Armour, 2005; Davies, 2005; Gilbert, 2004; "*The Jon Stewart*," 2004). Thus, this study predicts:

> H_1: Both the video and audio emphasis in *The Daily Show with Jon Stewart* will be on humor rather than substance.

The question remains, however, as to how this new source of political information will stack up to more traditional sources of television news as far as substantive political information is concerned.

Broadcast Television Network News as a Source of Campaign Information

Broadcast television networks were American's primary source of news and information about presidential elections for much of the second half of the 20th century (Baker & Dessart, 1998; "Despite Uncertain," 2000; Fox, Angelini, & Goble, 2005; Graber, 1993; Pew Research Center, 2002). In 2000, cable television news sources surpassed the broadcast television networks' as the primary source of political campaign information ("Despite Uncertain," 2000). Still, there are a number of compelling reasons to compare coverage of the most recent presidential election presented on the broadcast television networks and on *The Daily Show with Jon Stewart*.

First, the trend found in the Pew (2004a) study findings suggests that broadcast network news is being supplanted by comedy programs as a regular source of campaign information for young adults. Furthermore, the broadcast network newscasts still have millions more viewers than cable and still draw the largest audience for a news program at a particular time (Johnson, 2004; Lazaroff, 2004). Finally, given the passing of Peter Jennings and the retirements of Tom Brokaw and Dan Rather, all within 9 months of the 2004 presidential election, this particular election campaign marks a significant historic moment in broadcast journalism, as it was the last presidential election campaign that the three long-time broadcast television network news anchors covered.

A robust finding from previous studies since the 1970s has been the emphasis on hype rather than on more substantive matters, often described in terms of issue versus image, in the broadcast television networks' coverage of presidential election campaigns (Broh, 1980, 1983; Clancey & Robinson, 1985; Farnsworth & Lichter, 2003; Fox et al., 2005; Graber, 1976, 1980; Hofstetter, 1981; Lichter, Amundson, & Noyes, 1988; Lichter & Lichter, 1996; Patterson, 1977, 1980; Patterson & McClure, 1976). For example, an examination of the final 2 weeks of network coverage of the 1988, 1992, 1996, and 2000 election campaigns found the emphasis to be on horse race and hoopla rather than on campaign issues and candidate qualifications (Fox et al., 2005). While that study specifically examined the final 2 weeks of campaign coverage, other studies examining a longer period, for example from the traditional start of the general campaign after Labor Day, have found a similar emphasis on horse race over more substantive coverage during those years (Farnsworth & Lichter, 2003; Lichter & Lichter, 1996).

Given the lack of substantive coverage found in previous studies, this study is expected to replicate those findings. Specifically:

H_2: The video and audio emphasis in the broadcast network newscasts will be on hype rather than substance.

The bigger question posed here is whether there will be more substance in the broadcast television networks' coverage or in *The Daily Show with Jon Stewart*'s coverage. Given the long-established emphasis on hype rather than substance in television network campaign coverage, it is not at all clear whether a carefully conducted content analysis would find broadcast television network coverage to be more substantive than coverage on *The Daily Show with Jon Stewart*. While Stewart is the first to say that his program is a comedy show and not a news show (Davies, 2005; "*The Jon Stewart*," 2004), instances such as his telling the hosts of CNN's *Crossfire* that their show was hurting America and telling the host of NPR's *Fresh Air* that, in asking probing questions, he's doing what journalists often don't do clearly show his interest in substantive reporting (Cook, 2004; Davies, 2005; Ryan, 2005). Thus, this study poses the following research question:

> RQ[1]: Will there be more substance in the video and audio of the broadcast television networks' coverage than in the video and audio of *The Daily Show with Jon Stewart*'s coverage of the 2004 presidential election?

Method

This study compares the emphasis on hype versus substance in the broadcast television networks' coverage of the first presidential debate and the Democratic and Republican conventions in 2004, the emphasis on humor versus substance in the same debate and convention coverage on *The Daily Show with Jon Stewart*, and the substantive coverage presented on *The Daily Show with Jon Stewart* and in the broadcast television networks' coverage of the first debate and the party conventions.

Debate and Convention Coverage

As noted, other studies have sampled content from the final weeks of a campaign or from the general campaign time frame to examine political news coverage (Farnsworth & Lichter, 2003; Fox et al., 2005; Lichter & Lichter, 1996). However, there is also good reason to specifically examine coverage of debates and conventions. Conventions offer the candidates a chance to present their views on what they consider to be the important issues facing the nation (Scheele, 1984; Sesno, 2001; Trent & Friedenberg, 2004) and are critically important for shoring up political bases and reaching out to independent voters (Dearin, 1997). Political conventions increase voter attention to the campaign, often through news media coverage of the conventions rather than first-hand viewing of the convention proceedings (Jamieson, Johnston, Hagen, Waldman, & Kenski, 2000). As the election draws nearer, the candidates square off in the presidential debates, giving voters an opportunity to compare the candidates and their stands on issues (Just, Crigler, & Wallach, 1990). Although much of the information presented in the debates may have been presented earlier in the campaign, many voters are just beginning to pay attention to campaign messages during late September and October, when the debates are usually held (Jamieson & Adasiewica, 2000). While debates tend to reinforce preexisting candidate preferences, they are particularly important for activating supporters and can sway undecided voters (Kraus, 1979; Lang & Lang, 1961; Lowery & DeFleur, 1983; Middleton, 1962; Ranney, 1979; Salant, 1962; Willis, 1962).

Concept Operationalization

Following a coding scheme developed in previous research (Fox et al., 2005), substantive coverage, as a meta-concept, is categorized by the concepts of campaign issues and candidate qualifications while hype, as a meta-concept, is categorized by the concepts of horse race and hoopla. Indicators of campaign issues are references to or images of issues included in the party platforms such as defense and security, the economy, the environment, education, health care, and crime. Indicators of candidate qualifications are references to or images of the candidates' experience, such as political accomplishments and political positions held. Indicators of horse race are references to or images of the campaign contest, such as who's ahead and behind in the polls, campaign strategies and tactics, and political endorsements. Indicators of hoopla are references to or images of activities and items related to campaign events and their trappings, such as photo opportunities, rallies, flag-waving, hand-shaking, baby kissing, ball throwing, crowds, balloons, and celebrities.

This study also includes categories for humor, a meta-concept categorized by the concepts of joking and laughing. Joking is indicated by funny music, silly and untrue statements, silly voices, tone of voice (sarcastic or mocking or a sudden change in pitch or volume), silly faces (raised eyebrows or a skewed, wide-open or pinched mouth), mocking faces, silly or exaggerated gestures, and obviously altered images. Laughter is indicated by sounds of laughing or chuckling, smiling, and eye crinkling.

Sampling

For the convention coverage, this study used a saturation sample by examining all newscasts from ABC's *World News Tonight with Peter Jennings*, CBS's *Evening News with Dan Rather*, and NBC's *The Nightly News with Tom Brokaw* and all *The Daily Show with Jon Stewart* programs that covered the conventions; specifically, the study examined the broadcast television networks' nightly news programs on July 26–30, August 30 and 31, and September 1–3, and *The Daily Show with Jon Stewart* on July 27–30, August 31, and September 1–3.

Only the first presidential debate is examined in this study as the second debate, a town hall-style debate held on a Friday night, was not covered by ABC's *World News Tonight with Peter Jennings*, CBS's *Evening News with Dan Rather*, and NBC's *The Nightly News with Tom Brokaw* or *The Daily Show with Jon Stewart*, nor was the third debate covered by *The Daily Show with Jon Stewart*.

Coding

Because the audio and video channels in television news stories carry separate and sometimes conflicting messages (Fox et al., 2005), this study examines the coverage in the audio and video channels separately. The coding instrument was modified from one developed in a previous study (Fox et al., 2005) to include the additional categories of joking and laughing. Nominal codings were made for network, date, study coder, and whether the story was about the presidential election. Stories coded were read by the newscast anchors or were packaged by reporters, including the anchor lead-ins to reporters' stories. Story length (in seconds) was recorded for each story in each program in the study sample. In addition, the amount of time (in seconds) in the audio and video messages devoted to horse race, hoopla, campaign issues, candidate qualifications, joking, and laughter was also coded for stories about the presidential election. Coding directions, category definitions, examples, and sample coding sheets were provided to study coders during coder training.

Reliability

When coding interval or ratio-level data, such as the number of seconds of network evening news coverage devoted to a topic, Pearson's correlation coefficient (r) is used to measure the degree to which coders vary together in their observations (Riffe, Lacy, & Fico, 1998). This study uses Pearson correlation coefficients from distances correlations, which measure similarities or dissimilarities between pairs of cases based on particular variables of interest (Fox et al., 2005; Fox & Park, 2006). Here, pairs of coders were compared for similarities in their codings of the study categories—audio horse race, audio hoopla, audio issue, audio qualifications, audio joking, audio laughing, video horse race, video hoopla, video issue, video qualifications, video joking, and video laughing. The Pearson correlation for interval data is parsimonious in that it indicates how similar two coders are on all of these variables by rendering one statistic (Fox et al., 2005; Fox & Park, 2006). But this same statistic also provides a more complete picture of coder reliability compared to other measures as it provides detailed information about where reliability problems might be occurring among the particular study coders, unlike other measures of coder reliability for multiple coders that only render one statistic for the entire group of coders (Fox et al., 2005; Fox & Park, 2006). Study coders each coded a network newscast and one program of *The Daily Show with Jon Stewart* to test coder reliability. Pearson correlation coefficients from the distances correlations indicated that the data coders had both high intercoder reliability (Pearson correlation coefficients $r = .988$ or higher) and intracoder reliability (Pearson correlation coefficients $r = .975$ or higher).

Results

An analysis of variance was run prior to analyzing the data, using network as the independent variable, to examine whether the three broadcast television networks varied significantly in their coverage of the coding categories. No significant differences were found. In addition, separate analyses for each political convention found similar emphases on hype versus substance for the broadcast networks and similar emphases on humor versus substance for *The Daily Show with Jon Stewart* for both the Democratic and the Republican conventions.

Not surprisingly, the average amounts of video [60.27] and audio [114.73] humor were significantly more than the average amounts of video [2.16] and audio [19.78] substance in *The Daily Show with Jon Stewart* stories about the presidential election.

Also as predicted, the average amounts of video [58.18] and audio [80.69] hype were significantly more than the average amounts of video [2.2] and audio [26.13] substance in the broadcast network news stories about the presidential election.

Interestingly, the average amounts of video and audio substance in the broadcast network news stories were not significantly different than the average amounts of visual and audio substance in *The Daily Show with Jon Stewart* stories about the presidential election (see Table 1).

It should be noted that the broadcast network news stories about the presidential election were significantly shorter, on average, than were *The Daily Show with Jon Stewart* stories about the presidential election. Thus, the argument could be made that while the amount of substance per story was not significantly different, the proportion of each story devoted to substance was greater in the network news stories than in stories from *The Daily Show with Jon Stewart*. On the other hand, the proportion of stories per half hour program devoted to the election campaign was greater in *The Daily Show with Jon Stewart* than in the broadcast network newscasts. Thus, the analysis was run again using the half-hour program, rather than the story, as the unit of analysis. The results showed that there was still no significant difference in the average amounts of video and audio substance per program on *The Daily Show with Jon Stewart* and on the broadcast network newscasts (see Table 2).

Table 1

Substance in the Network News and *The Daily Show with Jon Stewart* Stories

RQ1: Audio/Video Substance	Network News		*The Daily Show*		Significance Test		
	M	*SD*	*M*	*SD*	*t*	*d*	*p (two-tailed)*
Video substance	2.29	5.37	2.16	8.95	−0.11	165	*p* = .91
Audio substance	26.13	33.38	19.78	36.05	1.00	165	*p* = .32

Table 2

Substance in the Network News and *The Daily Show with Jon Stewart* Programs

RQ1: Audio/Video Substance	Network News		*The Daily Show*		Significance Test		
	M	*SD*	*M*	*SD*	*t*	*d*	*p (two-tailed)*
Story length	135.40	60.20	233.16	80.00	−8.07	165	*p* < .011
Video substance	9.03	9.33	8.89	17.13	−0.3	40	*p* = .97
Audio substance	102.94	75.59	81.33	92.63	.73	40	*p* = .47

Discussion

At first blush, the increasing reliance among young voters on comedic sources of political information appears to turn the long-held assumption of rational citizens making informed, thoughtful decisions (Noelle-Neumann, 1995; Schudson, 1995) on its ear. Not surprisingly here, in keeping with Stewart's insistence that he is a comedian not a journalist, this study found considerably more humor than substance in *The Daily Show with Jon Stewart*'s political coverage. Yet, this study also found Stewart's program to be just as substantive as the broadcast networks' campaign coverage, regardless of whether the story or the program was used as the unit of analysis. As we've known for years that the broadcast networks place substantial emphasis on insubstantial information in their political coverage, this finding is perhaps not altogether surprising, either.

Although the two sources were found here to be equally substantive, are they equally informative? There is debate among scholars as to how well soft news shows, in which *The Daily Show with Jon Stewart* is categorized by some (Baumgartner & Morris, 2006), can inform their viewers. Baum (2002, 2003) concludes from survey research that soft news may help inform an otherwise inattentive public, although Hollander's (1995) survey data found viewing late-night programs was unrelated to general knowledge about the campaign. However, Hollander's study did not specifically examine viewing of *The Daily Show with Jon Stewart*. To the contrary, the University of Pennsylvania's National Annenberg Election survey found younger viewers of *The Daily Show with Jon Stewart* answered more political questions correctly than respondents who did not watch that show ("Stewart's 'stoned slackers,'" 2004).

Experimental research may well substantiate this correlational survey data suggestion that viewers may actually process and remember substantive information presented on *The Daily Show with Jon Stewart* better than when it is presented on more serious sources of political information. When viewers see positive messages they are appetitively activated (in an approach mode toward the message) and tend to encode more information than when they are aversively activated while viewing a negative message (Fox, Park, & Lang, 2006; Lang, 2006a, 2006b; Lang, Sparks, Bradley, Lee, & Wang, 2004). Previous studies have found that political coverage is often negative. For example, media coverage of presidential debates tends to include a greater proportion of attacks and a smaller proportion of acclaims compared to the actual candidate utterances during the debates (Benoit & Currie, 2001; Reber & Benoit, 2001). Thus, traditional television news campaign stories may activate the aversive motivational system. While such coverage is clearly different than, say, gory and graphic war coverage, which would clearly activate the aversive system, studies have found physiological indications of aversive system activation for socially as well as biologically threatening information (Blanchette, 2006; Lethbridge, Simmons, & Allen, 2002; McRae, Taitano, Kaszniak, & Lane), and in some cases the contemporary social threats elicited stronger responses than their biological counterparts (Blanchette, 2006). In contrast, although *The Daily Show with Jon Stewart* may also be negative in tone, the appetitive system is likely to be activated by the humor on *The Daily Show with Jon Stewart* and by the audience's laughter, which may elicit emotional contagion (McDonald & Fredin, 2001). Additionally, the audience laughter may elicit automatic attentional responses called orienting responses that bring additional processing resources to the viewing task (Lang, 2000).

For that matter, onset of visual information on screen also elicits orienting responses (Lang, 2000). Yet, in one of the limitations of this study, only the total time during which visuals were present on screen was coded here and not the frequency of visual onsets.

Clearly, there is much more to be examined in considering the phenomenon that *The Daily Show with Jon Stewart* has become, particularly experimental research to examine differences in the ways in which viewers process and remember political information presented on that show compared to more traditional, serious television newscasts. Also, other content analyses might examine differences in tone between *The Daily Show with Jon Stewart* and more traditional news sources, for example examining whether one source is more negative or more biased toward a particular political party. Other experiments might examine the impact of that emphasis on viewer attitudes, perhaps similar to Baumgartner and Morris's (2006) examination of effects on candidate evaluations and voter efficacy, but using a broader efficacy scale than used by those authors. Studies could also examine whether younger voters may be particularly susceptible to media dependency effects from *The Daily Show with Jon Stewart*. As Sears (1986) points out, this age group, particularly at the lower end of the age range, tends to have less "crystallized" social and political attitudes than older adults (p. 521). Previous studies have found that voters who are less partisan tend to be more influenced by media than those who are more set in their views (Chaffee, 2001; Chaffee & Choe, 1980; Lazarsfeld, Berelson, & Gaudet, 1944; Mendelsohn & O'Keefe, 1975). Thus, these younger voters, with more fluid social and political attitudes, may be even more susceptible to media dependency effects than their older counterparts. Indeed, a recent analysis (Baumgartner & Morris, 2006) of Pew Center (2004b) data found viewing *The Daily Show with Jon Stewart*, which regularly skewers traditional news media coverage (McKain, 2005), was significantly related to respondents 18–25 saying they were less likely to trust what news organizations say, but the same was not true for older viewers of the show.

In the meantime, the data reported here offer the first systematic comparison of substantive information presented in campaign coverage on *The Daily Show with Jon Stewart* and more conventional television news sources of political information. The results provide valuable information on the substantive quality of this increasingly important source of campaign information for young voters. The findings should allay at least some of the concerns about the growing reliance on this nontraditional source of political information, as it is just as substantive as the source that Americans have relied upon for decades for political news and information. However, while this is true in a comparative sense, in an absolute sense neither of the sources examined here was particularly substantive, which should give pause to broadcast news executives in particular, and more generally to all politicians, citizens, and scholars concerned with the important informative function that mass media, particularly television news sources, serve in this democracy.

References

Armour, T. (2005, April 24). It's a dirty job . . . *Chicago Tribune,* sec. 7, p. 18.

Baker, W., & Dessart, G. (1998). *Down the tube: An inside account of the failure of American television.* New York: Basic Books.

Ball-Rokeach, S. (1998). A theory of media power and a theory of media use: Different stories, questions, and ways of thinking. *Mass Communication and Society,* 1(1/2), 5–40.

Baum, M. (2002). Sex, lies, and war: How soft news brings foreign policy to the inattentive public. *American Political Science Review,* 96(1), 91–109.

Baum, M. (2003). Soft news and political knowledge: Evidence of absence or absence of evidence? *Political Communication,* 20, 173–190.

Baumgartner, J., & Morris, J. (2006). "The Daily Show" effect: Candidate evaluations, efficacy, and American youth. *American Politics Research,* 34(3), 341–367.

Benoit, W. L., & Currie, H. (2001). Inaccuracies in media coverage of the 1996 and 2000 presidential debates. *Argumentation and Advocacy,* 38(1), 28–39.

Blanchette, I. (2006). Snakes, spiders, guns, and syringes: How specific are evolutionary constraints on the detection of threatening stimuli? *The Quarterly Journal of Experimental Psychology,* 59(8), 1394–1414.

Broh, C. A. (1980). Horse-race journalism: Reporting the polls in the 1976 presidential election. *Public Opinion Quarterly,* 44, 515–549.

Broh, C. A. (1983). Presidential preference polls and network news. In W. C. Adams (Ed.), *Television coverage of the 1980 presidential campaign* (pp. 29–48). Norwood: Ablex Publishing Corporation.

Chaffee, S. (2001). Studying the new communication of politics. *Political Communication,* 18, 237–244.

Chaffee, S., & Cho, S. (1980). Time of decision and media use during the Ford-Carter campaign. *Public Opinion Quarterly,* 44, 53–69.

Clancey, M., & Robinson, M. J. (1985). General election coverage: Part I. In M. Robinson & A. Ranney (Eds.), *The mass media in campaign 84: Articles from Public Opinion magazine* (pp. 27–33). Washington, DC: American Enterprise Institute for Public Policy Research.

Comedy Central's *"The Daily Show with Jon Stewart" honored with four TCA awards nominations.* (2003, June 5). . . .

Cook, J. (2004, November 24). CBS' Rather to sign off as news anchor. *Chicago Tribune,* sec. 1, pp. 1, 14.

"The Daily Show's" Jon Stewart wins prestigious TCA award. (2005, July 25). . . .

Davies, D. (Host). (2005, July 22). *Fresh Air* [Radio broadcast]. Philadelphia, PA: WHYY.

Dearin, R. D. (1997). The American dream as depicted in Robert J. Dole's 1996 presidential nomination acceptance speech. *Presidential Studies Quarterly,* 27(1), 698–711.

DeFleur, M., & Ball-Rokeach, S. (1989). *Theories of mass communication* (5th ed.). White Plains, NY: Longman, Inc.

Despite uncertain outcome campaign 2000 highly rated. (2000). Washington, DC. Retrieved July 30, 2001, from Election turnout in 2004 was highest since 1968. (2005, January 16). *Hoosier Times*, p. A6.

Farnsworth, S. J., & Lichter, S. R. (2003). *The nightly news nightmare: Network television's coverage of U.S. presidential elections, 1988–2000.* Lanham, MD: Rowman & Littlefield Publishers, Inc.

Fleischer, M. (2004, November 3). *Youth turnout up sharply in 2004* [Press release]. Washington, DC: The Center for Information & Research on Civic Learning & Engagement.

Fox, J. R. (2003). The alarm function of mass media: A critical study of "The plot against America," a special edition of NBC Nightly News with Tom Brokaw. In N. Chitty, R. Rush, & M. Semati (Eds.), *Studies in terrorism: Media scholarship and the enigma of terror* (pp. 55–71). Penang, Malaysia: Southbound (in association with the *Journal of International Communication*).

Fox, J. R., Angelini, J. R., & Goble, C. (2005). Hype versus substance in network television coverage of presidential election campaigns. *Journalism and Mass Communication Quarterly, 82*(1), 97–109.

Fox, J. R., & Park, B. (2006). The "I" of embedded reporting: An analysis of CNN coverage of the "Shock and Awe" campaign. *Journal of Broadcasting & Electronic Media, 50,* 36–51.

Fox, J. R., Park, B., & Lang, A. (2006, June). *Complicated emotional messages produce liberal bias: Effects of valence and complexity on sensitivity and criterion.* Top paper presented to the Information Systems Division at the International Communication Association annual conference, Dresden, Germany.

Gilbert, M. (2004, December 30). Pop culture swung wildly left, right in election year. *Chicago Tribune*, sec. 2, p. 2.

Graber, D. A. (1976). Press and TV as opinion resources in presidential campaigns. *Public Opinion Quarterly, 40,* 285–303.

Graber, D. A. (1980). *Mass media and American politics.* Washington, DC: Congressional Quarterly Press.

Graber, D. A. (1993). *Mass media and American politics* (4th ed.). Washington, DC: Congressional Quarterly Press.

Hofstetter, C. R. (1981). Content analysis. In D. D. Nimmo & K. R. Sanders (Eds.), *Handbook of political communication* (pp. 529–560). Beverly Hills, CA: Sage Publications.

Hollander, B. (1995). The new news and the 1992 presidential campaign: Perceived vs. actual political knowledge. *Journalism and Mass Communication Quarterly, 72*(4), 786–798.

Jamieson, K. H., & Adasiewicz, C. (2000). What can voters learn from election debates? In S. Coleman (Ed.), *Televised election debates: International perspectives* (pp. 25– 42). New York: St. Martin's Press, Inc.

Jamieson, K. H., Johnston, R., Hagen, M. G., Waldman, P., & Kenski, K. (2000). *The public learned about Bush and Gore from conventions; half ready to make an informed choice.* Philadelphia: Annenberg Pubic Policy Center.

Johnson, S. (2004, November 28). The future of network news: Follow the money. *Chicago Tribune*, sec. 7, pp. 1, 8–9.

The Jon Stewart and undecided voter connection. (2004, September 20). New York: Fox News Network. . . .

Just, M., Crigler, A., & Wallach, L. (1990). Thirty seconds or thirty minutes: What viewers learn from spot advertisements and candidate debates. *Journal of Communication, 40*(3), 120–133.

Kraus, S. (Ed.). (1979). *The great debates: Carter v. Ford, 1976.* Bloomington: Indiana University Press.

Lang, A. (2000). The limited capacity model of mediated message processing. *Journal of Communication, 50*(1), 46–70.

Lang, A. (2006a). Motivated cognition (LC4MP): The influence of appetitive and aversive activation on the processing of video games. In P. Messarsis & L. Humphries (Eds.), *Digital media: Transformation in human communication* (pp. 237–254). New York: Peter Lang Publishing.

Lang, A. (2006b). Using the limited capacity model of motivated mediated message processing to design effective cancer communication messages. *Journal of Communication, 56*(Suppl.), S57–S81.

Lang, A., Sparks, J. V., Bradley, S. D., Lee, S., & Wang, Z. (2004). Processing arousing information: Psychophysiological predictors of motivated attention. *Psychophysiology, 41*(Suppl. 1), S61.

Lang, K., & Lang, G. E. (1961). Ordeal by debate: Viewer reactions. *Public Opinion Quarterly, 25*, 277–288.

Lasswell, H. (1948). The structure and function of communication in society. In L. Bryson (Ed.), *The communication of ideas* (pp. 37–51). New York: Harper and Row.

Lazaroff, L. (2004, November 24). Audience decline an old story. *Chicago Tribune,* sec. 3, pp. 1, 8.

Lazarsfeld, P., Berelson, B., & Gaudet, H. (1944). *The People's Choice.* New York: Columbia University Press.

Lethbridge, R., Simmons, J., & Allen, N. (2002). All things unpleasant are not equal: Startle reflex modification while processing social and physical threat. *Psychophysiology, 39*(Suppl. 1), S51.

Lichter, S. R., Amundson, D., & Noyes, R. (1988). *The video campaign: Network coverage of the 1988 primaries.* Washington, DC: American Enterprise Institute and the Center for Media and Public Affairs.

Lichter, S. R., & Lichter, L. S. (1996). Campaign '96 final: How TV news covered the general election. *Media Monitor.* Washington, DC: Center for Media and Public Affairs.

Lippmann, W. (1921). *Public opinion.* New York: Macmillan Company.

Lowery, S. A., & DeFleur, M. L. (1983). *Milestones in mass communication research.* New York: Longman.

McDonald, D., & Fredin, E. (2001, May). *Primitive emotional contagion in coviewing.* Paper presented to the Information Systems Division at the International Communication Association 51st annual conference, Washington, DC.

McKain, A. (2005). Not necessarily not the news: Gatekeeping, remediation, and *The Daily Show. The Journal of American Culture, 28*(4), 415–430.

McRae, K., Taitano, E., Kaszniak, A., & Lane, R. (2004). Differential skin conductance response to biologically and non-biologically relevant IAPS stimuli at brief exposure durations before a backward mask. *Psychophysiology, 41*(Suppl. 1), S60.

Mendelsohn, H., & O'Keefe, G. (1975). *The people choose a president: Influences on voter decision making.* New York: Praeger Publishers.

Middleton, R. (1962). National TV debates and presidential voting decisions. *Public Opinion Quarterly, 26,* 426–429.

Noelle-Neumann, E. (1995). Public opinion and rationality. In T. Glasser & C. Salmon (Eds.), *Public opinion and the communication of consent* (pp. 33–54). New York: The Guilford Press.

Patterson, T. E. (1977). The 1976 horserace. *The Wilson Quarterly, 1,* 73–79.

Patterson, T. E. (1980). *The mass media election: How Americans choose their president.* New York: Praeger Publishers.

Patterson, T. E., & McClure, R. D. (1976). *The unseeing eye: The myth of television power in national politics.* New York: Paragon Books.

Pew Research Center for the People & the Press. (2002, June 9). *Public's news habits little changed by September 11.* Washington, DC: Author. Retrieved August 15, 2002, from http://people-press.org

Pew Research Center for the People & the Press. (2004a, January 11). *Cable and Internet loom large in fragmented political universe: Perceptions of partisan bias seen as growing.* Washington, DC: Author. . . .

Pew Research Center for the People & the Press. (2004b, June 8). *Online news audience larger, more diverse.* Washington, DC: Author. . . .

Price, V., & Roberts, D. (1987). Public opinion processes. In C. Berger & S. Chaffee (Eds.), *Handbook of communication science* (pp. 781–816). Newbury Park, CA: Sage.

Ranney, A. (Ed.). (1979). *The past and future of presidential debates.* Washington, DC: American Enterprise Institute for Public Policy Research.

Reber, B. H., & Benoit, W. L. (2001). Presidential debate stories accentuate the negative. *Newspaper Research Journal, 22*(3), 30–43.

Rifle, D., Lacy, S., & Fico, F. (1998). *Analyzing media messages: Using quantitative content analysis in research.* Mahwah, NJ: Lawrence Erlbaum Associates, Inc.

Ryan, M. (2005, April 8). Good decision: Putting "Indecision" on DVD. *Chicago Tribune,* sec. 2, p. 2.

Salant, R. S., (1962). The television debates: A revolution that deserves a future. *Public Opinion Quarterly, 26,* 335–350.

Scheele, H. Z. (1984). Ronald Reagan's 1980 Acceptance Address: A focus on American values. *Western Journal of Speech Communication, 48*(1), 51–61.

Schudson, M. (1995). *The power of news.* Cambridge, MA: Harvard University Press.

Sears, D. (1986). College sophomores in the laboratory: Influences of a narrow data base on social psychology's view of human nature. *Journal of Personality and Social Psychology, 51*(3), 515–530.

Sesno, F. (2001). Let's cover the conventions. *The Harvard International Journal of Press/Politics, 6*(1), 11–15.

Stewart's "stoned slackers"? Not quite. (2004, September 28). Atlanta, GA: CNN. com. . . .

Trent, J. S., & Friedenberg, R. V. (2004). *Political campaign communication: Principles and practices* (5th ed.). Lanham, MD: Rowman & Littlefield.

Under-30 voters top 20 million. (2004, November 6). *The Herald-Times*, p. A5.

Williams, B., & Edy, J. (1999). Basic beliefs, democratic theory, and public opinion. In C. Glynn, S. Herbst, G. O'Keefe, & R. Shapiro (Eds.), *Public Opinion* (pp. 212–245). Boulder, CO: Westview Press.

Willis, E. F. (1962). Little TV debates in Michigan. *Quarterly Journal of Speech, 48,* 15–23.

Wright, C. (1974). The nature and functions of mass communication. In J. Civikly (Ed.), *Messages: A reader on human communication* (pp. 241–250). New York: Random House. (Reprinted from *Mass communication: A sociological perspective*, pp. 11–23, by C. Wright, Ed., 1959, New York: Random House).

Young America's news source: Jon Stewart. (2004, March 2). CNN.com. . . .

Barry A. Hollander   ⟶ **NO**

Late-Night Learning

The fragmenting mass media environment has created a host of new ways people say they learn about public affairs. In the early 1990s, researchers explored the role of the "new news" in U.S. politics, particularly the influence of talk radio (Hollander, 1994, 1995). An emerging body of scholarly work has expanded this analysis to entertainment-based television and how it affects political perceptions and knowledge. The scope ranges widely to include television talk shows (Prior, 2003), dramas such as *The West Wing* (Holbert, Pillion, et al., 2003; Parry-Giles & Parry-Giles, 2002; Rollins & O'Connor, 2003), situation comedies (Holbert, Shah, & Kwak, 2003), police dramas (Holbert, Shah, & Kwak, 2004), and the political content of late-night comedy shows (Moy, Xenos, & Hess, 2004; Niven, Lichter, & Amundson, 2003; Parkin, Bos, & van Doom, 2003).

Among the concerns is whether entertainment programs actually inform viewers, specifically younger people who may get their news from late-night television hosts such as Jay Leno or comedy programs like *The Daily Show*. Anecdotal evidence and surveys suggest that for many young people, such programs and their hosts are perceived as vital sources of political information and news (Pew Research Center, 2000, 2002, 2004). Not everyone is convinced, especially Stewart, the host of *The Daily Show*. "I still think that's a fallacy that they get most of their news from us," Stewart told television critics (McFarland, 2004, ¶ 14).

Not all knowledge is the same. Whether viewers of entertainment-based programs learn about public affairs is reminiscent of earlier concerns about the informative power of television news as compared to print sources, most often newspapers. Shoemaker, Schooler, and Danielson (1989) argued that medium differences and their subsequent effects were best addressed through understanding the differences between recall versus recognition of political information. This position is echoed by those who examined the differential effects of intentional and incidental exposure to information (Eagle & Leiter, 1964; Stapel, 1998). In brief, what viewers glean from such programs may be a function of many factors: the cognitive effort expended, political interest and sophistication, and exactly what kind of knowledge is tapped in surveys or questionnaires. This study presents two tests of knowledge—recall and recognition—and argues that entertainment-based programs are better suited for the latter in terms of understanding what they contribute to a viewer's public affairs knowledge, particularly for younger viewers.

Political Knowledge

An enlightened citizenry remains one of the foundations of a successful and thriving democracy, and yet the U.S. public is relatively uninformed about their political world (Bennett, 1996). Despite advances in education and an exploding number of available news sources, scholars have discovered no corresponding increase in political knowledge (Neuman, 1986; Smith, 1989). As Delli Carpini and Keeter (1992) noted: "To say that much of the public is uninformed about much of the substance of politics and public policy is to say nothing new" (p. 19).

Measures of newspaper use are often associated with political knowledge (Becker & Dunwoody, 1982; Chaffee & Tims, 1982; Chaffee, Zhao, & Leshner, 1994; Pettey, 1988; but see also Weaver & Drew, 1995). Exposure to or reliance on television news has not fared as well (Becker & Whitney, 1980; Patterson & McClure, 1976), although a few studies have uncovered a positive relationship (e.g., Zhao & Chaffee, 1995). To make sense of these findings, some have suggested that how people orient toward a medium (McLeod & McDonald, 1985), attend to a medium (Chaffee & Schleuder, 1986), or involve themselves with a medium (Shoemaker et al., 1989) can mask the existence of positive effects on knowledge. These approaches are similar to that of Salomon's (1983) position that people assess the amount of cognitive effort necessary for a particular medium and expend only that amount, with television perceived as requiring the least amount of effort and therefore leading to reduced learning as compared to print, which is perceived to require greater mental effort. The result is a self-fulfilling prophecy, with print information generating superior learning as compared to television or video presentations.

Taken together, these studies suggest that measures of recall alone may not be sensitive enough to uncover the effects of televised entertainment-based programming. Intention to learn or attention to a message is often associated with superior recall, whereas incidental exposure to a message leads to greater recognition of information (Beals, Mazis, Salop, & Staelin, 1981; Eagle & Leiter, 1964; Stapel, 1998). When involvement is high, measures of recall perform best, but in situations in which only marginal interest exists, recognition is often the best measurement strategy (Singh & Rothschild, 1983). Thus, television is ill suited for measures of recall as compared to print. Some argue the differences lie in left-brain versus right-brain processing, in which print learning is best tapped by asking recall questions and television learning is best tapped by recognition questions (Krugman, 1977, but see du Plessis, 1994, for an alternate view).

Entertainment Media and Politics

This discussion is particularly apt when considering the emergence of entertainment-based media as a form of political communication. Indeed, interpersonal conversations now rely on the fictional television content in addition to news as people make sense of their social and political world (Delli Carpini & Williams, 1996). Popular late-night and comedy programs have taken an increasingly political bent, with the number of political jokes on late-night TV steadily rising from 1989 to 2000 (Parkin et al., 2003). Thus, the audience is exposed to campaign politics and public affairs as part of the entertainment whole, but the quality of the information remains in doubt. Late-night humor's focus on the presidency and presidential candidates, for example, rarely includes issue content and instead highlights the miscues of political actors (Niven et al., 2003). The audience of such entertainment-oriented talk shows and comedy programs is often less educated and interested in politics than the mainstream news audience (Davis & Owen, 1998; Hamilton, 2003), suggesting viewers less capable of making sense of the political content. Indeed, in an examination of talk radio, Hollander (1995) found that among less educated listeners, exposure to such programs led to a sense of feeling informed but was unrelated to actual campaign knowledge. Among listeners of greater education, talk radio exposure was related to both the feeling of being informed and campaign information holding, suggesting that greater cognitive ability and motivation brought about by education increases the ability to glean useful information from such programs.

Most studies find no relationship between entertainment-based or "soft" news and political knowledge (Chaffee et al., 1994; Hollander, 1995; McLeod et al., 1996; Pfau, Cho, & Chong, 2001; Prior, 2003), and an analysis by Parkin et al. (2003) reports a negative relationship. This is not to say watching entertainment programs is unrelated to how people make sense of the political world. Such programs can influence perceptions of political actors or how people process political information (Moy et al., 2004; Pfau et al., 2001).

The question of how much is actually learned from entertainment television remains open to debate, and some argue that passive learning or awareness of issues does occur from casual television viewing (see Baum, 2003, for a discussion). As Shoemaker et al. (1989) noted in their examination of differences among newspaper-reliant and television-news-reliant respondents, the kind of knowledge one measures can help explain many of the confusing and contradictory findings from previous studies. In addition, the gratifications sought from such viewing can also play a role (Becker & Whitney, 1980), and thus, we need to consider more than mere exposure to a medium in order to understand how it may influence the ways in which people process public affairs information. Therefore, the following hypothesis was posited:

H_1: Viewing comedy and late-night programs for political information will be associated with recognition of campaign knowledge but not with recall of campaign knowledge.

A number of other factors can also influence processing strategies and information processing, such as political sophistication, cognitive ability, and motivation. The self-reported reliance of younger viewers on entertainment-based fare has drawn both popular and academic attention, making age a normative factor of interest and one often associated with political sophistication and motivation. Shoemaker et al. (1989) found age to be a significant factor in their recall and recognition study in terms of reliance on either newspapers or television news. Younger respondents recalled more election facts only if they relied on newspapers for their campaign information, suggesting that their peers who relied on television news were either unable or unmotivated to process information from that medium. In a similar vein, Young (2004) found people with greater political knowledge to be largely unaffected by late-night programming, but those with less knowledge were more volatile in their candidate evaluations depending on how much they watched such programming. Baum (2005) also found that politically unengaged voters who watch entertainment TV were more influenced by such heuristics in their perceptions of candidates. Given that age and political knowledge are often negatively correlated (Delli Carpini & Keeter, 1996) and that younger persons might be expected to rely on television-based fare for information, this suggests that younger respondents may be less successful at tests of recall as compared to recognition. Therefore, the following hypotheses were posited:

> H_2: Younger viewers of entertainment programs will be more likely than older viewers to identify such programs as a method of learning about political campaigns.

> H_3: Watching such programs for campaign information will be associated with recognition of campaign events for younger viewers but not with recall of campaign events.

Method

Data were drawn from the January 2004 Political Communications Study conducted by the Pew Research Center for the People and the Press. This national telephone survey of 3,188 adults includes a battery of questions tapping the use of various media sources, from print to television, and a small set of items asking for recall and recognition of events in the campaign for the Democratic Party nomination. In addition, the availability of a large number of demographic and political variables allows for stringent multivariate controls in subsequent analyses.

Entertainment Media Measures

Rather than focus on mere exposure to a medium or category of programs, the analysis here examines those who say they use various programs specifically for the purpose of keeping up with the election campaign. Survey respondents were asked a battery of possible sources of such information and whether they use them to "learn something about the presidential campaign or the candidates."[1] Responses could range from 1 (*never*) to 4 (*regularly*), creating a 4-point scale for each category of programming or specific program. The 15 possible sources include 2 of most interest here: late-night TV shows such as *Letterman* and *Leno* and comedy shows such as *Saturday Night Live* and *The Daily Show*. In addition, respondents answered questions about religious radio shows, talk radio, the Internet, local TV news, national network broadcast news, cable news networks, C-SPAN, TV magazine shows, NPR, public broadcasting news, morning TV news shows, political talk shows such as CNN's *Crossfire* and CNBC's *Hardball*, and Sunday morning network talk shows.

Political Knowledge

The survey provides a small set of questions that tap both recall and recognition of events tied to the Democratic Party as candidates vied for its nomination to face incumbent President George W. Bush. Recall is measured by two questions: one asking if a respondent can correctly identify which Democratic presidential candidate served as an Army general (Wesley Clark) and which served as majority leader in the House of Representatives (Richard Gephardt). Correct responses were coded as 1, and all other responses were coded as 0, with the responses summed to create an index that ranged from 0 (*none of the questions answered correctly*) to 2 (*both items answered correctly*). There is a strong relationship between answering these two questions correctly ($\chi^2 = 921.3$, $p < .001$, Kendall's τ_b ordinal-by-ordinal correlation = .54, $p < .001$, Cronbach's $\alpha = .70$). Recognition is measured by asking respondents if they had heard of Al Gore's endorsement of Howard Dean and of Dean's comment about wanting to win the votes of "guys with Confederate flags in their pickup trucks." Respondents were presented a 3-point scale ranging from 1 (*never heard of it*) to 3 (*heard a lot*). These responses were summed into a index with a range from 0 (*never heard of either incident*) to 6 (*heard a lot about both incidents*). The two items are highly correlated ($r = .46$, $p < .001$, Cronbach's $\alpha = .63$).

Analytic Strategy

The first step is to establish who uses the various media to learn about political campaigns through bivariate analysis in tandem with demographic and political variables, specifically whether younger respondents are more likely to identify late-night and comedy programs as sources of information. The true test of these relationships will follow with multivariate analysis in which the "usual suspects" of political knowledge research are used as either statistical controls or as interaction terms to address the three hypotheses. These controls are age, education, gender, income, race, campaign interest, newspaper exposure, political participation, strength of ideology, and strength of partisanship.[2] Newspaper exposure was included because among all media variables, it is the one that in the literature consistently predicts political knowledge. Interaction terms with age are also included to test the third hypothesis.

Results

Patterns of Media Use

Respondents who said they used late-night and comedy television programs to learn about the political campaign also tended to use other media for the same information.[3] Age was significantly associated with these two kinds of programming, with the younger the respondent, the more likely he or she was to name late-night and comedy programs as an information source, supporting the hypothesized relationships.[4] The audience of these two types of programming—at least those who identify it as an important source of campaign news—tended to be younger rather than older, minority, more male than female, leaning toward the Democratic Party, politically liberal rather than conservative, and somewhat more interested in political campaigns. Indeed, few significant differences exist between the audience of these two kinds of programming, although age has a greater association with comedy viewing ($r = -.32$, $p < .01$) than with late-night television viewing ($r = -.19$, $p < .01$).[5]

Overall, most respondents did not score well on the test of recall, with 62% unable to answer either of the two questions in the survey. The index created from these two items had a mean of 0.6 ($SD = 0.8$), whereas the recognition index had a mean of 3.6 ($SD = 1.3$). . . . Recall knowledge was negatively correlated with watching late-night programs ($r = -.09$, ns) and comedy programs ($r = -.05$, $p < .01$), whereas recognition was unrelated to either media variable ($r = .02$, ns, and $r = -.00$, ns, respectively). The lack of a relationship with recognition is at odds with other studies, which suggest that such a measure might be the best method for tapping the kinds of knowledge gleaned from such programs. It is also important to note that using the other media for campaign news was often positively associated with both recall and recognition. Given the high correlation between late-night and comedy viewing and the correlation patterns with the key dependent variables among the various media, these two sources appear to have more in common with each other than with other communication channels.

Multivariate Analyses

A more stringent test is provided by . . . regression, which statistically controls for the effects of demographic and political factors. . . . The predictive power demonstrated by the demographic factors [of age, education, income, sex, and race] is particularly revealing, with all five achieving statistical significance. The political factors perform less well, although campaign interest and reading newspapers do contribute significantly to the model. The final step [enters] the two entertainment-based media. . . . Despite the large number of statistical controls, watching late-night programming to learn about the news was significantly associated with recall and recognition, but in opposite directions as predicted by Hypothesis 1. Watching late-night programs was negatively associated with recall ($\beta = -.06$, $p < .01$) and positively associated with recognition ($\beta = .05$, $p < .01$). The results for comedy television use do not support the hypothesis, with use of these programs for campaign information being unrelated to both recall ($\beta = -.03$, ns) and recognition ($\beta = .01$, ns).

Hypothesis 2 predicted that age would be significantly associated with program viewing. By regressing the demographic and political factors listed previously on use of both programs, age was the most powerful predictor, far outstripping the predictive power of other variables.[6] This hypothesis was supported.

To answer Hypothesis 3 on whether age and viewing act together to explain campaign knowledge, interaction terms were created. The interaction of age and watching late-night programs for campaign news was negatively related to recall ($\beta = -.04$, $p < .05$) but not significantly associated with recognition ($\beta = -.02$, ns). . . . That is, for young people at the lowest and highest levels of viewing late-night programs, the recall of campaign information is relatively low as compared to more moderate viewing of such programs. Older respondents demonstrate more of a linear relationship. This suggests a function of diminishing returns for younger viewers in how much they actually learn from late-night programs. The interaction term of age with comedy television viewing created a similar result on recall ($\beta = -.05$, $p < .01$) but also achieved statistical significance on recognition as well ($\beta = -.04$, $p < .05$). Although comedy viewing alone was not associated with either knowledge measure, when combined with age the results suggest that young people do receive a modest benefit from viewing comedy programs in terms of both recall and recognition.

Summary

As predicted in the hypothesis, younger viewers identified comedy and late-night television programs as a source of political campaign news. In addition, there was some support for the prediction that the consumption of such programming, particularly late-night television shows, was more associated with recognition than recall. Little support was found, however, for the hypothesized interaction between age and media use in predicting recognition but not recall. For example, watching comedy programs for news improved both recognition and recall for younger viewers, but age made no difference in the relationship between watching late-night programs and recognition of political information. However, age did interact with late-night viewing and recall but not in the expected direction, with younger respondents contradicting the general tendency of a negative relationship between viewing such programs and recall of campaign information.

Conclusion

This study began with a basic question: Do young people learn about a political campaign from such entertainment fare as late-night and comedy television programs? That a younger audience is drawn to such content is without doubt, and in surveys and anecdotal accounts, they often identify *The Daily Show* and similar programs as the source of their political information. The research here supports the idea that younger people seek out entertainment-based programs to keep up with a political campaign and that watching such programs is more likely to be associated with recognition of campaign information than it is with recall of actual information. This is an important difference. Previous research has identified two key methods of measuring political knowledge— recall and recognition. Successful recall of factual information is often associated with use of the print media, particularly newspapers, and scholars suggest that lower motivation and differences in how information is processed makes tests of recognition the preferred method of measuring the effects of television news—and by extension such entertainment-based programming as comedy and late-night shows. In addition, some have found that age can play an important role in the ability to answer public affairs questions.

Overall, younger viewers do appear to get more out of such programs as compared to older viewers, although in some cases it is a matter of diminishing returns. Beyond moderate levels of viewing late-night programs, the improvement in recall disappears while the improvement in recognition increases. Or to put it another way, late-night television viewing increases what young people think they know about a political campaign but provides at best modest improvements to actual recall of events associated with the campaign.

Does political knowledge truly matter? As Rousseau (1762/1968) wrote: "The very right to vote imposes on me the duty to instruct myself in public affairs, however little influence my voice may have in them" (p. 49). Democratic theory rests on the assumption of an informed electorate, and there is some fear that viewers face a diet of empty calories and may "fill up" on programming that does little to actually improve their knowledge about public affairs and political campaigns, a finding reminiscent of Hollander's (1995) results concerning education and listening to talk radio and the effects on actual versus perceived knowledge.

Some 20 years ago, Postman (1985) warned that a reliance on perpetual entertainment and trivia will harm public conversation, placing the nation and its culture at risk. A demand that all content be entertaining, even the most serious questions of politics and public affairs, appears a trend that has captured the attention of the youngest in society. As the political content of comedy and late-night television programs continues to rise, as does an audience turned off by mainstream news sources, then the significance of this exposure increases to the point where, for many, they become the lone source of news. Such a possibility seems to stun host Jon Stewart, who says the possibility either "says something terrible about news organizations, or something terrible about the comedy we're doing, or terrible about teenagers" (McFarland, 2004, ¶ 9). There is some good news here, that young people are capable of gleaning at least modest amounts of campaign information from such content, but how competent it leaves them to participate in a meaningful manner remains an open question.

Notes

1. The items were randomized to control for the influence of question order. For some items, a split-method was used, meaning half of the respondents were randomly assigned to receive one of two program questions. The split variables are religious radio shows such as *Focus on The Family*, talk radio shows, local TV news about your viewing area, TV news magazine shows such as *60 Minutes, 20/20,* and *Dateline,* and morning television shows such as *The Today Show* and *Good Morning America.* In these cases, half of the 3,188 respondents received these items, and half did not.

2. The strength of partisanship and ideology measures are the typical folded scales in which extremes on party identification and political ideology are

scored as high, and scores in the middle of both measures are scored as low. These measures then set aside the direction of a respondent's ideological or partisan leanings and instead focus on how strongly they feel about either political factor.

3. Indeed there is some suggestion here of a response bias, given the positive correlations found between late-night and comedy viewing and all of the other media save one, a hardly surprising nonsignificant relationship between watching comedy programs and listening to religious radio programming. The most powerful correlation in the analysis, however, is between both late-night and comedy TV for information ($r = .50, p < .001$), suggesting a significant overlap in the viewing of these two genres to learn about campaign information.

4. However, age also is associated with using other channels for campaign information. Younger users are more likely to also report getting information from the Internet, C-SPAN, talk radio, NPR, and cable news channels such as CNN. Older respondents favor TV news magazines, religious radio, public broadcasting, Sunday morning political talk shows, local television news, and national television news broadcasts.

5. Minor differences can be found, although most are of little substantive difference. Newspaper exposure, for example, is negatively correlated with late-night viewing ($r = -.06, p < .01$) but is unrelated to watching comedy shows ($r = -.03, ns$). In addition, education is weakly but positively associated with comedy viewing ($r = .07, p < .01$) but not with late-night viewing ($r = .01, ns$). Overall, a weak trend in correlations suggests that late-night viewing, as compared to comedy viewing, is somewhat more tied to less use of regular news and less education. However, no differences can be seen in partisan or ideological strength, ties to a specific party or ideology, or in campaign interest, making any suggestion of audience differences here more speculative than likely.

6. No table provided. The top predictors of late-night television viewing were age ($\beta = -.20, p < .01$), income ($\beta = -.07, p < .01$), and campaign interest ($\beta = .07, p < .01$). The top predictors of comedy show viewing were age ($\beta = -.31, p < .01$), campaign interest ($\beta = .09, p < .01$), and race ($\beta = -.08, p < .01$). The only difference other than the relative predictive power of age between the two variables is the role of newspaper reading ($\beta = -.05, p < .01$, for late-night television, and $\beta = -.00, ns$, for comedy shows).

References

Baum, M. A. (2003). Soft news and political knowledge: Evidence of absence or absence of evidence? *Political Communication, 20*, 173–190.

Baum, M. A. (2005). Talking the vote: Why presidential candidates hit the talk show circuit. *American Journal of Political Science, 49*, 213–234.

Beals, H., Mazis, M. B., Salop, S. C., & Staelin, S. (1981). Consumer search and public policy. *Journal of Consumer Research, 8*, 11–22.

Becker, L. B., & Dunwoody, S. (1982). Media use, public affairs knowledge and voting in a local election. *Journalism Quarterly, 59*, 212–218.

Becker, L. B., & Whitney, D. C. (1980). Effects of media dependencies: Audience assessment of government. *Communication Research, 7*, 95–120.

Bennett, S. E. (1996). "Know-nothings" revisited again. *Political Behavior*, 18, 219–233.

Chaffee, S. H., & Schleuder, J. (1986). Measurement and effects of attention to media news. *Human Communication Research*, 13, 76–107.

Chaffee, S. H., & Tims, A. R. (1982). News media use in adolescence: Implications for political cognitions. In M. Burgoon (Ed.), *Communication yearbook 6* (pp. 736–758). Beverly Hills, CA: Sage.

Chaffee, S. H., Zhao, X., & Leshner, G. (1994). Political knowledge and the campaign media of 1992. *Communication Research*, 21, 305–324.

Davis, R., & Owen, D. (1998). *New media and American politics*. New York: Oxford University Press.

Delli Carpini, M. X., & Keeter, S. (1992). The public's knowledge of politics. In J. D. Kennamer (Ed.), *Public opinion, the press, and public policy* (pp. 19–40). Westport, CT: Praeger.

Delli Carpini, M. X., & Keeter, S. (1996). *What Americans know about politics and why it matters*. New Haven, CT: Yale University Press.

Delli Carpini, M. X., & Williams, B. A. (1996). Constructing public opinion: The uses of fictional and nonfictional television in conversations about the environment. In A. N. Crigler (Ed.), *The psychology of political communication* (pp. 149–175). Ann Arbor: University of Michigan Press.

du Plessis, E. (1994). Recognition versus recall. *Journal of Advertising Research*, 34, 75–91.

Eagle, M., & Leiter, E. (1964). Recall and recognition in intentional and incidental learning. *Journal of Experimental Psychology*, 68, 58–63.

Hamilton, J. T. (2003). *All the news that's fit to sell: How the market transforms information into news*. Princeton, NJ: Princeton University Press.

Holbert, R. L., Pillion, O., Tschida, D. A., Armfield, G. G., Kinder, K., Cherry, K., et al. (2003). The *West Wing* as endorsement of the American presidency: Expanding the domain of priming in political communication. *Journal of Communication*, 53, 427–443.

Holbert, R. L., Shah, D. V., & Kwak, N. (2003). Political implications of prime-time drama and sitcom use: Genres of representation and opinions concerning women's rights. *Journal of Communication*, 53, 45–60.

Holbert, R. L., Shah, D. V., & Kwak, N. (2004). Fear, authority, and justice: The influence of TV news, police reality, and crime drama viewing on endorsements of capital punishment and gun ownership. *Journalism and Mass Communication Quarterly*, 81, 343–363.

Hollander, B. A. (1994). Patterns in the exposure and influence of the Old News and the New News. *Mass Comm Review*, 21, 144–155.

Hollander, B. A. (1995). The new news and the 1992 presidential campaign: Perceived versus actual campaign knowledge. *Journalism and Mass Communication Quarterly*, 72, 786–798.

Krugman, H. E. (1977). Memory without recall, exposure without perception. *Journal of Advertising Research*, 17, 7–12.

McFarland, M. (2004). Young people turning comedy shows into serious news source. *Seattle Post-Intelligencer*. . . .

McLeod, J. M., Guo, Z., Daily, K., Steele, C. A., Horowitz, E., & Chen, H. (1996). The impact of traditional and nontraditional media forms in the 1992 presidential election. *Journalism and Mass Communication Quarterly, 73,* 401–416.

McLeod, J. M., & McDonald, D. G. (1985). Beyond simple exposure: Media orientations and their impact on political processes. *Communication Research, 12,* 3–33.

Moy, P., Xenos, M. A., & Hess, V. K. (2004, May). *Priming effects of late-night comedy.* Paper presented at the annual meeting of the International Communication Association, New Orleans, LA.

Neuman, W. R. (1986). *The paradox of mass politics: Knowledge and opinion in the American electorate.* Cambridge, MA: Harvard University Press.

Niven, D., Lichter, S. R., & Amundson, D. (2003). The political content of late night comedy. *Press/Politics, 8,* 118–133.

Parkin, M., Bos, A., & van Doom, B. (2003, November). *Laughing, learning and liking: The effects of entertainment-based media on American politics.* Paper presented at the annual meeting of the Midwest Political Science Association, Chicago.

Parry-Giles, T., & Parry-Giles, S. J. (2002). The *West Wing's* prime time presidentality: Mimesis and catharsis in a postmodern romance. *Quarterly Journal of Speech, 88,* 209–227.

Patterson, T. E., & McClure, R. (1976). *The unseeing eye: The myth of television power in national elections.* New York: Putman's.

Pettey, G. R. (1988). The interaction of the individual's social environment, attention and interest, and public affairs media use on political knowledge holding. *Communication Research, 15,* 265–281.

Pew Research Center for the People and the Press. (2000, February 5). *The tough job of communicating with voters. . . .*

Pew Research Center for the People and the Press. (2002, June 9). *Public's news habits little changed since September 11. . . .*

Pew Research Center for the People and the Press. (2004, January 11). *Cable and Internet loom large in fragmented political news universe. . . .*

Pfau, M., Cho, J., & Chong, K. (2001). Communication forms in U.S. presidential campaigns: Influences on candidate perceptions and the democratic process. *Press/Politics, 6,* 88–105.

Postman, N. (1985). *Amusing ourselves to death: Public discourse in the age of show business.* New York: Viking.

Prior, M. (2003). Any good news in soft news? The impact of soft news preference on political knowledge. *Political Communication, 20,* 149–171.

Rollins, P. C., & O'Connor, J. E. (2003). *The West Wing: The American presidency as television drama.* Syracuse, NY: Syracuse University Press.

Rousseau, J.-J. (1968). *The social contract* (M. Cranston, Trans.). Harmondworth, England: Penguin. (Original work published 1762)

Salomon, G. (1983). Television watching and mental effort: A social psychological view. In J. Bryant & D. R. Anderson (Eds.), *Children's understanding of television: Research on attention and comprehension* (pp. 181–198). New York: Academic.

Shoemaker, P. J., Schooler, C., & Danielson, W. A. (1989). Involvement with the media: Recall versus recognition of election information. *Communication Research, 16,* 78–103.

Singh, S. N., & Rothschild, M. L. (1983). Recognition as a measure of learning from television commercials. *Journal of Marketing Research, 20,* 235–248.

Smith, E. R. A. N. (1989). *The unchanging American voter.* Berkeley: University of California Press.

Stapel, J. (1998). Recall and recognition: A very close relationship. *Journal of Advertising Research, 38,* 41–45.

Weaver, D., & Drew, D. (1995). Voter learning in the 1992 presidential election: Did the "nontraditional" media and debates matter? *Journalism and Mass Communication Quarterly, 72,* 7–17.

Young, D. G. (2004). Late-night comedy in election 2000: Its influence on candidate trait ratings and the moderating effects of political knowledge and partisanship. *Journal of Broadcasting & Electronic Media, 48,* 1–22.

Zhao, X., & Chaffee, S. H. (1995). Campaign advertisements versus television news as sources of political issue information. *Public Opinion Quarterly, 59,* 41–65.

POSTSCRIPT

Does Fake News Mislead the Public?

Comedic news has captured the public imagination. The August 2007 *Critical Studies in Mass Communication* journal featured a humorous debate concerning Jon Stewart. Hart and Hartelius accuse Stewart of the sin of "unbridled political cynicism," luring youth into abandoning conventional society and attempting to foster social change, or shunning involvement in civic and political issues. Continuing with the lighthearted tone, but serious issues, Bennett defends the importance of comedy in an age of cynicism, and argues that it breeds instead an independence of perspective.

Robert Love in "Before Jon Stewart" (*Columbia Journalism Review*, March/ April 2007) outlines the history of fake news, ranging from Hearst to the "yellow press" to video news releases. He reveals a long and undistinguished history of journalistic fakes. John Pavlik in "Fake News" (*Television Quarterly*, 2005) details his experience as a interviewee for *The Daily Show*. His careful retelling of his experience, from the point of view of an established department head in a major mass communication program, is both humorous and troubling.

An interesting feature of Pew Research Center Online at http://www .pewresearch.org is the News IQ quiz that allows you to assess your level of political knowledge, and compares your results to a national sample. The Pew Internet and American Life Project at http://www.pewinternet.org offers many reports on uses and consequences of Internet and online activities for American life, including political concerns.

There are two issues entangled in these readings; the first has to do with the worth of fake news in contemporary society. Does it function to invite knowledge and debate within society, or is it mere entertainment? The lines between news and entertainment have long been blurred. Consider, just as one example, the frequent insertion of celebrity news into front pages of newspapers and packages on national newscasts. The line between journalists and the public is now blurring even more. Consider news and political bloggers, who have had major influence when they have upon occasion broken news stories before the mainstream media. Do we define journalism by where it appears or by how it functions in society?

The second has to do with the chief audience of the currently popular fake news: youth. Are they disadvantaged as citizens by their reliance on this form of news? Is it somehow less substantive than "real" news? Fox and colleagues think not. Does its presentation style inhibit learning? Hollander fears so. These are among the few works that have seriously studied this phenomenon, so additional research is needed. What are the questions that you think researchers need to ask? Part of what is implied by this concern for the youth audience is the fear that participation in the political life of our democracy will be harmed by nontraditional news sources. Is it information that threatens the political involvement of youth? What other factors influence youth engagement in political and civic issues? And most importantly, what can be done to enhance that engagement and participation?

ISSUE 10

Will Evolving Forms of Journalism Be an Improvement?

YES: Mark Deuze, Axel Bruns, and Christoph Neuberger, from "Preparing for an Age of Participatory News," *Journalism Practice* (vol. 1, no. 3, 2007)

NO: David Simon, from Testimony before the Senate Committee on Commerce, Science, and Transportation on the Future of Journalism, http://commerce.senate.gov/public/_files/DavidSimonTestimonyFutureof Journalism.pdf (May 6, 2009)

ISSUE SUMMARY

YES: Mark Deuze, Axel Bruns, and Christoph Neuberger conducted case studies of news organizations that developed extensive plans to incorporate participatory news practices. The case studies reveal the rewards and difficulties of these decisions.

NO: David Simon testified in May of 2009 to a Senate Committee examining the future of journalism. His conclusion was that high-end journalism was dying in America and could not be saved by the Internet and/or citizen journalists.

Has the time come to discard the journalistic models of the past? In this digital age, where new platforms for communication emerge routinely, what do the new models offer? Before you read further, take a moment to write one way in which you think journalism needs to improve. What change would you like to see?

A major change emerging in the digital age has been the rise of participatory journalism. "User generated content" is a broader term for all the ways in which individuals have expanded opportunity to produce and distribute their ideas and products across the Internet. Participatory journalism can take two forms: civic journalism and independent digital voices. Civic journalism refers to the journalistic practice of engaging communities in dialogue. Many media outlets have tried to strengthen their ties to the community by encouraging comment and reporting about important civic concerns. This can happen in a variety of ways, including inviting comment, convening citizen panels, changing journalistic practices to listen and reflect more thoroughly on citizen viewpoints, and surveying the community to identify community needs. Often these discussions take place on the media outlet's Web site. A concept that you may have heard used is "hyper local." A hyper local focus reports intensely on events and issues within a well-defined community and is intended primarily for consumption by residents of that community. It almost always relies on user-generated content as well as professionally developed reporting. Many believe that "localism" will save local newspapers, radio, and television stations because it will distinguish them from readily available national voices.

The second form of participatory journalism refers to the explosion of voices that have developed as independent news reporting and commentary. There are blogs, digital newsletters, Web sites, YouTube videos, and more, where individuals report and comment on the news. An early influential example was the Drudge Report. Many of these come from individuals; some have become large enough to style themselves as Internet newspapers and are now commercial enterprises.

Deuze, Bruns, and Neuberger offer case studies of three newspapers on three different continents that have adopted different approaches to participatory news. Deuze et al. view these as hybrids of the top-down process of traditional journalism and the bottom-up process of grassroots involvement. Professionals have had a rough time adapting to these changes, often because the practices and interests of citizen journalists clash with established journalistic norms. These case studies are particularly important because they reveal the realities of implementing ideas that are mostly untested.

David Simon, known currently as the writer and creator of the HBO series *The Wire*, represents the voice of the traditional newsroom. He readily admits that the industry has harmed itself with its business practices and failure to adapt to the digital environment. This does not, however, negate his fundamental concerns. With these evolutions, he asserts, high-end journalism is dying in America. This selection is his written testimony before a Senate Committee. In his oral testimony he noted the twin problems of management and Internet that have brought newspapers to this point. He clearly indicated his displeasure with the comment: "A plague on both their houses." His point is straightforward. Journalism is a profession. It requires full-time commitment and consistent attention. It cannot become the province of the occasional commentator.

As you read and debate these selections, return to the one suggestion you made about how journalism needs to improve. What kinds of changes could make your suggestion happen? Would citizen journalism help? Or would your suggestion require more traditional journalistic practice? Participatory journalism offers the hope of broader community engagement in civic issues. But are there downsides to this focus? Does journalism lose some of its autonomy if it allows citizens to lead in reporting decisions? Does citizen journalism run the risk of involving citizens, but having their input minimized by the news outlets? As we consider the comments of David Simon, we need to consider the willingness of the American public to pay for high-quality journalism. As an abstract concept, we would probably agree that we want quality, but how many of us are willing to pay for the subscription fees that newspapers now charge? How many of us are willing to pay for our news at all in this age of free access to information on the Internet? These and many other questions are all part of trying to envision a future for journalism in the digital age.

YES

Mark Deuze, Axel Bruns, and Christoph Neuberger

Preparing for an Age of Participatory News

In a time of declining public trust in news, loss of advertising revenue, and an increasingly participatory, self-expressive and digital media culture, journalism is in the process of rethinking and reinventing itself. In this paper, the authors explore how journalism is preparing itself for an age of participatory news: a time where (some of) the news is gathered, selected, edited and communicated by professionals and amateurs, and by producers and consumers alike. Using materials from case studies of emerging participatory news practices in the Netherlands, Germany, Australia and the United States, the authors conclude with some preliminary recommendations for further research and theorize early explanations for the success or failure of participatory journalism. . . .

Preparing for an Age of Participatory News

The rise of what has been described variously as public/civic/communitarian, people's, open source, participatory journalism, or citizen journalism provides a new challenge to a news industry which in many developed nations faces significant permanent problems. Readership for newspapers and viewership of television news are declining, especially among younger generations. The other market news companies serve—advertisers—are also retreating from the field of journalism, gradually shifting their attention to online or non-news channels. These long-term structural trends coincide with a steady outsourcing of production work to "produsers": the consumer-turned-producer or, as Rosen states, "the people formerly known as the audience."

In this paper we investigate the emergence of citizen journalism in three countries—Australia, Germany, and the United States—as a phenomenon that we consider an example of both top-down (industry-driven) customer-relationship management efforts and labor cost-cutting measures, as well as of bottom-up processes of individual and collective self-expression in the context of a participatory and exceedingly digital culture. Participatory news, citizen media, or what Jarvis defines as *networked* journalism "takes into account the collaborative nature of journalism now: professionals and amateurs working together to get the real story, linking to each other across brands and old boundaries to share facts, questions, answers, ideas, perspectives. It recognizes the complex relationships that will make news. And it focuses on the process more than the product." In earlier

From *Journalism Practice*, vol. 1, no. 3, October 2007, pp. 322–335 (excerpts; refs. omitted). Copyright © 2007 by Taylor & Francis Journals. Reprinted by permission via Rightslink.

work, *network* journalism has been defined as a convergence between the core competences and functions of journalists and the civic potential of online inter-active communication. Bardoel and Deuze predicted a new form of journalism that would embrace a cross-media functionality—publishing news across mul-tiple media platforms—as well as an interactive relationship with audiences—acknowledging the lowered threshold for citizens to enter the public sphere. Ultimately, digital and networked journalism in whatever shape or form must be seen as a praxis that is not exclusively tied to salaried work or professional insti-tutions anymore. Or, as former Reuters editor-in-chief Geert Linnebank stated at a conference in March 2007: "Now everyone can be a reporter, commentator or a film director—the days of owning and controlling these processes are over." Throughout this paper we will use the term participatory journalism, as we feel this allows us the widest possible freedom to consider any and all practices and cases within the range of more or less journalistic or "newsy" initiatives mush-rooming online.

Participatory Journalism

Participatory journalism is any kind of newswork at the hands of professionals and amateurs, of journalists and citizens, and of users and producers bench-marked by what Benkler calls commons-based peer production: "the net-worked environment makes possible a new modality of organizing production: radically decentralized, collaborative, and nonproprietary; based on sharing resources and outputs among widely distributed, loosely connected individu-als who cooperate with each other without relying on either market signals or managerial commands." An embrace of this environment by journalism challenges news organizations to extend the level of their direct engagement with audiences as participants in the processes of gathering, selecting, editing, producing, and communicating news. . . .

Recent years have seen a fine-tuning of the various models under which such sites are produced, employing various degrees of balance between ena-bling the open and direct participation of citizen journalist contributors in publicizing and discussing the news, and some level of editorial oversight by the operators or communities of participatory journalism sites. Indeed, the common use of "citizen journalism" as a blanket term for such news publish-ing models to some extent obscures the significant differences in approach between the various participatory news websites currently in operation. . . . The sites of the world-wide Independent Media Center (*Indymedia*) network, for example, largely continue to prefer an entirely open approach and immedi-ately publish all submitted stories to their newswires, while *OhmyNews* com-bines a growing army of tens of thousands of citizen contributors with a small team of professional content editors who ensure the quality of the published product. Each model has proven successful in specific contexts, and it there-fore remains important to study such approaches in some depth in order to identify their strengths and limitations. . . .

The two-tiered developments of participatory news are part of a convergence process: a convergence between top-down and bottom-up journalisms. Such convergence is driven both by commercial pressures on existing news organizations to arrest their decline in audience numbers, and by the sedimentation of participatory journalism projects as serious alternatives to the established news industry. . . . Convergence culture serves both as a mechanism to increase revenue and further the agenda of industry, while at the same time enables people—in terms of their identities as producers and consumers, professionals as well as amateurs—to enact some kind of agency regarding the omnipresent messages and commodities of this industry.

Convergence culture-based participatory news sites tend to emerge from institutions and organizations with a strong public service agenda or a strong connection to clearly defined local or interest communities, or are set up by commercial news organizations which see a thorough embrace of participatory journalism models as a clear competitive advantage in a shrinking market for journalistic work. Examples of such sites may include *NowPublic,* which acts as a platform for the aggregation and discussion of international news reports, the hub of *Backfence* communities in the United States serving as a DIY ("Do-It-Yourself") platform of local news, the British *BBC Action Network,* where local communities are encouraged to submit and discuss information of public interest under the banner—within the brand—of the nation's public broadcaster, or the Dutch site *Headlines,* sponsored by public broadcast news organization NOS, inviting especially younger people to contribute to the news by uploading their own written, audio or video reports. In each instance a professional media organization (top-down) partners with or deliberately taps into the emerging participatory media culture online (bottom-up) in order to produce some kind of co-creative, commons-based news platform.

Conceptual Approach

While a great deal of research into mainstream online journalism or oppositional alternative news models for collaborative or participatory journalism is readily available, the more recent hybrid forms of news sites which combine elements of participatory journalism with frameworks borrowed from or initiated by mainstream news media are yet to be studied in great detail. This essay serves as an initial step towards such enquiries; it examines three intermediary sites in functionally equivalent media cultures—the United States, Germany, and Australia—in order to outline the differences and similarities in the models these sites have chosen to adopt in pursuit of their aims. . . .

The sites chosen here were selected largely because of the distinctive operational approaches they employ; at least some of them (the Australian *On Line Opinion* and the German *Opinio*) have also risen to some degree of national recognition for the unique brand of quality citizen journalism and public intellectual debate which they provide. Our approach looks at successes and failures in order to identify contributing factors for such outcomes, whereas we make an effort to define what one could regard as signifying success or failure. Furthermore, we outline the parallels and distinctions between individual operational models.

Case Studies

The three cases in this paper were selected by the authors in their respective countries or residence (or origin) as useful, prominent and diverse examples of activities in between traditional first-tier and new second-tier news media. In every case, the approach to participatory journalism is a hybrid between institutional or commercial support and community engagement. Further, although in all cases the Internet plays a significant role, in several instances other media—cell phone, newspaper, and magazine—are also involved. The sites furthermore target a range of demographics: the young, the disenfranchised, pundits and politicians, middle-class families. We consider these cases exemplary, and assume that by putting the characteristics and (relatively short) histories of these initiatives side by side in an initial comparison, we can draw some inferences that help us to specify further hypotheses and research questions regarding the changes and challenges involved in re-connecting journalism with the citizenry it is supposed to serve articulated with the affordances of a participatory media culture. These case studies are based on (scholarly, trade and Web-based) literature reviews and in expert interviews. Aspects of investigation were: the degree of user participation, the role of the professional journalists, the motivation of suppliers and participants, conflicts between editors and users, and the perceived success or failure of the projects.

The US-based *Bluffton Today* complements and connects with the local newspaper, adding a citizen-produced dimension to journalistic coverage, and in the process furthering the cultural convergence between producer and consumer. The Dutch *Skoeps* site is an extension of a newspaper publisher (PCM) and a commercial broadcaster (Talpa), and sponsored by Vodafone. The site asks users to upload their own pictures and videos of newsworthy events. The organizations involved make money by reselling user-generated materials to third parties with 50:50 deals. The German online magazine *Opinio* has to date shied away from political discussion and instead focuses on lifestyle issues. *Opinio* is an Internet offshoot of the *Rheinische Post* newspaper which fills a magazine and a weekly newspaper page with the user-generated content from the website. By contrast, the Australian *On Line Opinion* (run by the non-profit organization National Forum) tackles politics head-on, and provides a space for public intellectualism which connects journalists, politicians, academics, and "average" citizens in a rich mix of political debate—but here, questions remain over whether in the process the site becomes simply yet another platform for the usual suspects: pundits who are already over-represented in political debates.

"Transparency and Dialogue": The American *Bluffton Today*

Bluffton Today is a combination of a free daily newspaper (launched April 4, 2005) and a community news website (which went online April 1, 2005), both published by the Morris Publishing Group (MPG). MPG was founded in 2001 and publishes 27 daily, 12 non-daily and numerous free community newspapers in the United States. . . . The tabloid-size newspaper *Bluffton Today* had an initial circulation of 16,500 and is distributed free to every home in the greater Bluffton, South Carolina area in the United States. Bluffton is a fast-growing affluent community with over 10,000 households on the Atlantic coast of South Carolina. What makes the paper and site a prime example of a true hybrid between professional and amateur participatory news is its deliberate choice to have (slightly edited) user-generated content as its prime source of news and information. According to Morris analyst Steve Yelvington, *Bluffton Today* is an "experiment in citizen journalism, a complete inversion of the typical online newspaper model," as staffers as well as registered community members get a blog, a photo gallery, read/write access to a shared public community calendar, a community cookbook, and an application that supports podcasting and the uploading of video clips. Regarding the paper, readers' online comments on stories that appear in the print edition are edited and printed in the hard copy of next day's newspaper.

Discussing his company's choices in an online convergence newsletter, Ken Rickard, manager of product strategy for Morris DigitalWorks, explicitly notes how *Bluffton Today* is an example of cultural rather than technological convergence: "The goals of *Bluffton Today* are quite simple: to become a part of the daily conversation in Bluffton. The paper needs to build trust, solicit feedback and help develop a sense of shared community. The motto of the Web site, then, is 'It's what people are talking about.' And that's where the convergence comes from. The Web site is entirely created by the residents of Bluffton; those who work for the newspaper and those who do not." Here Rickard ties convergence to the cultural phenomenon of blurring the boundaries between "producers" and "users" of content. During the first months, the site and paper were in "beta," which is software development jargon for operating in a test phase. Writing one month after the launch of the site and paper, Rickard goes on to explain how this ongoing testing and tweaking has garnered a crucial insight for the company: "the early results have been very promising. The most notable result has been largely unintended: there exists a level of transparency and dialogue about the creation of the newspaper that engenders a real sense of trust in the community."

For the purposes of this case study, it is important to note here how convergence culture seems to instill increased levels of transparency in the media system, where producers and consumers of content can "see" each other at work, as they both play each other's roles. In this context, Yelvington is quoted in an interview at the *Online Journalism Review* (of September 7, 2005) as saying how he believes that people are "living in this cable TV world of the outside observer instead of acting as participants. We're trying to make people come out of their gates and become players. We want a participative culture to evolve."

Participation seems to be key for understanding the success of both the industry initiative and the community's response. The news as reported on the *Bluffton Today* site mainly covers typical topics of local and particular interest: the opening of a new public school, declining (or increasing) church attendance, parades and other community events, a regional sports team. Occasionally, discussions on certain news topics—the election of a black (or white) school principal for example—can get quite heated, and thus serve to add a critical edge to the coverage. On the other hand, most of the community blogs and user-submitted audio or video are quite mainstreamed. The website is largely self-policed, with the editors calling on participants to "be a good citizen and exhibit community leadership qualities. . . . Act as you would like your neighbors to act." Indeed, the site reports that it only professionally edits stories that are repurposed for the newspaper. In a post on his weblog of July 6, 2006, Yelvington takes note of the fundamental discussions among the journalists about their role in all of this: "As they nurtured the idea that eventually became Bluffton Today, my friends in our newspaper division spent many months wrestling with basic questions about content, tone and especially civic processes. They didn't come up with a label, and they certainly didn't call it citizen journalism. But they did come up with a catchphrase: A community in conversation with itself." In doing so, they mirror an ideal voiced by the late James Carey: that in a democracy journalism is or should be all about amplifying the conversation society has with itself. . . .

"Authentic Life Stories": The German *Opinio*

In the German media the website *Opinio* run by *Rheinische Post* has received a lot of attention. This daily newspaper, published in Düsseldorf, is one of the regional dailies with the highest circulation figures in Germany. . . . This site shows the tendency to skip subjects like the economy or politics, preferring to focus on users' everyday living and leisure-time activities. . . .

The *Rheinische Post,* one of the first newspapers to go online in Germany, started the website *Opinio* in December 2004, on which users write for users exclusively. Beginning in February 2005 it published the print magazine "Opinio." . . . Since the autumn of 2005, it publishes only a weekly special section in the newspaper with articles from *Opinio*. The target group of *Opinio* is people between 30 and 39 years, who rarely read the printed newspaper. . . .

The former project manager Torsten Casimir said (in an interview in February 2006) that an aim of *Opinio* was to reach new advertisers. But to date *Opinio* has not been too successful in this regard. The number of authors, however, has increased steadily. In March 2007 there were about 2800 registered authors, which at that time had submitted about 26,000 articles. Little is known about their socio-demographic characteristics, however. According to Casimir, the core of the community numbers some 60–70 authors who are writing on a daily basis. Among those, there are many teachers, housewives and unemployed graduates. They have developed a community feeling which also finds its expression in participation at meetings, for example at *Opinio* parties. Among the most widely read authors are a hobby satirist and a single mother who is writing a kind of public diary. But the vast majority of the authors are writing only occasionally.

What motivates people to contribute to a participatory newspaper website such as *Opinio*? Casimir assumes that, on the one hand, the reputable environment, and on the other hand, the promise of "print publicity" with a high circulation, motivate users. A survey shows that about two-thirds of the authors of the website exclusively write for *Opinio*. Here they found their home on the Internet.

Registration is necessary to participate as an author. The staff of *Opinio* have the right to cancel articles and to eliminate participants in any case where the rules are violated. . . . In February 2006, the *Opinio* staff numbered one editor who was a regular employee, as well as several freelancers. Staff members propose subjects: they mostly ask for reports on personal experiences, advice for everyday life, and photos. And they select and edit (fact checking, shortening in most cases) the best and most read *Opinio* articles for the weekly page in the *Rheinische Post*.

The German left-alternative daily *Die Tageszeitung* criticized *Opinio* because of its lifestyle mixture of subjects and the lack of political discussions. The sections of *Opinio* (like dating & parties, traveling & excursion, sports & leisure time, love & partnership, body & health) show that the main focus is on the private sector of life. *Opinio* does not complement the newspaper with subjects in the "hard news" sections, but "with experiences, with authentic stories—that's new." The aim of the website seems not to be citizen journalism so much as a concern to gain new readers and advertisers.

A significant conflict between users and between users and editorial staff occurred during January 2006. One of the most widely read authors, publishing under the pseudonym "kiyan," started a discussion about the future of *Opinio* which continued for several days. In his article "OPINIO innovativ?" kiyan criticized the stagnancy of the website and the low quality of many contributions. He asked for a more restrictive policy on the part of staff members and a more intensive debate about quality between users. The subsequent discussion addressed the growing complexity of *Opinio,* an effect of the rising number of authors. Staff was blamed for increasing the number of authors haphazardly, with no regard for the quality of their contributions. One author surmised that one reason for criticism was a latent competition between older and younger authors. The discussion culminated in the question of whether interventions for the improvement of articles should be interpreted as "censorship" or "quality management." Some users asked for more transparency of and participation in the work of staff. Above all, the decision which articles are chosen for publication in the printed magazine was discussed controversially. Conflicts about questions like these seem to be typical for community websites at least in the early stage. They express the tension between the two tiers mentioned, between openness for the people and professional perceptions of quality content.

Even though *Opinio* does not cover its own costs yet, the project is not at risk. The *Rheinische Post* earned a great deal of additional reputation through its publication of *Opinio*. A large number of publishing houses from Germany, Austria and the Netherlands have shown interest in the project. A clear sign of acknowledgement is the European Newspaper Award of 2006, which *Opinio* received in the category "Innovations."

"Provoking Debate": The Australian *On Line Opinion*

Compared to the international counterparts we have discussed above, which are clear attempts by commercial journalistic entities to embrace the productive potential of participatory journalism, the Australian-based non-profit news and current events site *On Line Opinion* is perhaps most similar to the US website *MediaChannel* as it both covers the news in its own right, and acts as a watchdog and corrective to the mainstream media. However, *MediaChannel* combines the efforts of a small in-house staff with material sourced from its vast network of over 1000 affiliate news sites (including a number of *Indymedia* sites), from whom articles are drawn in a kind of internal gatewatching process. *On Line Opinion,* on the other hand, focuses mostly on original writing by staffers and invited commentators—who frequently include journalists from the Canberra press gallery, as well as government and opposition politicians, academics, and other noteworthy public figures. Such high-profile involvement demonstrates that the site plays an important role in Australian political discussion, even though it may not or not yet have achieved widespread public recognition beyond political elites.

Such content is further combined with unsolicited article submissions from visitors to the site, responses by readers that are attached, blog-style, as commentary to articles, discussion forums, an e-mail list, and further staff blogs. As a result, *On Line Opinion* provides a middle ground for an exchange and deliberation between those in power (or hoping to come to power), those reporting on the powerful, and those affected by their policies. This is in keeping with the publication's stated goal of providing "a forum for public social and political debate about current Australian issues. We publish articles to stimulate a public discourse on a range of topics. It is not the editors' intention to dominate these pages—these articles are gathered from a variety of independent sources and are published in the belief that ideas are the essence of progress and that issues and opinions should be addressed, not suppressed." Editors further stress their emphasis on providing a complement to the mainstream as well as alternative media: "we welcome any rational contribution to what has become a robust public debate not available in any other media or forum."

At present, the Australian political scene is characterized by a significant degree of polarization between the long-serving conservative federal government and its Labor opposition, and conversely between the unanimously Labor-run state and territory governments and their conservative oppositions, as well as by a persistent sense of bias towards one or the other political persuasion in the mainstream news media. In this context, then, *On Line Opinion* is particularly notable for its bipartisan stance—its contributors include commentators from both the left and right, and the debates carried out in its forums, though occasionally as riddled with personal invective and political rhetoric as those in many other discussion groups, nonetheless frequently feature an open engagement between participants of differing political and ideological background. Indeed, as *On Line Opinion* editor and publisher Graham Young believes, "the forceful expression of opposites is more likely to lead to the uncovering of truth than the rote recital of mantras of common faiths."

Although by ways other than they may have imagined, then, *On Line Opinion* flattens the hierarchy of both expert sources and dominant news frames. This is for example supported by the mode in which articles are presented on *On Line Opinion*'s front page, which merely lists topics and authors without highlighting whether authors are government ministers, senators, members of parliament, journalists, expert commentators, academics, or "mere" members of the public. Thus, opinions and knowledge expressed on the site articulate the experiences of the participants. Or, as Young puts it, "every idea has a place in the public debate and has a right to be expressed."

However, the extent to which sites such as *On Line Opinion* can realize a truly deliberative journalism continues to remain limited both by the operational parameters of the site, as well as by the extent to which its participants are willing and able to embrace this new form of journalism. To begin with, like *MediaChannel, On Line Opinion* is not open news: it does not offer a platform for the publication of their views to all comers, but instead retains a clear editorial presence. And even while Young states emphatically that *"On Line Opinion* believes evangelically that speech must be as close to absolutely free as possible,"* the very fact that stories for *On Line Opinion* are selected from all incoming submissions cannot but introduce at least a small amount of bias towards certain articles and topics. As Young also writes, "what we do is publish pieces of opinion from people in the community who know and understand what is happening"—and so there remains a relatively traditional journalistic selection process for newsworthy events here. This contrasts for example with the open news approach of sites such as *Indymedia,* where all incoming stories are posted automatically, the open publishing model of the *Wikipedia,* where users are able to create new entries on topics of interest to them instantaneously, or the steps towards open editing in sites such as *Kuro5hin* and *Plastic,* where submitted stories are processed and published by community consensus.

But as we have noted above, sites such as *On Line Opinion,* which bridge the gap between mainstream and alternative, and thus perhaps between (top-down) editorially controlled and (bottom-up) open news media, are to some extent perhaps forced to reflect this intermediary position in their editorial practices. At least in present form *On Line Opinion* is edited enough to ensure the participation of high-level public figures who would otherwise perhaps shy away from open publishing sites, while simultaneously being open enough to participants to attract strong discussion and deliberation on the topics covered on the site. What is of more concern for the effort to encourage broad public participation and deliberation, however, is the level of meaningful participation in public debate that may be possible for the "average" citizen. While *On Line Opinion* openly invites contributors—Young writes that "we are . . . continually looking for new voices and fresh points of view, so *previous experience is not necessary*"—people must still be able to express their views in a clear and engaging fashion, and this may limit public debate to the usual suspects. If Young calls for contributors to "have a combination of one or more of the following characteristics: Expertise in their field; Influence in their field; Writing skills; Interesting, even iconoclastic, ideas; The ability to provoke debate," then, there is a danger that those attracted by and matching these criteria are largely members of those social groups who are already over-represented in public debate, perhaps already participate on *On Line Opinion,* and could at any rate also find a pathway into other media forms for their work.

This dilemma is by no means limited to, or even caused by, *On Line Opinion:* similar criticisms have been leveled at publications ranging from the mainstream media (where journalists are sometimes said to represent the views only of those whose position in and outlook on life matches their own) through to blogs (where the blogosphere has been described as an echo chamber repeating commonly-held views *ad infinitum).* The challenge for all news media aiming to embrace a more deliberative style of journalism, then, is to attract a broader range of participants in the deliberation—and while they still have a long way to go, blogs, open news, and semi-open news publications like *On Line Opinion* do already contribute to this process by providing at the very least the tools, and increasingly also the incentive, for more contributors to join the debate.

Discussion

In their strengths and limitations, the case studies presented here indicate a variety of approaches to participatory news with which commercial and non-profit media organizations are currently experimenting. As Outing suggests, "citizen journalism isn't one simple concept that can be applied universally by all news organizations. It's much more complex, with many potential variations . . . from dipping a toe into the waters of participatory journalism to embracing citizen reporting with your organization's full involvement." It is important to study these different approaches in some detail—both as an object of study in their own right, in the context of social software and so-called "Web 2.0" phenomena, and as pathways towards future configurations for culturally convergent models of journalism.

News organizations do not necessarily engage the citizen on a more or less equal footing because the professionals involved are universally convinced that the breakdown between users and producers of news provides society with better information—often a clear commercial motive is at work: the potential to sell targeted advertising across online and offline media. *On Line Opinion* is an exception, although the site is sponsored by a host of traditional public institutions whose motives are at the very least not entirely altruistic. The overarching ideals that are embodied in each of the sites discussed here do in combination point to a trend towards a more participatory reconceptualization of news and information production and dissemination.

What is most important about these sites is that they provide clear and workable alternatives to the traditional separation of journalists, their sources, and the public. These are not utopian ideals. We have found practicable and (monetary, communal or intellectual) revenue-generating models for the production of news outside of or across the boundaries of the established news industry. At the same time, this convergence of industrial and participatory journalism cultures does not occur in a uniform, painless process—nor does it occur in a vacuum. Coping with the emergence of hybrid producer–user forms of newswork is easier for some than for others, and tends to clash with entrenched notions of professionalism, objectivity, and carefully cultivated arrogance regarding the competences (or talent) of "the audience" to know what is good for them. As the case studies above suggest to us, their areas of engagement are sometimes clearly demarcated—citizen participation may be sought mainly in "soft news" areas, while "hard news," and especially politics, is still regarded as too controversial to be opened to the involvement of news users as "produsers." It is also noteworthy that in sites where this limitation is not enforced, "soft" news still appears to dominate, suggesting that many people come to citizen journalism not to correct the "hard" news of the mainstream itself, but to *correct for* mainstream journalism's bias *towards* "hard" news itself by adding a greater amount of "soft" news. . . .

Ultimately, convergence culture in journalism relies on the readiness of both sides of the equation: participants must bring and/or build an understanding of how to operate in a news "produsage" environment just as much as journalists must develop a sense of how to reinvent themselves as co-creators of culture. Indeed, journalists as the traditional regulators and moderators of public discourse should particularly focus on solving the conflict between open access and the quality of communication. . . .

Conclusion

At the beginning of this paper, we noted the many problems currently faced by the news industry. We cannot frame participatory journalism in its pure bottom-up form as an entirely satisfactory answer to the decline of the news industry's marketability or credibility, nor is it likely to facilitate the survival of news formats outside of the online realm. For all its success, citizen journalism remains dependent to a significant extent on mainstream news organizations, whose output it debates, critiques, recombines, and debunks by harnessing large and distributed communities of users. At the same time, increasingly mainstream news is taking note of what the citizen journalists are saying, and uses content generated by users as an alternative to vox-pops, opinion polls, or in some cases as a partial replacement of editorial work. Whether the practitioners are enthusiast participants in the process or not, the process of increasing hybridization and convergence between the bottom-up and top-down models of newswork is already in full swing around the world. The fact that the sites which we have considered here manage to survive and, in some cases, to flourish in an already overcrowded attention economy, and furthermore seem to generate relevant news for the communities they serve, suggests that professionally enhanced participatory journalism has legitimacy as a form of news production in its own right—well beyond the apparent ambition of some news barons to harvest bottom-up news as a cheaper alternative to the content produced by costly in-house staff. . . .

From these admittedly cursory glances it seems evident that the professionals involved in all of these cases have had (and are still having) a rough ride. Participatory ideals do not mesh well with set notions of professional distance in journalism; notions which tend to exclude rather than to include.

Indeed, in the information age modern societies can ill afford a status quo which leaves large sections of the citizenry disenfranchised from participation in processes of journalistic and political deliberation. On the other hand, the professionalization of journalism is one of the few markers it can wield to defend its unique position in contemporary democracy. Perhaps at issue is whether to see journalism as it works today as a profession that is "finished," or as a trade that is continually evolving and therefore is ready to invest itself in its own development. . . .

Testimony of David Simon   ➡ **NO**

Senate Committee on Commerce, Science, and Transportation Subcommittee on Communications, Technology, and the Internet Hearing on the Future of Journalism, May 6, 2009

T hank you all for the invitation and opportunity to speak on this issue today, but I start by confessing reluctance.

My name is David Simon and I used to be a newspaperman in Baltimore. Head and heart, I was a newspaperman from the day I signed up at my high school paper until the day, eighteen years later, when I took a buyout from the *Baltimore Sun* and left for the fleshpots of Hollywood.

To those colleagues who remain at newspapers, I am therefore an apostate, and my direct connection to newspapering—having ended in 1995—means that as a witness today, my experiences are attenuated.

Ideally, rather than listening to me, you should be hearing from any number of voices of those still laboring in American journalism. I am concerned that the collective voice of the newsroom itself—the wisdom of veteran desk editors, rewrite men and veteran reporters is poorly represented in this process. But of course newspapers are obliged to cover Congress and its works, and therefore the participation of most working journalists in today's hearing would compromise some careful ethics. I know your staff tried to invite working journalists but were rebuffed on these grounds. And so, tellingly, today's witness list is heavy with newspaper executives on the one hand, and representatives of the new, internet-based media on the other.

And so, I've accepted the invitation, though to be honest, I'm tired of hearing myself on this subject; I've had my say in essays that accompany this testimony, and in the episodes of a recent television drama, and I would be more inclined to hear from former colleagues if they were in a position to speak bluntly.

I am glad, at least, to be testifying beside Steve Coll, who labored at the *Washington Post* for two decades and whose coverage of complex issues upholds the highest journalistic standards. And I will leave to Mr. Coll a more careful

U.S. Senate, May 6, 2009.

and considered analysis of where journalism and newspapering must travel. I fully agree with his fundamental argument that non-profit status is the industry's last hope, and I believe his thoughts on the subject are more advanced and detailed than my own.

If Mr. Coll can be prescriptive, I will do my best to be diagnostic. I'll set him up by concentrating on what went wrong in American newspapering.

What I say will likely conflict with what representatives of the newspaper industry will claim for themselves. And I can imagine little agreement with those who speak for new media. From the captains of the newspaper industry, you will hear a certain martyrology—a claim that they were heroically serving democracy to their utmost only to be undone by a cataclysmic shift in technology and the arrival of all things web-based. From those speaking on behalf of new media, weblogs and that which goes twitter, you will be treated to assurances that American journalism has a perfectly fine future online, and that a great democratization in newsgathering is taking place.

In my city, there is a technical term we often administer when claims are plainly contradicted by facts on the ground. We note that the claimant is, for lack of a better term, full of it. Though in Baltimore, of course, we are explicit with our nouns.

High-end journalism is dying in America and unless a new economic model is achieved, it will not be reborn on the web or anywhere else. The internet is a marvelous tool and clearly it is the informational delivery system of our future, but thus far it does not deliver much first-generation reporting. Instead, it leeches that reporting from mainstream news publications, whereupon aggregating websites and bloggers contribute little more than repetition, commentary and froth. Meanwhile, readers acquire news from the aggregators and abandon its point of origin—namely the newspapers themselves.

In short, the parasite is slowly killing the host.

It is nice to get stuff for free, of course. And it is nice that more people can have their say in new media. And while some of our internet commentary is—as with any unchallenged and unedited intellectual effort—rampantly ideological, ridiculously inaccurate and occasionally juvenile, some of it is also quite good, even original.

Understand here that I am not making a Luddite argument against the internet and all that it offers. But democratized and independent though they may be, you do not—in my city—run into bloggers or so-called citizen journalists at City Hall, or in the courthouse hallways or at the bars and union halls where police officers gather. You do not see them consistently nurturing and then pressing sources. You do not see them holding institutions accountable on a daily basis.

Why? Because high-end journalism—that which acquires essential information about our government and society in the first place—is a profession; it requires daily, full-time commitment by trained men and women who return to the same beats day in and day out until the best of them know everything with which a given institution is contending. For a relatively brief period in American history—no more than the last fifty years or so—a lot of smart and talented people were paid a living wage and benefits to challenge the unrestrained authority of our institutions and to hold those institutions to task. Modern newspaper reporting was the hardest and in some ways most gratifying job I ever had. I am offended to think that anyone, anywhere believes American institutions as insulated, self-preserving and self-justifying as police departments, school systems, legislatures and chief executives can be held to gathered facts by amateurs pursuing the task without compensation, training or for that matter, sufficient standing to make public officials even care to whom it is they are lying or from whom they are withholding information.

The idea of this is absurd, yet to read the claims that some new media voices are already making, you would think they need only bulldoze the carcasses of moribund newspapers aside and begin typing. They don't know what they don't know—which is a dangerous state for any class of folk—and to those of us who do understand how subtle and complex good reporting can be, their ignorance is as embarrassing as it is seemingly sincere. Indeed, the very phrase citizen journalist strikes my ear as nearly Orwellian. A neighbor who is a good listener and cares about people is a good neighbor; he is not in any sense a citizen social worker. Just as a neighbor with a garden hose and good intentions is not a citizen firefighter. To say so is a heedless insult to trained social workers and firefighters.

So much for new media. But what about old media?

When you hear a newspaper executive claiming that his industry is an essential bulwark of society and that it stands threatened by a new technology that is, as of yet, unready to shoulder the same responsibility, you may be inclined to empathize. And indeed, that much is true enough as it goes.

But when that same newspaper executive then goes on to claim that this predicament has occurred through no fault on the industry's part, that they have merely been undone by new technologies, feel free to kick out his teeth. At that point, he's as fraudulent as the most self-aggrandized blogger.

Anyone listening carefully may have noted that I was bought out of my reporting position in 1995. That's fourteen years ago. That's well before the internet ever began to seriously threaten any aspect of the industry. That's well before Craig's List and department-store consolidation gutted the ad base. Well before any of the current economic conditions applied.

In fact, when newspaper chains began cutting personnel and content, their industry was one of the most profitable yet discovered by Wall Street money. We know now—because bankruptcy has opened the books—that The *Baltimore Sun* was eliminating its afternoon edition and trimming nearly 100 editors and reporters in an era when the paper was achieving 37 percent profits. In the years before the internet deluge, the men and women who might have made *The Sun* a more essential vehicle for news and commentary— something so strong that it might have charged for its product online—they were being ushered out the door so that Wall Street could command short-term profits in the extreme.

Such short-sighted arrogance rivals that of Detroit in the 1970s, when automakers—confident that American consumers were mere captives—offered up Chevy Vegas, and Pacers and Gremlins without the slightest worry that mediocrity would be challenged by better-made cars from Germany or Japan.

In short, my industry butchered itself and we did so at the behest of Wall Street and the same unfettered, free-market logic that has proved so disastrous for so many American industries. And the original sin of American newspapering lies, indeed, in going to Wall Street in the first place.

When locally-based, family-owned newspapers like *The Sun* were consolidated into publicly-owned newspaper chains, an essential dynamic, an essential trust between journalism and the communities served by that journalism was betrayed.

Economically, the disconnect is now obvious. What do newspaper executives in Los Angeles or Chicago care whether or not readers in Baltimore have a better newspaper, especially when you can make more putting out a mediocre paper than a worthy one? The profit margin was all. And so, where family ownership might have been content with 10 or 15 percent profit, the chains demanded double that and more, and the cutting began—long before the threat of new technology was ever sensed.

But editorially? The newspaper chains brought an ugly disconnect to the newsroom, and by extension, to the community as well.

A few years after the A.S. Abell Family sold *The Sun* to the *Times-Mirror* newspaper chain, fresh editors arrived from out of town to take over the reins of the paper.

They looked upon Baltimore not as essential terrain to be covered with consistency, to be explained in all its complexity year in and year out for readers who had and would live their lives in Baltimore. Why would they? They had arrived from somewhere else, and if they could win a prize or two, they would be moving on to bigger and better opportunities within the chain.

So, well before the arrival of the internet, as veteran reporters and home-grown editors took buyouts, newsbeats were dropped and less and less of Baltimore and central Maryland were covered with rigor or complexity.

In a city in which half the adult black males are without consistent work, the poverty and social services beat was abandoned. In a town where the unions were imploding and the working class eviscerated, where the bankruptcy of a huge steel manufacturer meant thousands were losing medical benefits and pensions, there was no longer a labor reporter. And though it is one of the most violent cities in America, the Baltimore courthouse went uncovered for more than a year and the declining quality of criminal casework in the state's attorney's office went largely ignored.

Meanwhile, the editors used their manpower to pursue a handful of special projects, Pulitzer-sniffing as one does. The self-gratification of my profession does not come, you see, from covering a city and covering it well, from explaining an increasingly complex and interconnected world to citizens, from holding basic institutions accountable on a daily basis. It comes from someone handing you a plaque and taking your picture.

The prizes meant little, of course, to actual readers. What might have mattered to them, what might have made *The Baltimore Sun* substantial enough to charge online for content would have been to comprehensively cover its region and the issues of that region, to do so with real insight and sophistication and consistency.

But the reporters required to achieve such were cleanly dispatched, buy-out after buyout, from the first staff reduction in 1992 to the latest round last week, in which nearly a third of the remaining newsroom was fired. Where 500 men and women once covered central Maryland, there are now 140. And the money required to make a great newspaper—including, say, the R&D funding that might have anticipated and planned for the internet revolution—all of that went back to Wall Street, to CEO salaries and to big-money investors. The executives and board chairman held up their profit margins and got promoted; they're all on some golf course in Florida right now, comfortably retired and thinking about things other than journalism. The editors took their prizes and got promoted; they're probably on what passes for a journalism lecture circuit these days, offering heroic tales of past glory and jeremiads about the world they, in fact, helped to bring about.

But the newspapers themselves?

When I was in journalism school in the 1970s, the threat was television and its immediacy. My professors claimed that in order to survive, newspapers were going to have to cede the ambulance chasing and reactive coverage to TV and instead become more like great magazines. Specialization and detailed beat reporting were the future. We were going to have to explain an increasingly complex world in ways that made us essential to an increasingly educated readership. The scope of coverage would have to go deeper, address more of the world not less. Those were our ambitions. Those were my ambitions.

In Baltimore at least, and I imagine in every other American city served by newspaper-chain journalism, those ambitions were not betrayed by the internet. We had trashed them on our own, years before. Incredibly, we did it for naked, short-term profits and a handful of trinkets to hang on the office wall. And now, having made ourselves less essential, less comprehensive and less able to offer a product that people might purchase online, we pretend to an undeserved martyrdom at the hands of new technology.

I don't know if it isn't too late already for American newspapering. So much talent has been torn from newsrooms over the last two decades and the ambitions of the craft are now so crude, small-time and stunted that it's hard to imagine a turnaround. But if there is to be a renewal of the industry a few things are certain and obvious:

First, cutting down trees and printing a daily accounting of the world on paper and delivering it to individual doorsteps is anachronistic. And if that is so, then the industry is going to have to find a way to charge for online content. Yes, I have heard the post-modern rallying cry that information wants to be free. But information isn't. It costs money to send reporters to London, Fallujah and Capitol Hill, and to send photographers with them, and to keep them there day after day. It costs money to hire the best investigators and writers and then to back them up with the best editors. It costs money to do the finest kind of journalism. And how anyone can believe that the industry can fund that kind of expense by giving its product away online to aggregators and bloggers is a source of endless fascination to me. A freshman marketing major at any community college can tell you that if you don't have a product for which you can charge people, you don't actually have a product.

Second, Wall Street and free-market logic, having been a destructive force in journalism over the last few decades, are not now suddenly the answer. Raw, unencumbered capitalism is never the answer when a public trust or public mission is at issue. If the last quarter century has taught us anything—and admittedly, with too many of us, I doubt it has—it's that free-market capitalism, absent social imperatives and responsible regulatory oversight, can produce durable goods and services, glorious profits, and little of lasting social value. Airlines, manufacturing, banking, real estate—is there a sector of the American economy where laissez-faire theories have not burned the poor, the middle class and the consumer, while bloating the rich and mortgaging the very future of the industry, if not the country itself? I'm pressed to think of one.

Similarly, there can be no serious consideration of public funding for newspapers. High-end journalism can and should bite any hand that tries to feed it, and it should bite a government hand most viciously. Moreover, it is the right of every American to despise his local newspaper—for being too liberal or too conservative, for covering X and not covering Y, for spelling your name wrong when you do something notable and spelling it correctly when you are seen as dishonorable. And it is the birthright of every healthy newspaper to hold itself indifferent to such constant disdain and be nonetheless read by all. Because in the end, despite all flaws, there is no better model for a comprehensive and independent review of society than a modern newspaper. As love-hate relationships go, this is a pretty intricate one. An exchange of public money would pull both sides from their comfort zone and prove unacceptable to all.

But a non-profit model intrigues, especially if that model allows for locally-based ownership and control of news organizations. Anything that government can do in the way of creating non-profit status for newspapers should be seriously pursued. And further, anything that can be done to create financial or tax-based incentives for bankrupt and near-bankrupt newspaper chains to transfer or even donate unprofitable publications to locally-based non-profits should also be considered.

Lastly, I would urge Congress to consider relaxing certain anti-trust prohibitions with regard to the newspaper industry, so that *The Washington Post*, *The New York Times* and various other newspapers can sit down and openly discuss protecting their copyright from aggregators and plan an industry wide transition to a paid, online subscriber base. Whatever money comes will prove essential to the task of hiring back some of the talent, commitment and institutional memory that has been squandered.

Absent this basic and belated acknowledgment that content has value— if indeed it still does after so many destructive buyouts and layoffs—and that content is what ultimately matters, I don't think anything else can save high-end, professional journalism.

Thank you for your time and again, for your kind invitation.

POSTSCRIPT

Will Evolving Forms of Journalism Be an Improvement?

For another perspective on whether emerging forms of journalism will be an improvement, consider the views of Eran Ben-Porath in his article "Internal Fragmentation of the News: Television News in Dialogical Format and Its Consequences for Journalism," *Journalism Studies* (2007). He argues that the primary change in journalism in this era has been the shift from traditional practices to dialogic formats in which conversationally based news has become predominant. When dialogue, rather than reporting, is the format, the authority of the journalist is lessened, conversationalists are often not journalists but commentators or partisan spokespersons, and the audience changes from receivers of information to witnesses of conversation. In addition to diminished authority of the reporter, Ben-Porath argues for diminished authority and accountability for the news organization; the organization did not make the "claims"; their guests did. Thus the organization's accountability for accuracy is diminished. He also asserts that question asking becomes the norm rather than fact-checking. These changes are taking place most visibly in television news, but are also playing out extensively on the Internet. Does this mean that the evolving forms of journalistic practice will continue this drift to conversation rather than reporting? As a colleague said, "News is expensive; opinion is cheap."

As a student of mass communication, media literacy is almost certainly a goal of your course. Media literacy refers to the ability to analyze and evaluate the media messages within our society. Media literacy refers to the ability to establish expectations of news organizations and the capacity to critically evaluate the many professional and participatory messages that are available. Consider what your standards or expectations will be. This and other issues within this volume should help you define your own criteria for excellence.

To pursue some of these themes, you might want to read *Hot Air: All Talk, All the Time* by Howard Kurtz (1997). You may also enjoy his 2007 *Reality Show: Inside the Last Great Television News War,* an insider look at news production and judgment at the three legacy networks. For a look at how the state of newspaper journalism has changed in the Internet age, see *The Washington Post* editors Downie and Kaiser's *The News about the News: American Journalism in Peril.* To read more extensively about the hope that online journalism will fundamentally change journalism in a positive manner, see Dan Gillmor's *We the Media: Grassroots Journalism by the People, for the People* (2006).

Internet References . . .

American Civil Liberties Union

This official site of the ACLU provides a general introduction of issues involving individual rights.

http://www.aclu.org

Fairness and Accuracy in Reporting (FAIR)

FAIR is a national media watch group that offers criticism of media bias and censorship. FAIR advocates for greater diversity in the press and scrutinizes media practices that marginalize public interest, minority and dissenting viewpoints.

http://www.fair.org

The Federal Communications Commission (FCC)

This official cite of the FCC provides comprehensive information about the rules and guidelines, official inquiries, and other operations of this complex agency.

http://www.fcc.gov

Freedom Forum

Freedom Forum is a nonpartisan international foundation dedicated to free press and free speech, and to helping media and the public understand one another. The Web site includes extensive resources and excellent discussion of issues of free speech and press, as well as religion, technology, and international issues. The Press Watch area is intriguing.

http://www.freedomforum.org

CQ Researcher

Type "Broadcast Indecency" into the search engine for access to a full report on issues of broadcast indecency including extensive background material, a historical recap, an analysis of current issues, and additional resources.

http://library.cqpress.com/cqresearcher/

UNIT 4

Law and Policy

*F*or the media, the First Amendment entails both rights and responsibilities. How to ensure that these responsibilities will be met is the subject of much of communications law and legislative action. What are the valid limits of the rights of free press? How should society respond when First Amendment rights are in conflict with other individual rights? What changes will new technology force upon our operation of these rights? The issues in this section deal with who should be responsible for media content and with the rights of groups who find that content inappropriate.

- Should the Public Support Freedom of the Press?
- Is Hate Speech in the Media Directly Affecting Our Culture?
- Has Industry Regulation Controlled Indecent Media Content?

ISSUE 11

Should the Public Support Freedom of the Press?

YES: Jeffrey J. Maciejewski and David T. Ozar, from "Natural Law and the Right to Know in a Democracy," *Journal of Mass Media Ethics* (vol. 21, no. 1, 2006)

NO: First Amendment Center, from *State of the First Amendment: 2004* (Freedom Forum, 2004)

ISSUE SUMMARY

YES: Citizens' "right to know" in a democratic society is a foundation of freedom of the press. Jeffrey J. Maciejewski and David T. Ozar examine multiple meanings of the concept of right to know, asking what this implies about conduct at the personal and institutional level. Maciejewski and Ozar then situate the concept in natural law and applies that understanding to journalistic decisions.

NO: In contrast, the *State of the First Amendment: 2004* report reveals lackluster support for the First Amendment in general and its application to controversial cases in particular. Few know the freedoms guaranteed or care passionately about them—almost one-third feel the freedom granted under the First Amendment "goes too far." Moreover, Americans seem less supportive of freedom of the press than of any other freedoms guaranteed in our Bill of Rights.

The First Amendment to the U.S. Constitution states:

> Congress shall make no law respecting an establishment of religion, or prohibiting the free exercise thereof; or abridging the freedom of speech, or of the press; or the right of the people peaceably to assemble, and to petition the government for a redress of grievances.

Thomas Jefferson said, "Were it left to me to decide whether we should have government without newspapers, or newspapers without government, I should not hesitate a moment to prefer the latter." Yet freedoms are never absolute. Justice Holmes was writing for the Supreme Court in 1919 when he said: "The most stringent protection of free speech would not protect a man in falsely shouting fire in a theater and causing a panic. . . . The question in every case is whether the words are used in such circumstances and are of such a nature as to create a clear and present danger that they will bring about the substantive evils that Congress has a right to prevent." Yet Benjamin Franklin cautioned, "Those who give up essential liberty for a little safety deserve neither."

In the United States, we have been loath to create systems to control or restrict these freedoms. The First Amendment guarantees freedom of speech and of the press, as well as of religion, the right to assemble and the right to petition the government. This discussion will focus on the rights of speech and press. In general, attempts to regulate communication always generate questions about the First Amendment, but words such as "regulation" or "restriction" bring to mind the guarantee of free press and speech that is at the heart of so many of our communication laws.

Maciejewski and Ozar argue that the basis of First Amendment rights is in the concept of the public's right to know. Rarely will you read an article that is so explicit in outlining its underlying premises. Outline what these authors are putting forward, in order to understand the important distinctions they make. But, ask your own questions. Do you agree with their fundamental presuppositions? Is the right to know both clear and valid? Can you derive other possible dimensions of analysis than those given? And, would you select the same possibilities to define the concept? This article outlines the importance of the right to know, locates it in natural law, and establishes, for the authors, the important parameters of the law. So why do we find so many, in the following article, willing to give up these rights when we move from the abstract concept to its operationalization in contemporary society?

The First Amendment Center report describes a population grappling with practical issues and generally unimpressed with current media practices. Potential harm to vulnerable populations, such as children, is one area where much of the public is willing to accept some restrictions. Offensiveness is another area of confusion: what can you say or write, and when does it cross over into something that should not be allowed? Long ago when I was in college, a local woman tried to prevent our university from bringing to campus a speaker on socialist and communist ideas. Students protested this attempt, and the university supported the students against the community outcry. A speech that would have attracted about 20 students brought out hundreds in protest—and I got my first lesson in appreciating something only when it could be taken away.

YES ↵

Jeffrey J. Maciejewski and
David T. Ozar

Natural Law and the Right to Know in a Democracy

Journalists frequently accept burdens and defend actions risking harm or ill-will from others on the basis of "the public's right to know." The Code of Ethics of the Society of Professional Journalists, which many American journalists take very seriously, refers twice to this right (Society of Professional Journalists, 1996). . . . This article asks what "the public's right to know" might mean (i.e., what its moral implications are and also whether there is a sound basis for thinking there is such a right).

The first part of the article will use a simple philosophical interpretive tool to explore 12 possible meanings of "the public's right to know." This will bring to light a set of core questions that anyone referring to this right ought to be asking. . . . Part 2 focuses on . . . particular interpretation of this right . . . in an effort to identify an appropriate moral foundation for this right. [The] article examines in more detail . . . the moral implications of this right and a reason for thinking there is such a right (i.e., a reason for thinking that, in the sense specified, the public does have a "right to know"). Part 3 of the article discusses implications and offers a number of applications based on our interpretation.

Part 1

Some Preliminaries

Ethical and social policy issues can be parochial when formulated as rights issues, adopting uncritically a particular understanding of rights or of their foundations. . . .

A truly complete account of "the public's right to know" would need to be sensitive to the many ways in which rights and their foundations have been understood; that enterprise is well beyond the scope of this article. In the interests of transparency and clarity, however, it is important to state several presuppositions of the questions this article has posed for itself, although it is beyond its scope to defend them.

First, this article will be examining "the public's right to know" from the point of view of a democratic polity in which there is a widely shared conviction that extensive freedom in the open sharing of information and opinion by

From *Journal of Mass Media Ethics*, vol. 20, nos. 2 & 3, September 2005, pp. 121–138. Copyright © 2005 by Taylor & Francis. Reprinted by permission via Rightslink.

the populace, both by individual persons and by groups and organizations, is a valuable feature of society and is important to the workings of democratic government. This does not imply a presumption that the United States is an ideal democracy. However it does mean that an image of a well functioning democracy is at work in the background of this article's reflections. Those for whom the ideal polity has a significantly different character might reject the article's conclusions on this basis, or they might find that the article's conclusions translate more or less effectively into another system of political organization.

Second, this article presupposes that, at least in the long run when the human community has engaged fully in respectful dialogue on how to live together, a shared set of ethical and social standards for individuals and for organizations is possible and that natural law is worth exploring as such a moral framework. The article therefore formulates its questions as part of just such a search and offers its conclusions as hypotheses for consideration by others engaged in the same search.

Thinkers not willing to presume affirmatively that such a set of standards might ever be grasped, but still willing to say that the possibility of this remains an open question, should read the reflections offered here as hypothetical in two ways. First, the article formulates an hypothesis about how to understand "the public's right to know" and about whether there is any basis for affirming such a right. Second, the article itself is an effort to explore the very possibility of current social and ethical reflection and dialogue making genuine progress, albeit on a small, carefully circumscribed issue.

With these as framing comments, the next task is to explore 12 possible meanings of "the public's right to know" and thereby to identify a set of core questions about such a right.

Rights Talk

Rights talk is powerful talk. To say something is a right is to say that it is the most important moral consideration in the matter at hand. That is why a person who can assert a right so often acts as if the moral debate is now over. Political philosopher Dworkin (1978) expressed this point by describing rights as "moral trump." When you can play a trump in a card game, you expect to win the trick because the trump suit is the most powerful suit. However, it is important to remember that you cannot play a trump in cards whenever you wish, just to assert your power. The same is true of rights talk (Ozar, 1986).

A rights claim must be appropriate in two distinguishable ways to have moral power. First, the rights claim must be clear in what it implies about conduct. Second, the rights claim must be valid, true, resting on a sound basis. As an example, consider the legal right to free speech in the United States. We all know that a person having this right means that everyone is legally obligated not to interfere in the person expressing his or her mind, at least within certain limits. However, the meaning of this right does not include anyone having a legal obligation to assist a hesitant or ill-trained speaker in stating his or her views. The meaning of this right is quite clear in this regard. Rights' scholars will note that the analysis here is in terms of what Hohfeld (1923) called "rights in the strict and narrow sense," or claim rights. This form of analysis has been deemed sufficient for these purposes.

Second, we all know the basis of this legal right in our society, in the language of the Constitution, in statutes, judicial opinions, executive orders, and so on. Moreover, if this right is asserted in a particular case, we have well understood procedures for determining if there is a basis in law for that particular application of it. Precisely because it is a legal right, its basis is to be found in the law.

However, the meaning and the basis of "the public's right to know" are not so clear. What does this right imply about conduct? What is the basis of this right? Why should we think there is such a right, within whatever limits we have identified for its scope? To explore these questions, the next section offers a test to unpack possible meanings of "the public's right to know." The test works like this: Whenever anyone makes a rights claim, he or she is implying that someone else, either an individual or a group, has an obligation to either act or refrain from acting in some way. Therefore the question is "If the public has 'a right to know,' then who has obligations to act or refrain how?"

Twelve Possible Meanings

There is not one clear answer. There are at least 12 possible interpretations of "the public's right to know" in terms of who has obligations to act or refrain how, all of which make some sense. It will be useful to examine and compare these 12 interpretations.

Possibility 1.   If the public has a right to know, then everyone is obligated not to interfere at all with a person's taking action to learn something that the person values learning.

Possibility 2.   If the public has a right to know, then everyone is obligated not to interfere with a person's taking action to learn something that the person values learning, provided that the actions being taken by the person are not themselves harmful (by some appropriate standard) to other persons or institutions.

Comment.   Notice the question that differentiates Possibility 1 from 2. Is the right we are referring to unconditional? Or is this right conditional, dependent on the actions undertaken in the name of the right being harmless (by some appropriate standard) to other persons and institutions? This is a question anyone referring to "the public's right to know" needs to think about.

Possibility 3.   If the public has a right to know, then all persons are obligated to actively share with the public any information they control that the public (or a significant portion of the public) values knowing.

Possibility 4.   If the public has a right to know, then everyone is obligated to actively share with the public any information he or she controls on which the well-being (or the basic needs) of the public (or a significant portion of the public) is significantly dependent.

Comment.   Possibilities 3 and 4 differ from 1 and 2. . . . The first two possibilities focused on not interfering; the second pair propose the people have an obligation to actively assist in other people's obtaining of knowledge. Anyone who talks about "the public's right to know" needs to think about this difference between an obligation to refrain from interfering and an obligation to actively assist in the acquisition of information.

In addition, Possibility 4 introduces a possibility not mentioned in 1, 2, or 3; namely, that what "the public's right to know" is about knowledge on which the well-being (or the basic needs) of the public (or a significant portion of the public) is significantly dependent. Those who talk about "the public's right to know" need to think about this distinction as well.

Possibility 5.   If the public has a right to know, then everyone is obligated not to interfere at all with the community's efforts to establish institutions to communicate to the public anything that the public happens to value learning.

Possibility 6.   If the public has a right to know, then everyone is obligated not to interfere at all with the community's efforts to establish institutions to communicate to the public information on which the well-being (or basic needs) of the public (or a significant portion of the public) is significantly dependent.

Comment.   Possibilities 5 and 6 introduce the theme of institutions whose social role is to provide the public with information. Is the public's right to know what journalists talk about really more about a society's journalistic institutions than it is about any particular individual's acquisition of information? Note also the difference between 5 and 6. It is again the distinction between the social value of whatever information people happen to value and the social value of information on which the well-being or basic needs of the public depends. In addition, Possibilities 5 and 6 focus on the establishment of such institutions rather than on their daily activities. The daily activities of such institutions are the focus of the six possibilities that follow.

Possibility 7A.   If the public has a right to know, then everyone is obligated to not interfere at all with the efforts of institutions (and those who carry out their mission) established to communicate to the public anything that the public happens to value learning.

Possibility 7B.   If the public has a right to know, then everyone is obligated to not interfere with the efforts of institutions (and those who carry out their mission) established to communicate to the public anything that the public happens to value learning, provided that the actions being taken by the institution (or its representatives) are not themselves harmful (by some appropriate standard) to other persons or institutions.

Possibility 7C.   If the public has a right to know, then everyone is obligated to actively assist community-established institutions (and those who carry out their mission) that have been established to communicate to the public anything that the public happens to value learning.

Possibility 8A.   If the public has a right to know, then everyone is obligated to not interfere at all with the efforts of institutions (and those who carry out their mission) established to communicate to the public information on which the well-being (or basic needs) of the public (or a significant portion of the public) is significantly dependent.

Possibility 8B.   If the public has a right to know, then everyone is obligated to not interfere with the efforts of institutions (and those who carry out their mission) established to communicate to the public information on which the well-being (or basic needs) of the public (or a significant portion of the public) is significantly dependent, provided that the actions being taken by the institution (or its representatives) are not themselves harmful (by some appropriate standard) to other persons or institutions.

Possibility 8C.   If the public has a right to know, then everyone is obligated to actively assist community-established institutions (and those who carry out their mission) that have been established to communicate to the public information on which the well-being (or basic needs) of the public (or a significant portion of the public) is significantly dependent.

Comment.   What distinguishes Possibilities 7A through 7C from Possibilities 8A through 8C is again the difference between the social value of whatever information people happen to value and the social value of information on which the well-being or basic needs of the public depends. Then, within each of these sets, three different interpretations of the implied obligation are considered: (a) an unconditional obligation to refrain from interfering, (b) a conditional obligation to refrain from interfering (i.e., unless the action undertaken in the name of the right is, by some appropriate standard, harmful), and (c) an obligation to actively assist in the process of providing information. References to "the public's right to know" need to be clear about which of these kinds of conduct is implied by this right when it is invoked.

Five Crucial Questions

From this comparison of possible interpretations, five crucial questions have come to light that all who speak of the public's right to know will need to address if their words are to be clear enough to guide conduct. These questions are as follows:

1. Does the proposed right imply an obligation that someone act positively toward the right holder or only refrain from acting in certain ways?

2. Is the proposed right unconditional or does its implied obligation to act or refrain apply only under certain conditions? If the latter, what are the conditions (e.g., the proviso that the actions being taken by the person acted for or not interfered with are not themselves harmful, by some appropriate standard, to other persons or institutions)?

3. Does the "knowing" that the proposed right fosters or protects include whatever the right holder happens to value knowledge of, or does the knowing that is protected or fostered include only certain classes of knowledge? If the latter, which classes of knowledge (e.g., knowledge on which the well-being or the basic needs of the public or of a significant portion of the public is significantly dependent)?

4. Is the proposed right directly a right of journalists (so the rights specifically obligate others to act positively toward or to refrain from interfering with journalists), or are journalists involved more indirectly because the right is understood literally as a right of "the public," whose access to truth depends on certain kinds of institutions whose proper functioning depends in turn on the actions of journalists?

5. If the proposed right is about the public's access to truth through appropriate institutions, then is its focus on the establishment and general maintenance of such institutions, or is its focus on the daily operations of such institutions where journalists obviously play a direct role, or is its focus some combination of these two?

Selecting a Focus: An Interpretation Worth Examining

Some who examine the public's right to know might well conclude that this idea is hopelessly vague and that we should speak of our moral concerns about journalistic practice and the public's desire or need for information in other moral terms than these. Others are confident that there is a deep moral basis for this right and that careful social and ethical reflection can uncover it even if, in most ordinary usage, it is often difficult to know what the expression is intended to mean.

The position taken in this article is that there is one particular focus among the 12—or rather a combination of two of them—that offers a clear set of moral implications and articulates some very important moral content about human society, journalistic institutions, and the role of journalists in society. The proposed interpretation is a combination of what were labeled Possibility 6 and Possibility 8B. Both of these rights refer to "institutions to communicate to the public information on which the well-being (or basic needs) of the public (or a significant portion of the public) is significantly dependent."

Possibility 6 could be labeled the "establishment right" for such institutions. It held "If the public has a right to know, then everyone is obligated not to interfere at all with the community's efforts to establish institutions to communicate to the public information on which the well-being (or basic needs) of the public (or a significant portion of the public) is significantly dependent."

Possibility 8B could be labeled the "limited practice right" for such institutions. It held "If the public has a right to know, then everyone is obligated to not interfere with the efforts of institutions (and those who carry out their mission) established to communicate to the public information on which the well-being (or basic needs) of the public (or a significant portion of the public) is significantly dependent, provided that the actions being taken by the institution (or its representatives) are not themselves harmful (by some appropriate standard) to other persons or institutions."

The establishment right emphasizes the importance for a society of institutions whose social role is to communicate to the society information on which the public's well-being, especially its ability to fulfill its most basic needs, depends. Included in such information is surely information about the conduct of government, the kinds of information on which the functioning of democracy depends and in terms of which most First Amendment debates are conducted. . . .

In terms of the establishment right, when people refer to the public's right to know, one thing they should be referring to is the social value of institutions that fill this kind of need in society. It is surely impossible for members of the public to fill this need without the aid of institutions and therefore this right posits obligations on individuals and institutions (including and perhaps especially the institutions of government) to at least not interfere in the establishment of such institutions.

The implications of the "limited practice right" concern the daily practice of these institutions; they cannot fulfill their role day-in and day-out if they and those who represent them are interfered with. So the focus is on an obligation of not interfering. However, an unconditional obligation of non-interference would be excessive because we know that these institutions have the potential to cause harm, deliberately or inadvertently, to other persons and institutions. Therefore the limited practice right implies that the daily efforts of these institutions, and of those who represent them, are not to be interfered with unless they are harmful (by some appropriate standard) to other persons or institutions. . . .

Thus the interpretation of the public's right to know that will be the subject of the remainder of this article (the combination of Possibility 6, the establishment right and Possibility 8B, the limited practice right) is the following:

> If the public has a right to know, then (a) everyone is obligated not to interfere at all with the community's efforts to establish institutions to communicate to the public information on which the well-being (or basic needs) of the public (or a significant portion of the public) is significantly dependent, and (b) everyone is obligated to not interfere with the efforts of institutions (and those who carry out their mission) established to communicate to the public information on which the well-being (or basic needs) of the public (or a significant portion of the public) is significantly dependent, provided that the actions being taken by the institution (or its representatives) are not themselves harmful (by some appropriate standard) to other persons or institutions.

Part 2

Some Preliminaries on Natural law

We now turn to the task of explicating a moral foundation for the right to know as we have proposed it. We maintain that any moral foundation for the right to know must not only lend itself to the general moral convictions espoused by democracy, but it must be congruent with the very notion of rights (and the moral "trump" implied by them) to begin with. We propose that one such moral paradigm that fits these two criteria is natural-law theory.

We must, however, make one important caveat: Our task here will not be to suggest that the right to know may be universalized as some "natural right," a claim that might apply to all individuals. Rather, we will suggest that the moral principles that support the right to know are congruent with the moral foundations of democracy and offer moral justification for the right to know.

Natural Law and Democracy

Natural law theory has been positively associated with American conceptions of democracy through much of the latter's history. Its association with a representative form of government has stemmed primarily from what has been seen as a natural tendency of humans to associate and a concomitant need for a mechanism by which liberty may be assured when such associations occur and are formalized. By exploring the link between natural law and democracy, it is possible to see with greater clarity a strong moral justification for the right to know.

Although "it is well known that the Declaration of Independence was based on the natural rights philosophy of John Locke" (Sigmund, 1982, p. 98), the framers of democracy in the United States also looked to writers in the natural law tradition such as Grotius and Pufendorf for justification for their actions. By reason of our fundamental tendency to associate with one another, Pufendorf (1994) held that democracy is "the most ancient [form of government] among most nations" (p. 226).

At the forefront of such thoughts is the concept of liberty. The doctrine that the natural benefits of association need to be joined with the protection of liberty was extracted, in major part, from the Lockean (Loke, 1966) discussion of "state of nature," a state that

> all men are naturally in, and that is a state of perfect freedom to order their actions and dispose of their possessions and persons as they think fit, within the bounds of the law of nature, without asking leave, or depending upon the will of any other man. (p. 287)

The philosophical purpose of this state of nature was to highlight the essential role of natural liberty in social thinking. In the Lockean state of nature, liberty and freedom were inexorably linked. Freedom was viewed as "natural and therefore inalienable" (Murray, 1991, p. 191), derived from a single law, the law of nature, which was based on a single precept: self preservation or the preservation of one's own life, liberty, and property. Such was the Lockean influence on early American democratic thought . . . expressed eloquently in the Declaration of Independence.

Inasmuch as freedom necessitated the preservation of liberty in the midst of association, it paradoxically required that individuals, in accordance with the principle of self-preservation, sacrifice a portion of their natural liberty to civil government. Hamburger (1993) wrote that this in turn made necessary a written Constitution to keep a proper balance.

Among the freedoms not to be given up were freedom of speech and freedom of the press, and it is important for the purpose of this article to ask why this is so. Indeed, freedom of speech and press were themselves broadly thought of as natural rights, freedoms that individuals could enjoy as humans in the absence of government. However, in describing what portions of natural liberty would have protection, American constitutionalists appear to have referred to a limited form of the freedom of speech and press, not every aspect of these liberties that might have been possible in the state of nature. "For example, as historians have pointed out, Americans frequently said or assumed that certain types of speech and press—including blasphemous, obscene, fraudulent, or defamatory words—lacked or should lack protection" (Hamburger, 1993, p. 935). Such limitations were deemed necessary, according to Jefferson, to prevent the publishing of "false facts affecting injuriously the life, liberty, property or reputation of others or affecting the peace of the confederacy with foreign nations" (Hamburger, 1993, note 83, p. 936).

Natural Law and the Right to Know

Despite the limitations placed on freedom of speech and freedom of the press, "evidence suggests that some of the framers intended to embody a 'right to know' in the first amendment" (Olsen, 1979, p. 507). For if natural law prescribed that democracy was arguably the form of government most conducive to the preservation of the natural liberties, if freedom of speech and freedom of the press constituted one such liberty (its constitutional limitations notwithstanding), then by implication it would follow that individuals ought to be at liberty (i.e., not interfered with) to receive information.

This "new" element of freedom actually has two parts: The first is that information itself is a necessary constituent of the exercise of liberty; receiving information is viewed as being necessary to preserve it . . .

Bollan and Alexander, appealing to free expression, believed in "the necessity and right of the people to be informed of the conduct of their governors so as to shape their own judgments on 'Publik Matters' and be qualified to choose their representatives wisely" (Levy, 1960, p. 137).

Second, information has been seen as being not only necessary to choose democratic officers and representatives and to evaluate their conduct in office, but also in order for human beings in association to function properly in the first place (Messner, 1949, p. 565). Therefore, a right to know (or, more accurately, a right to receive information) is consistent with a form of government derived from natural rights and liberties and related freedoms. Within the context of representative government, a right to receive information, particularly concerning the functioning of government, was clearly deemed necessary to assure the liberty the framers sought.

However, what of a right to create institutions that are responsible for delivering information? Although freedom of the press was conceived to protect the "marketplace of ideas" . . . in and to protect the dialectic that is the hallmark of participatory government, one might assert that if indeed freedom of the press was a natural right, it was so by virtue of its communicative function. Here, as Hamburger (1993) suggested, the freedoms of speech and press are very much related to one another. The former was intended to put "the decision as to what views shall be voiced largely into the hands of each of us, in the hope that use of such freedom will ultimately produce a more capable citizenry and more perfect polity" (Olsen, 1979, note 3, p. 506). Whereas, in tandem with free speech, freedom of the press was intended to produce a more capable citizenry by virtue of being informed and thus expression the people's will. According to Madison . . .

> The liberty of the press is expressly declared to be beyond the reach of this Government; the people may therefore publicly address their representatives, may privately advise them, or declare their sentiments by petition to the whole body; in all these ways they may communicate their will. (note 4, p. 506)

So although the framers were likely not aware that they were articulating a right to create the institutions of information (i.e., the press), the freedoms of speech and press nevertheless refer to both aspects of the interpretation of "the people's right to know" formulated previously. This right, so interpreted, aims to secure, in the context of the values and attendant risks of association, several key liberties that are at the basis of the practice of democracy and that are in turn manifestations of the sort of natural-law inspired rights that serve as the moral foundation for our form of representative government.

Part 3

Some Implications

Two things have been argued for in Part 2 that are relevant as bases of the specific right proposed at the conclusion of Part 1. First, it has been argued that certain characteristics of democratic polity either are themselves aspects of human experience valuable in themselves or have extremely important instrumental value in humans' pursuit of the activities. . . . Furthermore, it has been argued that these elements of democratic society are impossible to achieve and secure without the proper functioning of those social institutions by which truth is disseminated. Therefore there are strong moral reasons not to interfere with the creation and functioning of such institutions. . . .

Second, it has been argued that for anyone who considers the activity of pursuing truth to be valuable in itself, those social institutions by which truth is disseminated and on which the members of society are therefore dependent have extremely important instrumental value. Thus there will be strong moral reasons not to interfere with the creation and functioning of such institutions, in the interest of humans' fulfillment of their efforts to pursue truth. Similarly, these moral reasons may not overrule all other moral considerations. However only other moral reasons of high social and human importance will weigh favorably in comparison.

What are some of the implications of this right, assuming that it has a sound moral basis? Although detailed implications of this right for particular concrete situations cannot be described in advance, some important characteristics of conduct conforming to and respectful of this right can still be identified.

Example and Variations

Suppose a meteor or comet was threatening life on earth. What would the proposed interpretation of the public's right to know imply about conduct in such a situation? That is, if there is such a right, who has an obligation to act or refrain how?

If the object hit earth without anyone's prior knowledge, it would be difficult for anyone to claim that rights to knowledge had been violated. However, suppose someone did know in advance about the event. Suppose, for example, that scientists at NASA knew about the inbound object. Almost certainly, if the NASA scientists were going to inform the public of the risk, they would use—and indeed would almost have to use—social institutions specifically designed for the dissemination of information. Suppose that, by reason of the actions of powerful persons or organizations in the society, there were no such institutions for the NASA scientists to use. Or suppose that the efforts of persons or groups to create such institutions were so regularly hindered by powerful individuals or groups in the society that the institutions of information that did exist were unable to function with any efficiency, and suppose that, as a consequence, the efforts of the NASA scientists to inform the public of the risk were ineffective.

On either of these scenarios, the public's right to know as interpreted in Part 1 (i.e., the combination of the establishment right and the limited practice right) would be violated. The value of knowledge, especially knowledge essential for life, means that the institutions that a complex society needs to have access to that knowledge have extremely high moral value and that parties who would use their power to prevent such institutions from coming into being or from performing their social function effectively (provided these institutions are not doing other forms of harm, for this is a conditional right) are violating that value for the public.

Or suppose that the institutions were in place, but that, for personal reasons of some sort, a NASA scientist charged with communicating the risk to the media refrained from doing so. Or suppose a journalist who received the information did not report it responsibly for some reason. Here too the proposed right would be violated.

Now consider some variations on this scenario. Suppose the reason that government officials were hindering the institutions that would disseminate the NASA information is that the nation was then under direct military attack from an enemy and publishing the information about the meteor would inform the enemy of the existence of NASA's satellite systems so as to severely compromise our nation's defensive abilities. Now, even though the same values of public knowledge are at risk as in the previous scenario, other extremely important public values are also at risk. . . . In such a situation, even though the public's right to know as interpreted here is certainly at stake, it may be that this particular right does not trump all the other moral considerations in the case. In a similar way, suppose the journalist who is given the information about the meteor by NASA is briefed by the mentioned military strategists and warned of the serious dangers of informing the enemy of NASA's satellite network. Again the right being considered here would be relevant, but would not necessarily be the determining factor for ethically appropriate conduct by the journalist.

The point of discussing these variations is that, even when a soundly based right with a clear general meaning is at risk, there may well be other moral considerations of sufficient moral weight that alternative courses of action have to be carefully weighed to determine the morally best course of action. This is particularly true when complex institutions with multiple stakeholders are involved. The moral "overriding-ness" of rights does not change the moral complexity of human life, even if it does sometimes provide a clear answer about conduct in a simple case.

Implications for Professional Journalists

The single most important source of guidance for journalists and journalistic organizations trying to determine how to act in a morally complex situation remains the standards of ethical conduct for the profession of journalism. Neither the existence of a sound basis for the proposed right nor the meaningfulness and moral significance of any other possible interpretations of the public's right to know changes this reality for journalistic practice.

That is, if a journalist or an organization wants to know whether a particular action is morally or ethically appropriate in a given situation, the first question to ask is whether it is in accord with the standards of professional practice. The Code of Ethics of the Society of Professional Journalists (Society of Professional Journalists, 1996) is a useful summary statement of these standards for journalists in the United States. However, it is important to remember that no such summary is exhaustive, and concrete situations often need careful examination from the point of view of many stakeholders and the multiple core values of professional journalistic practice to be properly judged. In any case, questions about whether the issues at hand violate the public's right to know should always come second to a careful examination of the situation from the perspective of the professional obligations of journalistic practice.

Unfortunately, not a few journalists employ the notion of the public's right to know as if it was their personal right and a mandate for them to conduct the business of journalism as they see fit. Some news organizations defend their actions in similar terms. However, this is clearly a mistake if the meaning of the public's right to know is interpreted as proposed in this article. In other words, the right whose moral basis has been argued for in Part 2 is not a right of journalists as such. It is a right, in the first line of argument, of the members of a democratic polity (or, if certain elements of democratic polity are held to be valuable in themselves, then of all persons in their pursuit of these aspects of social life) and, in the second line of argument, of humans as pursuers of truth in a complex society. However, when this right implies an obligation not to interfere with journalists' professional efforts, it is not because the journalists involved have such a right in their role as journalists. They do have a right to know, and the implications of proposed right apply to them in that respect, but they have this right only and precisely as members of a democratic polity. In neither case may a journalist or organization properly assert this right as if it were a right of journalists or journalistic organizations as such.

Conclusions

There are therefore good reasons to be skeptical about the moral or ethical weight of claims that journalists or journalistic organizations make in terms of the public's right to know. . . . Careful moral argument is needed to demonstrate that a proposed right has a sound moral basis, and such argument depends in turn on complicated claims of what is of value in human life and what institutions or other means are necessary for its achievement. Journalists and organizations who employ appeals to the public's right to know need to assure their audiences that their appeal to this moral standard . . . is made only after the situation has been fully and carefully examined from the perspective of the professional standards of journalistic practice.

     . . . There is an interpretation of the public's right to know that is clear in its meaning and general implications and that rests on a defensible foundation of moral reflection. Therefore, when journalists and journalistic organizations—who have already done the careful ethical reflection on professional standards that is their first recourse in ethically complex situations—appeal to the public's right to know, so interpreted, that appeal is something of great moral importance and should be taken very seriously.

References

Corbin, A. L. (1919). Legal analysis and terminology. *Yale Law Journal, 29,* 163–173.

Dworkin, R. (1978). *Taking rights seriously.* Cambridge, MA: Harvard University Press.

Hamburger, P. A. (1993). Natural rights, natural law, and American constitutions. *Yale Law Journal, 102,* 907–960.

Hohfeld, W. (1923). *Fundamental legal conceptions.* New Haven, CT: Yale University Press.

Levy, L. (1960). Legacy of suppression: Freedom of speech and press in early American history. Cambridge, MA: Harvard University Press.

Locke, J. (1966). *Two treatises of civil government.* Cambridge, England: Cambridge University Press.

Madison, J. (1910). Letter from James Madison to W. T. Barry (Aug. 4, 1822). In G. Hunt (Ed.), *Writings of James Madison* (Vol. 9, p. 103). New York: Putnam.

Messner, J. (1949). *Social ethics: Natural law in the modern world.* St. Louis, MO: Herder.

Murray, J. C. (1991). The doctrine lives: The eternal return of natural law. In C. E. Curran & R. A. McCormick, S.J. (Eds.), *Natural law and theology* (pp. 184–220). New York: Paulist.

Olsen, E. G. (1979). Note, the right to know in First Amendment analysis. *Texas Law Review, 57,* 505–521.

Ozar, D.T. (1986). Rights: What they are and where they come from. In P. Werhane, A. R. Gini, & D. Ozar (Eds.), *Philosophical issues in human rights: Theories and application* (pp. 3–25). New York: Random House.

Pufendorf, S. (1994). On the law of nature and of nations in eight books. In C. Carr (Ed.), *The political writings of Samuel Pufendorf* (pp. 95–269). New York: Oxford University Press.

Sigmund, P. E. (1982). *Natural law in political thought.* Washington, DC: University Press of America.

Society of Professional Journalists. (1996). *Code of ethics.* Available at www.spj.org/ethics_code.asp

United Nations. (1948). *Declaration of human rights.* Available at www.un.org/overview/rights.html

State of the First Amendment: 2004

T he First Amendment to the U.S. Constitution has long been considered a fundamental pillar in the American scheme of ordered liberties, and a guiding influence in American life. Those on all sides of the political spectrum hail its guarantees of protection for the individual from government censorship and official efforts to curb reasonable and fair dissent. Of course at various times in our nation's history, some of the amendment's provisions have come into conflict with what many perceive to be national security interests. In the minds of some, the terrorist attack of Sept. 11, 2001, led some federal government officials to subordinate civil liberties in the name of fighting a heightened war on terrorism. The broadcast media's inundation of the airwaves with material that may be inappropriate to children also has been the subject of recent controversy. Devices such as the v-chip allow parents to monitor materials viewed at home.

How cherished are our First Amendment guarantees? To date, only a handful of detailed and comprehensive surveys on issues pertaining to the First Amendment have ever been conducted. Few, if any, of those surveys follow the state of the First Amendment over an extended period of time. While some civil libertarians contend that First Amendment freedoms are being threatened on a daily basis, others believe the First Amendment enjoys unprecedented strength in the American constitutional system.

Since 1997, the First Amendment Center has sought to discover American attitudes toward the First Amendment by asking a series of questions designed to evaluate both general and specific First Amendment issues. For the third consecutive year, the First Amendment Center has been joined by *American Journalism Review* in this effort. Together, they commissioned the Center for Survey Research & Analysis at the University of Connecticut to conduct this year's survey. Along with asking a number of important new questions, the 2004 survey sought to trace trends in public attitudes over time by repeating some of the more important questions asked in previous surveys.

This report presents the findings from the 2004 survey and includes noteworthy comparisons from seven earlier polls. . . . Although the First Amendment itself encompasses numerous specific rights (including the right of people to peaceably assemble and to petition the government), we targeted for intensive study the freedoms of speech and press. . . .

Report by the Center for Survey Research & Analysis at the University of Connecticut, excerpts pp. 10–11, 13–19. Copyright © 2004 by Freedom Forum. Reprinted by permission.

Recent revelations that reporters in *The New York Times* and other newspapers falsified stories have gotten considerable attention. The 2004 survey considered the degree to which those problems have influenced perceptions of local media. Has the falsifying or making up of stories become a widespread problem?

The v-chip and other forms of technology now make it possible for parents to regulate media to their children. Should it be their responsibility? Are government regulations of the media justified when applied to broadcast media in the daytime and early evening, when children are most likely to be tuning in? The 2004 survey paid special attention to these as well other issues concerning the status of the First Amendment.

Specifically, the 2004 survey addressed the following issues:

- Do Americans know the freedoms guaranteed to them by the First Amendment? Does the American educational system do a good enough job teaching students about these freedoms?
- Are Americans generally satisfied with current levels of First Amendment freedom afforded to individuals in society, or is there a sense that there is overall too much or too little of these freedoms in America?
- Should people be allowed to say offensive things in public? Should musicians be allowed to sing offensive songs? Should flag burning as a means of political dissent be protected under the Constitution?
- Is it important that the news media act as a watchdog on government? Have recent revelations about the falsification of news stories in *The New York Times* and elsewhere undermined the people's trust in their own local media? Is such falsification of stories considered a widespread problem? Overall, do the media enjoy too much freedom to publish?
- Should government officials have the power to regulate basic television, cable television, and radio programming that contain references to sexual activity? At what times of the day should such regulations be allowed? Who should be responsible for keeping inappropriate print or broadcasted materials away from children? Is the v-chip being used? . . .

The First Amendment Center/*American Journalism Review* poll on the First Amendment was conducted under the supervision of the Center for Survey Research & Analysis at the University of Connecticut. A random sample of 1,002 national adults age 18 and over were interviewed between May 6 and June 6, 2004. Sampling error is ± 3.1% at the 95% confidence level. For smaller groups, the sampling error is slightly higher. Weights were assigned to reflect the characteristics of the adult U.S. population. . . .

General Orientations toward the First Amendment

Highlights:

- 30% of those surveyed in 2004 indicated that the First Amendment goes too far in the rights it guarantees. That's slightly less than the

34% who responded that way in 2003, and a significant drop from the 49% in the 2002 survey. Meanwhile, 65% disagreed that the First Amendment goes too far, the highest percentage recorded since 2000, and an 18-point jump from two years ago.

- Education is a key factor in determining levels of public satisfaction with the First Amendment. Those respondents who graduated from college are significantly more likely (77%) to disagree with the premise that the First Amendment goes too far than those who never advanced beyond high school (57%). Young adults aged 18–30 (74%) are also more likely to disagree that the First Amendment goes too far than do senior citizens (47%).
- Just 58% of those surveyed were able to name freedom of speech as one of the specific rights guaranteed by the First Amendment. Still, no other right was named by even one in five respondents, and freedom of the press was identified by just 15% of those surveyed.
- Americans expressed greater satisfaction with current levels of free speech and religion than with current levels of press freedom. While less than half (46%) indicated the nation currently has the right amount of press freedom, 60% said we have the right amount of free speech and 64% said we have the right amount of religious freedom. Interestingly, 28% said Americans have too little freedom to speak freely, the highest percentage in the last seven surveys.
- Dissatisfaction with First Amendment education practices rose: 35% rated the American educational system as "poor" in teaching students about First Amendment freedoms, compared with less than 30% who rated it that low in 2002 and 2003, and 24% who rated it as poor in 2001.

In every survey conducted since 1999, the First Amendment Center has investigated the public's overall perceptions of the First Amendment. Do Americans respond positively or negatively to its words? More specifically, do Americans think the First Amendment "goes too far in the rights it guarantees"?

In the 2004 survey, 65% of those surveyed disagreed with the premise that the First Amendment goes too far, more than twice the percentage (30%) that agreed with that premise. This represents the highest level of general satisfaction registered with the First Amendment since 2000, when 74% disagreed with the statement that the First Amendment goes too far. Even more stark, the 65% figure represents an 18-point jump in disagreement from 2002, when 47% said the First Amendment goes too far in the rights it guarantees.

"The First Amendment became part of the U.S. Constitution more than 200 years ago. This is what it says: 'Congress shall make no law respecting an establishment of religion or prohibiting the free exercise thereof, or abridging the freedom of speech or of the press, or the right of the people peaceably to assemble, and to petition the government for a redress of grievances.' Based on your own feelings about the First Amendment, please tell me whether you agree or disagree with the following statement: The First Amendment goes too far in the rights it guarantees."

Education is a key determinant of satisfaction with the First Amendment: 77% of those who attended college or beyond disagreed with the premise that the First Amendment goes too far in the rights it guarantees, as compared to 57% among those who never advanced beyond high school. Meanwhile, fundamentalist/evangelicals (41%) and senior citizens (44%) were far more likely than the general public to agree that the First Amendment goes too far.

Recognition for First Amendment rights other than freedom of speech was low. While 58% were able to identify freedom of speech as a specific right guaranteed by the First Amendment, not even one in five respondents could name any other right, including freedom of the press (15%), freedom of religion (17%) and the right of free assembly (10%). And 35% could not name even one right afforded to them under the First Amendment to the U.S. Constitution.

Among the various freedoms contained within the First Amendment, the public generally registers far greater satisfaction with freedom of speech and freedom of religion than it does with freedom of the press. The majority of respondents (64%) said the religious freedom afforded to Americans under the Constitution is "about right," and six in 10 were similarly satisfied with their current amount of freedom to speak freely. If anything, Americans would prefer even more freedom in this regard. Almost four times as many people said Americans have too little religious freedom (27%) as think they have too much religious freedom (7%). Meanwhile, 28% indicated Americans have too little freedom to speak freely, compared to 11% who said they receive too much of such freedom.

Not surprisingly, greater amounts of religious freedom are especially favored by fundamentalist/evangelicals, 37% of whom said there is too little such freedom. (By contrast, 16% of Catholics felt that way.)

As for freedom of the press, less than half of those surveyed (46%) said Americans have the right amount of that freedom, and 36% said Americans have too much press freedom—more than twice the percentage indicating that there is too little of such freedom. When phrased as a freedom that belongs to the press (as opposed to Americans), dissatisfaction increases even further: 42% of respondents said that the press has too much freedom to do what it wants. Of those with a college education, 28% felt the press has too much freedom.

Additionally, respondents exhibited increased levels of frustration with the overall quality of First Amendment education. Specifically, 35% rated the educational system as "poor" in teaching students about First Amendment freedoms. By contrast, less than 30% rated it as poor in the previous three years of the survey, with not even a quarter (24%) of respondents ranking it as poor in 2001.

Freedom of Speech

Highlights:

- Not all forms of controversial speech draw significant levels of support from Americans. A majority (54%) agreed that people should be allowed to say things in public that might be offensive to religious groups. By contrast, 35% said people should be allowed to say things that might be offensive to racial groups.

- Nearly six in 10 agreed that musicians should be allowed to sing songs with lyrics that others might find offensive; 38% disagreed with that right.
- 53% opposed amending the U.S. Constitution to prohibit flag burning, as compared to 45% who said they favor such an amendment. Three years ago, before the events of Sept. 11, 59% opposed a flag-burning amendment, significantly more than the 39% who favored an amendment at that time. Of the various subgroups surveyed, fundamentalist/evangelicals (36%) were least likely to oppose such an amendment.
- Nearly twice as many people (29%) said students in public high schools have too little freedom to express themselves as said that students have too much freedom (15%). 51% said the amount of freedom they have to express themselves is about right.
- A substantial majority (72%) opposed allowing public school students to wear a T-shirt with a potentially offensive message or picture, with a majority saying they strongly disagree with that right.

Although Americans continue to exhibit strong support for the freedom of speech in the abstract, a significance percentage of the public still exhibits a reluctance to extend protection to some forms of controversial speech, including those which offend various groups. For example, while nearly six in 10 said they support the right of musicians to sings songs that may have offensive lyrics, 38% disagreed with that right, and more than a quarter (26%) strongly disagreed with that right.

The public is more split on whether people should be allowed to say things in public that might be offensive to religious groups. While 54% said they favored such a right, 44% of Americans disagreed, led by those with incomes under $40,000 per year (53% of that subgroup disagreed with the right) and fundamentalist/evangelicals (52% said they would not support such a right).

Meanwhile, when it comes to speech that might be offensive to racial groups, there is no split in public opinion. The public overwhelmingly opposed such speech by a margin of 63% to 35%, with nearly half (49%) strongly disagreeing with that right. Here too, education plays a significant role in explaining levels of tolerance. Almost three in four (74%) of those surveyed who never advanced beyond high school disagreed with the right to say things that may be offensive to racial groups, while less than half (46%) of those who graduated college were opposed to that right. Thus while the less educated lead the way in opposition, the more educated are almost split on whether such free speech rights should be allowed.

For the fifth consecutive year, a majority of those surveyed (in 2004 it was 53%) opposed amending the Constitution to specifically prohibit flag burning or desecration. Opposition to such an amendment reached a zenith in the last survey conducted before the Sept. 11 terrorist attacks, as 59% opposed such an amendment in the spring of 2001. In recent years this percentage has dipped slightly, though never below a majority.

Among the various subgroups surveyed, fundamentalist/evangelicals are most likely to support an amendment to prohibit flag burning: While 36% said they opposed such an amendment, 58% said they favored it. Additionally, those who completed a college education (66%) are far more likely to oppose that constitutional amendment than those who never went beyond high school (48%). And Midwesterners (60%) are far more resistant to such an amendment than those who hail from any other region; Northeasterners actually support the amendment by a margin of 51% to 47%.

A slim majority (51%) also said that students in public high schools have "the right amount" of freedom to express themselves. Meanwhile, for the second year in a row, those who believe students have "too little freedom" (29%) outnumber those who think they have "too much freedom" (15%) by an approximately 2-1 margin.

Finally, for the third time in the history of the survey, the First Amendment Center inquired as to whether public school students should be allowed to wear a T-shirt with a message or picture that others might offensive. As was indicated in the 1997 and 1999 surveys, the public overwhelmingly opposes granting public students such a right. In all, 72% said they did not think students should be allowed to wear such controversial T-shirts, and a majority (51%) strongly disagreed with that right. Not surprisingly, 57% of those aged 18–30 (the subgroup that most recently attended high school) opposed the wearing of T-shirts under those circumstances, while 83% of the senior citizens surveyed expressed similar opposition.

Freedom of the Press

Highlights:

- Nearly half of those surveyed (49%) said the media have too much freedom to publish whatever they want; 15 points greater than the percentage (34%) that indicated there is too much government censorship. Republicans (64%) are far more likely than Democrats (43%) and Independents (43%) to indicate the media has too much freedom to publish.
- 77% said it is important for our democracy that the news media act as a watchdog on government. Still, 39% said the news media try to report the news without bias.
- 70% said journalists should be allowed to keep a news source confidential. That is a slight drop from 2000, when 77% agreed with this policy.
- 56% said that newspapers should be allowed to freely criticize the U.S. military about its strategy and performance.
- Meanwhile, Americans remain split over issues of access to information about the war on terrorism: Half said they have too little access to such information, as compared with 46% who said we have "too much" or "just about the right amount" of access.

- 52% followed reports concerning the falsifying of news stories in 2004. Among those, 30% said such incidents have decreased the level of trust they have in their local newspaper. Meanwhile, 59% believed the falsifying of stories in the news media has become a widespread problem.

As was noted earlier, Americans are generally less supportive of press freedoms in the abstract than they are of other First Amendment freedoms. Distrust of the media is one source of the problem. When forced to choose between competing problems, more respondents tend to think there is "too much media freedom" (49%) than think there is "too much government censorship" (34%). A partisan divide on this issue is evident. While 64% of Republicans said there is too much media freedom, 43% of those identifying themselves as Democrats and Independents felt that way.

Still, citizens continue to express support both for a principle justification that underlies press rights in this country, and to a lesser degree, for the rights of the press to engage in specific activities that may appear controversial to some.

More than three in four respondents (77%) agreed that it is important for our democracy that the news media act as a watchdog on government, with 49% indicating that they strongly adhered to that principle. Although support for this premise was widespread across the populace, it was especially well-pronounced among Democrats (84%) and non-whites (83%). Perhaps some of that intense support arises out of those groups' distaste for the Republican administration and the current Congress.

With regard to more specific press functions, public support for First Amendment rights is once again evident, although not to the degree detected in past surveys. Exactly seven in 10 agreed that journalists should be allowed to keep a news source confidential, a slight drop from the 77% who felt that way in 2000 and a substantial drop from the 1997 survey, when 85% supported that right. Additionally, while 42% said they strongly agreed with the right to keep sources confidential, that's quite a bit less than in 2000, when more than half (52%) indicated that they strongly supported the right to maintain the secrecy of sources.

The war on terrorism has heightened tensions between freedom of press and the need for the military to control information. Since Sept. 11, 2001, Americans have only narrowly supported the right of newspapers to freely criticize the U.S. military about its strategy and performance—in this year's survey 56% supported the right, while 41% opposed it. Support for the newspapers in this context is especially weak among those who never attended college (46% of that subgroup support the press's right to criticize the military) and among Republicans (42% support the right).

Americans are also split on whether there is too little access to information about the war on terrorism. Exactly half said there is too little access; 46% said that there is either "too much" access or that the current amount of access is "about right." By contrast, in 2002, four in 10 thought there was "too little access" to such information.

Concerns about media bias also have received considerable attention in recent years. Not even four in 10 (39%) said the media tries to report the news without bias. One finds a partisan divide on this question, as 28% of Republicans said the news media is free of such biased motives (48% of Democrats felt that way). More interesting, however, is the income divide revealed on this issue: those with higher incomes ($75,000 or more) are even less trusting of media motives, as just 27% of that subgroup said the media try to report the news without bias.

What about the recent newspaper scandals implicating Jayson Blair of *The New York Times* and others? More than half (52%) of those surveyed said they've heard or read about reports concerning the falsifying of facts and columns in newspapers. Of that number, three in 10 said those incidents have decreased the level of trust they maintain in their local newspapers. As for the population as a whole, 59% of those surveyed indicated that the falsifying or making up of stories in the American news media is now a "widespread problem." These suspicions are especially rampant among those who never advanced beyond high school, as 68% of that less educated group believes falsification is a widespread problem.

Government Regulation of the Media

Highlights:

- Nearly six in 10 said they are satisfied with the current amount of regulation of entertainment programming on both television and radio.
- With regard to programming that contains references to sexual activity, respondents favor government regulation of broadcast television (65%) and radio programming (63%) during the morning, afternoon and early evening hours. By contrast, 55% favor government regulation of such sexual material on basic cable television programs during those same hours.
- Respondents favor expanding the reach of the "do not call" registry, as 62% said they favor adding charities and other nonprofit organizations to the current lists, as compared to 36% who opposed such expansion.
- A vast majority of those surveyed said parents should be primarily responsible for keeping all forms of inappropriate material away from children. The public places tremendous responsibility on parents in monitoring inappropriate printed materials in particular: 87% said parents should be primarily responsible for keeping those materials away, as compared to 10% who said it should be the primary responsibility of publishers.
- 35% of respondents said that their television is equipped with a v-chip. Of those, less than a quarter (24%) indicated that they are currently using the v-chip to monitor programs in their household.

Apparently there exists no public groundswell to overthrow the current system of regulating entertainment television and radio. Nearly six in 10 (58%) said the current amount of government regulation of entertainment television is "about right," nearly three times the percentage (21%) who said there is too little of such regulation. Similarly, 59% are satisfied with the current amount of government regulation of entertainment programming on the radio.

But what about more controversial content that is published or broadcast on the air? In an age where the public as a whole has unprecedented access to materials featuring explicit references to sexual activity, some have started to look to the government for assistance in monitoring and filtering such materials before they reach the hands of consumers, especially children. Is this an appropriate function for government? Do government efforts to impose restrictions on such materials run up against public concerns that free speech rights not be violated?

Explicit references to sexual activity have become a staple of many prime time shows. Still, the public draws critical distinctions between the time of day and the type of medium in which such references should be allowed. Not even half of those surveyed (49%) said government officials should have the power to regulate such programming by over-the-air television networks (ABC, CBS, etc.) during the late evening and overnight hours, and even fewer (45%) would tolerate similar regulations of basic cable television programming during late hours.

Meanwhile popular support for regulation of programs that contain references to sexual activity increases substantially when it applies to programming during the morning, afternoon and early evening: 65% would afford the power to regulate over-the-air network broadcasts during those earlier hours, and a majority (55%) would even favor regulation of basic cable television networks such as CNN, ESPN, etc., that air sexual references during the morning, afternoon and early evening.

The public also distinguishes between regulations of radio programs that contain references to sexual activity at different times of the day. Sixty-three percent approved of such regulations during the morning, afternoon and early evening, while only half favored regulations of radio programming during the late evening and overnight hours.

One of the more popular laws passed in recent years created a "do not call" registry, which allows individuals to block many telemarketers from making calls. A majority (62%) favored adding charities and other non-profit organizations to the list of those who must defer to the registry, with 42% indicating that they strongly favor such an expansion. Only 36% opposed any such expansion.

Who should be responsible for keeping inappropriate content away from children? Americans overwhelmingly favor placing such responsibility with parents themselves. A vast majority (87%) indicated parents should be responsible for keeping inappropriate printed materials away from children, almost nine times the number that would prefer publishers to be primarily responsible. Among subgroups, whites (90%) are more likely to identify parents for this task than non-whites (78%). And parents of children under age 6 (94%) are especially likely to think that parents in general should primarily assume that role.

The public is nearly as adamant that parents maintain the primary responsibility for keeping away from children inappropriate television programming (81%), inappropriate radio programming (77%), and even inappropriate movies shown in theaters (71%). In the latter category, 19% would make theater owners and operators responsible for keeping inappropriate movies away from children, and 3% would place that responsibility with government officials.

How can parents keep track of their children's television viewing habits? In recent years the v-chip has gotten considerable attention. Yet just 35% of those surveyed said their television sets are equipped with a v-chip, and of those, only 24% admitted to using the v-chip to monitor programs being viewed in their household. If parents are truly assuming the responsibility for monitoring their children's viewing habits, it is largely happening without the benefits of this new technology. . . .

POSTSCRIPT

Should the Public Support Freedom of the Press?

Maciejewski and Ozar remind us of the philosophy behind the public right to know. What are the obligations of individuals and institutions to not interfere with the individuals or institutions that fulfill that need? The First Amendment Report pulls us into the practical applications of these principles to complex issues. Beyond the thorny philosophical questions of "What constitutes freedom?" and "What constitutes protection?" lurk some surprisingly practical issues. Does pretrial publicity bias juries? Should journalistic sources be protected? Offensive jokes, pornography in an office setting, ethnic slurs, online discussions, and even public meetings can pose problems about restriction on freedom of speech. Can speech be sexual harassment? Should libraries restrict Internet sites available to children? If so, should they do the same thing with the sensitive books on their shelves? When do the rights of the individual take precedence over the general rights guaranteed by the First Amendment?

These are important questions for debate. Decisions can be difficult when you have a constitutionally guaranteed right that becomes very complicated in the specific context, and in which rights may conflict with each other. Sometimes it is easy to support the First Amendment in general, until you are personally made uncomfortable or offended by the exercise of these unrestricted rights. Just as sometimes it is easy to ignore rights until they are taken away.

Those who argue that freedom must be absolute often invoke the concept of the "slippery slope." Any defection from absolute adherence to total freedom of expressions is attacked. It is too easy a move from credentialing reporters, to licensing newspapers, to yanking the credentials and licenses of those who are troublesome. Is it a short step from limiting Internet access of children, to removing similarly troublesome materials from the library bookshelves, or making them only available by special request? Once you start, the argument goes, each step is easier and soon freedom slips away. What restrictions or regulations on absolute freedom of speech and press would you support, and why?

Issues of speech and press freedom are global. The Committee to Protect Journalists maintains a chilling Web site, www.cpj.org. Type "Attacks on the Press in 2006" into the search box for a report on who is killing and incarcerating journalists and why. Throughout the globe, journalists face oppression, incarceration, and even death to report on issues of importance. In many cases governments and their policies fail to protect journalists. Think about what is needed to have a free and independent press: decriminalization of media output, so that you can't legally be jailed for writing something that others disagree with; rule of law, so that these laws are followed; perhaps some form of private ownership; professionally trained journalists; a business model that works. What would you think to be essential? *Freedom of the Press 2006* by Freedom House (available at http://www.freedomhouse.org under publications) talks about the development of media independence, and the many legal, business, and social areas that must converge to allow that development.

So the simple question: Do we really need the First Amendment? How much should we bother about its application to complex issues in our society? Do you count yourself among those who really care?

ISSUE 12

Is Hate Speech in the Media Directly Affecting Our Culture?

YES: Henry A. Giroux, from "Living in a Culture of Cruelty: Democracy as Spectacle," *Truthout* (September 2, 2009)

NO: Georgie Ann Weatherby and Brian Scoggins, from "A Content Analysis of Persuasion Techniques Used on White Supremacist Websites," *The Journal of Hate Studies* (vol. 4, 2005–2006)

ISSUE SUMMARY

YES: In this essay, scholar Henry Giroux questions how and why our culture has become so mean spirited. By addressing media content in news and popular fare, he analyzes how the politics of a "pedagogy of hate" has become an exercise in power that ultimately has created a "culture of cruelty." As part of this imposed philosophy, citizens have begun to question and undermine our government's responsibility to protect their interests.

NO: Georgie Ann Weatherby and Brian Scoggins examine the content of the Web pages of four extremist groups on the Internet and discuss the persuasive techniques each uses. They find that the sites draw from traditional tactics that "soft-pedal" positions that emphasize recruiting, while downplaying the messages of hate.

$\mathbf{T}$he term "hate speech" often means different things to different people. The First Amendment to the Constitution ensures freedom of speech, but, in general, hate speech is exempted from the First Amendment. What actually constitutes hate speech is where the difficulties begin. In most cases, hate speech demonstrates some level of contempt for other people, but the term is meant to convey the deliberate bias toward and discrimination against persons that could be incited because of the form of hate speech. This definition becomes murkier when we think of the political ideology behind criticizing others, or the levels to which persuasive tactics may hide the actual intention of hate.

In these selections, the authors do not quarrel with the intentions of hate speech, but rather with the way disguised forms of hate speech exist in different forms of media. Henry Giroux is highly critical of popular media that mask the politics of hate in the process of understanding the production of cultural meaning. By examining specific media texts, he identifies how information and entertainment media normalize a culture of cruelty by disguising meanness and power in entertaining ways, thereby creating cultural products that value the beating of homeless people, contempt for noncommercial public spheres, and scorn for those who are disenfranchised.

Arguing from the perspective of the indirect, or limited, effects of media, Georgie Ann Weatherby and Brian Scoggins investigate how four white supremacist Web sites present information that may appear benign but mask the ideologies of the groups they represent. They investigate the persuasive tactics of The National Alliance, which is part of the neo-Nazi movement; the Imperial Klans of America, which is connected to the Ku Klux Klan; the Aryan Nations, which is a part of the Christian Identity movement; and a less well-known site called Stormfront. By presenting their ideas to the mainstream society, these groups attempt to gain compliance from persons who may be recruited to the extremist group's side.

In the United States, our history of hate speech legislation often is targeted toward groups that exhibit bigotry or contempt for racial, ethnic, religious, or gender groups. In particular, we have had a long history of extremist groups of all kinds, hoping to use the media to defend their positions and recruit new members. When the ideas or methods of a group are viewed as possibly contemptuous, the case usually reaches the courts. In 1989, the Ku Klux Klan approached a cable television company in Kansas City, Missouri, for the purpose of showing a program on the local community access station. The city council decided to withdraw the public access channel completely (*Missouri Knights of the Ku Klux Klan v. Kansas City*, 723 F. Supp. 1347, 1989). The Klan sued the city based on their denial of First Amendment right to fee speech and won. The city had to reinstitute the public access channel, and the Klan was able to run their program.

This type of right to free speech exists in most forms of media in the United States, but the issue has become even more extreme in the case of the Internet, where there is so much freedom to post information. In both mainstream media (as Giroux writes) and on the Internet where extremist Web sites exist (as Weatherby and Scoggins write), we can see how hate speech is sanctioned, practiced, and, in some cases, endorsed by the public. Is hate speech infiltrating our society? We think that these selections pose this important question as well as many others.

YES

Henry A. Giroux

Living in a Culture of Cruelty: Democracy as Spectacle

Under the Bush administration, a seeping, sometimes galloping, authoritarianism began to reach into every vestige of the culture, giving free rein to those anti-democratic forces in which religious, market, military and political fundamentalism thrived, casting an ominous shadow over the fate of United States democracy. During the Bush-Cheney regime, power became an instrument of retribution and punishment was connected to and fueled by a repressive state. A bullying rhetoric of war, a ruthless consolidation of economic forces, and an all-embracing free-market apparatus and media driven pedagogy of fear supported and sustained a distinct culture of cruelty and inequality in the United States. In pointing to a culture of cruelty, I am not employing a form of left moralism that collapses matters of power and politics into the discourse of character. On the contrary, I think the notion of a culture of cruelty is useful in thinking through the convergence of everyday life and politics, of considering material relations of power—the disciplining of the body as an object of control—on the one hand, and the production of cultural meaning, especially the co-optation of popular culture to sanction official violence, on the other. The culture of cruelty is important for thinking through how life and death now converge in ways that fundamentally transform how we understand and imagine politics in the current historical moment—a moment when the most vital of safety nets, health care reform, is being undermined by right-wing ideologues. What is it about a culture of cruelty that provides the conditions for many Americans to believe that government is the enemy of health care reform and health care reform should be turned over to corporate and market-driven interests, further depriving millions of an essential right?

Increasingly, many individuals and groups now find themselves living in a society that measures the worth of human life in terms of cost-benefit analyses. The central issue of life and politics is no longer about working to get ahead, but struggling simply to survive. And many groups, who are considered marginal because they are poor, unemployed, people of color, elderly or young, have not just been excluded from "the American dream," but have become utterly redundant and disposable, waste products of a society that no longer considers them of any value. How else to explain the zealousness in which social safety nets have been dismantled, the transition from welfare to

From *Truthout*, September 2, 2009 (notes omitted). Copyright © 2009 by Henry A. Giroux. Reprinted by permission. www.truthout.org

workfare (offering little job training programs and no child care), and recent acrimony over health care reform's public option? What accounts for the passage of laws that criminalize the behavior of the 1.2 million homeless in the United States, often defining sleeping, sitting, soliciting, lying down or loitering in public places as a criminal offence rather than a behavior in need of compassionate good will and public assistance? Or, for that matter, the expulsions, suspensions, segregation, class discrimination and racism in the public schools as well as the more severe beatings, broken bones and damaged lives endured by young people in the juvenile justice system? Within these politics, largely fueled by market fundamentalism—one that substitutes the power of the social state with the power of the corporate state and only values wealth, money and consumers—there is a ruthless and hidden dimension of cruelty, one in which the powers of life and death are increasingly determined by punishing apparatuses, such as the criminal justice system for poor people of color and/or market forces that increasingly decide who may live and who may die.

The growing dominance of a right-wing media forged in a pedagogy of hate has become a crucial element providing numerous platforms for a culture of cruelty and is fundamental to how we understand the role of education in a range of sites outside of traditional forms of schooling. This educational apparatus and mode of public pedagogy is central to analyzing not just how power is exercised, rewarded and contested in a growing culture of cruelty, but also how particular identities, desires and needs are mobilized in support of an overt racism, hostility towards immigrants and utter disdain, coupled with the threat of mob violence toward any political figure supportive of the social contract and the welfare state. Citizens are increasingly constructed through a language of contempt for all noncommercial public spheres and a chilling indifference to the plight of others that is increasingly expressed in vicious tirades against big government and health care reform. There is a growing element of scorn on the part of the American public for those human beings caught in the web of misfortune, human suffering, dependency and deprivation. As Barbara Ehrenreich observes, "The pattern is to curtail financing for services that might help the poor while ramping up law enforcement: starve school and public transportation budgets, then make truancy illegal. Shut down public housing, then make it a crime to be homeless. Be sure to harass street vendors when there are few other opportunities for employment. The experience of the poor, and especially poor minorities, comes to resemble that of a rat in a cage scrambling to avoid erratically administered electric shocks."

A right-wing spin machine, influenced by haters like Rush Limbaugh, Glenn Beck, Michael Savage and Ann Coulter, endlessly spews out a toxic rhetoric in which: all Muslims are defined as jihadists; the homeless are not victims of misfortune but lazy; blacks are not terrorized by a racist criminal justice system, but the main architects of a culture of criminality; the epidemic of obesity has nothing to do with corporations, big agriculture and advertisers selling junk food, but rather the result of "big" government giving people food stamps; the public sphere is largely for white people, which is being threatened by immigrants and people of color, and so it goes. Glenn Beck, the alleged voice of the common man, appearing on the "Fox & Friends" morning show, calls President Obama a "racist" and then accuses him of "having a deep-seated hatred for white people or the white culture." Nationally syndicated radio host Rush Limbaugh unapologetically states that James Early Ray, the confessed killer of Martin Luther King Jr., should be given a posthumous Medal of Honor, while his counterpart in right-wing hate, talk radio host Michael Savage, states on his show, "You know, when I see a woman walking around with a burqa, I see a Nazi. That's what I see—how do you like that?—a hateful Nazi who would like to cut your throat and kill your children." He also claims that Obama is "surrounded by terrorists" and is "raping America." This is a variation of a crude theme established by Ann Coulter, who refers to Bill Clinton as a "very good rapist." Even worse, Obama is a "neo-Marxist fascist dictator in the making," who plans to "force children into a paramilitary domestic army." And this is just a small sampling of the kind of hate talk that permeates right-wing media. This could be dismissed as loony right-wing political theater if it were not for the low levels of civic literacy displayed by so many Americans who choose to believe and invest in this type of hate talk. On the contrary, while it may be idiocy, it reveals a powerful set of political, economic and educational forces at work in miseducating the American public while at the same time extending the culture of cruelty. One central task of any viable form of politics is to analyze the culture of cruelty and its overt and covert dimensions of violence, often parading as entertainment.

Underlying the culture of cruelty that reached its apogee during the Bush administration was the legalization of state violence, such that human suffering was now sanctioned by the law, which no longer served as a summons to justice. But if a legal culture emerged that made violence and human suffering socially acceptable, popular culture rendered such violence pleasurable by commodifying, aestheticizing and spectacularizing it. Rather than being unspoken and unseen, violence in American life had become both visible in its pervasiveness and normalized as a central feature of dominant and popular culture. Americans had grown accustomed to luxuriating in a warm bath of cinematic blood, as young people and adults alike were seduced with commercial and military video games such as "Grand Theft Auto" and "America's Army," the television series "24" and its ongoing Bacchanalian fête of torture, the crude violence on display in World Wrestling Entertainment and Ultimate Fighting Championship, and an endless series of vigilante films such as "The Brave One" and "Death Sentence," in which the rule of law is suspended by the viscerally satisfying images of men and women seeking revenge as laudable killing machines—a nod to the permanent state of emergency and war in the United States. Symptomatically, there is the mindless glorification and aestheticization of brutal violence in the most celebrated Hollywood films, including many of Quentin Tarantino's films, especially the recent "Death Proof," "Kill Bill" 1 & 2, and "Inglorious Bastards." With the release of Tarantino's 2009 bloody war film, in fact, the press reported that Dianne Kruger, the co-star of "Inglorious Bastards," claimed that she "loved being tortured by Brad Pitt [though] she was frustrated she didn't get an opportunity to get frisky with her co-star, but admits being beaten by Pitt was a satisfying experience."

This is more than the aestheticization of violence, it is the normalization and glorification of torture itself.

If Hollywood has made gratuitous violence the main staple of its endless parade of blockbuster films, television has tapped into the culture of cruelty in a way that was unimaginable before the attack on the US on September 11. Prime-time television before the attacks had "fewer than four acts of torture" per year, but "now there are more than a hundred." Moreover, the people who torture are no longer the villains, but the heroes of prime-time television. The most celebrated is, of course, Jack Bauer, the tragic-ethical hero of the wildly popular Fox TV thriller "24." Not only is torture the main thread of the plot, often presented "with gusto and no moral compunction," but Bauer is portrayed as a patriot, rather than a depraved monster, who tortures in order to protect American lives and national security. Torture, in this scenario, takes society's ultimate betrayal of human dignity and legitimates the pain and fear it produces as normal, all the while making a "moral sadist" a television celebrity. The show has over 15 million viewers, and its glamorization of torture has proven so successful that it appears to have not only numbed the public's reaction to the horrors of torture, but it is so overwhelmingly influential among the US military that the Pentagon sent Brig. Gen. Patrick Finnegan to California to meet with the producers of the show. "He told them that promoting illegal behavior in the series . . . was having a damaging effect on young troops." The pornographic glorification of gratuitous, sadistic violence is also on full display in the popular HBO television series "Dexter," which portrays a serial killer as a sympathetic, even lovable, character. Visual spectacles steeped in degradation and violence permeate the culture and can be found in various reality TV shows, professional wrestling and the infamous Jerry Springer Show. These programs all trade in fantasy, glamorized violence and escapism. And they share similar values. As Chris Hedges points out in his analysis of professional wrestling, they all mirror the worst dimensions of an unchecked and unregulated market society in which "winning is all that matters. Morality is irrelevant. . . . It is all about personal pain, vendettas, hedonism and fantasies of revenge, while inflicting pain on others. It is the cult of victimhood."

The celebration of hyper-violence, moral sadism and torture travels easily from fiction to real life with the emergence in the past few years of a proliferation of "bum fight" videos on the Internet, "shot by young men and boys who are seen beating the homeless or who pay transients a few dollars to fight each other." The culture of cruelty mimics cinematic violence as the agents of abuse both indulge in actual forms of violence and then further celebrate the barbarity by posting it on the web, mimicking the desire for fame and recognition, while voyeuristically consuming their own violent cultural productions. The National Coalition for the Homeless claims that "On YouTube in July 2009, people have posted 85,900 videos with 'bum' in the title [and] 5,690 videos can be found with the title 'bum fight,' representing . . . an increase of 1,460 videos since April 2008." Rather than problematize violence, popular culture increasingly normalizes it, often in ways that border on criminal intent. For instance, a recent issue of Maxim, a popular men's magazine, included "a blurb titled 'Hunt the Homeless' [focusing on] a coming 'hobo convention' in Iowa and says 'Kill one for fun. We're

87 percent sure it's legal.'" In this context, violence is not simply being transformed into an utterly distasteful form of adolescent entertainment or spectacularized to attract readers and boost profits, it becomes a powerful pedagogical force in the culture of cruelty by both aligning itself and becoming complicit with the very real surge of violence against the homeless, often committed by young men and teenage boys looking for a thrill. Spurred on by the ever reassuring presence of violence and dehumanization in the wider culture, these young "thrill offenders" now search out the homeless and "punch, kick, shoot or set afire people living on the streets, frequently killing them, simply for the sport of it, their victims all but invisible to society." All of these elements of popular culture speak stylishly and sadistically to new ways in which to maximize the pleasure of violence, giving it its hip (if fascist) edginess.

Needless to say, neither violent video games and television series nor Hollywood films and the Internet (or for that matter popular culture) cause in any direct sense real world violence and suffering, but they do not leave the real world behind either. That is too simplistic. What they do achieve is the execution of a well-funded and highly seductive public pedagogical enterprise that sexualizes and stylizes representations of violence, investing them with an intense pleasure quotient. I don't believe it is an exaggeration to claim that the violence of screen culture entertains and cleanses young people of the burden of ethical considerations when they, for instance, play video games that enabled them to "casually kill the simulated human beings whose world they control." Hollywood films such as the "Saw" series offer up a form of torture porn in which the spectacle of the violence enhances not merely its attraction, but offers young viewers a space where questions of ethics and responsibility are gleefully suspended, enabling them to evade their complicity in a culture of cruelty. No warnings appear on the labels of these violent videos and films, suggesting that the line between catharsis and desensitization may become blurred, making it more difficult for them to raise questions about what it means "to live in a society that produces, markets, and supports such products." But these hyper-violent cultural products also form part of a corrupt pedagogical assemblage that makes it all the more difficult to recognize the hard realities of power and material violence at work through militarism, a winner-take-all economy marked by punishing inequalities and a national security state that exhibits an utter disregard for human suffering. Even the suffering of children, we must note, as when government officials reduce the lives of babies and young children lost in Iraq and Afghanistan to collateral damage. Tragically, the crime here is much more than symbolic.

The ideology of hardness and cruelty runs through American culture like an electric current, sapping the strength of social relations and individual character, moral compassion and collective action, offering up crimes against humanity that become fodder for video games and spectacularized media infotainment, and constructing a culture of cruelty that promotes a "symbiosis of suffering and spectacle." As Chris Hedges argues,

> Sadism is as much a part of popular culture as it is of corporate culture.
> It dominates pornography, runs . . . through reality television and trash-
> talk programs and is at the core of the compliant, corporate collective.

Corporatism is about crushing the capacity for moral choice. And it has its logical fruition in Abu Ghraib, the wars in Iraq and Afghanistan, and our lack of compassion for the homeless, our poor, the mentally ill, the unemployed and the sick.

Bailouts are not going to address the ways in which individual desires, values and identities are endlessly produced in the service of a culture of cruelty and inequality. Power is not merely material; it is also symbolic and is distributed through a society in ways we have never seen before. No longer is education about schooling. It now functions through the educational force of the larger culture in the media, Internet, electronic media and through a wide range of technologies and sites endlessly working to undo democratic values, compassion and any viable notion of justice and its accompanying social relations. What this suggests is a redefinition of both literacy and education. We need, as a society, to educate students and others to be literate in multiple ways, to reclaim the high ground of civic courage, and to be able to name, engage and transform those forms of public pedagogy that produce hate and cruelty as part of the discourse of common sense. Otherwise, democracy will lose the supportive institutions, social relations and culture that make it not only possible but even thinkable.

Georgie Ann Weatherby
and Brian Scoggins

→ **NO**

A Content Analysis of Persuasion Techniques Used on White Supremacist Websites

The Internet has made it possible for people to access just about any information they could possibly want. Conversely, it has given organizations a vehicle through which they can get their message out to a large audience. Hate groups have found the Internet particularly appealing, because they are able to get their uncensored message out to an unlimited number of people. This is an issue that is not likely to go away. The Supreme Court has declared that the Internet is like a public square, and it is therefore unconstitutional for the government to censor websites (*Reno et al. v. American Civil Liberties Union et al.* 1997). Research into how hate groups use the Internet is necessary for several reasons. First, the Internet has the potential to reach more people than any other medium. Connected to that, there is no way to censor who views what, so it is unknown whom these groups are trying to target for membership. It is also important to learn what kinds of views these groups hold and what, if any, actions they are encouraging individuals to take. In addition, ongoing research is needed because both the Internet and the groups themselves are constantly changing.

The research dealing with hate websites is sparse. The few studies that have been conducted have been content analyses of dozens of different hate sites. The findings indicate a wide variation in the types of sites, but the samples are so broad that no real patterns have emerged.

This study will focus on the content and the use of persuasive techniques of four major white supremacist websites. Three of them are major groups connected to larger movements: the National Alliance connected to the Neo-Nazi movement, the Imperial Klans of America connected to the Ku Klux Klan, and the Aryan Nations connected to the Christian Identity movement. In addition, the study will be examining a large site named Stormfront that is not affiliated with any group.

This study will catalogue what parts of the site hate groups use for attracting people, how their extremist views are disguised, what types of age, gender, and educational demographics they are appealing to, and what kinds of attempts they make to recruit potential members. Its primary focus is to

From *Journal of Hate Studies*, vol. 4, no. 1, 2005–2006, pp. 9–13, 17–18, 20–23 (refs. omitted). Copyright © 2006 by Gonzaga University Institute for Action Against Hate. Reprinted by permission.

examine the efforts that are made on the site to indoctrinate visitors into white supremacist beliefs. Since the views expressed on the sites are extremist, it is hypothesized that the compliance techniques of foot-in-the-door technique (when something small is requested first to make compliance more likely for a larger request) and low-ball technique (when only part of what a request entails is made known) will be used. This study will examine the extent to which these techniques are present on the sites.

Literature Review

The theories in which this study is grounded are compliance techniques that, if present on the website, would serve to make the site more appealing to potential members of mainstream society. Foot-in-the-door technique is a theory of social psychology that holds that a person will be more likely to accede to a request if he or she previously has agreed to a smaller, related request. Generally, gaining compliance with a request is the purpose of foot-in-the-door technique. It is not a new idea to use this technique to change people's perspectives. It is believed to be one of the basic tactics used in Korean brainwashing. Furthermore, it is one of the techniques that Nazi propaganda minister Joseph Goebbles used in his attempts to spread the racism that was vital to Hitler's rise to power.

Low-ball technique is a technique wherein compliance is gained by not telling the person the whole story. This method is often intertwined with foot-in-the-door technique. This is in fact how most propaganda works. The person or organization trying to persuade tells only part of the story. Low-ball technique includes the site's explanations and a defense of the viewpoints expressed on it. In telling only one side, the websites are more likely to sound reasonable and appealing to others. When people do not know both sides or the whole story, they are much more likely to comply, and compliance will change their self-perception.

Freedman and Fraser did pioneering work with foot-in-the-door technique. Their study included two experiments in which they compared the likelihood of people's complying with a large request if they were first asked to comply with a smaller request and if they were not. They found that only 22% of people who were asked only the large request agreed to it, whereas 53% of the people who agreed to the initial small request agreed to the large request. When the researchers controlled for the variable of familiarity with the experimenter, they found it to be insignificant, which indicates that people do not comply because they feel as if they know the person making the request. When they looked at the factor of merely agreeing to the request and not actually following through, they found that it was only slightly less of an indication of compliance. This means that just the act of agreeing to the request is a significant part of the effect.

This study was very significant in that it uncovered some of the basic principles concerning how and why foot-in-the-door technique works. The basic idea was that once someone has agreed to any action, no matter how small, he tends to feel more involved than he did before, which leads to a change in self-perception and attitude. This is very relevant to the present study, because this is the kind of self-perception change that is hypothesized to take place when the foot-in-the-door technique is used on websites.

Bem found that cognitive dissonance is a necessary element when changing one's self-perception, if the changed perception conflicts with the person's original beliefs. Cognitive dissonance occurs when a person holds two views that are in conflict with one another. The way a person deals with this dissonance will vary, but regardless of that, it causes a person anxiety, and therefore he or she will want to resolve it. When trying to appeal to potential members, these groups will structure their websites to make them appear more likeable and less extreme; this would be an example of low-ball technique. A change in self-perception comes about more easily if a person does not have set beliefs about something. In this case, cognitive dissonance may not occur and a change in beliefs could come as soon as some propaganda gets its foot in the door.

The people that are most likely to be susceptible to this technique are those with low self-esteem or values that, while mainstream, remain closer to those of extremists. Bramel found that when something is in conflict with a person's self-perception, it causes more arousal and subsequently is viewed as bad. However, the opposite is true as well: the more closely an idea matches a person's self-perception, the more likely it is to be viewed as not as bad. Thus hate groups seeking to recruit people from the mainstream are likely to have greater success if they are welcoming, and downplay or disguise their actual beliefs, as McDonald has already observed. This is why foot-in-the-door and low-ball techniques are expected to be prevalent.

There are three other major compliance techniques as well: door-in-the-face, pique, and that's-not-all techniques. Door-in-the-face technique is demonstrated when someone initially is asked to perform a large request, and then is asked to perform a smaller one. Pique technique refers to arousing someone's interest with something unusual. In that's-not-all technique, a rather large request is made, followed by the offering of incentives for following the request. These techniques are not considered in this study, for the reason that they would not be effective in changing people's beliefs. This is so because in this situation, extremists are striving to make their viewpoint look appealing to those in the mainstream. These other techniques, if used, would further polarize the group from the mainstream, making its members seem more extreme or outlandish, which would not cause people to sympathize or associate with them; consequently, they would not change anyone's self-perception.

The Internet has become an excellent medium for recruitment. However, recruitment was not the main goal of these groups at first. Even today, there are many other ways in which white supremacist sites use the Internet. The history of white supremacist groups on the Internet began in 1983 when George Dietz put up a computer bulletin board system named Liberty Bell. The West Virginian Neo-Nazi used it to post various white supremacist information such as holocaust denial, racist, and anti-Semitic material.

A year later, the Aryan Nations and White Aryan Resistance set up bulletin boards of their own in an attempt to help connect right-wing extremists from all over. Included in the content of the postings on the Aryan Nations site were listings of various Jewish headquarters, with messages attached encouraging surfers to take action against them.

The White Aryan Resistance was even more focused on inciting violence; however, their activities caught up with them when they were held liable for the death of an Ethiopian immigrant at the hands of two skinheads for the amount of $12.5 million. Already by 1985, hate groups online were being monitored by watchdog groups such as the Anti-Defamation League.

By the early 1990s, bulletin boards were being replaced by discussion boards. These allowed more people the opportunity to contribute their own extremist views. By this time, the Internet was also being used by hate groups to encourage their strategy of leaderless resistance. The goal was to have people take matters into their own hands, operating in underground cells unaffiliated with any particular group. William Pierce's 1978 novel, the *Turner Diaries,* is a model of this tactic. In the book, the main character starts a race war by bombing the FBI building (this was the model Timothy McVeigh used in his attack on the Federal Building in Oklahoma City). Other groups have promoted RAHOWA (or racial holy war) on their sites and generally encouraged leaderless resistance.

The Internet offers groups the opportunity to reach unprecedented numbers of people with these ideas. It further allows groups to implicitly encourage leaderless resistance, glorifying real-life terrorists such as Robert Mathews, Gordon Kahl, and David Tate. It allows lone wolves the ability to keep up on events, stay informed about the group, and get ideas while protecting the group from liability.

Now that the Internet is more widely used and accessible, groups use it for many of the same purposes, but have expanded its role to include more intricate methods of recruiting. Groups are able to appeal to a wide range of age groups and people with different ideologies by allowing them easy access to what interests them.

There are hundreds of racist websites, all of which have different objectives and means by which they attempt to arrive at those objectives. . . . Grant and Chiang . . . looked at 157 racist websites. They found that recruitment appeared to be a main objective for many sites that were making attempts to reach more impressionable surfers. These attempts occasionally included kids' pages, but much more commonly were links to multimedia, merchandise, racist music, and video games.

The Internet allows hate groups to control their image in terms of how they wish to appear to the public. Groups are able to appear much more respectable, and nearly all are choosing to take this route. Among the sites included in this analysis, overt support of violence (even by violent groups) was seen infrequently, and claims that groups were unbiased, not racist, and not hate groups were made fairly often. Indeed, a great many sites were lacking in overt bigotry, especially on the home page.

An ostensibly non-offensive and objective site is one of the things that is effective in preparing to use foot-in-the-door and low-ball technique. The first step is to make the site friendlier and apparently closer to people's mainstream views. Doing so will make the ideas presented more likely to be considered, as they are perceived as being closer to people's self-perception. . . .

The National Alliance is the largest Neo-Nazi group in the U.S., despite the death of its leader and founder, William Pierce, in 2002. The West Virginia-based group was founded in the 1970s and since then has grown a great deal, thanks to Pierce. Erich Gliebe took over as the head of the NA after Pierce's death. The group uses several mediums in addition to the Internet, including radio, flyers, video games, magazines, and newsletters. . . . One of the main focuses of the National Alliance is recruiting: "To attract new followers, NA leaders and members have used billboards, hung organizational banners in prominent locations, rented booths at gun shows, posted their propaganda materials on public property and distributed NA literature in suburban neighborhoods and on college campuses." In addition, the National Alliance owns Resistance Records, a label for white power music meant to attract younger people. It also publishes Pierce's books, the *Turner Diaries* and another book called *Hunter,* which details a race war. These measures have influenced a number of terrorist acts and hate crimes. All of these efforts toward recruitment are intended to get NA members' foot in the door so that they can attract a greater number of people. The National Alliance takes a much less direct approach when it comes to letting people know they are out there. Thus we surmise that the group is more concerned with recruitment and indoctrination than they are with spreading a hateful message.

The Aryan Nations was chosen for this study because, while it has ties to Neo-Nazis, it is one of the largest and most visible representations of the Christian Identity movement. The Christian Identity Church is based on the presupposition that Aryans are God's chosen people and Jews are the offspring of Satan. The Aryan Nations was established in the mid-1970s by Richard Butler, and since then it has grown under his leadership. At the time of Butler's death in 2004, the group was bankrupt as a result of a Southern Poverty Law Center lawsuit against it; currently the group is run by August Kreis, who has led it into disarray. The mediums for recruitment used by this group are Internet websites, posters, videos, chat rooms, conferences, and online bulletin boards. Its members can also be linked to numerous hate crimes and terrorist acts that have occurred since the 1970s.

The Ku Klux Klan is a group that is fragmented into many various factions. In general, its members all share the same beliefs and ideologies. Their basic goal since the group's genesis in 1866 has been to lash out at minority groups who they feel are responsible for any change in lifestyle or hardship they experience. Today their focus appears (at least to the outside observer) to be inward, on such things as taking pride in their heritage. They have also made an effort to clean up their image in order to mainstream the organization. This study will examine the Imperial Klans of America, chosen because they are the largest single group within the KKK. The mediums they use to reach people are leaflets, mass mailings, the Internet, and rallies. All of these rely on compliance techniques; however, this study is concerned only with those used on the Internet. Most of these techniques would not be effective in changing a person's self-perception, and therefore are not effective methods of recruitment. They are used simply to let the public know that the Klan is out there.

Stormfront.org is the largest white supremacist site on the Internet. Don Black is the founder and operator of the website. It has numerous links to sites all across the world. It can most accurately be described as a forum, but what makes Stormfront unique is that it is very inclusive of all other white supremacist sites. It was chosen for the very fact that it is by far the largest white supremacist site on the Internet. . . .

The findings of this study were for the most part what was expected. The sites appear to be used largely as recruiting tools. There were many examples of foot-in-the-door technique and low-ball technique. Stormfront had the most instances of the techniques with 154; next was the National Alliance with 76; then came the Imperial Klans of America with 72; and last was the Aryan Nations with 40 instances. When contrasted with examples of overtly racist or offensive parts of the site, it was found that the overwhelming majority of the content for three of the sites paints their parent group in a positive light. Stormfront had only 2 examples of overtly racist or offensive material, the Imperial Klans of America 3, and the National Alliance 0. What was unexpected was the open virulence of the Aryan Nations, who had 20 overtly racist and offensive portions on their site. The quantity of racist and offensive portions of the site is important to note because even a few instances of a site's overtly stating its message have a strong impact on the viewer. Such directness serves to negate many of the efforts of the sites to appear mainstream and reasonable.

There are many differences and similarities that were found between the sites. The National Alliance separated itself from the other sites by its complete lack of overtly offensive areas on its website. That is not to say that there is nothing offensive about the message of the site; however, to a person with little or no knowledge of white supremacism looking at the site, it might not immediately appear offensive and racist. The site lacked any racial epithets; instead, it explained why the group holds its beliefs and cites evidence to support those beliefs. The absence of overt hostility makes it impossible to place the site in a ratio. It appears to be appealing most to a better-educated, middle-class demographic. Evidence for this assertion can be gleaned from a section in which the group profiles those involved in the National Alliance. In the profile section two middle-class housewives explain why they wanted to join. The National Alliance owns a rather extensive publishing company, Vanguard books. There are 600 books available through the site, many of which appear to be unaffiliated with the white supremacy movement. Both of these are examples of foot-in-the-door technique, but the member profile is also an example of subculture theory being used. It is interesting that two women are profiled. The choice of female profiles shows whom the group is trying to target: people who would not normally be associated with an extremist group. Another telling fact was that there was no link to the group's music label, Resistance Records. The absence of the link has changed since December of 2003. The missing link is further evidence that the group is targeting exclusively an older, more educated generation. The same is true of their radio show, which appeals to people who would have the time and desire to listen to such things during the day. It is clear from this study that the National Alliance is the group in the study that is most heavily focused on trying to appear mainstream.

The Imperial Klans of America and Stormfront have very similar approaches when it comes to attracting people. As was stated earlier, the overtly racist and offensive parts of the site have a huge impact. So even though there is a large discrepancy between the ratios, it does not appear that great when visiting the sites. Stormfront has a ratio of 77:1, the IKA a ratio of 24:1. Stormfront covers all of the demographics. It has discussion forums for teens and for women, as well as an entire kids' site.

Among the more notable parts of the site is the section for the scholarship essay competition. An essay is a small request, yet the power to change someone's self-perception through getting him to agree to write one is a huge step in indoctrinating young minds. Using this same principle, the kids' page attached to the site suggests that any students having to do a report on Martin Luther King would do well to use the resource of martinlutherking .org. This is a site that appears legitimate, but makes Martin Luther King out to be a villain and hate-monger. It is also noteworthy that the kids' page has a large collection of writings explaining the history of the white race. Stormfront makes great use of low-ball technique. The site goes to extreme lengths to explain the group's views and the problems caused by minorities. This lowball technique accounts for 111 of the 154 instances of efforts to recruit used on this site.

Stormfront has a variety of areas that are dedicated to all age groups and genders. Furthermore, there are discussion forums for all sorts of different interests. There are forums for health and fitness, homemaking, business, poetry, theology, and personal ads, just to name a few. It is a very inclusive site with respect to white supremacists.

It was somewhat surprising that a site unaffiliated with any particular groups would have so much of its content tailored to prospective members. This suggests that Don Black, the site's creator, is more concerned with changing people's beliefs than with having them take any sort of action, such as joining a particular group or committing a certain act. This orientation is similar to that of the IKA.

The Imperial Klans of America have made a distinct effort to separate themselves from their menacing past. This was evident from the disclaimer on the site, which stated that the group does not condone any acts of violence whatsoever. This claim is ironic because historically the Klans are the oldest and most violent group. The reason for the disclaimer is to protect the group from legal liability if a person was to commit a hate crime based on the information on their site. The disclaimer also serves a secondary purpose: to give the impression that the IKA is nonviolent. Like Stormfront, they have a broad discussion forum, though it is somewhat smaller. They have a selection of specific forums to choose from, such as homemaking, Bible studies, education and home schooling, and unrevised history, to name a few. These categories are evidence that they are trying to appeal to women as well. This site had no specific section for young kids, but promoted Nordic Fest, a White Power music festival that would appeal to teens in general.

In keeping with tradition, their primary enemies were blacks. They have a very long section entitled "Black Hate Crimes Against Whites," in which they explain how the crime statistics people see are skewed toward favoring blacks. The different points made here accounted for 19 different examples of the efforts to recruit. Nothing was overtly racist; rather, it was made to look well-researched and scholarly. As one example, on the part entitled "Martin Luther King, The Truth," which tells about the torture of whites in South Africa at the hands of blacks, there is a toll-free hotline at the bottom of the page. Its mere presence made the group appear to be a reputable organization.

While much of the site was professionally done and much of the work appeared scholarly, there were some blatantly racist and offensive images. There were pictures up from a recent cross "lighting" the group had held. There were also advertisements for Nordic Fest, the annual White Power music festival sponsored by the IKA. By far the most offensive material on the site was the printable flyers. These flyers could not possibly be intended for anything other than shock value and for threatening minorities. It is clearly this group's goal to have people distribute the flyers in order to harass the groups depicted in them. Often they depicted minorities in a dehumanizing fashion, as ready to prey on whites.

The Aryan Nations was the black sheep of the sites studied, with a ratio of 2:1. Half of their 40 instances of foot-in-the-door or low-ball technique were different writings explaining the national socialist movement. The rest were simple things like links to contact them and the implication of a nonprofit .org URL. There were very few efforts to appeal to a broader range of people. It should be noted that several of the links that would likely have led to parts of the site that could have been coded as attempts to recruit did not work. The faulty links are most likely a result of the internal disarray that plagues the group. Consequently they are probably not devoting much time or effort to the upkeep of the website. . . .

POSTSCRIPT

Is Hate Speech in the Media Directly Affecting Our Culture?

Hate speech is almost always evaluated based upon the context in which it is presented. The Supreme Court has adjudicated many cases in which the debate around messages has revolved around the meaning of "free speech" and "hate speech." As articulated in the First Amendment, is "free speech" extended to everyone, or just to those who have the responsibility of informing the public of the surveillance of the environment and of the impact of social movements? Are bloggers given the same rights as journalists, and do regular citizens have the right to "free speech" in both public and private communications?

Hate speech has always been an important topic on campuses where speech codes often exist to protect people. Timothy C. Schiell's *Campus Hate Speech on Trial* (University of Kansas, 2009) is an in-depth analysis of a number of important situations in which controversial positions on hate speech have become prevalent on campuses.

In a 2008 public symposium in New York City, organized by New Criterion and the Foundation for Defense of Democracies, the issue of hate speech and Islam/U.S. relationships in media was addressed in *Free Speech in an Age of Jihad: Libel Tourism, "Hate Speech" and Political Freedom*. A collection of problems of hate speech and media images in popular culture was produced by Janis L. Judson and Donna M. Bertazzoni, called *Law, Media, and Culture, the Landscape of Hate* (Peter Lang, 2002).

Many excellent Web sites can also provide further information on various approaches toward freedom of speech on the Internet, including the Electronic Freedom Foundation's site (http://www.eff.org/) and a collection of sites produced by the University of Illinois at (http://education.illinois.edu/wp/censorship/resources/general.html).

ISSUE 13

Has Industry Regulation Controlled Indecent Media Content?

YES: Rhoda Rabkin, from "Children, Entertainment, and Marketing," *Consumer Research* (June 2002)

NO: Karen E. Dill and Lisa Fager Bediako, from Testimony to the Hearing before the Subcommittee on Commerce, Trade, and Consumer Protection, "From Imus to Industry: The Business of Stereotypes and Degrading Images" (September 25, 2007)

ISSUE SUMMARY

YES: Rhoda Rabkin strongly defends the industry system of self-censorship, and feels that any government intervention toward monitoring media content is doomed to failure. She examines a number of media forms and claims that any time there has been a question about content, the industry generally re-packages the products for different audiences and age groups. She advocates for voluntary codes of conduct over federal censorship of entertainment.

NO: Shortly after radio shock-jock Don Imus lost his job for comments considered to be inappropriate for the air, the House of Representatives held a hearing at which different individuals from industry, academe, and social interest groups commented on inappropriate content. Karen Dill commented on the psychological processes of media images and the way they influence girls and women. Lisa Fager Bediako, president of Industry Ears, a group dedicated to examining the images of persons of color, testified that degrading images of violence, sexism, racism, and hate are rampant in contemporary media.

Since the early days of the Hays Commission in Hollywood, the controversy over what type of content should be available to different consumers has plagued the relationship of media industries, the public, and the FCC. As industries attempt to self-regulate and keep government from exercising what would probably be much stricter regulation over content that could be understood to be violent, racist, sexist, or hateful, we see the conflict over appropriate content and First Amendment right to freedom of expression. While the FCC is

273

structurally the "regulator" of media, the commission has never been comfortable in the role of arbiter of consumer taste, and now that so much media come to us over distribution forms that are less likely to be regulated (like the Internet), the question of appropriate content has become even more controversial.

In April 2007, popular shock-jock disc jockey Don Imus was fired by CBS after he casually called the Rutgers University women's basketball team a group of "nappy-headed ho's" on his radio program. His comments drew immediate outrage from the National Association of Black Journalists, who demanded a "sincere and unequivocal apology" and called for a boycott of Imus's show. Immediately, the media picked up on the type of language Imus regularly used on his radio show, and attention was focused on the racial, ethnic, and sexist slurs of Imus and other radio and television personalities too.

The House of Representatives called for an inquiry into industry practices, and at the hearing, several individuals from media industries discussed the difficulty of controlling on-air personalities, but for the most part, they attempted to isolate this incident from the wide range of media available today. Some of the most compelling testimony came from people who felt that the government should require greater control over disturbing language and images. Karen Dill discussed the social and psychological problems that can result with relation to sexist stereotypes and the impact of violent language and images in a variety of media forms.

Lisa Fager Bediako, president of an organization called Industry Ears, discussed the negative consequences of harmful media messages and images on children, particularly children of color. She discussed the after-effects of the Imus incident and the disproportionate impact of negative media on the African American community. Her take on the problem was that big media conglomerates exert power over the powerless by sanctioning shock-jock language; and other forms of media like record labels, radio stations, and music video channels all profit from such negative content while undermining communities of persons of color.

Rhoda Rabkin, however, writes of the industry's ability to monitor its own content and therefore sees the ongoing controversy about controversial content as a moot point. Complaints result in fewer problematic issues and act as a self-regulating mechanism for all media industries. She discusses the attempts to control children's content and the on-going problem of legislating culture.

YES ↵

Rhoda Rabkin

Children, Entertainment, and Marketing

Most American parents want to restrict children's access to entertainment glamorizing violence, sex, drug use, or vulgar language. Ideally, purveyors of "mature" entertainment would voluntarily adhere to a code of advertising ethics. Self-regulation would obviate the need for burdensome government regulation. In practice, threats of legal restriction have always played an important role in persuading "morally hazardous" industries to observe codes of conduct and to avoid aggressive marketing to young people. Specifically, self-regulation on the part of makers of entertainment products (for example, movies and comic books) has allowed Americans to shield children and adolescents from "mature" content with minimal recourse to government censorship.

This tradition may, however, be about to change. In April 2001, Sen. Joseph Lieberman (D-Conn.) introduced the Media Marketing Accountability Act (MMAA)—a bill to prohibit the marketing of "adult-rated media," i.e., movies, music, and computer games containing violent or sexual material, to young people under the age of 17. The MMAA would empower the Federal Trade Commission to regulate the advertising of entertainment products to young people. The proposed legislation, if enacted, would inject a federal agency into decisions about the marketing of movies, music, and electronic games—and thereby potentially into decisions about what sorts of movies, music, and games are produced. Lieberman's hearings, well publicized at the time, provided a valuable forum for exposing entertainment industry practices to public scrutiny. Even so, the expansion of the federal government's regulatory powers in the area of entertainment and culture is undesirable compared to the traditional, and still-workable, system of industry self-censorship. It is worth noting that the FTC itself, in its testimony before the House Commerce Subcommittee on Telecommunications in July 2001, did not seek regulatory authority over the marketing of entertainment products, and in fact argued, in view of the First Amendment protections enjoyed by these products, that industry self-regulation was the best approach.

Why voluntary ratings? Even in the 1930s, when America was a much more conservative country (at least in terms of popular culture) than it is today, public outrage over the emphasis on sex and crime in the movies led not to censorship by the federal government but to a system wherein Hollywood regulated

From *Consumers' Research,* June 2002, pp. 14–18, 29. Copyright © 2002 by Rhoda Rabkin. Reprinted by permission of the author.

itself. The movie moguls created their own Production Code Administration (PCA) in 1930, supervised first by William Hays and later, in 1934, with more seriousness, by Joseph Breen.

The so-called Hays Code presumed that movies were far more influential than books and that standards of cinematic morality consequently needed to be much stricter than those governing novels and other literature. The code forbade any mention at all of certain controversial topics, such as "illegal drug traffic," "sex perversion," "white slavery," and "miscegenation." The code did allow for the depiction of some crime and some immorality (such as adultery), but stipulated that no presentation should encourage sympathy for illegal or immoral acts.

The American film industry has a long history of self-censorship for the simple reason that offending audiences has never been in its self-interest. Business concern for the bottom line, not moral sensitivity, dictated the willingness of the film industry to regulate itself. For example, during the 1920s and 1930s, Hollywood seldom produced mass market movies with dignified portrayals of black Americans. Scenes of racial mixing on terms of social equality were avoided because they were known to offend white Southern audiences. By the 1940s, however, tentative efforts at more dignified portrayals could be seen, and soon the industry was censoring itself to avoid offending black Americans. The National Association for the Advancement of Colored People's threat of a boycott caused Walt Disney to withdraw *Song of the South* (1946), a partly animated musical based on the Uncle Remus stories. The NAACP found the film's depiction of happy slaves demeaning. For a long time, this feature was available only on a Japanese laserdisc, and even today one can obtain a video version only from Britain or Germany.

The Hays Code assumed that adults and children would and should share the same entertainment at the movie theater. But the code applied only to American-made films, and in the 1950s and '60s, Hollywood found itself losing box office share to "sophisticated" European imports. In 1968, the movie industry abandoned its code of conduct approach and replaced it with a system of age-based ratings devised by Jack Valenti, then (as now) president of the Motion Picture Association of America.

The history of the comic book industry also illustrates the effectiveness of industry self-regulation in shielding the young from "mature" content. Public concern about crime and horror comics in the 1950s led to congressional hearings sponsored by Sen. Estes Kefauver (D-Tenn.) The hearings did not come close to proving that lurid comics caused juvenile delinquency, but in the face of negative publicity, an embarrassed comic book industry opted for self-regulation. The system was voluntary, but the fact that most retailers chose not to display or sell comics without the industry seal of approval meant that objectionable comics soon languished, unable to reach their intended market.

Television greatly reduced the popularity of comic books among children, but the comic book medium did not die. Instead, a new reading audience for "adult" comics came into being. In the 1970s and '80s, as graphic violence became more acceptable in movies and on television, the industry rewrote its code to be more permissive. In September 2001, the largest comic book company, Marvel, released several new lines (Fury, Alias, and U.S. War Machine) completely without code approval. The new titles, which allowed for profanity, sexual situations, and violence, were big sellers. But they are not sold at newsstands, airports, or convenience stores; they are distributed through specialized comic book stores which tend to be patronized by older purchasers (average age: 25).

An age-based classification system has also been employed since 1994 by the video and computer games industry, which has an Entertainment Software Rating Board. The board classifies products as EC (everyone including young children), E (everyone), T (teen), M (mature—may not be suitable for persons under 17), and AO (adults only).

The oppositional music industry Of all branches of entertainment, the music recording industry has been least responsive to parental concerns and most resistant to self-regulation. The best explanation is that "oppositional" teenage music, although far from the whole of youth-oriented recordings, accounts for a significant proportion of sales. Many music performers who cater to the adolescent audience view themselves as anti-establishment rebels, and this self-image is inseparable from their marketing strategies. Irreverence and defiance seem grown-up and sophisticated to many teenagers.

What comic books were to young people in the 1930s and '40s, popular music is to today's generation of adolescents. Many adults focus on television as a baleful influence on the younger generation, but this is just a sign of how out of touch with teenagers they are. Survey evidence indicates that, in terms of both hours logged and overall meaningfulness, music listening has an importance in the lives of many adolescents far beyond what most parents understand. Parents can easily monitor what their children watch on television, but most adults find it impossible to listen to teenage "noise" on the radio or CD, let alone distinguish among the many varieties, such as album rock, alternative, grunge, world beat, progressive rock, salsa, house, technopop, etc. Yet involvement in a particular subgenre of music is often an important aspect of adolescent social identity. Conversance with popular culture seems to enhance a teenager's social contacts and status, and contrariwise, the young person who remains aloof from pop music is likely to be excluded from many teen peer groups.

One should not assume that music with lyrics featuring profanity, violence, casual sex, drug use, and so on is itself the cause of negative behaviors. Adolescence is a time of life when young people must adjust to startling discoveries about sex, violence, and other potentially troubling aspects of the real world. Just as many adults enjoy watching movies about gangsters, with no inclination toward becoming gangsters themselves, many teenagers find in their music a safe way to satisfy curiosity about the darker aspects of life. The key to understanding this segment of the entertainment industry is that "mature" content actually signifies the opposite, a puerile interest in everything so taboo that parents will not discuss it with their children. The good news is that the teenager who does not die first (or become pregnant or addicted to drugs) almost always grows out of it. On the other hand, undoubtedly some troubled teenagers focus on music with morbid, aggressive, profane, or vulgar lyrics because it seems to legitimize their impulses—in which case the music may indeed reinforce their predispositions. Many different forms of music are popular with teenagers, so preoccupation with "oppositional" music should draw parental attention—which does not mean that underlying problems are addressed by simply prohibiting a form of music.

Movies were controversial from their inception. Comic books were born innocent, but aroused parental concern when they began to exploit themes of violence and sex. Scantily clad women and heads dripping blood came as a shock to adults who had thought comics were about funny talking animals. Similarly, coarse, violent, misogynistic lyrics (to say nothing of offensive references to race, religion, and sexual orientation) prevalent in some youth-oriented music came as a shock to many parents raised on the "outrageous" music of their day, 1950s rock and roll.

Back in 1985, when Tipper Gore, together with several other Washington wives of politicians, founded the Parents Music Resource Center (PMRC), their new organization successfully drew public attention to the problematic content of rock lyrics, particularly those of heavy metal groups with names like Twisted Sister, Black Sabbath, Judas Priest, etc. In the view of the PMRC, it was a straightforward issue of consumers' rights that parents know about references to sex, drugs, alcohol, suicide, violence, and the occult in their children's music. The PMRC proposed that music companies affix warning labels to their products to alert parents about questionable content (for example, V for violence, X for sexually explicit lyrics, O for occult).

Defenders of the music industry predictably accused the PMRC of advocating censorship. The charge was unfair, but the music industry was right that there were real problems with the PMRC approach, which viewed any reference to a topic, regardless of how the topic was treated, as cause for a warning label. Thus, an anti-drug song would call for a warning sticker the same as a song that promoted drug use. This was one of the problems with the Hays Code and the comics code as well. For years, movie executives shied away from *The Man with the Golden Arm*, until Otto Preminger made this powerful anti-drug drama and successfully released it without PCA approval. In 1970, after receiving a letter from the Department of Health, Education, and Welfare, Marvel Comics incorporated an anti-drug story into its popular Spider-Man series, but had to release the titles without code office approval.

Another difficulty that arises with attempts at age-classification of music lyrics is the problem of double meanings, which have a long tradition in songwriting. John Denver testified to good effect at the 1985 hearings that his song "Rocky Mountain High" about the beauty of nature had been unfairly banned by some radio stations out of misplaced zeal against drug references. But those responsible for age-ratings will have to face such issues as what Marilyn Manson means when he sings about someone who "powders his nose." Most parents will not have a problem with children hearing Bessie Smith sing: "Nobody in town can bake a sweet jelly-roll like mine"—but of course she meant something by that, too. The enterprise of routing out double-entendres can quickly turn ridiculous, seeming to prove the truth of Lenny Bruce's observation: "There are no dirty words; there are just dirty minds."

In response to the 1985 Commerce Committee hearings, and because of a wave of local prosecutions (utilizing charges of obscenity) against retailers, in 1990, the Recording Industry Association of America (RIAA) announced that it had designed a "Parental Advisory/Explicit Lyrics" label, with a distinctive logo. But whereas the movie industry's trade association, the MPAA, rates individual movies, the RIAA created no guidelines or recommendations and left the use of the labels to the discretion of the individual recording companies. "This consistent reference to parents is offensive. We are all parents," said RIAA president Hilary Rosen. "I don't want to tell parents whether Chuck Berry is singing about his ding-a-ling."

The PMRC was disturbed by the lyrics of heavy metal rock groups, but many parents soon would be concerned by the violence and sexual vulgarity in a new form of teenage music: hip-hop, or as it is sometimes (though not accurately) called, rap music. And with this new form of music, the question of morality in music became entwined in questions about racism and double standards.

Sen. Lieberman did not invite Russell Simmons, a longtime hip-hop entrepreneur and chairman of the Hip-Hop Summit Action Network, to testify at his hearings. But Simmons attended anyway and managed to speak. Simmons complained that Lieberman had unfairly targeted hip-hop as objectionable. In *The New York Times,* he wrote: "hip-hop is an important art form, really the first new genre of music to emerge since rock and roll. . . . To deny its power and artistic merit in an attempt to silence it is downright dangerous." Criticism of violent, profane, and vulgar music lyrics, Simmons implied, betrays unconscious racism because black performers are the main creators of "gangsta rap" and hip-hop.

Simmons was wrong to equate Lieberman's proposed legislation with censorship but still had a point worth considering: Many parents upset by hip-hop would not be similarly disturbed by traditional songs, such as "Whiskey in the Jar," an Irish song that celebrates drinking or "Tom Dooley," a Civil War-era song (which became a popular hit for the Kingston Trio in the early 1960s) that recounts a murder. Of course, some parents would be equally disturbed by these songs (just as some are offended by the "occult" in a children's classic such as *The Wizard of Oz*). Many parents believe that evil has enormous inherent attractiveness, so that any depiction of wicked conduct is morally dangerous. But should the law require the makers of all such recordings and videos to affix a warning sticker and submit their advertising plans to federal supervision?

There is some basis for optimism that the value of voluntary labeling has become apparent even to the music industry. A hip-hop summit held in July 2001 brought recording company executives together with established black organizations, such as the NAACP. The three-day conference (at which Minister Louis Farrakhan spoke and urged the musicians to display more "responsibility") led to considerable reflection within the hip-hop community. Industry representatives at the summit agreed on a uniform standard for the "Parental Advisory" label, which should be one size, plainly displayed, and not removable, on the cover art of the recordings and visible on all advertising as well. The RIAA continues to insist, however (as noted critically in the FTC's December 2001 report), on its right to market labeled music aggressively to young people.

The tobacco model   As it turns out, the music industry was right to argue that any concession to parental interest in labeling would stimulate additional demands for regulation of entertainment. One of the most well-respected citizen groups concerned with media, the National Institute on Media and the Family (NIMF), has paid considerable attention to media ratings and is dissatisfied with the current system. The NIMF, along with other children's health advocates, has argued for an independent ratings oversight committee and a unified media ratings system to cover movies, television programs, music, and games.

Some politicians and children's "advocates" seem entranced by the prospect of identifying the entertainment industry in the public mind as the successor to Big Tobacco as a threat to the health of young people. In the late 1990s, Sen. Sam Brownback (R-Kan.) helped persuade the American Medical Association to assert a causal connection between violent entertainment and individual acts of aggressiveness and violence. In fact, an impressive list of highly respectable organizations, such as the National Institute of Mental Health, the National Academy of Sciences, the American Psychological Association, and the American Academy of Pediatrics, are on record agreeing that exposure to media violence presents a risk of harmful effects on children. These claims in turn help support litigation that seeks tort damages from the producers of violent entertainment. For example, families of victims of the Paducah, Ky. school shooting filed lawsuits against entertainment companies on the grounds that their products created a mindset that led to murder. Thus far, lawsuits of this nature have been dismissed in court, but then, so were tobacco suits—until they weren't.

Many essentially moral concerns tend to be packaged and presented in terms of concern for danger to "children's health." And there is no shortage of experts whose research alleges that violence (and sometimes sex) in entertainment presents proven health hazards analogous to cigarette smoking. According to Harvard researcher, Dr. Michael Rich: "The findings of hundreds of studies, analyzed as a whole, showed that the strength of the relationship between television exposure and aggressive behavior is greater than that of calcium intake and bone mass, lead ingestion and lower IQ, condom nonuse and sexually acquired HIV, or environmental tobacco smoke and lung cancer, all associations that clinicians accept and on which preventive medicine is based." Of course, some experts have come to the opposite conclusion about the effects of media on behavior. The September 2000 FTC report acknowledged that there are abundant studies on both sides of the issue.

It is possible that, even if passed, the Media Marketing Accountability Act would be found unconstitutional in the first federal court to hear a challenge to it. In one recent case, *Lorillard v. Reilly* (2001), which involved efforts by Massachusetts to restrict the advertising of tobacco products, the Supreme Court stated that retailers and manufacturers have a strong First Amendment interest in "conveying truthful information about their products to adults." Supreme Court decisions in recent years have tended to expand protection for commercial speech, even when the advertising in question is for products recognized as presenting moral hazards.

"Marketing to children" is not a clear, unambiguous concept. Many adults watch children's programming, such as "The Wonderful World of Disney," and more than two-thirds of the audience for MTV consists of viewers aged 18 or older. The FTC objected to the industry practice of showing movie trailers for R-rated movies before G- and PG-rated movies. But as Valenti testified, "the R rating does not mean 'Adult-Rated'—that is the province of the NC-17 rating. Children are admitted to R-rated movies if accompanied by a parent or adult guardian. The rating system believes that only parents can make final decisions about what they want their children to see or not to see." A Pennsylvania statute banning the practice of showing previews for R-rated features at G- and PG-rated movies was ruled unconstitutional by a federal court. Some industry executives responded to complaints about movie trailers for R-rated movies by asking where the regulation of advertising would stop: Should R-rated movies be removed from newspaper ads? But Jack Valenti eventually responded to congressional criticism by promulgating new MPAA guidelines, including: "Each company will request theater owners not to show trailers advertising films rated R for violence in connection with the exhibition of its G-rated films. In addition, each company will not attach trailers for films rated R for violence on G-rated movies on videocassettes or DVDs containing G-rated movies." This suggests that parent groups have enough clout to persuade the entertainment industry that it should voluntarily refrain from advertising R-rated movies in certain venues.

Valenti, representing the movie industry at the Senate hearings on the Media Marketing Accountability Act, argued convincingly that the proposed legislation would likely jeopardize the voluntary ratings system on which the FTC regulatory regime is supposed to be based. As Valenti noted, "the bill immunizes those producers who do not rate their films." "Why," he asked, "would sane producers continue to submit their films for voluntary ratings when they could be subjected to fines of $11,000 per day per violation?" A good question. What seems likely is that Lieberman's approach requires the creation of a different, compulsory ratings system staffed not by unaccountable, anonymous industry insiders but by "members of the entertainment industry, child development and public health professionals, social scientists and parents," as one witness recommended.

If children's "health" is the primary concern, there is no reason to expect such an independent board to stop with rating entertainment for violent content when there are so many other "threats" to the health of young people and so many pressure groups concerned with such health. What would certainly follow would be calls for adding a ratings category to restrict the depiction of tobacco and alcohol products. There would also be pressure to address other social problems as well, such as eating disorders among teenage girls allegedly promoted by unrealistically slender actresses. Health-oriented raters might consider "safe sex" scenes with condoms more youth-appropriate than sexual depictions without them. Racial, religious, and sexual stereotyping also present a threat to the health of children, to be dealt with accordingly.

In Britain and Canada, where age rating has legal force, all kinds of issues, such as cruelty to animals, racial slurs, and even "presentation of controversial lifestyles" can be grounds for restriction. At least in those countries, local authorities have the final say, an important check on the system lacking in Lieberman's plan to give the FTC regulatory authority.

The bull in the (video) shop   Representatives of the entertainment industry have deployed two serious arguments against the MMAA: first, that violence in entertainment does not cause young people to behave violently; and second, that the proposed legislation excessively empowers government to control speech and art through control over the marketing of entertainment.

Entertainment executives are right that media messages have a complex, indirect relationship to behavior. Consequently, our society wisely vests control over the entertainment choices of young people in their parents using common sense, not in a clumsy, heavy-handed government bureaucracy relying on the latest, and soon to be controverted, social science research. A sense of proportion is needed if we are to reinforce parental authority without attempting to supplant it. Self-regulation is a system in which all citizens assume civic responsibility. The MMAA, by contrast, assumes that young people are helpless victims of the advertising and media to which they are exposed. Much of the rhetoric supporting the legislation is uncomfortably reminiscent of the campaigns directed at tobacco products, junk foods, and guns. One collateral result is likely to be encouragement for lawyers to sue entertainment companies.

What cannot be achieved by the heavy hand of the law can be achieved by industry self-regulation—but this requires the cooperation of the regulated. Lieberman's bill does not seem well thought out. It would punish companies that rate their material, but no law can compel the companies to rate their material satisfactorily in the first place. What is involved here obviously calls for much more complex judgments than, for example, listing the alcohol content of a beverage or the nicotine content of a cigarette. If the music or movie industry resists rating because it leads to punitive fines, the next step would have to be rating by quasi-official "independent" boards whose judgments would then be utilized by FTC regulators. Self-censorship would give way to federal regulation. Congress will have performed its usual sorry trick—enact a vague regulatory regime and then settle back as lobbying interest groups funnel money to Washington politicians in hope of gaining favorable treatment.

The MMAA empowers the FTC only to regulate advertising to young people, so the legislation would not truly establish a system of federal censorship over entertainment. But it would bring us much closer to such a system than we have ever come in our history. Averting this outcome is in everyone's interest, but the entertainment industries themselves have the greatest responsibility to do so—through voluntary observance of codes of conduct acceptable to American parents.

Karen E. Dill and
Lisa Fager Bediako

 **NO**

Testimony to the Hearing Before the Subcommittee on Commerce, Trade, and Consumer Protection, "From Imus To Industry: The Business of Stereotypes and Degrading Images"

. . . Americans spend two-thirds of our waking lives consuming mass media. Be it television, movies, music, video games or the internet, media consumption is the number one activity of choice for Americans—commanding, on average, 3,700 hours of each citizen's time annually. The average American child devotes 45 hours per week to media consumption, more time than she spends in school.

Since culture is our shared reality, created and sustained through common experience, American culture is now largely that which is shaped and maintained by the mass media. Television, video games, music and other forms of media create meaning including shared beliefs, values and rules. Television, games, songs and movies tell stories, project images and communicate ideas. Since we are social creatures, it is natural for us to learn who we are, how we should act, feel, think and believe through the stories of our common culture.

This creation of culture through popular media was sadly exemplified recently when radio personality Don Imus referred to a college women's basketball team as "nappy-headed ho's." Sadder still, many responded that the racist and sexist language was acceptable because that type of language is used by minorities in rap music. Unfortunately racist and sexist slurs influence real people, for example sending the message to girls that this is how our society views them and causing issues with self esteem and identity.

When people say that media messages do not matter, they do not understand the psychology behind the media. For example, research on the third person effect has shown repeatedly that people believe that they themselves are immune to being affected by negative media content such as media violence, but that they believe other people, especially children, are affected. A recent study showed that the more violent video games you play, the less likely you are to believe that you are affected by video game violence. Reasons for these misperceptions include 1) the natural tendency to reject the notion that

U.S. House of Representatives, September 25, 2007.

our habits are harmful 2) a mistaken view of how media effects work (e.g., that media violence effects are always immediately observable and extreme such as murder) and 3) that media are produced primarily to entertain us (rather than to make a profit) and 4) that media do not affect the viewer (including the tendency to believe that important effects such as violence must have an important cause, not a trivial cause such as watching television).

Research on music has demonstrated that exposure to violent rap videos increases adversarial sexual beliefs (viewing men and women as enemies in the sexual sphere), negative mood, and acceptance of relationship violence (for example, believing it is acceptable for a boyfriend to shove his girlfriend out of jealousy). Additionally, violent music lyrics have been shown to increase aggressive thoughts and feelings. Across a number of studies in which researchers controlled for artist, style and other relevant factors, results showed conclusively that it was the aggressive content that caused the observed changes.

In 2007, the **APA Task Force on the Sexualization of Girls** found that when girls are exposed to images in the media of females as sex objects, a variety of negative outcomes follow. Sexualization is linked to negative consequences for cognitive and emotional functioning (including impaired performance on mental activities), mental health (including eating disorders, low self esteem, and depression), physical health, and healthy sexual development.

To understand the psychological research on media and women's issues, it is important to keep in mind that one major motive for aggression is a desire for power, control and dominance. For example, current research characterizes domestic violence as motivated primarily by a man's desire to dominate and control his wife. Theoretically, both sexism and racism in the media are examples of social influence—degrading women and minorities through sexist and racist language and imagery is a way to keep women and minorities "in their place."

Research spanning different forms of media has clearly demonstrated that sexist content causes negative effects on girls and women. What follows is representative of research findings that relate to media and aggression against women:

Those who watch more TV are more likely to hold dysfunctional beliefs about relationships and are more accepting of sexual harassment against women. Seeing ads where women are portrayed as sex objects increases rape-supportive attitudes in men. Similarly, violent video game players are more likely than non-players to believe "rape myths" such as the idea that sometimes women "deserve" rape and to hold sexist beliefs such as the idea that men are more capable as leaders and professionals, and that women deserve less freedom than men and are subservient to men.

My colleagues and I exposed young people to either sexist stereotypes—violent, "macho" males and sexually-objectified women—or to professional men and women (members of the US Congress). Next, participants read a true story where a male college professor sexually harassed a young female college student—he put his hand on her thigh and she protested. Young men who had seen the sexist images were less likely to say the event really was sexual harassment, to say it was serious and damaging, and to show empathy for the victim. They were more likely to blame the victim and to choose less severe punishments for the perpetrator. In another phase of the study, males and females who were exposed to the sexist images were more likely to endorse rape-supportive beliefs such as the ideas that women like sexual force, that men should dominate women and that leading a man on sexually justifies sexual force. These findings are especially relevant given that recent research shows that the overwhelming majority of video game characters are presented in stereotypical ways, and that general youth audiences are aware of these stereotypes.

Similar to representations of women, media representations of minorities have traditionally been stereotypical. Recent research on common depictions of popular video game characters shows blatant stereotyping. Black males are more likely than other characters to carry guns (especially extreme guns) and to fit the definition of a "thug" or "gangsta," and much more likely to be depicted as athletes. This is troubling given that research shows that simply knowing a society's endorsement of a "Black criminal" stereotype is enough to make video game players shoot more unarmed Black targets than unarmed White targets.

We enjoy freedom of expression in this country, but no country can grant us freedom from consequences. Scientists call it cause and effect. To put it more poetically, you reap what you sow. If you want peace, plant peace. If you want justice, grow justice. If we plant the seeds of violence and hate, we, as a culture, will reap what we have sown.

My message today is that violence, hatred, racism and sexism in the media do matter. One way our government can ameliorate this situation is to act on the research findings by planning legislation and regulation accordingly. Beyond that, we have a dire need in our schools to implement a curriculum that teaches how the media work (known as *media literacy* training) so that if a child hears these messages she is better equipped to deal with them. We need to make our priorities protecting and empowering children and all people rather than placing emphasis on protecting the rights of special interests to profit from selling messages of hate and injustice. We also need to recognize the deception involved with defending these harmful messages as freedom of expression. . . .

Testimony of Lisa Fager Bediako

. . . Industry Ears is a nonprofit, nonpartisan and independent organization which has focused on the impact media has on communities of color and children since 2003. My co-founder, Paul Porter and I, have, collectively, more than 40 years of experience working for media and entertainment companies including Black Entertainment Television, Clear Channel Communications, Emmis Communications, Discovery Communications, CBS radio, Capital-EMI records, Def Jam Records, AOL, NBA Entertainment, Radio One, Discovery.com, and Inner City Broadcasting. Using our insiders' knowledge, we created Industry Ears and industryears.com to address the myths and misconceptions about how media and the entertainment industry operate; and, more importantly, to develop effective means to combat the negative consequences of harmful media messages and images on children, particularly children of color.

My testimony today will focus on the following: 1) the fallout following the Imus incident, including the identity of the real culprits, and their roles in perpetuating stereotypes; 2) the disproportionate impact of negative media on the African American community; 3) the beneficiaries of negative and stereotypical media messages; and finally, some Industry Ears recommendations to address these problems.

The now-infamous "Imus Incident" is intriguing in that it has created strange bedfellows: it has unified both conservative and liberal media in invoking Hip Hop music as the veritable poster child of all that is wrong with society. That is, a popular argument made in the throes of Imus' oft-repeated "nappy-headed hoes" comment is that such language pales in comparison to the content of most commercialized Hip Hop music. The idea is that if radio stations and Viacom music channels can play the "bitch, ho, nigga" content of gangsta rappers, then what is so bad about Imus' comment? If the Black community apparently accepts such language from its own, then why get upset when Don Imus says it?

It is easy for me to understand why Black folk would be in an uproar over a White man referring to young Black women as "nappy headed hoes" on a nationally syndicated radio show; as a Black woman, that part should be intuitive. However, what appears to be more difficult to understand—especially to our friends in the news media—is that there exists a large cadre of individuals and organizations that represent communities of color that *also* are in an uproar when media permits content that is degrading to women and people of color to be broadcast. Note that, unlike the conservative and liberal media hypes, our concern is not simplistically directed at the artists who produce such material; our concern is also directed towards the record labels, radio stations, and music video channels (*i.e., the corporations*) that are profiting from allowing such material to air.

This is the fact that often gets overlooked in the mainstream media. Not all Black people and not all lovers of Hip Hop endorse the materialism, violence, and misogyny that characterize commercial rap music. Organizations and campaigns such as industry Ears, Enough Is Enough, Social Action Coalition, Youth Media Council, Third World Majority, Woman's Coalition for Decency and Dignity, REACHip Hop, Free Mix Radio and many individuals have been challenging such content for years, but their visibility has been blocked by the mainstream media. For example, during the week in which Imus was suspended and subsequently fired by CBS, I was called by three national news outlets to speak about the Hip Hop music issue. However, each outlet only wanted me to defend the commercialized Hip Hop industry; no one was interested in the fact that I also agreed that "bad" content applies across the board and should also be dealt with. The message is clear: If you do not fit the "role" media has created for ratings you lose your opportunity to be heard.

It is time to wake up and see the real issue—that media conglomerates are the gatekeepers of content and in essence control what opinions receive airtime. The deletion of the Fairness Doctrine and passage of the 1996 Telecommunications Act helped to create incredibly powerful, big media corporations by eliminating the requirement that balanced viewpoints be presented, and by relaxing rules placing limits on how much media a single corporation could own. Further, by repealing the tax certificate program, which successfully—if temporarily—increased ownership of media outlets by people of color, we have ensured that these big media corporations do not represent the diversity of society. Then, with control of so much media concentrated in the hands of the very few, we are at the mercy of big media and rely on companies to serve in the best interest of the public while also serving their bottom line.

As might seem obvious, what best serves the public, and what best serves the bottom line are not always the same. This is evidenced by the fact that CBS fired Imus only when corporate sponsors started to pull out; Imus has made offensive and derogatory statements before. Commercialized Hip Hop has flourished in this environment, giving public perception that what you see and hear on radio and TV has been set as community standard. The Federal Communications Commission (FCC) states that it is a federal violation to broadcast indecent or sexually explicit content between the hours of 6 a.m. and 10 p.m. However, songs that discuss explicit sexual situations including oral sex, rape, casual sex and gang sex receive daily spins on radio stations and video music channels that cater to the 12–17 year old demographic.

Freedom of speech has been spun by industry conglomerates to mean the *b-word, n-word* and *ho* while censoring and eliminating Hip Hop music that discusses Hurricane Katrina, the Iraqi War, Jena 6, dangers of gun violence and drugs and songs that contains words like "George Bush" and "Free Mumia." In 2005, MTV and radio stations around the country self-regulated themselves to remove the words "white man" from the Kanye West hit single *All Fall Down*. The lyrics demonstrated the far reach of capitalism by exclaiming /*Drug dealers buy Jordans, crackheads buy crack/And a white man get paid off of all of that/*. When asked why they decided to dub "white man" from the lyrics the response from MTV was "we didn't want to offend anyone."

Today, Hip Hop is bombarded by the demeaning images of the black male thug and the sleazy video vixen. Record labels and their executives choose to support and promote these images for airplay solely as if these are the only images that represent black people.

I understand that payola is out of the scope of this subcommittee; however I think it is important to mention, because it is a major contributor to how music receives radio and video airplay. . . .

All over the country you have identical playlists from station to station no matter what the radio format and it's no coincidence. Payola is no longer the local DJ receiving a couple dollars for airplay; it is now an organized corporate crime that supports the lack of balanced content and demeaning imagery with no consequences. Broadcaster claims that this is what listeners want to hear is not honest. Radio stations only research the songs that are currently being played on the radio (*i.e. songs that are paid for*). New artists with new songs do not get tested. This explains the identical playlists and the exclusion of local and regional artist airplay on radio stations.

Stereotypes and degrading images in both radio and television disproportionately impact the African American community. There are a wealth of shows on networks like Viacom that capitalize and profit from demeaning women and black people, including the following examples:

- *Flavor of Love,* which stars former Public Enemy artist Flavor Flav, as a modern buffoon, focused solely on the objectification of women;
- *Where My Dogs At* is an animated program which includes an episode where a rapper leads black women on leashes, like dogs, down a red carpet, where one of the women defecates on the floor;
- *Yo Momma* pits teens against each other to yell disrespecting and sometimes racist insults; and
- *We Can Do Better aka a Hot Ghetto Mess* demeans and makes fun of everyday people all in the name of entertainment. The cumulative effect suggests to the targeted audience that this is the way things are and how they should act.

A good example of records, radio and corporate partnerships includes a song on Virgin Records label called "Ms. New Booty." This song, performed by a white rapper was silly and tasteless, but the promotion by the record label and partnership with *Girls Gone Wild* was truly offensive. A local Washington DC DJ at 5 p.m. promoted the tune by suggesting he likes to visit the MsNewBooty .com website to masturbate. The website created by Virgin Records asked girls to enter a contest for the "best new booty." Girls were required to take photos of their butts and post them online. Each week people would vote for the best "booty" of the week with the winner receiving a chance to be in a music video. It was obvious that girls under 17 were entering the contest (some even listed their myspace accounts making it easy for child predators). The *Girls Gone Wild* partner was listed at the top of the website and linked making it easy for pre-teens and others to access. I wrote an open letter to Virgin records and Jermaine Dupri, President of urban music, responded by saying, "It was all in fun and it wasn't about sex." Later that same month Jermaine Dupri appeared in an article in Billboard magazine and stated "Southern Hip Hop is inspired by strip clubs."

It is important to note that African American children listen and watch more radio and television than any other demographic. Although Top 40 and Hip Hop radio stations claim to target the 18–34 demographic their largest audience share are the 12–17 year old segment. Recording companies, radio stations and Viacom networks are aware of their audience but have chosen to put the bottom line above the welfare of their audiences. In the documentary, *Hip Hop: Beyond Beats and Rhymes,* a group of white teens are asked what they think about Hip Hop. They explained, "Hip Hop gives a better insight into black culture and what it's like to grow up in the ghetto," as if all black people had the same experience. Bakari Kitwana, professor and author of several books dealing with Hip Hop and politics, said when he was researching information for his next book he asked white women from all of the country what they felt about rappers who used the b-word to describe women. The overwhelming majority responded by saying, "They were not offended because the rappers weren't describing them; they were only talking about black women."

These perpetuated stereotypes and demeaning images are reflective in the behavior and attitudes of children and specifically children of color. We see an increase in risky sexual behavior—black girls 15–24 years old represent the fastest growing segment of HIV patients, devaluing of education and rise in the dropout rate—reports show as high as 75% dropout rate among black 9th grade boys, unhealthy interpersonal relationships, increase in aggression, a normalization of criminal activity and materialism.

In sum, because I'm sure the industry will shrug at the notion that their actions have led to or influenced any of this behavior, I strongly suggest that a research study look at the direct impact of degrading and stereotypical images on children and adults. This study will help us understand the direct implications and back up the policy and regulations that need to be implemented and enforced. . . .

POSTSCRIPT

Has Industry Regulation Controlled Indecent Media Content?

The history of questionable media content and the desire of some groups to exercise control over content has a long, bumpy history. Even different constituents at the FCC have trouble finding one answer to the myriad problems of questionable content. While extreme cases of content are easier to deal with, many of the subjects discussed in these selections show that even word choice or suggestion might be problematic in some contexts. And, while more media industries have attempted to use ratings systems to attempt to control access to material that may be inappropriate for some audiences, the number of problems seems to grow.

Perhaps the "poster boy" for questionable content is Howard Stern, though Don Imus is not far behind him. Stern had a very successful radio show and television show until after the Super Bowl incident of 2004, in which Justin Timberlake bared one of Janet Jackson's breasts in a "wardrobe malfunction" during the half-time entertainment. This incident prompted the FCC to issue more fines for indecent content, and Stern ultimately decided to leave broadcast radio and opt for a satellite service, which is unregulated by the FCC, and where he would have greater control over the content of his programs.

Once again, the issues become even more complicated when we consider how often children have access to media content that may not be supervised. Probably the best answer might be to have the parents control what their children see and hear, and discuss the content with them, but, unfortunately, that easy answer is often very difficult to ensure.

If you are interested in how the controversy over "appropriate" children's programming has fared, you might want to read *The Faces of Television Media: Teaching Violence, Selling to Children,* by Edward L. Palmer and Brian M. Young (Erlbaum, 2003), or *Saturday Morning Censors: Television Regulation Before the V-Chip,* by Heather Hendershot (Duke University Press, 1998). John A. Fortunato's book, *Making Media Content: The Influence of Constituency Groups on Mass Media* (Erlbaum, 2005), deals more specifically with issues of content for more mature audiences. The Don Imus case in particular has been analyzed by Michael Awkward in *Burying Don Imus: Anatomy of a Scapegoat* (University of Minnesota Press, 2009).

Internet References . . .

National Association of Broadcasters (NAB)

The NAB is an organization dedicated to promoting the interests of broadcasters. Some of the pages include information such as TV parental guidelines, laws and regulation, research, and current issues.

http://www.nab.org

National Cable TV Association (NCTA)

The NCTA is an organization dedicated to promoting the interests of the cable industry. See their Web page for discussion of current issues, and updates on issues of importance to cable.

http://www.ncta.com

Television Bureau of Advertising

The Television Bureau of Advertising is a non-profit trade association of the broadcast television industry. This Web site provides a diverse variety of resources to help advertisers make the best use of local television. Go to "television facts" for useful information.

http://www.tvb.org

Yahoo Finance

From the site below, click through investing to industries to the industry center where you can access information on individual companies, industry rivals, strategies and value, and stock prices. This is an invaluable resource for learning more about specific firms and their markets.

http://www.finance.yahoo.com

IFPI Music Market Statistics

IFPI (International Federation of the Phonographic Industry) is an industry association. As part of their services, the statistics section provides a "comprehensive range of global industry statistics." The goals of this association are to promote the value of recorded music, safeguard the rights of record producers, and expand the commercial uses of recorded music.

http://www.ifpi.org/content/section_statistics/index.html

Cynopsis

Cynopsis is a free daily trade publication for the television industry. There are four daily early morning editions—**Cyn**opsis, **Cyn**opsis: Kids, **Cyn**opsis: International, and **Cyn**opsis: Digital—that can be read on the Web or sent via email.

http://www.cynopsis.com

Media Business

*I*t is important to remember that media industries are businesses and that they must be profitable in order to thrive. Changes in ownership rules have resulted in a new group of media companies and corporations. Newspapers may be the first major industry to fail. Most have retooled and have focused on smaller, targeted audiences. In this section we discuss what has changed in traditional media outlets, and how new special-interest groups and new technologies are changing the type of media that is available to the public. Are changes to traditional industries inevitable? Are there evolving models of business for the digital age? What aspects of law, regulation, and business practices have come together to change the nature of the media "playing field?" How likely are new services to survive? Is the era of mass media now over?

- Can the Independent Musical Artist Thrive in Today's Music Business?
- Should Newspapers Shut Down Their Presses?
- Do New Business Models Result in Greater Consumer Choice of Products and Ideas?

ISSUE 14

Can the Independent Musical Artist Thrive in Today's Music Business?

YES: Chuck Salter, from "Way Behind the Music," *Fast Company* (February 2007)

NO: Eric Boehlert, from "Pay for Play," *Salon.com* (March 14, 2001)

ISSUE SUMMARY

YES: Chuck Salter looks at the way musical artists have had to become business people to control the branding of their "products." He examines the business model established by John Legend, and describes how today's musical artists must retain control of their brand to survive in the music industry today.

NO: Eric Boehlert describes why radio has become so bad, with regard to diversity of music, and how little opportunity there is for new artists to get their music on the air. He describes what has happened to the traditional music industry/radio alliance, and how independent record promoters have influenced both businesses.

For many years, the Recording Industry Association of America (RIAA) has vigorously fought the use of the Internet to distribute music. Though the RIAA could not prohibit the use of MP3 technology and file sharing, they did mount an attack on individuals who apparently downloaded large files of music. One of the RIAA's chief claims was that free downloading of music punished the musical artist, who would no longer make any royalties on his or her work. As you read these selections, you'll see that the legality of downloading music is not really a concern of these writers. Instead, each focuses on the Internet's impact in one way or another on consumption practices and music, and how new business models have emerged that influence what we hear.

What the RIAA was really concerned about was how the Internet would influence the sale of records and CDs, thus affecting the entire structure of the RIAA. But the Internet alone was not to blame for changes to the recording industry. New business models, like those in these selections, have emerged to shift power away from the traditional RIAA structure, and put the power into other hands. The selections in this issue focus on how that power has shifted, for whom, and with what effect.

Chuck Salter describes how entrepreneurs in the music business have had to learn how to conduct the business that corporations and the RIAA once controlled. Many artists now control every aspect of their enterprises, from recording their music to selling products with their logos, tour merchandise, and controlling their brand. While this model helps established artists, it also gives new hope to emerging artists and allows them to market themselves in a way that gives them a greater opportunity to succeed. The Internet, then, becomes a distribution agency for music, products, publicity, fan clubs, and more.

Eric Boehlert examines the music industry from a different perspective. As large corporations bought smaller record labels, the role of the independent record promoter shifted enormous power to people who would pay to have records played on certain radio stations. The indie promoter then earned money on how many plays he could arrange, and fewer new groups could get to be heard on radio. Boehlert describes what happened to the disc jockey's choices about music, and traces the money trail to see what happened to the recording industry in the process.

Probably the most common defense for downloading music for free is that "I'm a student, and I don't have any money." But at the same time, changes in industries are created because purchasing patterns change. Both of these authors show how the recording industry has undergone shifts in recent years, in part because of the Internet, but also because of corporate greed that has given us music that is packaged for consumption by the greatest number of individuals, at the lowest cost to producers. It's important for us to realize that whenever there is one shift to an industry, it doesn't take much to search for other seismic encounters.

As you consider the positions taken by these authors, remember that the recording industry and the radio industry are always changing. What may be true today can also change again tomorrow. This is particularly important for anyone who wishes to work in these ever-changing industries, and understanding how and why industries change is important for understanding the impact the industries have on our culture, but also to understand the dynamics that are in play in the world of media, popular culture, and business.

YES ↩

Chuck Salter

Way Behind the Music

If there's any musician who can make sense of the tectonic upheaval in the industry, it's John Legend. Before teaming with Kanye West and Snoop Dogg on his major-label debut, *Get Lifted*, the ultrasmooth R&B singer-songwriter worked as an associate consultant for the Boston Consulting Group (under his given name, John Stephens). When the recording sold north of 3 million copies worldwide—and snagged a trio of 2006 Grammys, including best new artist—John Stephens the consultant had some cautionary words for John Legend the musician: Protect your brand. It was some of the best advice he'd ever gotten.

Legend, who's 28, knew people would be lining up to take a piece of every dollar he could pull down, and that if he went the traditional route, there wasn't much he could do to stop them. After all, it was the label, retailers, and ticket companies in the sweet spot at the center of every transaction with his fans. "I can't let someone else have more control over the relationship people have with my music than I do," he says.

So Legend took control in a way that would have been unthinkable for a new artist just 10 years ago. He still releases music through a major label, Sony BMG, but last fall he formed John Legend Ventures with two friends and began researching how other bands were creating their own businesses and increasing their leverage in the market.

They found that the Internet has become not only a channel for distributing music but one for insinuating bands into the lives of their most enraptured fans. They found that the efficiencies of the Web are such that for very little cost, an artist can build his own online operation and outsource everything, from peddling "merch" to boosting the fan club to ticketing and marketing. And they found a full-service company that had built an infrastructure so vast and so efficient that no one could rival it.

Legend's new partner is a virtual unknown outside the industry. The machine, by design, remains invisible. It's called Musictoday.

Founded by Coran Capshaw, the storied but reticent manager of the Dave Matthews Band, Musictoday works behind the scenes to fashion an online identity for artists, then connects them with fans—and drives commerce. It feeds the sort of passion, or obsession, that turns a $20 teddy bear in a Dylan shirt or a $45 Red Hot Chili Peppers messenger bag into a necessity. It fulfills fantasies: owning Carlos Santana's black fedora, say, or playing blackjack and softball with the Backstreet Boys, or sitting in on a soundcheck with John Mayer. Musictoday can even help fans become part of the music itself, as when Christina Aguilera incorporated their voice-mail messages into "Thank You," a song on *Back to Basics*, her most recent release. "This is all about taking your fans behind the velvet rope," says Matt Blum, Musictoday's fan-club manager.

While the big money is still in touring, Musictoday rechannels revenue streams—merchandise margins and ticket fees that traditionally padded someone else's pocket—in the talent's direction. For new or lesser-known bands, that money could mean the difference between touring and trading in that Stratocaster for a busboy tray. "Somebody you've never heard of will sell $10 million in merchandise in two years," says Jim Kingdon, executive vice president. And for megabands like Dave Matthews, which has more than 80,000 fans paying $35 a year for fan-club membership alone, the money can snowball.

"We're heading to a do-it-yourself world where artists will be taking more control of their careers," says Michael McDonald, John Mayer's manager. Or as Legend puts it: "In the not-too-distant future, this could mean you won't need a label anymore. That's the pot of gold at the end of the rainbow."

In the Foothills of the Blue Ridge Mountains, in an unmarked former chicken-pot-pie plant outside Charlottesville, Virginia, the music revolution is humming along nicely. Here in Musictoday's 350,000-square-foot headquarters, that revolution is most visible in the plastic bins filled with stuff: shower slippers, coasters, and leather coats plastered with the Rolling Stones' wagging-tongue logo. Eminem bobbleheads. Phish onesies. Snoop Dogg rubber wrist bands. Carole King yoga pants. As harmless, even useless, as these tchotchkes may seem, they are upending the industry for one simple reason: Traditional retailers aren't selling them—the artists themselves are. "That direct interaction is unique," says Capshaw. "It's a bonding experience."

Of course, this direct interaction involves some sleight of hand. Behind any given band's online store, it's Musictoday that actually performs the "unfun, unsexy part of the business," says Bruce Flohr, an executive with Red Light Management, one of Capshaw's many ventures. Musictoday's 200 employees are responsible for emailing fans, processing orders, printing tickets, mailing merchandise, fielding complaints, monitoring message boards—all of it. "When you stand in that warehouse, you realize the industry is healthy," says Flohr, who also manages several bands. "It no longer hinges on a silver disc."

But there's a compelling lesson here for any company that makes a product: If you control a piece of the transaction, you understand more about your customers. By aggregating fan data that artists haven't usually been privy to, Musictoday can help shape decisions such as where to tour, advertise, or deploy superfans to evangelize. Considering that an estimated 60% of concert tickets typically go unsold every year, that kind of targeting is no small contribution. "We're able to say to artists, 'We know more about your fans than you do,'" says Nathan Hubbard, 31, who runs Musictoday as Capshaw's chief of staff. "Let's put our heads together and figure out how to monetize this relationship."

Monetize it they have. Musictoday's roster now counts more than 700 clients using some combination of its services. ("We're a little embarrassed by our scale," says Hubbard, "but it helps.") That list includes newcomers like Legend, legacy bands like the Doors, and everyone in between—Kenny Chesney, Justin Timberlake, Taylor Hicks, Janet Jackson, Britney Spears. The company has also begun expanding beyond music, nabbing Tiger Woods, the Miami Heat's Dwyane Wade, Maria Sharapova, the New York Knicks, comedian Dane Cook, and CNN chatterbox Glenn Beck. "We're genre agnostic," says Hubbard. Fans are fans.

And revenue is revenue. By the end of 2006, Musictoday was on pace to sell more than $200 million worth of concert tickets, CDs, merchandise, and fan-club memberships, roughly twice what it sold the previous year. In keeping with its low profile, the seven-year-old company remains tight-lipped about earnings and its cut of online purchases, other than to say it has been profitable for several years and expects to keep growing. That seems a safe bet given that in September, Live Nation, the industry's largest concert promoter, acquired a majority stake in Musictoday (it won't disclose the purchase price). Live Nation, which does about $3 billion in annual sales and produces more than 33,000 shows a year, is eager to keep moving into Live recordings and other concert-related goods. "There's a lot of fragmentation right now, a lot of new products," says Michael Rapino, CEO of Live Nation. "Artists are looking for partners who can deliver these products to their fan base. It's what the labels did for so long. Musictoday is a mile ahead of anyone else."

Capshaw's long, strange journey from fan to mogul began years earlier with the Grateful Dead. "I went to a lot of their shows," he says, "and was exposed to the do-it-yourself model." Jerry Garcia and the boys, whose instrumental jams shot the bird at the radio-hit formula, were touring tour de force. But behind the reefer haze was a larger, iconoclastic strategy. Deadheads were encouraged to tape shows, which fostered a tribe of bootleggers. The Dead shrugged at the lost record revenue and cashed in by selling its tickets and merchandise directly to fans.

Capshaw didn't consider managing until the early 1990s, when the Dave Matthews Band became a Tuesday night fixture at Trax, one of his two clubs in Charlottesville. He'd gotten into the business as a student at the University of Virginia back in the late 1970s, booking bands for fraternity parties. Eventually, he became a nightclub owner, one with an innate sense of how to take care of the talent: Ann Jones Donohue, now director of sales at Musictoday, started out by researching the artists' favorite foods and preparing home-cooked meals. Grilled seafood for the Neville Brothers. Barbecue for Jane's Addiction's Perry Farrell. "They came to town expecting a deli tray," she says.

Dave Matthews's crew reminded Capshaw of the Dead. How they thrived onstage, improvising, giving a different performance each night. How the crowds grew, attracting fans from around the state. How they taped shows, which Capshaw and the band encouraged to gin up word of mouth. It was a prototypical social network. "I remember talking to Coran once, and he held his phone outside his office for me to hear them," says Donohue. "He said they were going to be huge."

The first time he met Capshaw, Flohr recalls, "I was scared s—tless." It was 1993. Flohr was then vice president of A&R (artists and repertoire) at RCA and had come to Charlottesville hoping to sign Matthews. Capshaw had deliberately avoided a recording contract; the band was playing 200 or so gigs a year across the Southeast, building a rabid, mostly collegiate audience. "We needed them more than they needed us," Flohr admits. At dinner, Capshaw wavered, but eventually the two hammered out a deal largely influenced by the Dead's philosophy. "Rather than the label's saying, 'Here's what we're going to do with you,' they called the shots," Flohr recalls. "They said, 'We'll take some of your money, we'll put out an independent record, and we'll tour—boom, boom, boom.'" Boom is right: *Under the Table and Dreaming*, the group's first album for RCA, has sold nearly 7 million copies to date, and the band has become one of the industry's top-grossing concert acts.

The incident revealed what has become a recurring theme in Capshaw's career: a tenacity and talent for challenging the status quo, finding a soft spot in the industry's armor, and ultimately exploiting it to secure power for the artist. RCA got recording rights, but Dave Matthews retained merchandise and online rights. Later, the band negotiated the ability to release its own live recordings. Piece by piece, Capshaw was crafting a highly profitable and largely independent operation. Within a few years of teaming up with RCA, Matthews had produced three multimillion-selling albums and was filling football stadiums (and selling half of those tickets). Along the way, Capshaw built the mechanism for recording live shows (ATO Records, which now boasts more than a dozen acts, including David Gray and My Morning Jacket) and selling shirts, CDs, and tickets (Red Light Management).

Those early CDs contained the seed of what Musictoday would eventually become, in the form of a mail-order insert for merchandise. Capshaw and the band were designing and selling their own goods and pocketing "the retail spread." As that business expanded, it outgrew the spare room at Trax. Then, in the late 1990s, they began offering items online—and the bigger picture revealed itself. The infrastructure had fallen into place for a much bigger operation. "I realized that we could do it with more than just Dave Matthews," says Capshaw. "We had the potential to help other bands."

It wasn't just the artists' interests he was thinking of; Capshaw's a fan himself and wanted to change an industry that all too often took people like him for granted. His "pre-sale," for example, was a reward for a band's most loyal fans, a way of giving them the first shot at great seats for a few bucks less (typically, half the usual surcharge) before the public sale. By winning over more bands to the concept, Capshaw was in position to propel broader changes in the industry. But not before encountering big-time resistance. In 2002, Ticketmaster—the Microsoft in that space—sensed a potentially lethal threat and deployed its lawyers. "They tried to shut down the artist-to-fan concept," Capshaw says matter-of-factly. "There was a series of letters they sent to promoters and venues, some back and forth there." Pause. "But we worked it out."

Ulysses S. Grant couldn't have said it better. As part of an exclusive agreement, Ticketmaster would allow Musictoday to sell 10% of tickets for its clients' shows. That sounds modest, but it represented a seismic power shift, as even Ticketmaster will tell you: "Musictoday went up against a big entrenched company and got it done," says David Marcus, Ticketmaster's vice president of music. "That requires a serious amount of fighting and skirmishing. You have to give them credit for shining a light on the path to the future. Coran's an aggressive, smart entrepreneur. Sometimes it takes small innovators to get mature companies back to innovating again."

Capshaw doesn't come across as the skirmishing type. Sitting in the top-floor conference room of Red Light Management, in downtown Charlottesville, he seems every bit the 48-year-old Deadhead, as laid-back as his black Lab Emmy (as in singer Emmylou Harris). He has thick, bushy gray hair, a reflective manner, and a deep voice softened by a slight drawl. *C-Ville Weekly*, a local paper, once called Capshaw the Donald of Charlottesville because of his many real estate projects, which include this very office building, an amphitheater, various apartments, several restaurants, a club, and a microbrewery. ("We joke that Coran pays you on Friday, and you give it back to him over the weekend," says Donohue.)

In fact, Capshaw, Pollstar's manager of the year in 2004, is notoriously media shy. It took more than a year to arrange this interview, which proceeds with all the brio of a Quaker meeting. However detached he may seem, Capshaw is intimately familiar with every gear in the machine. "He gets the same reports every day that I do," Hubbard says. Capshaw will weigh in on the wording of a fan email, the timing of a promotion. "He'll ask, 'What was Robert Randolph's ticket count Saturday night in DC?'" says Flohr. "'What was Trey Anastasio's pre-sale?'"

Flohr's so confident in Capshaw's model that he switched sides. Four years ago, he left RCA and came to work for him.

What the Musictoday machine does particularly well is tame the chaos inherent in the unfun, unsexy part of the business. In early November, once again it's fans of the Dave Matthews Band triggering a frenzy in the warehouse, this time with pre-orders for its latest live compilation, *The Best of What's Around, Volume 1*. Tens of thousands of orders pile in, many to be delivered on the exact release date. (In the past, as many as 70,000 of the 470,000 or so CDs sold in the first week were purchased through the band's site.)

This massive facility, with white-tile walls from its days as a frozen-food factory, is the clincher for visiting band managers, agents, and artists—the part of the tour that seals the deal. Often, bands have come after trying to run their own stores and getting overwhelmed. "Sometimes we're competing against somebody's uncle who makes the band's T-shirts in his garage," says Hubbard. "In many ways, this is still an unsophisticated business."

Musictoday couldn't possibly coordinate orders of this scale, complexity, and precision without state-of-the-art warehouse-management software and equipment, such as handheld scanners and a $200,000 automated packing machine. The logistics are made even gnarlier by the special offers that bundle in exclusive knick-knacks and routinely turn the sale of a single CD into a shopping spree. It's a fine example of Capshaw's vision of the symbiotic artist-fan relationship—fans get special items, the artist gets the profits. But that kind of customization creates a fulfillment nightmare that would challenge any retailer—and bring a hungover band to its knees. All the more amazing that Musictoday boasts "a 98.4% to 99.8% accuracy rate," according to Chief Operations Officer (COO) Del Wood.

The other side of the warehouse is like the stash of some obsessive-compulsive collector: 30,000 items from about 400 clients. The shelves, lined with different-colored bins, keep going and going. Ramones flip-flops. Cans of Arnold Palmer iced tea. AC/DC boxer shorts. And behind a locked door, pricier items, like a $5,000 lithograph signed by the Stones. The inventory, too, is organized for maximum efficiency, with the fastest-moving items on the front racks, within easy reach—"nose to knees," as Hubbard says.

Logistically, selling tickets is equally complex, with even less room for error. Just ask U2, not a Musictoday client. In 2005, it had to issue an apology when fans were left in the lurch by scalpers who'd infiltrated its site. "When we screw up, fans don't blame Musictoday," says Hubbard. "They blame the artist." So the company's system is built to handle near-instantaneous sell-outs as well as several hundred simultaneous events. It sells tickets for its clients as well as handling all the ticketing for certain arenas. The arena business is sure to grow since Live Nation owns, operates, or has booking rights at 170 venues worldwide, and its Ticketmaster contract expires next year. "Our system runs like a Ferrari," says Wood. For an Eric Clapton concert in October, it allocated 15,000 seats in 15 seconds.

Before acquiring Musictoday, Rapino, Live Nation's CEO, visited Charlottesville. "I was blown away," he says. "This is not a business you can dabble in. You have to invest in the infrastructure or you can't execute, and they have." The company's remote location has built-in cost advantages, namely affordable space and a top-flight young talent pool at UVA. In that sense, says Rapino, Musictoday "is impossible to replicate."

A few years ago, Nikki Vinci heard a song by a little-known rock band called the Damnwells and "fell in love." She went to the group's site and bought a T-shirt. "I felt like I was supporting them," she says. Without knowing it, though, Vinci had become a Musictoday customer. Now she manages dozens of Musictoday online stores—for Tiger Woods, Led Zeppelin, the Bonnaroo Music & Arts Festival . . . , even her beloved Damnwells. "I never forget what it feels like to he a fan," she says.

That sort of empathy is another key ingredient in the Musictoday formula. Employees are focused on being "artist friendly" and "fan friendly," the bedrock of Capshaw's philosophy. They're expected to be kindred spirits as well as music experts. Each band, after all, has its own subculture, with certain rules and tastes. ("Incense, rolling papers, and shot glasses won't work with Christina Aguilera," says Dave Kostelnik in client services, "but they will for the Black Crowes.") Dozens of employees play in bands of their own, including Hubbard, who's half of the acoustic duo Rockwell Church and a Musictoday client (its CDs, alas, don't qualify for "knees to nose"). They even get two "concert days" apiece every year. And they, like their boss, are discreet, refusing to dish on clients. "We're an invisible service provider," says Hubbard.

Although the music business traditionally revolves around product cycles, Musictoday takes a longer view, developing what Donohue calls "a fan for life." Staying on the radar. Creating products in between CDs and tours.

Vinci follows her clients and their fans like a dogged reporter. She checks in with artist management, sometimes several times a day, to learn what the talent is up to. She reviews dozens of Google alerts on her clients. Most nights and weekends, she pores through magazines online and off (the usual suspects, plus *Filter, Relix,* and *Paste*), industry trade journals (*Billboard, Pollstar*), message boards, and a couple of dozen blogs (An Aquarium Drunkard, Coolfer, Stereogum). "That's why they're partners with us," she says. "They know I'll find out what's going on and call."

With the right touch, says Hubbard, this sort of micromanaged online presence can prolong a musician's career. And he's not kidding: Frank Zappa—dead since 1993—is a client. The challenge, then, is not to taint the relationship by coming on too strong. So Musictoday tries to be more like a church that happens to sell communion wafers. "It sounds schlocky," says Kingdon in corporate strategy, "but we're trying to maximize that fan relationship, not maximize sales. If you do the first part, the rest will take care of itself. But if it smacks of commerce, you risk diluting the brand."

To fend off the competition spawned by its own success, Musictoday is always looking for ways to deepen its relationship with artists. The latest is by being a "strategic consultant," says Hubbard. The company's data mining could provide customer insight to drive decisions beyond ticketing or merchandise. "There's always been a real shoot-from-the-hip mentality in this business," he says. "Gut, not data." By mapping merch or ticket sales by geography, for instance, Musictoday can identify where marketing dollars are needed or where an artist should tour. "If you know you're drawing fans from Utah to drive to shows out of state," says Hubbard, "you need to add that 43rd tour date in Salt Lake City."

The Live Nation acquisition should crank up Musictoday's volume even further, like plugging an acoustic guitar into an amp. Live Nation gives it "a broader reach," says Capshaw. Yeah, broader by about 30 million potential customers. According to Live Nation, more than half of its fans visited an artist's Web site last year. "What was it five years ago, zero?" says Rapino. "This channel is as big as you can make it."

That's music to John Legend's ears. His Musictoday paid membership site . . . was slated to launch in December. In November, he posted a preview. Riding his tour bus through a snowstorm in Wisconsin, he filmed a video clip, singing a few bars of a Christmas carol and signing off: "God bless y'all, I love y'all, I appreciate y'all—Peace." Musictoday allows him to add messages himself—immediate, unfiltered access to his supporters. The idea, he says, "is to let them get to know me better."

And vice versa. *Get Lifted* may have sold 3 million copies, but Legend didn't own those sales data, so he had no way of contacting those fans. When people join his new club, they provide demographic information, which he hopes to build a business around. "You need to know who those people are, where they're from," Legend says. "What if you could find out what other products they like to buy? You might use that information to approach other brands—clothing and car companies that want to cater to the same market."

Legend pauses, reins in his inner consultant. "But if I don't make good music, none of this stuff is going to work. I never forget that."

Eric Boehlert

→ **NO**

Pay for Play

Does radio seem bad these days? Do all the hits sound the same, all the stars seem like cookie cutouts of one another?

It's because they do, and they are.

Why? Listeners may not realize it, but radio today is largely bought by the record companies. Most rock and Top 40 stations get paid to play the songs they spin by the companies that manufacture the records.

But it's not payola—exactly. Here's how it works.

Standing between the record companies and the radio stations is a legendary team of industry players called independent record promoters, or "indies."

The indies are the shadowy middlemen record companies will pay hundreds of millions of dollars to this year to get songs played on the radio. Indies align themselves with certain radio stations by promising the stations "promotional payments" in the six figures. Then, every time the radio station adds a Shaggy or Madonna or Janet Jackson song to its playlist, the indie gets paid by the record label.

Indies are not the guys U2 or Destiny's Child thanked on Grammys night, but everyone in the business, artists included, understands that the indies make or break careers.

"It's a big f---ing mudball," complains one radio veteran. At first glance, the indies are just the people who grease the gears in a typical mechanism connecting wholesaler with retailer. After all, Pepsi distributors, for example, pay for placement in grocery stores, right?

Except that radio isn't really retail—that's what the record stores are. Radio is an entity unique to the music industry. It's an independent force that, much to the industry's chagrin, represents the one tried-and-true way record companies know to sell their product.

Small wonder that the industry for decades has used money in various ways to influence what radio stations play. The days are long gone when a DJ made an impulse decision about what song to spin. The music industry is a $12 billion-a-year business; today, nearly every commercial music station in the country has an indie guarding its playlist. And for that right, the indie shells out hundreds of thousands of dollars a year to individual stations—and collects a lot more from the major record labels.

Indeed, say many industry observers, very little of what we hear on today's radio stations isn't bought, one way or another.

This article first appeared in *Salon.com*, March 14, 2001. An online version remains in the Salon archives. Copyright © 2001 by Salon Media Group, Inc. Reprinted with permission.
www.Salon.com

The indie promoter was once a tireless hustler, the lobbyist who worked the phones on behalf of record companies, cajoling station jocks and program directors, or P.D.s, to add a new song to their playlists. Sure, once in a while the indies showed their appreciation by sending some cocaine or hookers to station employees, but the colorful crew of fix-it men were basically providing a service: forging relationships with the gatekeepers in the complex world of radio, and turning that service into a deceptively simple and lucrative business. If record companies wanted access to radio, they had to pay.

In the 1990s, however, Washington moved steadily to deregulate the radio industry. Among other things, it removed most of America's decades-old restrictions on ownership. Today, the top three broadcasters control at least 60 percent of the stations in the top 100 markets in the U.S.

As that happened, indie promoters became big business.

Drugs and hookers are out; detailed invoices are in. Where indies were once scattered across the country, claiming a few dozen stations within a geographic territory, today's big firms stretch coast to coast, with hundreds of exclusive stations in every major format.

In effect, they've become an extraordinarily expensive phalanx of toll collectors who bill the record company every time a new song is added to a station's playlist.

And the indies do not come cheap.

There are 10,000 commercial radio stations in the United States; record companies rely on approximately 1,000 of the largest to create hits and sell records. Each of those 1,000 stations adds roughly three new songs to its playlist each week. The indies get paid for every one: $1,000 on average for an "add" at a Top 40 or rock station, but as high as $6,000 or $8,000 under certain circumstances.

That's a minimum $3 million worth of indie invoices sent out each week.

Now there's a new and more ominous development. There are rampant industry rumors that Clear Channel Communications, the country's largest radio station owner, is on the verge of formalizing a strategic alliance with one of the biggest indie promotion firms, Tri State Promotions & Marketing. The Cincinnati indie company has been closely aligned with the radio chain for years; now, sources suggest, Clear Channel will be using Tri State exclusively for the company's hundreds of music stations.

If the talk proves to be true, the move would dramatically alter radio's landscape in several ways—and raise new questions about the effect of the nation's payola laws at a time when the Federal Communications Commission has seemingly given up on regulating radio.

According to the FCC, there's nothing wrong with a radio station's accepting money in exchange for playing a song. The payment only becomes payola—and illegal—if the station fails to inform listeners about the cash changing hands.

But stations, of course, are reluctant to pepper their programming with announcements like "The previous Ricky Martin single was paid for by Sony Records." Besides that, stations want to maintain the illusion that they sift through stacks of records and pick out only the best ones for their listeners.

The secretive, and at times unseemly, indie system has been in place for decades. Rock radio pioneer Alan Freed was convicted in 1960 for accepting bribes in exchange for playing records. (What became known as the payola laws were passed as a response soon afterward.) More recently, legendary indie heavyweight Joe Isgro battled prosecutors for nearly a decade over payola-related charges before they were dismissed in 1996.

Isgro's tale of money, drugs and the mob was told in "Hit Men," Fredric Dannen's revealing 1991 book about the world of independent promoters and the extraordinary power they wielded over record companies.

Amazingly, says one radio veteran, "nothing's changed since 'Hit Men.' The cast of characters is different, but nothing's really changed."

One major-label V.P. agrees: "It's only changed color and form, but in essence it's the same. It's nothing but bullshit and operators and wasted money. But it's very intricate, and the system has been laid down for years."

Some in the increasingly sophisticated and global music business wonder if the time has finally come to break free from the costly chains of independent promotion. After all, no other entertainment industry vests so much power and pays so much money to outside sources who do so little work. Yet just-released figures indicate music sales were soft last year. Will record companies have the power, or the nerve, to walk away?

"Labels claim they're trying to cut back on indies, but everybody just laughs," says one radio veteran, who has both programmed stations and done indie promotion work. (He, like most of the people interviewed for this story, asked that his name not be used.) Adds another veteran: "Labels are pissed off and want to cut back, but they're powerless to do anything about it."

"The labels have created a monster," agrees longtime artist manager Ron Stone. Nevertheless, Stone views indies as an important insurance policy for his clients. "I never want to find out after the fact that we should've hired this indie or that indie. I want to cover all the bases.

"Because you only get 12 weeks for your record to get any traction at radio. After 12 weeks the next wave of record company singles come over the breach and if you don't have any traction you get washed away. But now it's become even more complicated and expensive because of consolidation. It's a high-stakes poker game."

Playing off record industry insecurities, indies have been winning this poker game for decades.

The Clear Channel/Tri State move would be a watershed. Arguably the most powerful force in the music business, Clear Channel's multibillion-dollar assets include 60 percent of the United States' rock-radio business and the leading Top 40 stations in major markets across the country, including KIIS Los Angeles, WHTZ New York, WJMN Boston, WKSC-FM Chicago, KHKS-FM Dallas and WHYI Miami. The company also has extensive holdings in concert venues, concert production firms and outdoor advertising companies, stemming from its merger with the SFX conglomerate last year.

In that arena, Tri State would appear to be a minor player. But by maintaining a close relationship with Clear Channel as the conglomerate mushroomed and bought hundreds of new radio stations in recent years, Tri State has become synonymous with Clear Channel in the industry.

That relationship has translated into power and wealth. "Tri State's billings are probably up more than 1,000 percent since deregulation, considering how many more stations they have influence over," says one indie promoter.

Tri State's chiefs, Lenny Lyons and Bill Scull, did not return phone calls seeking comment.

Clear Channel stations not already using Tri State exclusively are likely to have to terminate their contracts with indie competitors, such as longtime powerhouse Jeff McClusky & Associates. That already may be happening. "They're clearing the decks," says one person who works at a major-label radio promotion department. (McClusky declined to comment.)

The move could mean higher indie fees for record companies. Tri State was charging labels $1,000 an add at some stations, but sources say those rates could jump considerably if Clear Channel and Tri State join forces.

Indeed, particularly in this deregulatory era, Clear Channel can basically charge whatever it wants. Why? Because record companies realize they can't create a hit without help from the conglomerate.

With that kind of clout, Clear Channel, through Tri State, could institute national buys for new singles. "Labels would pay $100,000 or $200,000 to get a single added to all the Clear Channel format stations one week," suggests one radio source. "And if they don't pay, there is no chance in hell they're getting that song on the radio without Tri State. If it's not on the list, it's not on stations."

And if the song isn't played on the radio, chances are it's not going to make the record company any money.

That raises real red flags at the record companies. "Tolls go up if there's only one road into town. And today you cannot have a hit record without Clear Channel or Tri State," says one record company president whose label recently scored a top-five hit on pop radio with the help of indie promoters. "That allows for an abusive type of toll collections. It seems to be getting out of hand. It's creating burdensome costs and it's screwing with the economics of the music business."

And perhaps most important, any long-term deal between Clear Channel and Tri State would essentially eliminate the all-important middleman. Record companies would instead be paying Tri State for airplay on Clear Channel stations. "That would put it into the realm of payola," says one record company promotion exec.

Clear Channel CEO Randy Michaels recently told the *Los Angeles Times* that the company does want a piece of the promotional pie, but only through an odd new twist: It plans to sell promotional packages to record companies that would identify the artist after each song is played.

But in a business swimming in money, some doubt things could become that cut and dried. For instance, what Clear Channel is proposing is something stations usually do for free; it's called "back-announcing," letting listeners know which artist they just heard. Will Clear Channel stations now only I.D. songs if the labels pay for the service?

"It sounds like extortion to me," says a former programmer. (Clear Channel executives were not available for comment.)

If the practice takes hold, look for competing groups, like Viacom's Infinity Broadcasting, to start hitting up labels for similar commercial buys. "It will throw the whole system into chaos," fears one indie.

⋅⟨⊙⟩⋅

The indies' power illustrates just how crucial radio, especially Top 40, is in generating CD sales. (U.S. consumers bought more than 700 million CDs last year.) Steady touring, an Internet presence, glowing press and MTV help, of course, but mainstream radio play is still the engine that drives the music business.

Yet radio has traditionally been a brood of literally thousands of sometimes spatting siblings, each typically run by a P.D. with high self-regard.

The problem for record companies has always been that there are too many radio stations—and too many egos—nationwide for label staffers to keep close tabs on. So they need to hire indies, people with close business relationships in different markets. (Third-party indies have traditionally insulated labels from direct involvement in any payola activity as well.)

Here's how the game is played today:

The reality is, disc jockeys were cut out of music-making decisions at stations many years ago. Virtually all commercial radio airplay is determined by program directors, who typically construct elaborate schedules directing the DJs what to play and when.

Today, thanks to consolidation, even station program directors often get their playlist cues from above—from general managers, station owners or, in this age of consolidation, regional program directors.

So many indies no longer bother to target the P.D.s. Instead, they go straight to the general managers or owners and cut deals, typically guaranteeing a station in a medium-sized market roughly $75,000 to $100,000 annually in what is termed "promotional support." The station claims that the money goes to buying new station vans, T-shirts or giveaway prizes; in reality, the station spends the cash any way it wants.

That payment makes the indie the station's exclusive point man, the only one (or at least the first one) its programmers will talk to about adding new singles. Once that indie has "claimed" a station, he (there are very few shes in the business) sends out a notice to record companies, letting them know he will invoice them every time the station adds a song to its playlist.

"The truth is, you could [be] making a handsome living, and have a gigantic house in Greenville, S.C., for instance, if you have just six exclusive stations there," explains one industry veteran. (Arbitron ranks Greenville as the 61st largest radio market, with a metro population of 750,000.) "You could gross between half a million and 1 million dollars each year. That's with no staff—just a couple of phones and a fax machine. Because somebody is going to pay you $1,000 every time one of those Greenville stations adds a song. And that $1,000 is just the average. Columbia records may be dying to get a single on, so they say, 'We'll pay you $2,500 for this add.' "

Do the math: six stations in a market like Greenville adding three songs a week, 50 weeks of the year. That represents about $900,000 worth of invoiced adds. If the indie is paying each station $75,000 a year in "promotional support," that leaves him with $450,000.

But that's just the beginning. There are additional sources of indie income, including retainers, "bill-backs" and "spin maintenance." Along with being paid on a per-add basis, some indies earn a retainer (roughly $800 a week) just to call stations on behalf of a song. Bill-backs are essentially second invoices—to cover "promotional purposes"—that indies send to record companies on top of the one for the add. If the add cost $2,000, the indie often sends a $1,000 bill-back invoice as well.

Meanwhile, the cost of the add covers just that: getting the song added to the playlist. If labels want to increase the spins (or number of times a song is played each week), that costs money, too. "There are spin programs you can buy," explains one record company source, such as "$4,000 to make the song top 15 at the station."

In the past, if indies wanted to increase their billings by getting stations to add more songs, they could employ "paper adds." Stations would notify labels that a song was on the playlist so the indie got paid, but in reality the single never got spun. Today, however, all key radio stations are monitored electronically by a company called Broadcast Data Service, which gives labels a detailed readout of actual airplay. Paper adds no longer pass the test.

The solution? A so-called lunar rotation.

"I've got one station that during crunch time in September and October, when every label is desperate for fourth-quarter adds, will do eight adds a week for four weeks in a row at $2,000 a pop," says one label source. That's 32 added songs—and $64,000 in indie invoices—for just one month. But the station's playlist could never support that many new songs. (With today's tightly controlled playlists, any new song is a risk that can cause listeners to switch to a channel with an older and more comforting hit.) Most of these new "adds" are played only in the early-morning hours, or in the "lunar rotation." They are detected by BDS, but don't really affect the station's playlist or ratings.

For record companies, indie costs can be staggering. Just to launch a single at rock radio over several weeks can cost between $100,000 and $250,000 in indie fees. What exactly do labels get in return? "I'll be damned if I know," says artist manager Stone. "It's bizarre." (Labels can sometimes get artists to pay the indie promotion costs, but not always.)

Regardless, the No. 1 rule of radio promotion is that the indie always gets paid. Even if rock programmers discover a good song by a new band on their own, and add it to their playlists because they like it, the station's indie gets paid for it.

Even if someone at Universal Records persuades a pop station to play Nelly's new single "Ride Wit Me," the indie gets paid. Even if the song is a sure hit that needs almost no promotion, like Aerosmith's latest, "Jaded," the indie gets paid. "Either way the invoices arrive and you pay, in the interest of keeping everybody happy," says one former programmer.

The fear is that if a label tangles with an indie over billing, he could torpedo the label's next project by bad-mouthing a new single or keeping it off the air until his previous invoice is paid. As messy as the relationship can be, the third-party arrangement between labels, indies and stations is crucial for appearance' sake. Today, indies pay stations for "access," not airplay. At least in theory.

"Everyone says indies don't force stations to add records. That's ridiculous," says one rock programmer who has worked in a Top 10 market. "Because [if there is friction] the indie will get on the phone with the station G.M. and say, 'Look, your P.D. has not been cooperative over the last few months on adds I need.' The G.M. either says to the indie, 'Our relationship is about access, not influence,' or he caves. Most G.M.s cave and have a word with the P.D.: 'Look, we have $100,000 a year riding on this relationship with our indie.' Then suddenly—bam—a song you know the P.D. hates shows up on the air."

"Record companies say, 'We're not doing anything illegal; we're just paying indies to promote the records," says another programmer. "And indies say we're not doing anything wrong; we're just helping market a radio station. Everybody toes the company line on this.

"But indies are like money launderers; they make sure record company money gets to radio stations, but in a different form."

POSTSCRIPT

Can the Independent Musical Artist Thrive in Today's Music Business?

Both of the authors speaking to this issue focus on a different aspect of how the music industry is changing. One looks at the entrepreneurial activity that new artists can avail themselves of, and the other looks at the role of the indie record promoter and that person's influence on what does, or does not, get played on the radio. Obviously, the recording industry has undergone many changes since the development of the Internet, and these examples represent only two of the many business models that are emerging at this time in history. Since Eric Boehlert's article, the FCC has attempted to crack down on the practice of justified payola—which is the term given to the way indie record promoters work. But despite a short flurry of activity with threats of penalties and greater regulation, little has been effective to curb the "pay for play" model.

The digital technologies used for recording today have drastically changed the way the recording industry operates. Not only does downloading digital information result in high-quality copies, but the number of musical artists who have access to low-cost recording devices is growing. There is probably no other media industry that has changed as rapidly as the recording industry, but others are not far behind.

One matter that will still be debated is the ownership of digital material. The Digital Millennium Copyright Act (DMCA) has attempted to clarify who controls what in the recording and re-recording of material, but the act is still vague and subject to many revisions in the future. Encryption technologies and dissolving digital signals may be short-term solutions for the industry to control content, but even these methods can be easily overwritten by a knowledgeable consumer.

Some good sources address the changing music business. Steve Gordon has written *The Future of the Music Business: How to Succeed with the New Digital Technologies* (Backbeat Books, 2005), which specifically says that "copyright is the basis of virtually every music business transaction." In a little more progressive vein, Dave Kusek and Gerd Leonhard have written *The Future of Music: Manifesto for the Digital Music Revolution* (Berlee Press, 2005) in which they envision "a future in which music will be like water: ubiquitous and free-flowing." A DVD featuring Russell Simmons and Lyor Cohen called *The Industry* (Kwame Amoaku, director, 2005) portrays the executive side of the music industry and the stresses of working in that industry today.

Students should also become familiar with some of the trade magazines in the industries they hope to pursue. If you are interested in the recording industry or radio, you should familiarize yourself with *Record World* and *Billboard*. Both are required reading for people who work in these industries (and also have job listings in the classified sections).

ISSUE 15

Should Newspapers Shut Down Their Presses?

YES: Clay Shirkey, from "Newspapers and Thinking the Unthinkable," at http://www.shirky.com/weblog/2009/03/newspapers-and-thinking-the-unthinkable/

NO: Paul Farhi, from "A Bright Future for Newspapers," *American Journalism Review* (June/July 2005)

ISSUE SUMMARY

YES: Clay Shirkey argues that the old economies of newspapers are destroyed in the digital age. This is a revolution similar to that which occurred with the invention of the printing press. No one knows what the future will hold, but we can only hope that journalism is not lost with the demise of newspapers.

NO: All news media are facing challenges in these difficult economic times. Paul Farhi, a *Washington Post* staff writer, argues that newspapers have unique competitive advantages that should assure that the worst case won't happen.

$\mathbf{A}$re newspapers dying? The press is filled with reports of calamity. The *Rocky Mountain News*, a daily Denver newspaper, shut down in February of 2009. *The Christian Science* Monitor ceased daily print publication in March 2009, moving to an online daily offering. *The State of the News Media 2009* (www .stateofthemedia.org/2009) reports a drop from 49.3 billion in advertising revenue in 2006 to 38 billion in 2008—a decline of 23 percent. These losses come from loss of classifieds to online competitors such as Craig's List and the loss of lucrative employment, auto, and retail advertising. Yet despite these dire figures, the majority of newspapers remain profitable—although not nearly as profitable as previously. High debt loads are one cause of financial problems for some papers. But the longer-term issue is whether the traditional business model of printed newspapers delivered to homes will continue to be viable.

At one level, the question is simple. Which is the better idea: to print papers using expensive ink and paper and to transport them daily to people's homes at substantial delivery costs, or to put that information online for virtually no reproduction or distribution costs? Clay Shirky thinks the unthinkable in his blog. Newspapers anticipated the transformational nature of the Internet, but they could not find a business model to profit from it. Would it be walled content, micropayments, nonprofit status? Shirkey compares this to the revolution wrought by the printing press. What happens now will be as chaotic and unanticipated as the events following Gutenberg's invention.

Farhi does not see such a bleak future. Certainly circulation is down, advertising has dropped, and a heavy debt load threatens some newspaper companies. But Farhi challenges the reader to compare the newspaper to other traditional media, which are experiencing similar problems. And new media are not the panacea, failing even now to advance a profitable business plan for news. Newspapers carry an important tradition of localism and public service, and typically field the largest reporting staffs within their area. They have a tradition of profitability fueled by attractive numbers, the demographics of their readers, and the commitment of those readers to the product. Are newspapers troubled? Yes, but they have every resource to respond to the current situation and continue into the coming decades.

The economics of this prediction haven't changed, according to Alan Mutter, a self-styled Newsosaur who explains "why it would be suicidal for any reasonably profitable publisher to stop its presses." (See "Why Newspapers Can't Stop the Presses," *Reflections of a Newsosaur*, February 1–4, 2009: http://newsosaur.blogspot.com/2009/02/why-newspapers-cant-stop-presses.html.) He offers a complex economic analysis of the flaws in plans to stop the presses. Because newspapers generate about 90 percent of revenue from print advertising, he argues that transitioning to Web-only would produce at best 10 percent of the cash generated by the print-online model. From such drastic reductions in revenue, the only option would be to drastically reduce the remaining major expense center—the newsroom. His analysis challenges easy assumptions that the move to Web-only papers would be easy and would generate savings to cancel lost revenue.

John Carroll provides a clear statement of the business and professional issues that make this such an important debate. In a speech at the University of Kentucky titled "The Future (We Hope) of Journalism," he asks three crucial questions: Who, in the digital future, will do the reporting? What principles, if any, will guide the journalism of the digital age? and Will we have journalistic institutions that are strong enough, and independent enough, to serve as a counterweight to big government and big corporations? You can find this speech at www.poynter.org.

You will notice that several issues are related in this volume. Issue 8 asks about why the press has lost its credibility and how that can be restored. Issue 10 asks how journalistic practice will change in the digital age. This selection asks us to consider the dramatic changes in how newspapers will operate. All share a similar concern with the future of newspapers and journalism in the digital age. Before you delve into these selections, ask yourself a question that is truly unthinkable to all of the authors in the issues noted above: If newspapers collapse, would quality journalism die?

YES

Clay Shirky

Newspapers and Thinking the Unthinkable

Back in 1993, the Knight-Ridder newspaper chain began investigating piracy of Dave Barry's popular column, which was published by *The Miami Herald* and syndicated widely. In the course of tracking down the sources of unlicensed distribution, they found many things, including the copying of his column to alt.fan.dave_barry on usenet; a 2000-person strong mailing list also reading pirated versions; and a teenager in the Midwest who was doing some of the copying himself, because he loved Barry's work so much he wanted everybody to be able to read it.

One of the people I was hanging around with online back then was Gordy Thompson, who managed internet services at *The New York Times:* I remember Thompson saying something to the effect of "When a 14 year old kid can blow up your business in his spare time, not because he hates you but because he loves you, then you got a problem." I think about that conversation a lot these days.

The problem newspapers face isn't that they didn't see the internet coming. They not only saw it miles off; they figured out early on that they needed a plan to deal with it, and during the early 90s they came up with not just one plan but several. One was to partner with companies like America Online, a fast-growing subscription service that was less chaotic than the open internet. Another plan was to educate the public about the behaviors required of them by copyright law. New payment models such as micropayments were proposed. Alternatively, they could pursue the profit margins enjoyed by radio and TV, if they became purely ad-supported. Still another plan was to convince tech firms to make their hardware and software less capable of sharing, or to partner with the businesses running data networks to achieve the same goal. Then there was the nuclear option: sue copyright infringers directly, making an example of them.

As these ideas were articulated, there was intense debate about the merits of various scenarios. Would DRM or walled gardens work better? Shouldn't we try a carrot-and-stick approach, with education *and* prosecution? And so on. In all this conversation, there was one scenario that was widely regarded as unthinkable, a scenario that didn't get much discussion in the nation's newsrooms, for the obvious reason.

The unthinkable scenario unfolded something like this: The ability to share content wouldn't shrink; it would grow. Walled gardens would prove unpopular. Digital advertising would reduce inefficiencies, and therefore profits. Dislike of micropayments would prevent widespread use. People would resist being educated to act against their own desires. Old habits of advertisers and readers would not transfer online. Even ferocious litigation would be inadequate to constrain massive, sustained law-breaking. (Prohibition redux.) Hardware and software vendors would not regard copyright holders as allies, nor would they regard customers as enemies. DRM's requirement that the attacker be allowed to decode the content would be an insuperable flaw. And, per Thompson, suing people who love something so much they want to share it would piss them off.

Revolutions create a curious inversion of perception. In ordinary times, people who do no more than describe the world around them are seen as pragmatists, while those who imagine fabulous alternative futures are viewed as radicals. The last couple of decades haven't been ordinary, however. Inside the papers, the pragmatists were the ones simply looking out the window and noticing that the real world was increasingly resembling the unthinkable scenario. These people were treated as if they were barking mad. Meanwhile the people spinning visions of popular walled gardens and enthusiastic micropayment adoption, visions unsupported by reality, were regarded not as charlatans but saviors.

When reality is labeled unthinkable, it creates a kind of sickness in an industry. Leadership becomes faith-based, while employees who have the temerity to suggest that what seems to be happening is in fact happening are herded into Innovation Departments, where they can be ignored *en masse*. This shunting aside of the realists in favor of the fabulists has different effects on different industries at different times. One of the effects on the newspapers is that many of their most passionate defenders are unable, even now, to plan for a world in which the industry they knew is visibly going away.

⁕

The curious thing about the various plans hatched in the '90s is that they were, at base, all the same plan: "Here's how we're going to preserve the old forms of organization in a world of cheap perfect copies!" The details differed, but the core assumption behind all imagined outcomes (save the unthinkable one) was that the organizational form of the newspaper, as a general-purpose vehicle for publishing a variety of news and opinion, was basically sound, and only needed a digital facelift. As a result, the conversation has degenerated into the enthusiastic grasping at straws, pursued by skeptical responses.

"*The Wall Street Journal* has a paywall, so we can too!" (Financial information is one of the few kinds of information whose recipients don't want to share.) "Micropayments work for iTunes, so they will work for us!" (Micropayments work only where the provider can avoid competitive business models.) "*The New York Times* should charge for content!" (They've tried, with QPass and later TimesSelect.) "*Cook's Illustrated* and *Consumer Reports* are doing fine on subscriptions!" (Those publications forgo ad revenues; users are paying not just for content but for unimpeachability.) "We'll form a cartel!" (. . . and hand a competitive advantage to every ad-supported media firm in the world.)

Round and round this goes, with the people committed to saving newspapers demanding to know "If the old model is broken, what will work in its place?" To which the answer is: Nothing. Nothing will work. There is no general model for newspapers to replace the one the internet just broke.

With the old economics destroyed, organizational forms perfected for industrial production have to be replaced with structures optimized for digital data. It makes increasingly less sense even to talk about a publishing industry, because the core problem publishing solves—the incredible difficulty, complexity, and expense of making something available to the public—has stopped being a problem.

❧

Elizabeth Eisenstein's magisterial treatment of Gutenberg's invention, *The Printing Press as an Agent of Change*, opens with a recounting of her research into the early history of the printing press. She was able to find many descriptions of life in the early 1400s, the era before movable type. Literacy was limited, the Catholic Church was the pan-European political force, Mass was in Latin, and the average book was the Bible. She was also able to find endless descriptions of life in the late 1500s, after Gutenberg's invention had started to spread. Literacy was on the rise, as were books written in contemporary languages, Copernicus had published his epochal work on astronomy, and Martin Luther's use of the press to reform the Church was upending both religious and political stability.

What Eisenstein focused on, though, was how many historians ignored the transition from one era to the other. To describe the world before or after the spread of print was child's play; those dates were safely distanced from upheaval. But what was happening in 1500? The hard question Eisenstein's book asks is "How did we get from the world before the printing press to the world after it? What was the revolution *itself* like?"

Chaotic, as it turns out. The Bible was translated into local languages; was this an educational boon or the work of the devil? Erotic novels appeared, prompting the same set of questions. Copies of Aristotle and Galen circulated widely, but direct encounter with the relevant texts revealed that the two sources clashed, tarnishing faith in the Ancients. As novelty spread, old institutions seemed exhausted while new ones seemed untrustworthy; as a result, people almost literally didn't know what to think. If you can't trust Aristotle, who can you trust?

During the wrenching transition to print, experiments were only revealed in retrospect to be turning points. Aldus Manutius, the Venetian printer and publisher, invented the smaller *octavo* volume along with italic type. What seemed like a minor change—take a book and shrink it—was in retrospect a key innovation in the democratization of the printed word. As books became cheaper, more portable, and therefore more desirable, they expanded the market for all publishers, heightening the value of literacy still further.

That is what real revolutions are like. The old stuff gets broken faster than the new stuff is put in its place. The importance of any given experiment isn't apparent at the moment it appears; big changes stall, small changes spread. Even the revolutionaries can't predict what will happen. Agreements on all sides that core institutions must be protected are rendered meaningless by the very people doing the agreeing. (Luther and the Church both insisted, for years, that whatever else happened, no one was talking about a schism.) Ancient social bargains, once disrupted, can neither be mended nor quickly replaced, since any such bargain takes decades to solidify.

And so it is today. When someone demands to know how we are going to replace newspapers, they are really demanding to be told that we are not living through a revolution. They are demanding to be told that old systems won't break before new systems are in place. They are demanding to be told that ancient social bargains aren't in peril, that core institutions will be spared, that new methods of spreading information will improve previous practice rather than upending it. They are demanding to be lied to.

There are fewer and fewer people who can convincingly tell such a lie.

⋅◆⋅

If you want to know why newspapers are in such trouble, the most salient fact is this: Printing presses are terrifically expensive to set up and to run. This bit of economics, normal since Gutenberg, limits competition while creating positive returns to scale for the press owner, a happy pair of economic effects that feed on each other. In a notional town with two perfectly balanced newspapers, one paper would eventually generate some small advantage—a breaking story, a key interview—at which point both advertisers and readers would come to prefer it, however slightly. That paper would in turn find it easier to capture the next dollar of advertising, at lower expense, than the competition. This would increase its dominance, which would further deepen those preferences, repeat chorus. The end result is either geographic or demographic segmentation among papers, or one paper holding a monopoly on the local mainstream audience.

For a long time, longer than anyone in the newspaper business has been alive in fact, print journalism has been intertwined with these economics. The expense of printing created an environment where Wal-Mart was willing to subsidize the Baghdad bureau. This wasn't because of any deep link between advertising and reporting, nor was it about any real desire on the part of Wal-Mart to have their marketing budget go to international correspondents. It was just an accident. Advertisers had little choice other than to have their money used that way, since they didn't really have any other vehicle for display ads.

The old difficulties and costs of printing forced everyone doing it into a similar set of organizational models; it was this similarity that made us regard

Daily Racing Form and *L'Osservatore Romano* as being in the same business. That the relationship between advertisers, publishers, and journalists has been ratified by a century of cultural practice doesn't make it any less accidental.

The competition-deflecting effects of printing cost got destroyed by the internet, where everyone pays for the infrastructure, and then everyone gets to use it. And when Wal-Mart, and the local Maytag dealer, and the law firm hiring a secretary, and that kid down the block selling his bike, were all able to use that infrastructure to get out of their old relationship with the publisher, they did. They'd never really signed up to fund the Baghdad bureau anyway.

ꞏ◄◉►ꞏ

Print media does much of society's heavy journalistic lifting, from flooding the zone—covering every angle of a huge story—to the daily grind of attending the City Council meeting, just in case. This coverage creates benefits even for people who aren't newspaper readers, because the work of print journalists is used by everyone from politicians to district attorneys to talk radio hosts to bloggers. The newspaper people often note that newspapers benefit society as a whole. This is true, but irrelevant to the problem at hand; "You're gonna miss us when we're gone!" has never been much of a business model. So who covers all that news if some significant fraction of the currently employed newspaper people lose their jobs?

I don't know. Nobody knows. We're collectively living through 1500, when it's easier to see what's broken than what will replace it. The internet turns 40 this fall. Access by the general public is less than half that age. Web use, as a normal part of life for a majority of the developed world, is less than half *that* age. We just got here. Even the revolutionaries can't predict what will happen.

Imagine, in 1996, asking some net-savvy soul to expound on the potential of craigslist, then a year old and not yet incorporated. The answer you'd almost certainly have gotten would be extrapolation: "Mailing lists can be powerful tools," "Social effects are intertwining with digital networks," blah blah blah. What no one would have told you, could have told you, was what actually happened: craiglist became a critical piece of infrastructure. Not the idea of craigslist, or the business model, or even the software driving it. Craigslist itself spread to cover hundreds of cities and has become a part of public consciousness about what is now possible. Experiments are only revealed in retrospect to be turning points.

In craigslist's gradual shift from 'interesting if minor' to 'essential and transformative,' there is one possible answer to the question "If the old model is broken, what will work in its place?" The answer is: Nothing will work, but everything might. Now is the time for experiments, lots and lots of experiments, each of which will seem as minor at launch as craigslist did, as Wikipedia did, as *octavo* volumes did.

Journalism has always been subsidized. Sometimes it's been Wal-Mart and the kid with the bike. Sometimes it's been Richard Mellon Scaife. Increasingly, it's you and me, donating our time. The list of models that are obviously working today, like *Consumer Reports* and NPR, like ProPublica and WikiLeaks, can't be expanded to cover any general case, but then nothing is going to cover the general case.

Society doesn't need newspapers. What we need is journalism. For a century, the imperatives to strengthen journalism and to strengthen newspapers have been so tightly wound as to be indistinguishable. That's been a fine accident to have, but when that accident stops, as it is stopping before our eyes, we're going to need lots of other ways to strengthen journalism instead.

When we shift our attention from 'save newspapers' to 'save society,' the imperative changes from 'preserve the current institutions' to 'do whatever works.' And what works today isn't the same as what used to work.

We don't know who the Aldus Manutius of the current age is. It could be Craig Newmark, or Caterina Fake. It could be Martin Nisenholtz, or Emily Bell. It could be some 19 year old kid few of us have heard of, working on something we won't recognize as vital until a decade hence. Any experiment, though, designed to provide new models for journalism is going to be an improvement over hiding from the real, especially in a year when, for many papers, the unthinkable future is already in the past.

For the next few decades, journalism will be made up of overlapping special cases. Many of these models will rely on amateurs as researchers and writers. Many of these models will rely on sponsorship or grants or endowments instead of revenues. Many of these models will rely on excitable 14 year olds distributing the results. Many of these models will fail. No one experiment is going to replace what we are now losing with the demise of news on paper, but over time, the collection of new experiments that do work might give us the journalism we need.

Paul Farhi

→ **NO**

A Bright Future for Newspapers

Philip Meyer, who has studied the newspaper industry for three decades, can see the darkness at the end of the tunnel. If present readership trends continue indefinitely, says the University of North Carolina professor, the last daily newspaper reader will check out in 2044. October 2044, to be exact. "I use that as an attention-getting device," says Meyer, whose latest book, "The Vanishing Newspaper: Saving Journalism in the Information Age," spells out the bad news in elaborate detail. "It's shocking, but that's what the numbers say."

It's not hard to understand how we could get from here to there. The media have been covering the bad news about newspapers for years. To see and read these accounts is to encounter an industry that seems on the verge of crisis, and possibly on the edge of the abyss. "In many U.S. markets, the dominant paper is a fading enterprise," wrote Slate media critic Jack Shafer this spring. "In the long run, no newspaper is safe from electronic technologies." *Barron's Online* columnist Howard R. Gold put it this way recently: "A crisis of confidence has combined with a technological revolution and structural economic change to create what can only be described as a perfect storm. . . . [P]rint's business model is imploding as younger readers turn toward free tabloids and electronic media to get news." *The Washington Post* was more succinct: "The venerable newspaper is in trouble," it declared in a long feature story in February.

Wait a second. Newspapers, which predate the founding of the American republic, are "imploding," "in trouble" and staring at oblivion? Is the future really so bleak?

To be certain, all is not as well as it once was at the average daily. Circulation, which has been on an orderly downward trajectory for two decades, has lately shown signs of free fall. (Daily newspaper circulation dropped 1.9 percent in the last year, according to the Audit Bureau of Circulations numbers.) Young readers are scarce, newsroom budgets are tight, and the competition remains unrelenting. Newspapers have wounded themselves with a series of credibility-shredding scandals and screwups—from Jayson Blair's and Jack Kelley's fictions to Judith Miller's mistaken WMD stories to last year's Enron-style circulation-inflation mess. The Internet, with its vastness, its vibrancy and its immediacy, does seem poised to blow away the snoozy old newspaper.

And yet all of this misses a bigger, more positive picture. Media accounts of the rise and fall of newspapers are greatly exaggerated, if not flat wrong. The case for the survival of the daily paper is at least as compelling as the one for its much-reported demise. Considering the hurricane of change that is buffeting all segments of the news media these days, I'd argue that no part of the business is as firmly anchored as the average daily newspaper. Rather than accepting their own mortality, newspapers may have the best chance of any of the old media to survive in a new-media world.

All of the pessimistic assessments of the newspaper industry's future invite a simple rejoinder: Compared with what? Since all traditional media—newspapers, magazines, radio, TV, etc.—are gradually losing readers, listeners and viewers, assessing any single medium in isolation provides a flawed and distorted picture. Compared with the rest of the media industry, newspapers are doing no worse, and in some respects quite a bit better, than the competition, including the Internet.

Let's take a quick tour.

Cable TV news? Except for the surge in interest late last year due to the presidential election, the three news channels—Fox News Channel, CNN and MSNBC—likely would have experienced their third no-growth year in a row.

In any case, the audience trends in cable news aren't promising. For one thing, cable news viewing is subject to extreme volatility—people come and go, driven to the set by the big breaking stories but paying only sporadic attention the rest of the time. More important, cable and the all-news networks it carries are at saturation. Cable's audience grew during the last decade partly as a result of expanded distribution—as more households could receive Fox News or CNN, more people watched. However, the wiring of America is all but complete now. So cable companies have had to look for new ways to grow, and they're doing so by expanding the number of channels available to their existing household customers. This can only mean more audience fragmentation, as viewers click around their new digital channels. Since new viewers aren't rushing to watch the all-news channels (and the audience for cable news is small to begin with—between 2 million and 3 million people at a time), the only way a network can grow is by cannibalizing the other guy's audience. Hardly a vibrant scenario.

The broadcast networks and local stations? They've been shedding viewers for years. It's not just the networks' prime time entertainment schedules that have been faltering; sports, soap operas, talk shows and game shows have been, too. Over the past two decades, the networks' news programming has lost viewers at a much faster pace than newspapers have been losing their readers. The Big Three still command the attention of roughly 29 million people each weeknight—but that's down 10 million, or 26 percent, from as recently as the mid-1990s.

Unlike cable, the broadcast networks still have a massive audience, and thus have further to fall. But TV networks are hypersensitive to even small movements in the Nielsen numbers these days. It's easy to lament, but not hard to understand, ABC's deliberations over the fate of "Nightline." In the past decade, the program has lost almost 40 percent of its audience (it still averages a respectable 3.8 million viewers per night). Journalists may shudder at the possible cancellation of "Nightline," but competence and prestige are no longer guarantees of survival on network TV.

Radio? Long ago, in a quainter, slower America, radio was a significant source of news and information. But since deregulation and consolidation, hundreds of commercial stations have dropped news, even the most rudimentary rip-and-read kind. The audience for all-news radio has remained relatively stable (and in the case of stations carrying NPR programming has actually grown). But conventional over-the-air radio seems to be in about the same position now as broadcast television was a couple of decades ago—on the verge of huge change. New technologies—satellite radio, multichannel digital terrestrial radio, podcasting, even enhanced cell phones—are already starting to chip away at radio's car-bound audience.

Magazines? They're also losing their claim on the ever-shortening attention span of Americans (a Pew Research Center for the People & the Press survey reports that only a quarter of Americans said they read a magazine "yesterday," down from a third that reported the same thing in 1994). Magazines have always lived in a world of ferocious competition and fragmentation—they're easy to start and can be tailored for readers interested in almost any subject. But the magazine industry is, in many respects, among the least economically healthy segments of the media. Consider: There were nearly one-third fewer titles being published in 2004 than there were in 1999, according to the National Directory of Magazines.

The most interesting and complicated case is the New News Media. Despite the hype, the Internet isn't swallowing everything in its path. A mere 2 percent of the people surveyed by Pew last year said the Internet was their only regular news source. The appetite for news from the Internet is growing, but it's just one part of a varied diet. The average person gets news from a variety of sources—some online, some from TV or radio, some from newspapers and magazines, Pew's figures show. The Internet is actually a small part of that; the average amount of time spent reading the news online was just seven minutes a day last year. No question Internet advertising is growing rapidly, but from a base of almost nothing just a few years ago.

Unlike TV, which created instant and sustained riches, Internet news pioneers are still grasping for a sustainable business model 10 or so years into the online era. Only a few news Web sites earn their keep—and prominent on this list are the online versions of print-and-ink newspapers. This is not to say that the Internet, with its speed and near-zero distribution costs, won't someday dominate news delivery. It could, but it's still hard to see how that day will come about. Will people pay for content online, or is the free model an established fact of life? If it is, will there be enough advertising, at high enough prices, to support as many reporters and editors as now staff even a small newspaper? Will general one-stop, online newspapers amass enough visitors (and enough geographically concentrated visitors at that) to attract lost print subscribers and local advertising? And with people spending relatively few minutes a day on news sites, will anyone be sitting still long enough to see an online ad in the first place?

A couple of aspects of the changing media landscape plainly seem hyped, or maybe just misreported. One is that young people don't read newspapers. They don't, to a shocking degree (just 23 percent of people under 30 said they had read a newspaper the day before they were interviewed, according to the Pew survey). But here's the other part of the picture: The same survey says young people aren't very interested in news from any source, electronic or print. The time spent watching or reading the news by adults under 30 has dropped by about 16 percent in the past decade. The advent of online news hasn't helped reverse the trend.

The major fear in the newspaper industry is that today's young people won't grow into the next generation of readers. That's a reasonable concern, but the evidence suggests it's far too narrowly focused. If young people are less interested in consuming news of any kind, isn't this a problem for news organizations of all types, including those on the Web? Some of the "young reader" problem is self-correcting; people tend to become more interested in the world around them as they buy houses, pay taxes, raise families and generally settle down. Some of these people will probably read the paper, someday. Where will the rest seek news and information (if they go anywhere at all)? How about the Internet? If that is the case, newspapers are as well positioned as anyone at the moment to offer the most comprehensive package of daily local news and features on the Web. Forget paper and ink; journalists (and publishers) have to be ready to deliver the goods via whatever delivery system "end users" want it in.

The other piece of misinformation is the kind spread by the blogosphere about the blogosphere. Despite their role in fanning a few important stories (such as Dan Rather's flawed "60 Minutes II" report on President Bush's National Guard service), bloggers seem at best a part of the news media's future, not the future itself. At the moment, most people have never even heard of blogs. Fifty-six percent of all adults polled by CNN/USA Today/Gallup said in February that they had no knowledge of blogs, and fewer than a third (32 percent) said they were very or somewhat familiar with them. For all their self-infatuation and all their (often useful) criticism of the Old Media, many bloggers would be out of business without the traditional media. Blogs draw their lifeblood from the raw material served up each day by conventional news organizations.

So how do newspapers fit into this dynamic cosmos? Nicely, I'd say. Consider just a few unique competitive advantages that newspapers (still) enjoy:

- **Monopoly status.** A hundred-plus years of competition have left most American cities with just one newspaper. This is, by far, a newspaper's biggest competitive advantage and the source of even the lowliest daily's fat profits.
- **Newsgathering power.** Local newspapers typically still have the largest reporting staffs in town of any single news outlet, print or electronic. This (coupled with wire sources) enables a newspaper to produce the broadest range of daily news and features of any single news outlet. In a world of specialty, there's still great value and convenience in such a general package. Think of the retail analogy: Some

people prefer shopping at boutiques and specialty stores, but lots of people still patronize supermarkets and department stores.

- **Localism.** Readers will always want to know about the schools, government, businesses, taxes, entertainment and teams closest to home. No news organization is better equipped or staffed to supply this information than a newspaper.

- **The best customers.** Newspapers typically beat their direct competition in both the quantity of customers (i.e., readers) and their quality (i.e., demographics). Even with declining circulation, this advantage remains relatively stable. As traditional newspaper advertisers—airlines, retailers, banks, auto dealers, etc.—undergo their own transformation, newspaper advertising remains one of the most efficient ways to reach relatively large numbers of educated, affluent people. Young people may not read the newspaper much, but in strictly business terms, this is somewhat irrelevant. Advertisers already know this. They buy newspaper space to sell goods and services aimed at an older, more moneyed crowd.

- **Lots of attention.** Newspapers no longer play the central role in people's daily lives they once did, but they are far from irrelevant. Some 42 percent of adults surveyed by the Pew researchers in 2004 reported that they had read a newspaper "yesterday" (a figure that rose slightly over 2002). With the exception of local TV news, no other news source reaches so many people on a given day.

- **Brand-name recognition.** Newspapers big and small have spent millions of dollars over the years reminding people what they do. This has created a vast but hard-to-measure reservoir of goodwill for newspapers and represents a major strategic advantage over, say, the latest shopper startup or flashy Web site. It partly explains why, even today, no one has been able to create a local news site that outdraws the newspaper's own on the Internet (and Microsoft and America Online have tried).

- **Historic profitability.** Thanks to all of the above, newspaper companies enjoy profit margins unmatched not just by most other news media but by most other industries. Industrywide, newspapers reaped about 23 cents of profit for every dollar they took in last year, according to Merrill Lynch analyst Lauren Rich Fine. Newspaper revenues and profits are rising even as readers are deserting. This could be because newspapers are raising prices while skimping on long-term investment in their plants and people—harvesting the assets," in business speak.

Of course, the newspaper industry's high profitability cuts both ways, as many newsroom managers know. The need to maintain those margins to satisfy the short-term demands of stockholders and Wall Street analysts compels some companies to cut back on hiring, newsgathering and the size of the newshole. This can create its own vicious cycle: As the amount of news shrinks thanks to the pursuit of higher profits, readers despair and depart, thereby undermining the basis for higher profits.

Washington Post Associate Editor Robert G. Kaiser, the coauthor (with Post Executive Editor Leonard Downie Jr.) of "The News About the News: American Journalism in Peril," calls the huge profit margins enjoyed by newspapers both arbitrary and pernicious. Once newspapers began regularly achieving these profit levels in the early 1980s, Kaiser says, many publishers became unwilling to settle for anything less and began shortchanging their newsrooms in the drive to achieve them.

"The question we need to ask is, 'What's an appropriate profit for a newspaper?'" says Kaiser. "If you went to a newspaper publishers' meeting in 1975 and told them their papers could make 15 percent profits, they would have been overjoyed. Now, the standard is 20 percent, 30 percent. Why? Because it's possible, for no other reason."

But the thing about obscenely high profits is they're a whole lot better than no profit at all. For newspapers, they can be the seed that provides tomorrow's harvest. Wisely reinvested, today's profits could prevent the day Philip Meyer believes is coming. To be fair, many newspaper companies aren't sitting still. They've beefed up their Web offerings and expanded their Internet "footprint" by buying independent sites (see "Dotcom Bloom," June/July 2005). Dow Jones recently purchased MarketWatch.com, *The New York Times* nabbed About.com, and the Washington Post Co. bought *Slate* from Microsoft. Major industry players also are embracing ethnic media (primarily Spanish-language) and niche publications like real-estate shoppers. The hottest single publishing market of the moment may be the battle for young readers (see "Hip—and Happening," April/May 2005). In Dallas, the *Morning News* started *Quick*, an easy-to-read freebie. In Chicago, both the *Tribune* and the *Sun-Times* have similar papers. *The Washington Post* launched *Express*, beating to the punch a new tabloid called *The Washington Examiner,* which is delivered free to mostly affluent families and is not aimed squarely at the young. Critics can argue about the quality of these papers, but their existence does say something about the prospects for print. *The Examiner,* for one, is the brainchild of billionaire Philip Anschutz, who has revived the moribund *San Francisco Examiner* and registered the *Examiner* trademark in some 70 cities nationwide. While the extent of Anschutz's publishing ambitions remain a mystery, his moves raise a larger question: Why does a billionaire think investing in newspapers is a good idea right now? Similarly, executives at fast-growing Lee Enterprises see newspapers as a growth industry (see "Lee Who?" June/July 2005).

Ultimately, some in the industry believe newspapers will have to rethink much of what they do to survive. A recent white paper by the Newspaper Association of America suggested, among other things, publishing smaller editions some days of the week and charging higher subscription fees to offset ad losses. Kaiser says it's a lot simpler than that. The best defense, he says, is a great offense. Put more money back into the newsroom and build up the journalistic firepower—and the community credibility—that many newspapers have been frittering away for years.

He'll get no argument from Phil Meyer on this. The premise of Meyer's most recent book is that high-quality journalism—accurate, clear and in-depth—strongly correlates with, if it doesn't create, market success (see Books, February/March 2005). He worries, however, that even quality may not be enough to save newspapers. Meyer sketches a "tipping point" scenario that would hasten the end—the day when a paper's slide is so prolonged and deep that a critical mass of advertisers concludes it's no longer worth supporting it. Maybe. But the mistake the newspapers-are-dead crowd makes is believing that trend lines continue in the same direction forever. It pays to remember that new communications media rarely eliminate the old ones; the old simply adapt to accommodate the new. So movies didn't eliminate novels and TV didn't eliminate movies or radio.

It could be just as likely, therefore, that the worst case doesn't happen. Maybe newspapers will find stability and equilibrium with a core of loyal, demographically attractive readers. Old habits do die hard. In a world of ever-expanding choice, many people—pressed for time and seeking the trusted and familiar—may just stick with what they already know and respect.

Without doubt, it will take skill, vision and creativity for newspapers to survive. But I'd bet on success sooner than I'd bet on failure. It may be that newspapers are dinosaurs. But then again, dinosaurs walked the earth for millions of years.

POSTSCRIPT

Should Newspapers Shut Down Their Presses?

$\mathbf{T}$he selections you've read introduce a number of ideas that might save newspapers. These include micropayments, walled content, portable reading devices, and nonprofit status.

If news content is available online, will we be willing to pay for it? The outlook seems dim; we are used to free access to information online. One suggestion is micropayments, which would require the payment of small amounts of money to read content online. Some have dubbed it an iTunes or PayPal model. Free access to some stories or to limited content would be available; to follow the story in more depth a small amount would be charged for access. For more information see the Nieman Journalism Lab Web site, which defines their efforts as a collaborative attempt to figure out how quality journalism can survive and thrive in the Internet age. Go to www.niemanlab .org and search for "Micropayments for news: The Holy Grail or just a dangerous delusion?" Spend some time checking out the many other issues that are discussed.

Related to micropayments are suggestions about the use of walled or paid content. Generally speaking, this would involve purchasing a subscription that would allow access to any material behind the wall. *The Wall Street Journal* has been somewhat successful with this approach online. *The New York Times* uses it for some limited content. The PBS Mediashift site discusses many aspects of changing media in the digital age. Go to www.pbs.org/mediashift and search for "The Great Debate on Micropayments and Paid Content." Again, it is worth spending some time looking at the variety of topics discussed. For journalism and mass communication majors, there is an excellent section on education.

A related suggestion is that readers may be willing to give up the printed paper if they can receive that material on a portable reading device such as a Kindle. This retains the portability of a paper and still requires readers to subscribe. There are a number of studies in progress, examining reader responses to news on these devices. See *The New York Times* for an interesting article on whether the Kindle can save newspapers at http://www.nytimes.com/2009/05/04/technology/companies/04reader.html?_r=1.

Reorganizing newspapers into nonprofit corporations is being widely discussed. It remains a controversial suggestion with significant concerns about the independence of newspapers in this organizational configuration. Go to www.newyorker.com to read Steve Coll's blog on "Nonprofit Newspapers." Coll argues that nonprofit status can be the future because it will allow the independent journalism that commercial pressure does not support. Guensburg in

American Journalism Review (February/March 2008) examines both sides of the "Nonprofit News" argument.

For historical and conceptual insights into these issues, read *The Vanishing Newspaper: Saving Journalism in the Information Age* (2004) by Philip Meyer, referenced in Farhi's selection. *Digitizing the News: Innovation in Online Newspapers* (2005) by Pablo Boczkowski is praised for tracing the short and varied history of how newspapers have responded to the digital challenge. Joseph Epstein's piece in *Commentary* (January 2008) is titled "Are Newspaper Doomed?" It reminds us that issues of readership retention in newspapers were grave, even before the recent economic downturn.

ISSUE 16

Do New Business Models Result in Greater Consumer Choice of Products and Ideas?

YES: Chris Anderson, from "The Long Tail: How Technology Is Turning Mass Markets into Millions of Niches," *The Long Tail: Why the Future of Business Is Selling Less of More* (Hyperion, 2006)

NO: Kathryn C. Montgomery, from "Social Marketing in the New Millennium," *Generation Digital: Politics, Commerce, and Childhood in the Age of the Internet* (MIT Press, 2007)

ISSUE SUMMARY

YES: Chris Anderson, an editor of *Wired* Magazine, writes of the decline of the mass market and the rise of niche markets. He claims that the future of business, particularly in book, music, and DVD sales, will shift toward selling a wider range of media to audiences that have much broader interests.

NO: Professor Kathryn Montgomery looks at the cooperative relationships between social interest groups and media content providers, to better understand how themes with social objectives permeate media content.

For several years, pundits have been predicting the death of newspapers, the music industry, television, and the decline of reading in America. But in this issue, we explore how legacy industries have been changing over the years. The two selections provide different scenarios for the consumer; Chris Anderson examines how consumer choice can keep the legacy recording industry profitable, and Kathryn Montgomery addresses the relationships behind the scenes to better understand why some television content seems to promote particular ideals. Both authors look to legacy industries and document how more digitally oriented migrations of content target specific audiences.

Many people flippantly say, "The media only give us what we want," but the complex nature of media industries actually reframes that statement so that a more accurate assessment might be that the media give us what we're willing to take. The various business models in media respond to the pressure from other forms of media and new distribution channels. As Anderson writes, "The sales data and trends from [these] services and others like them show that the emerging digital economy is going to be radically different from today's mass market." The social marketing campaigns studied by Montgomery show that multiplatform media content geared to teens has resulted in "public-education strategies [that] have been evolved into highly sophisticated inter-active campaigns, often employing the same tools of the trade that advertisers use to promote brands to young people."

Chris Anderson discusses how legacy industries can successfully adapt their business models to online sales, and actually increase their profits by sell-ing less of a wider range of products to niche audiences. Kathryn Montgomery explores how nonprofit organizations have been collaborating with the creators of prime-time TV and soap operas to influence teens' attitudes and behaviors. While she does not reference "product placement" or "product enhancement" as direct marketing tools that are being used, she does chronicle how attitudes toward sex, pregnancy, drug abuse, and smoking can use similar techniques to get the teen audiences' attention and promote particular values.

Both of these selections demonstrate that media business is always expe-riencing change—whether it is a migration to a different distribution form of music, or the behind-the-scenes cooperative ventures that influence social norms and mores. Together they raise questions about media businesses that either drive consumer expectations or respond to consumer demand, and pose situations that make us think about our relationship to the products and images we see in media. Both of the ideas supported by these authors demon-strate how complicated media business is and how the history of media images and products continually changes with the distribution forms and content available at any given time.

YES ↩

Chris Anderson

The Long Tail: How Technology Is Turning Mass Markets into Millions of Niches

In 1988, a British mountain climber named Joe Simpson wrote a book called *Touching the Void*, a harrowing account of near death in the Peruvian Andes. Though reviews for the book were good, it was only a modest success, and soon was largely forgotten. Then, a decade later, a strange thing happened. Jon Krakauer's *Into Thin Air*, another book about a mountain-climbing tragedy, became a publishing sensation. Suddenly, *Touching the Void* started to sell again.

Booksellers began promoting it next to their *Into Thin Air* displays, and sales continued to rise. In early 2004, IFC Films released a docu-drama of the story, to good reviews. Shortly thereafter, HarperCollins released a revised paperback, which spent fourteen weeks on the *New York Times* best-seller list. By mid-2004, *Touching the Void* was outselling *Into Thin Air* more than two to one.

What happened? Online word of mouth. When *Into Thin Air* first came out, a few readers wrote reviews on Amazon.com that pointed out the similarities with the then lesser-known *Touching the Void*, which they praised effusively. Other shoppers read those reviews, checked out the older book, and added it to their shopping carts. Pretty soon the online bookseller's software noted the patterns in buying behavior—"Readers who bought *Into Thin Air* also bought *Touching the Void*"—and started recommending the two as a pair. People took the suggestion, agreed wholeheartedly, wrote more rhapsodic reviews. More sales, more algorithm-fueled recommendations—and a powerful positive feedback loop kicked in.

Particularly notable is that when Krakauer's book hit shelves, Simpson's was nearly out of print. A decade ago readers of Krakauer would never even have learned about Simpson's book—and if they had, they wouldn't have been able to find it. Online booksellers changed that. By combining infinite shelf space with real-time information about buying trends and public opinion, they created the entire *Touching the Void* phenomenon. The result: rising demand for an obscure book.

This is not just a virtue of online booksellers; it is an example of an entirely new economic model for the media and entertainment industries, one just beginning to show its power. Unlimited selection is revealing truths about *what* consumers want and *how* they want to get it in service after service—from DVDs at

From *The Long Tail: Why the Future of Business Is Selling Less of More,* Hyperion Books, 2006, pp. 15–20, 22–26 (excerpts). Copyright © 2006 by Chris Anderson. Reprinted by permission of Hyperion Books. All rights reserved.

the rental-by-mail firm Netflix to songs in the iTunes Music Store and Rhapsody. People are going deep into the catalog, down the long, long list of available titles, far past what's available at Blockbuster Video and Tower Records. And the more they find, the more they like. As they wander farther from the beaten path, they discover their taste is not as mainstream as they thought (or as they had been led to believe by marketing, a hit-centric culture, and simply a lack of alternatives).

The sales data and trends from these services and others like them show that the emerging digital entertainment economy is going to be radically different from today's mass market. If the twentieth-century entertainment industry was about *hits,* the twenty-first will be equally about *niches.*

For too long we've bebn suffering the tyranny of lowest-common-denominator fare, subjected to brain-dead summer blockbusters and manufactured pop. Why? Economics. Many of our assumptions about popular taste are actually artifacts of poor supply-and-demand matching—a market response to inefficient distribution.

The main problem, if that's the word, is that we live in the physical world, and until recently, most of our entertainment media did, too. That world puts dramatic limitations on our entertainment.

The Tyranny of Locality

The curse of traditional retail is the need to find local audiences. An average movie theater will not show a film unless it can attract at least 1,500 people over a two-week run. That's essentially the rent for a screen. An average record store needs to sell at least four copies of a CD per year to make it worth carrying; that's the rent for a half inch of shelf space. And so on, for DVD rental shops, video-game stores, booksellers, and newsstands.

In each case, retailers will carry only content that can generate sufficient demand to earn its keep. However, each can pull from only a limited local population—perhaps a ten-mile radius for a typical movie theater, less than that for music and bookstores, and even less (just a mile or two) for video rental shops. It's not enough for a great documentary to have a potential national audience of half a million; what matters is how much of an audience it has in the northern part of Rockville, Maryland, or among the mall shoppers of Walnut Creek, California.

There is plenty of great entertainment with potentially large, even rapturous, national audiences that cannot clear the local retailer bar. For instance, *The Triplets of Belleville,* a critically acclaimed film that was nominated for the best animated feature Oscar in 2004, opened on just six screens nationwide. An even more striking example is the plight of Bollywood in America. Each year, India's film industry produces more than eight hundred feature films. There are an estimated 1.7 million Indians living in the United States. Yet the top-rated Hindi-language film, *Lagaan: Once Upon a Time in India,* opened on just two screens in the States. Moreover, it was one of only a handful of Indian films that managed to get *any* U.S. distribution at all that year. In the tyranny of geography, an audience spread too thinly is the same as no audience at all.

Another constraint of the physical world is physics itself. The radio spectrum can carry only so many stations, and a coaxial cable only so many TV channels. And, of course, there are only twenty-four hours of programming a day. The curse of broadcast technologies is that they are profligate users of limited resources. The result is yet another instance of having to aggregate large audiences in one geographic area—another high bar above which only a fraction of potential content rises. . . .

However, most of us want more than just the hits. Everyone's taste departs from the mainstream somewhere. The more we explore alternatives, the more we're drawn to them. Unfortunately, in recent decades, such alternatives have been relegated to the fringes by pumped-up marketing vehicles built to order by industries that desperately needed them. . . .

This is the world of *scarcity*. Now, with online distribution and retail, we are entering a world of *abundance*. The differences are profound.

For a better look at the world of abundance, let's return to online music retailer Rhapsody. A subscription-based streaming service owned by RealNetworks, Rhapsody currently offers more than 1.5 million tracks. . . .

So although there are millions of tracks in the collective catalogs of all the labels, America's largest music retailer, Wal-Mart, cuts off its inventory pretty close to the Head. It carries about 4,500 unique CD titles. On Rhapsody, the top 4,500 albums account for the top 25,000 tracks. . . . In Wal-Mart's inventory, . . . the top 200 albums account for more than 90 percent of the sales.

Focusing on the hits certainly seems to make sense. That's the lion's share of the market, after all. Anything after the top 5,000 or 10,000 tracks appears to rank pretty close to zero. Why bother with those losers at the bottom? . . .

What's extraordinary is that virtually every single one of those tracks will sell. From the perspective of a store like Wal-Mart, the music industry stops at less than 60,000 tracks. However, for online retailers like Rhapsody the market is seemingly never-ending. Not only is every one of Rhapsody's top 60,000 tracks streamed at least once each month, but the same is true for its top 100,000, top 200,000, and top 400,000—even its top 600,000, top 900,000, and beyond. As fast as Rhapsody adds tracks to its library, those songs find an audience, even if it's just a handful of people every month, somewhere in the world.

This is the Long Tail.

You can find *everything* out here in the Long Tail. There's the back catalog, older albums still fondly remembered by longtime fans or rediscovered by new ones. There are live tracks, B-sides, remixes, even (gasp) covers. There are niches by the thousands, genres within genres within genres (imagine an entire Tower Records store devoted to eighties hair bands or ambient dub). There are foreign bands, once priced out of reach on a shelf in the import aisle, and obscure bands on even more obscure labels—many of which don't have the distribution clout to get into Tower at all.

Oh sure, there's also a lot of crap here in the Long Tail. But then again, there's an awful lot of crap hiding between the radio tracks on hit albums, too. People have to skip over it on CDs, but they can more easily avoid it online, where the best individual songs can be cherry-picked (with the help of personalized recommendations) from those whole albums. So, unlike the CD—where each crap track costs perhaps one-twelfth of a $15 album price—all of the crap tracks online just sit harmlessly on some server, ignored by a marketplace that evaluates songs on their own merit.

What's truly amazing about the Long Tail is the sheer size of it. Again, if you combine enough of the non-hits, you've actually established a market that rivals the hits. Take books: The average Borders carries around 100,000 titles. Yet about a quarter of Amazon's book sales come from *outside* its top 100,000 titles. Consider the implication: If the Amazon statistics are any guide, the market for books that are not even sold in the average bookstore is already a third the size of the existing market—and what's more, it's growing quickly. If these growth trends continue, the potential book market may actually be half again as big as it appears to be, if only we can get over the economics of scarcity. Venture capitalist and former music industry consultant Kevin Laws puts it this way: "The biggest money is in the smallest sales." . . .

When you think about it, most successful Internet businesses are capitalizing on the Long Tail in one way or another. Google, for instance, makes most of its money not from huge corporate advertisers, but from small ones (the Long Tail of advertising). EBay is mostly Tail as well—niche products from collector cars to tricked-out golf clubs. By overcoming the limitations of geography and scale, companies like these have not only expanded existing markets, but more important, they've also discovered entirely new ones. Moreover, in each case those new markets that lie *outside* the reach of the physical retailer have proven to be far bigger than anyone expected—and they're only getting bigger.

In fact, as these companies offered more and more (simply because they *could*), they found that demand actually followed supply. The act of vastly increasing choice seemed to unlock demand for that choice. Whether it was latent demand for niche goods that was already there or the creation of new demand, we don't yet know. But what we do know is that with the companies for which we have the most complete data—Netflix, Amazon, and Rhapsody—sales of products *not offered* by their bricks-and-mortar competitors amounted to between a quarter and nearly half of total revenues—and that percentage is rising each year. In other words, the *fastest-growing* part of their businesses is sales of products that aren't available in traditional, physical retail stores at all.

These infinite-shelf-space businesses have effectively learned a lesson in new math: A very, very big number (the products in the Tail) multiplied by a relatively small number (the sales of each) is still equal to a very, very big number. And, again, that very, very big number is only getting bigger.

What's more, these millions of fringe sales are an efficient, cost-effective business. With no shelf space to pay for—and in the case of purely digital services like iTunes, no manufacturing costs and hardly any distribution fees—a niche product sold is just another sale, with the same (or better) margins as a hit. For the first time in history, hits and niches are on equal economic footing, both just entries in a database called up on demand, both equally worthy of being carried. Suddenly, popularity no longer has a monopoly on profitability. . . .

The Hidden Majority

One way to think of the difference between yesterday's limited choice and today's abundance is as if our culture were an ocean and the only features above the surface were islands of hits. There's a music island composed of hit albums, a movie island of blockbusters, an archipelago of popular TV shows, and so on.

Think of the waterline as being the economic threshold for that category, the amount of sales necessary to satisfy the distribution channels. The islands represent the products that are popular enough to be above that line, and thus profitable enough to be offered through distribution channels with scarce capacity, which is to say the shelf space demands of most major retailers. Scan the cultural horizon and what stands out are these peaks of popularity rising above the waves.

However, islands are, of course, just the tips of vast undersea mountains. When the cost of distribution falls, it's like the water level falling in the ocean. All of a sudden things are revealed that were previously hidden. And there's much, much more under the current waterline than above it. What we're now starting to see, as online retailers begin to capitalize on their extraordinary economic efficiencies, is the shape of a massive mountain of choice emerging where before there was just a peak.

More than 99 percent of music albums on the market today are not available in Wal-Mart. Of the more than 200,000 films, TV shows, documentaries, and other video that have been released commercially, the average Blockbuster carries just 3,000. Same for any other leading retailer and practically any other commodity—from books to kitchen fittings. The vast majority of products are *not* available at a store near you. By necessity, the economics of traditional, hit-driven retail limit choice.

When you can dramatically lower the costs of connecting supply and demand, it changes not just the numbers, but the entire nature of the market. This is not just a quantitative change, but a qualitative one, too. Bringing niches within reach reveals latent demand for noncommercial content. Then, as demand shifts toward the niches, the economics of providing them improve further, and so on, creating a positive feedback loop that will transform entire industries—and the culture—for decades to come.

Kathryn C. Montgomery

NO

Social Marketing in the New Millennium

When it premiered on MTV in 1992, *The Real World* generated mixed reviews from TV critics. A cross between a soap opera and a documentary, the show recruited seven people in their twenties and set them up in a plush apartment, where their lives were videotaped, day and night, for the next four months. The edited footage, with its steamy sex and raunchy language, was then set to a rock soundtrack featuring the latest hot music groups. "This is not reality as we know it," wrote Ginny Holbert in the *Chicago Sun-Times*, "but a highly artificial setup designed to turn ordinary life into an extended music video." Despite its obviously contrived nature, the show's success helped usher in a new genre of "reality programming" that by the end of the decade had begun to dominate programming schedules. With no union writers to pay, these shows—*Big Brother, Survivor, American Idol,* and the like—proved cheap to produce as well as highly popular with younger demographics.

By 2002, *The Real World* had become one of MTV's staple shows, selecting a fresh new cast of young people each year to act out their lives before millions of television viewers. Among the seven strangers thrown together that season—this time in a posh Las Vegas apartment—was Trishelle, a young woman from the rural town of Cutoff, Louisiana. Within the first few episodes, she succumbed to several serious temptations. She fell for a married man, got drunk, and had sex, all against her better judgment. She even kissed another girl, even though she was not gay. In angst, she called home to confide in her stepsister, only to have her father lambaste her for what he saw as sinfulness. Then, on top of everything else, her period was late.

It took Trishelle three episodes to get up the courage to take a pregnancy test. To her great relief, it turned out negative, but before the series ended that year, MTV turned the pregnancy scare into an educational opportunity. "Have you ever been late?" the show's Web site asked MTV's young viewers. "If so, you're not alone. To find out how to prevent being late or what to do if you are, click here." The next link provided a toll-free number for Planned Parenthood, advice on birth-control methods, and a hotline for access to emergency contraception. Viewers also were invited to take part in an online talk show with Trishelle, other cast members, and a representative of Planned Parenthood, who was on hand to answer questions about pregnancy prevention, sexually transmitted diseases (STDs), and communication strategies for dealing with sex partners.

From *Generation Digital: Politics, Commerce, and Childhood in the Age of the Internet* by Kathryn C. Montgomery (MIT Press, 2007), pp. 141–153 (excerpt; notes omitted). Copyright © 2007 by Massachusetts Institute of Technology. Reprinted by permission of MIT Press.

These efforts were part of the multimillion dollar public-education initiative Fight for Your Rights: Protect Yourself. A partnership between MTV and the Kaiser Family Foundation, the project's goal was to educate young people about sexual health and to promote safe sex. Because the campaign targeted teens and young adults through their own media, it was able to address sensitive sexual themes and controversial topics that might have sparked an outcry if they were more visible to the public.

For decades, youth have been the target of hundreds of "social marketing" campaigns, aimed at such vexing problems as teen pregnancy, drug abuse, and smoking. Over the years, nonprofit groups and government agencies have produced public-service advertising messages aimed at teens and young adults, often enlisting popular celebrities to promote pro-social messages in television spots, billboards, and magazine ads. In the new fragmented digital-media universe, these public-education strategies have evolved into highly sophisticated interactive campaigns, often employing the same tools of the trade that advertisers use to promote brands to young people. Just as marketers follow youth through the new digital landscape, closely tracking their every move, and inserting sales pitches into every possible venue, social marketers have crafted their campaigns to mesh with the media habits and journeys of teens and young adults. With the growth of the Internet and the proliferation of teen TV, public-health and social-issue organizations are able to incorporate their messages throughout the youth media culture, reaching their demographic targets with precision. Interactive media also make it possible to engage young people as never before, enlisting them in the campaigns, and encouraging them to spread the word among their peers. Sometimes these efforts generate controversy over their unorthodox methods and edgy messages. But much of the time they operate freely within the confines of a youth media world where adults seldom venture, addressing topics in a frank and direct manner that would be taboo in the mainstream media.

Sex Ed in the Digital Age

In August 1996, less than a month before the Democratic National Convention, President Clinton signed the Personal Responsibility and Work Opportunity Reconciliation Act of 1996 (commonly called the Welfare Reform Act), fulfilling a campaign promise he had made in 1992 to "end welfare as we know it." The landmark law eliminated more than sixty years of federally guaranteed assistance to the poor and enabled states to develop their own programs to move people from welfare to work. The legislation triggered a fiery debate in the midst of this election year. Clinton's support for the law prompted outcries from liberal groups, including the Children's Defense Fund and the National Organization for Women, who charged the White House with abandoning the Democratic Party's long-standing commitment to women, children, and the poor.

Among the law's new federal mandates was a little-known provision that had been pushed by conservative groups and slipped into the legislation at the last minute, requiring that $50 million a year be made available to the states to fund "abstinence-only" sex education. The new program, to be administered through schools, public agencies, and community organizations, was designed to deliver a clear and consistent message to young people: abstaining from sexual activity was the "only certain way" to avoid pregnancy and sexually transmitted diseases; the "expected standard" for sexual activity was "a monogamous relationship within the context of marriage"; and extramarital or premarital sex was likely to be "psychologically and physically harmful." Since passage of the law, abstinence-only programs grew in the nation's schools. A 2002 survey found that 23 percent of high school sex-education programs were teaching abstinence-only curricula, compared to only 2 percent in 1988.

But by the 1990s, neither schools nor parents held the exclusive franchise on sex education. The mass media already were eclipsing these traditional institutions. A national survey in 1997 found that more than half of high school boys and girls were learning about birth control, contraception, or pregnancy prevention from television, while two thirds of the girls and 40 percent of the boys had learned about these topics from magazines. Scholars studying the impact of television on teens found that messages in entertainment programming could affect attitudes, expectations, and behavior. Since the 1970s, a handful of nonprofit organizations had been collaborating with the creators of prime-time TV and soap operas to insert dialogue and storylines into programming, in order to educate youth about birth control, drunk driving, and other social issues. Over the years these efforts grew into an entire infrastructure of "entertainment-education" initiatives, part of the landscape of the television industry.

Advocates for Youth was one of the pioneers in the entertainment-education movement, establishing a Los Angeles office in the 1970s to encourage producers and writers to incorporate messages about birth control, abortion, and sexually transmitted diseases into their TV programs. By the mid-1990s, the group's Media Project was an established presence in the entertainment community, conducting informational workshops, consulting on scripts, and handing out awards for responsible and "balanced" depictions of sex. After passage of the abstinence-only legislation, Advocates for Youth's work in Hollywood became a key component in its political fight against the law. The group argued that young people had a right to a full spectrum of sexual information, including lifestyle options, birth control, abortion, and sexually transmitted diseases. By collaborating with creators of popular TV programs, the Media Project sought to communicate directly to teens, circumventing the restrictive curricula that many schools adopted in the wake of the new law.

With the growing number of entertainment programs created exclusively for teenagers, the project found a stable of willing and eager producers with whom to forge partnerships, developing ongoing storylines and characters that could help educate the loyal teen following. Project staff worked closely with producers of popular teen shows such as *Dawson's Creek* and *Felicity* to develop episodes dealing with teen sexual health and date rape. The project's Web site featured detailed lists of specific program episodes that the group felt had done a good job of dealing with sexual issues. "Whether dealing with sexual abuse, contraception, or unplanned pregnancy or portraying strong parent-child communication or peer pressure resistance, the producers and writers of these programs have a right to be proud." The list included dozens of news and entertainment shows, with synopses of the episodes, as well as the ratings figures. For example, in a 2003 episode of *The Gilmore Girls* on the WB network, "Paris confides to Rory that she had sex for the first time, leading to a conversation about how the right time is different for everyone." The project commended a 2003 episode of *The Simpsons* in which Homer and Marge separate and Homer moves in with two gay guys, learning "to be more accepting of gays and lesbians." On ABC's *All My Children*, "JR gives Jamie a condom in preparation for him 'getting lucky' at a party." Among the shows to receive the Media Project's SHINE Awards (for Sexual Health IN Entertainment) were: *Any Day Now, Sunset Beach, ER, The West Wing, Popular, Dawson's Creek, Will & Grace, Dateline NBC, That 70s Show,* and *Moesha.*

But addressing matters of sex in the context of prime-time television can be tricky business. Conservative media watchdog groups keep a close watch on television programs, taking their complaints to the government. In 2002, a storyline about oral sex (on which Advocates for Youth had consulted) was featured in the Fox Television series *Boston Public.* Aired at 8:00 p.m., the program sparked an outcry from fifteen conservative groups, including Focus on the Family, Christian Coalition, and the American Family Association. The organizations petitioned the FCC to enforce its rules governing indecent content on television and radio. Though the commission levied no fines against the network, the steady drumbeat for government intervention into sexual content on television would grow.

While continuing to work with TV producers, Advocates for Youth also turned to the Internet, using its Web site not just as an educational vehicle, but also as an organizing tool in the fight against the abstinence-only policy. "End Censorship in America's Schools," students were urged. "Join other youth activists in the My Voice Counts! Campaign, as they raise their voices about the need for honest sex education in communities in the U.S. and abroad." As more and more young people were going online to seek out resources and support for a range of health issues, those with limited knowledge of such matters at home or school now had unprecedented access to a wealth of information about sexual behavior, sexual lifestyles, and sexual health. Dozens of sites were set up to provide discussion forums on sexual issues, access to experts and community resources, as well as opportunities to be involved in the policy debate about sex education. At the Live Teen Forum page of . . . created by the American Social Health Association, teenagers could communicate directly with a health specialist about their own sexual-health concerns, through e-mail or a toll-free phone number. Rutgers University's Network for Family Life Education created . . . which quickly became a popular source of lively discussion and information among teens. The site included polls, surveys, and other interactive components to enable teenagers to voice their opinions on sex, sexually transmitted disease, and sex education policies. Sex, etc. also offered a downloadable "Teen Guide to Changing Your School's Sex Ed," with detailed instructions about building a local coalition, staging a community forum, drafting resolutions, and working with the press.

Youth seeking information and support about sexual-identity issues could find a new world online. "For homosexual teenagers with computer access," wrote Jennifer Egan in the *New York Times* magazine, "the Internet has, quite simply, revolutionized the experience of growing up gay." For those "with the inhospitable families and towns in which many find themselves marooned," she explained, "there exists a parallel online community—real people like them in cyberspace with whom they can chat, exchange messages, and even engage in (online) sex." Outproud.org, a Web site created by the National Coalition for Gay, Lesbian, Bisexual & Transgender Youth was one of hundreds of resources in this "parallel online community." It was set up "to help queer youth become happy, successful, confident and vital gay, lesbian and bisexual adults." The site offered "outreach and support to queer teens just coming to terms with their sexual orientation and to those contemplating coming out." Youth could find fact sheets and statistical information "to help make your case why supporting gay, lesbian, bisexual and transgender youth is important to your school." A Coming Out Archives provided a fully search-able database of hundreds of personal narratives, designed to "provide you with the benefit of the experiences of the millions of others who have found the right words on their own journeys. Sometimes things go well, sometimes they don't—whatever the results, they're here for you to see." Youth were also invited to share their own coming out stories on the Web site.

The explosion of new media technologies has created both opportunities and challenges for health educators. The Internet and cable television can be used to circumvent the mainstream media, providing a relatively unfet-tered arena for addressing otherwise taboo topics. However, with the growing number of media available to teenagers, there is no guarantee that certain health messages will reach most or all teens. Media researchers have found that individual teenagers are customizing their own "sexual media diets," selecting from a growing menu of available TV programs, Web sites, music, and movies to suit their own needs, tastes, and desires for sexual information.

"I Want My MTV!"

Executives at the Henry J. Kaiser Family Foundation took these trends into account when designing their public-education campaign on sexual health in the late 1990s. As Vicky Rideout, vice president and director of Kaiser's Pro-gram for the Study of Entertainment Media and Health, explained, the foun-dation's strategy was to "surround youth with a variety of messages in many different forms and styles." With assets of more than a half billion dollars, the Kaiser Foundation was in a particularly unique and powerful position to carry out its goal. The California-based philanthropic organization functions mainly as an "operating foundation," which means that, rather than just giving out grants to nonprofits, it can design its own large-scale public-education and research initiatives, often in partnership with other influential organizations. The foundation has been particularly effective at commanding the attention of the media, promoting widespread coverage of its research on such topics as health-care policy, women's health, HIV/AIDS, and minority health.

Because television still plays a central role in the media diets of teens, part of Kaiser's effort has been aimed at the Hollywood creative community. The foundation followed the lead of other entertainment-education projects to encourage the television industry to use its programs as a way to educate youth about sexual-health issues. But with more resources than many nonprofits, the foundation has been able to develop a more comprehensive initiative for influencing entertainment television, combining its work to influence the producers of popular prime-time series with formal research that assessed the impact of its efforts on both the viewers and the programming. Foundation staff worked regularly with the producers of the NBC prime-time series *ER*, helping them insert storylines on a variety of health-related issues, including episodes that dealt with emergency contraception and sexually transmitted diseases. Follow-up surveys of viewers of these programs showed that the depictions helped increase awareness of the issues, prompted discussions among friends and family members, and in some cases helped people make decisions about their own health care. For several years, Kaiser underwrote Advocates for Youth's Media Project in Los Angeles. The foundation also has tracked the sexual content of entertainment television programming, conducting biennial studies to measure levels and kinds of sexual activity, in addition to depictions of "safe-sex" practices.

To reach its target audience more directly, Kaiser partnered with popular teen magazines such as *Teen People, TM,* and *Seventeen,* working with editors to develop special features on sexual-health issues and reader surveys about sexual behavior. The foundation's most ambitious effort for reaching young people is through its partnership with MTV. Launched in 1981, MTV is the number-one cable network among 12–24-year-olds, and the network has become "nearly synonymous with youth." Its global reach (in 2006) includes more than 400 million subscribers in more than 164 countries.

Sexual issues are front and center in the lives of the MTV Generation. The proportion of sexually active girls age 15–19 rose from 47 percent in 1982 to 55 percent by 1990. Although rates of teen pregnancy declined somewhat since the high point in 1990, more than one million pregnancies still occurred in teenagers between ages 15 and 19, with nearly 30,000 in girls under 15. And a quarter of sexually active teenagers contracted a sexually transmitted disease every year. As far as teens are concerned, explained MTV's Jaime Uzeta, director of strategic partnerships and public affairs, sexual health is "public health #1." For many social critics, however, MTV was part of the problem. Since the cable channel began, its 24/7 stream of graphic sexual images had sparked protests from parents groups and conservative Christians. But for Kaiser, the pervasive sex on the cable network created an opportunity. Since MTV already was promoting sexual activity, it could be persuaded, with some financial incentives, to add responsible messages to the mix.

For years, nonprofit organizations seeking to use the mass media for their social-marketing campaigns often relied on the goodwill of the television networks and local stations (and encouragement by federal regulators) to provide free airtime. But many public-service announcements (PSAs) have been buried in the wee hours before dawn. With deregulation of the broadcasting industry in the 1980s, the number of PSAs that networks and stations were willing to run at all declined sharply. Many nonprofits turned to paid advertising to get their messages on at a desirable time. But the TV industry still was reluctant to air controversial PSAs. This was especially true with sexual issues.

The Kaiser Foundation's strategy with MTV was a deliberate departure from traditional public-service campaigns. The foundation entered into a business relationship with the cable channel, offering financial and organizational support to sweeten the deal. This arrangement became the model for Kaiser's other media efforts over the years. "Kaiser has approached its entertainment media partnerships as business propositions with a philanthropic purpose," foundation executives explained. Kaiser crafts its agreements in "formal memoranda of understanding," offering an appealing package to its media partners that includes support for: "issues research; briefings for writers and producers, and other media staff; substantive guidance on message development; and funds to support program production and the creation of information resources for consumers." In return for this financial commitment from the foundation, media companies contribute "creative and communications expertise; on-air programming on the issues addressed by the campaign; and guaranteed placement of the PSAs and other content to reach target audiences." Kaiser's campaigns are "undertaken in much the same way that any commercial product would be marketed—by using the best creative teams to help develop compelling messages for the target audience and securing commitments that ensure that they are seen on the right television shows in the right time slots." Kaiser's "product" is not "sneakers or beer" however, but "awareness and prevention."

The Be Safe campaign was launched in 1997 with a series of hip PSAs, a toll-free hotline, and the booklet "It's Your (Sex) Life," offering detailed advice and information about how to avoid getting sexually transmitted diseases. In the first six months, 150,000 viewers called the hotline, and more than 100,000 of them requested a copy of the Kaiser booklet. By 2002, the effort had been "rebranded" under MTV's existing Fight for Your Rights pro-social initiative with a new tag line added: Protect Yourself. Fight for Your Rights: Protect Yourself soon became a recognizable brand on its own, woven throughout the TV schedule and Web site on the popular youth network. The campaign themes and messages became a pervasive presence on MTV, appearing in PSAs, interactive Web features, and print materials, as well as on-the-ground, grassroots activities. The Kaiser Foundation spent $440,000 on its partnership with MTV in its initial year.

Though carefully framed as a public-health initiative, the campaign was not without controversy. In 1998, Christian right-to-life group Rock for Life, a division of the American Life League, attacked the Kaiser/MTV campaign for promoting sexual behavior among teens. "MTV has no business teaching kids about sexual relationships and promoting abortion," the group charged. "MTV is trying to take over the role of the parents and families and teach deadly values to kids under the disguise of looking out for their welfare." The group charged that by sending out informational materials directly to teens on abortion and contraception, it was attempting to undermine parents.

Despite these initial complaints, the campaign not only continued, but also expanded. During the first five and a half years, more than sixty public-service ads were produced, airing more than 4,600 times. The videos were much edgier, realistic, and graphic than anything that could run on broadcast television. Through research, the campaign also was able to identify specific subsegments of the MTV audience, tailoring PSAs to gays and lesbians, Latinos, females, and African Americans. One of the ads, for example, featured an inner-city Latino rocker speaking directly to the camera, trying to convince himself that he would know if he had a sexually transmitted disease. "If I was feeling weak, or had a rash downstairs—I'd definitely know something," he assures himself. But the voice-over announcer warns: "Most people with STDs show no symptoms at all. Get perspective. Get tested. For more information go to Fight for Your Rights @ MTV.com."

Programming on MTV is an integrated multimedia effort, employing cross-platform promotion strategies that have become standard operating procedure for entertainment-media companies in the digital era. The network takes full advantage of the multitasking media habits of youth to extend the reach of its brand and ensure maximum exposure and ongoing relationships with its viewers. These same strategies were central to the Fight for Your Rights: Protect Yourself campaign. Branded sexual-health messages were woven throughout the MTV franchise. Through interactive media, teens could discuss sex and sexual-health issues candidly with experts as well as peers, without fear of parental interference. Public-service advertising and TV programs featured links to the special Web site created for the campaign, itsyoursexlife.com, where viewers could access a wealth of online resources, including: "e-PSAs"; a searchable nationwide database of HIV- and STD-testing facilities; an interactive guide to sexual health; a sexual-health news site; monthly features that provide the latest information about HIV/AIDS and other topics; and 24-hour message boards where viewers could meet and discuss sexual-health-related issues in an ongoing dialogue. Through a toll-free hotline run by the Kaiser Foundation, teens could receive the free "Sex Life" booklet, and be "connected immediately to a live operator at the CDC's National HIV/AIDS or STD hot lines or to their local Planned Parenthood clinic."

In keeping with MTV's edgy, rebellious-youth image, the campaign encouraged its viewers to become engaged in sexual politics. The project's Web site featured a Take Action section, where MTV's other partners, including Advocates for Youth, offered opportunities to become involved in grassroots efforts. "Find out where you can be trained as a peer educator, learn how to take political action both locally and nationally, and get inspired by checking out what other young activists are doing," the Web site urged. But Kaiser was careful to distance itself from these overtly political aspects of the initiative, frequently pointing out that it neither engaged in nor funded advocacy. In its report "Reaching the MTV Generation," for example, among the specials listed as part of the campaign were several MTV broadcasts that directly took on the controversial policies around abstinence-only education. One was the 2002 MTV/*Time* magazine special "Sex in the Classroom." The program dealt with abstinence-only and comprehensive sex-ed curricula in the nation's schools, and it included sections where "students, educators, and experts speak out." Though the foundation listed this broadcast among the campaign's programmatic accomplishments, it noted that the special was "produced independently of the Foundation, but aired as part of the Fight for Your Rights campaign."

Dozens of TV programs were produced dealing with sexuality and sexual-health issues. During the 2002–2003 season, the network's documentary series *True Life* featured several episodes with sexual themes. In the episode "I Need Sex RX," camera crews followed several young people as they visited doctors and health-care centers, providing an up-close-and-personal view of one woman having her first gynecological exam and another getting tested for HIV. "It Could Be You" featured two young HIV-positive women on a road-trip around the country, meeting up with others who had tested positive for the disease. The special *9 Things You Need to Know before You're Good to Go* featured R&B/hip-hop star Tweet offering practical advice on how to have sex without getting an STD. The documentary *Dangerous Liaisons* examined the consequences of mixing drugs and alcohol with sex. And on *Live Loveline*, comedian Adam Carolla and MTV's sex doctor, Drew Pinsky, answered studio-audience and call-in questions about STDs. *MTV News* ran stories about teen pregnancy, STDs, HIV/AIDS, and other sexual-health issues. During the 2000 presidential election, the MTV special *Choose or Lose: Sex Laws* addressed such hot political issues as abortion, sex-ed policy, gay rights, and age of consent. The network's global reach enabled it to stage live, large-scale, international media events. The 2001 broadcast of *Staying Alive* 3, a special about young people and HIV/AIDS, aired in 150 countries, including South Africa, Kazakhstan, Russia, and China.

On-air specials frequently were coordinated with "offline" community events, in partnership with local chapters of Planned Parenthood and other sexual-health groups. Youth also could take part in live, online "e-discussions" about the TV programs on the MTV Web site. To kick off the 2002 campaign, MTV broadcast a live one-hour special called the "National Sex Quiz," promoting it in advance both on the air and online: "When it comes to sex, everybody thinks they know the score. You know everything you need to know . . . right? You sure? Prove it: Take MTV's 21-question pop quiz on sex and health, and then tune in to our live special on April 20 to find out if you know as much as you think (and get schooled if you don't!)." More than 700,000 viewers participated in the event, according to MTV executives. Inserts on "safer sex" were distributed in MTV's "Party to Go" CDs, as well as the *Real World* video, reaching 117,000 individuals. As part of MTV's 1998 Campus Invasion concert tour, "sexual information" tents were set up at thirty different colleges and universities around the country, staffed by college health counselors who distributed free literature and condoms.

But while TV specials and Web-site materials can offer fairly straightforward information on sexual health, incorporating the campaign's themes into unscripted reality shows sometimes can result in a muddled and confused message. With its rotating stable of eager young participants, *The Real World* has been a hotbed of topical issues confronting teens and young adults, making it a natural venue for pro-social messages. Over the years, the show has featured young people dealing with a variety of problems, including AIDS, sexual identity, and alcohol abuse. According to Kaiser executives, sexual-health themes have been "placed" in the popular series. Since it is a reality show, however, the issue cannot be written into scripts. Rather, when characters confront sexual issues on the show, the incidents can be linked to a more deliberate pro-social message.

So, when Trishelle went through her pregnancy scare, MTV put the young woman on an "online talk show," where she could debrief with her *Real World* viewers, accompanied by an expert to provide additional health information. But as Trishelle answered questions, it became clear that the fishbowl nature of the show itself may have contributed to her problem. When asked by the moderator why they did not use a condom when they had sex, Trishelle replied: "I think the first time we had sex it wasn't planned. And . . . the fact we had cameras on us, no one wanted to get up and get a condom. Then the camera crews would know that we were definitely having sex." The Planned Parenthood representative quickly intervened with her own advice: "The good news is most people don't have cameras on them when they're having sex. It's still a good idea to have condoms nearby if there's any chance you'll get involved in sexual behavior." After hearing the Planned Parenthood expert reel off a long list of birth control methods, the moderator asked Trishelle: "Did you consider going on the birth control pill?" The young woman replied that she had planned to go on the pill, but because she had to make a hasty move to Las Vegas in order to be on the show, she was having trouble getting her prescription transferred.

The *Real World* incident underscored what some media critics see as a contradiction in the Kaiser/MTV initiative. The highly popular youth network is a perfect venue for reaching the audience that Kaiser seeks to influence, but embedding socially responsible messages into a channel known for its titillating and graphic sexual content may send a double message to young people. "It's tremendously ironic," Bob Thompson, director of Syracuse University's Center for the Study of Popular Television, commented to the press. "The campaign is working with a network whose programming features exactly the opposite messages." But Kaiser officials counter that teens and young adults already are heavy viewers of MTV, "so the bottom line is, are they better off with this information included or without it?" Kaiser's Vicky Rideout told the press. "And the answer is that those who get our materials are more likely to see a doctor, talk to their parents and use birth control as a result."

Whether one agrees with the approach or not, the campaign's message appears to have gotten through. According to research released by the Kaiser Foundation, "a majority (52%) of all 16–24-year-olds in the country say they have seen sexual health ads on MTV, and a third (32%) say they have seen full-length shows." The research also found that "nearly two-thirds (63%)" of those who saw the campaign personally learned from it, and many told researchers they had become more cautious and careful in their own sexual behaviors, as a result of paying attention to the campaign. The campaign has won numerous awards, including an Emmy and a Peabody award in 2004. . . .

POSTSCRIPT

Do New Business Models Result in Greater Consumer Choice of Products and Ideas?

It's probably not too surprising that Chris Anderson is an editor of *Wired* Magazine, which often makes predictions about the future of media, consumerism, and new technology. In addition to many articles in *Wired*, Chris Anderson is a prolific author of books too. His most recent book, *Free: The Future of a Radical Price* (Hyperion, 2009), extends the metaphor of the Long Tail to examine how free products on the Internet (including media) could be the new economic model for our future. If he's right, the legacy industries will undoubtedly look toward greater diversification and divestiture, or, they may crumble.

Kathryn C. Montgomery takes a different approach, but discusses how nonprofit companies influence social campaigns. The partnership between MTV and the Kaiser Family Foundation's "Fight for Your Rights: Protect Yourself" program is typical of partnerships that take into consideration the vulnerability of children and teens. Are these programs, then, public service announcements or television content?

There is an emerging literature on e-commerce, the companies, and the individuals who made them possible. John Battelle's book, *The Search: How Google and Its Rivals Rewrote the Rules of Business and Transformed Our Culture* (Portfolio, 2005), is a comprehensive analysis of Google's rise and power. James Marcus' *Amazonia: Five Years at the Epicenter of the Dot.com Juggernaut* (New Press, 2004) is an entertaining story of the founding of Amazon and its slow rise before finally becoming a profitable company.

Social marketing is now an emerging field, though it has roots back to the 1970s when health care industry professionals sought to use traditional marketing strategies to influence attitudes and behaviors. Over the years, some of the most well known campaigns have resulted in anti-smoking campaigns, anti-drinking, anti-drug use, and health and wellness campaigns. Today, however, social networking, especially the use of Twitter, has become a method of immediate, direct marketing to the consumer. While many articles have been written about social marketing, books have been slower to appear. Among the new lists is Chel Holtz and John C. Havens' *Tactical Transparency: How Leaders Can Leverage Social Media to Maximize Value and Build Their Brand* (Josey-Bass, 2009).

Internet References . . .

Center for the Digital Future

Maintained by the University of Southern California, the Center for the Digital Future is a research and policy institute seeking to maximize the positive potential of the mass media and our rapidly evolving communication technologies.

http://www.digitalcenter.org

Electronic Frontier Foundation

Electronic Frontier Foundation is a nonprofit civil liberties organization working to protect free expression and access to public resources and information online and to promote responsibility in the new media.

http://www.eff.org

Yahoo International

The Yahoo service can access a number of countries, provide information about the media systems, and list media programming.

http://www.yahoo.com/Regional/Countries/

The Media Lab

MIT's Media Lab allows you to glimpse the many ways that researchers are thinking about the digital media future. Look at the research groups listed in the research section of the Web site, and then visit the group Web sites of the ones that interest you.

http://www.media.mit.edu

Pew Internet and American Life Project

An outstanding source for up-to-date reports on issues of Internet use and its integration into American society. Those interested in research can download surveys and data for secondary analysis.

http://www.pewinternet.org

Life in the Digital Age

*P*redictions of a world that is increasingly reliant upon media and communication technologies have generally provided either utopian or dystopian visions about what our lives will be like in the future. New media distribution technologies present new options for traditional ways of doing things. Not too many years ago, people were talking about the possibility of an information superhighway. Today, people talk about Facebook and Twitter. Although we are still learning how electronic communication may change our lives and the ways we work and communicate, many questions have not changed. Will new ways of communication change the way individuals interact? Will we find ways to protect the individual in this arena? Will the decision making of citizens change? Will everyone have access to the services and technologies that enable more immediate information exchange? What will new technologies mean to us as individuals as we live in the information age?

- Are Online Services Responsible for an Increase in Bullying and Harassment?

- Are People Better Informed in the Information Society?

ISSUE 17

Are Online Services Responsible for an Increase in Bullying and Harassment?

YES: **Penny A. Leisring**, from "Stalking Made Easy: How Information and Communication Technologies Are Influencing the Way People Monitor and Harass One Another," in Sharon Kleinman, ed., *The Culture of Efficiency* (Peter Lang, 2009)

NO: **Amanda Lenhart**, "Cyberbullying and Online Teens," Pew Internet and American Life Project (June 27, 2007)

ISSUE SUMMARY

YES: Penny Leisring discusses negative effects of using online technology to cyberstalk or harass someone. Use of social networking, e-mail, GPS systems, cell phone spamming, and caller ID all can be used to create a threatening or hostile environment for those people who use them for antisocial purposes. The author also addresses the situations that lend themselves most often to these undesirable uses of communication technology, such as in the break-up of romantic relationships, abusive relationships, or just plain hostile behaviors and interactions.

NO: Amanda Lenhart reports the findings of a Pew Internet & American Life Project that investigated the likelihood of teen harassment and cyberbullying and finds that the most likely candidates to experience online abuse are girls between the ages of 15 and 17, though the reported statistics for all teens of both genders are disturbing. However, Amanda Lenhart reports that, still, more teens report being bullied offline than online.

Online services are a wonderful way to communicate with others inexpensively and in real time, but the substitution of face-to-face communication often brings problems too. In this issue we explore the phenomenon of online communication from the perspective of technology that actually causes potential problems for the senders and receivers of messages that would otherwise be monitored by face-to-face communication, including nonverbal cues, gestures, and the presence of the body.

Parents and educators have become very concerned about the use of online technologies that exacerbate antisocial childhood behavior. When greater use of e-mail, social networks, and other forms of online communication is used to harass or bully someone, the children who are the victims often fear telling parents or teachers because they are afraid that their access to the technology might be curbed.

There have been many tragic situations in which an impressionable youth has been bullied, harassed, or intimidated to such a degree that he or she experiences physical and mental problems. Perhaps one of the most well-publicized tragedies is that of the young Megan Meier, a socially awkward 15-year-old who was the victim of a hoax that created so much distress for her that she committed suicide. The situation involved an adult's creation of a fictitious boy who romantically flirted with Megan, and then broke up with her online and told her that she was such a loser that she would be better off dead. The adult was indicted of computer fraud and in 2009 was acquitted. In the meantime, the "Megan Meier Cyberbullying Prevention Act (H.R. 1966)" has been introduced in the U.S. House of Representatives, which would make it a crime to knowingly transmit communication "intended to coerce, intimidate, harass, or cause substantial emotional distress to another person, using means to support severe, repeated, and hostile behavior."

Cyberbullying and online harassment are also increasing in the workplace, as more personal interactions take place on social networks, and companies are now dealing with the creation of policies that prohibit the creation of a hostile workplace. Harassment is now viewed as an act of discrimination that can be viewed as a part of the Civil Rights Act of 1964. Lewd remarks, offensive jokes, and unwanted physical contact are some of the ways in which a hostile work environment can be created, but the use of e-mail for images, jokes, and even gossip and rumors can also target an individual and fall into the category of cyberbullying and harassment.

While discourse about the impact of technology has moved far beyond the debate of the "positive" and "negative" qualities and characteristics of some communication forms, the distancing of activities beyond the interpersonal realm is increasingly viewed as an alienating effect of technology. As we live, work, and play more and more online, we need to become aware of how easy it is to let the technology do the work, and how easy it is to exercise those qualities that make us civil human beings in the increasingly technologized world. These selections raise these questions and more.

YES

Penny A. Leisring

Stalking Made Easy: How Information and Communication Technologies Are Influencing the Way People Monitor and Harass One Another

Your phone rings and obscene callers are on the line. Strangers show up repeatedly in the middle of the night at your door wanting to force themselves on you sexually. This is what happened to the victim in the first case prosecuted under California's cyberstalking law. Randi Barber was being cyberstalked by a man from her church, Gary Dellapenta, who was posting things about her on the Internet. After Barber rejected Dellapenta's romantic overtures, Dellapenta posed as Barber in Internet chat rooms and announced that she had fantasies about men raping her. He posted her home address and phone number online and urged men to show up at her home in the middle of the night. He even told them how to break into her apartment and bypass her home security system. Dellapenta told the men that her refusals were part of her fantasy but that she really wanted the men to force themselves on her. Six men showed up at her home. Barber was traumatized. She lost 35 pounds, lost her job, and moved out of her home. Dellapenta was sentenced to six years in prison for stalking and for soliciting others to commit rape.

This case illustrates one way that people use the Internet to stalk and harass others. Information and communication technologies such as computers, cell phones, and BlackBerry-like devices are making stalkers more efficient. Remarkably, a "stalker's home page" exists on the Internet, containing information and Web links for people interested in stalking others. Cyberstalking is "easier and less risky" to engage in than more traditional offline forms of stalking. Stalking with technology—cyberstalking—is common, especially among college students. Most cyberstalking is perpetrated by someone who knows the victim, and often cyberstalking, like other forms of stalking, is perpetrated by an ex-partner after a romantic relationship ends. Some ex-partners hope to rekindle the relationship. Computer-mediated communication may "promote a false sense of intimacy and misunderstanding of intentions." If a person's messages are responded to, their hope and behavior may persist or increase. According to Brian Spitzberg's review of offline stalking methods, stalking often lasts for almost two years. Paul Bocij suggests that cyberstalking typically lasts about four months.

All 50 states in the U.S. have laws against stalking, and the Federal Violence Against Women Act now includes cyberstalking. Stalkers have used a variety of methods to monitor and harass their victims, including phone calls, in-person contact, and surveillance methods. The Internet has expanded stalking methods, and now people can stalk others anonymously or pseudonymously. Cyberstalkers may send repeated e-mails, chat requests, or text messages, or they may make repeated cell phone calls to the victim. Some monitor the victim's activities by reading the victim's e-mails; online "away messages," which sometimes reveal the current location and behavior of the victim; and postings to social networking Web sites, such as MySpace and Facebook. Some perpetrators use global positioning system (GPS) devices to track their target's physical location, and they may even use computer spyware to monitor their victim's Web activity or computer keystrokes. When victims discover these activities, it can lead to tremendous fear and distress, especially for female victims. . . .

Types of Stalking with Technology

The ways in which information and communication technologies are being used to stalk and harass others are numerous. Cindy Southworth and Sarah Tucker have provided an excellent review of many cyberstalking methods. Stalkers may use cell phones to repeatedly call or send text messages to their victims. Fax machines may be used to send messages and the header on faxes may reveal the location of a victim, if she sends a fax to the stalker. Stalkers may use computers to send e-mail or instant messages to the victim or to post information about the victim on Web pages, bulletin boards, or blogs (Web logs). Spoofing is another technique used by cyberstalkers, which involves impersonating the victim online. Some stalkers have used anonymous re-mailers, e-mail forwarding services that mask the originating address of e-mail messages so that the sender cannot be traced. Others have spammed victims by sending hundreds of e-mail messages to clog up the victim's e-mail inbox or have signed the victim up for numerous online mailing lists so that the victim is flooded each day with e-mail. Some cyberstalkers purposely e-mail the victim files containing computer viruses. Some stalkers send pornography to their victims. Some even enlist third parties to stalk their victims, which Paul Bocij refers to as "stalking by proxy."

The Internet with its search engines and databases is also used to collect information for the purpose of monitoring or tracking victims. Vanessa Bufis, Penny Leisring, and Jessica Brinkmann found that many college students view the online "away messages" of their ex-partners. In these messages, people often reveal what they are doing and where they are located. Many college students also acknowledged checking their ex-partners' pages on social networking sites for information.

Perpetrators who are the former romantic partners of their victims may know their victims' passwords and personal identification numbers, which they could use to gain access to the victims' e-mail and voice mail accounts. One stalker accessed his victim's e-mail account and, impersonating the victim, sent threatening messages to himself that he took to the police. Technologies used by deaf individuals such as teletypewriters (TTY) and telecommunication devices for the deaf (TTD) record and save transcripts of all phone conversations, which makes it easy for stalkers to monitor victims' communications if they have access to the victims' devices. Such systems have also been used to impersonate victims. One perpetrator, pretending to be his victim, made a call to a prosecutor using the victim's TTY. The call indicated that the victim would commit suicide if charges against the perpetrator were not dropped. When help arrived it became apparent that the victim had been sleeping and had not made the call.

Stalkers sometimes resort to even more extreme measures, such as installing keystroke loggers or spyware on computers or cell phones belonging to their victims. Keystroke loggers require that the perpetrator have physical access to the victim's computer. Once installed, all keys pressed on the victim's computer are recorded, giving a perpetrator access to a lot of information, including confidential passwords. Spyware, which can be installed remotely, allows the perpetrator to track Web sites visited and e-mails sent and received by the victim. According to Bruce Gross, some spyware allows the user to access all files on the victim's computer and will search for passwords. Spyware is sometimes configured to reinstall itself if it is deleted. Small cameras can be remotely installed and activated that would allow the perpetrator to actually see inside the victim's home. Mapping sites like Google Earth (Atkinson et al., 2007) and GPS devices are used to track victims' physical locations. In addition, some new Caller Identification (ID) systems show the caller's address as well as phone number. Thus, if the victim calls the perpetrator, the victim's address will be revealed. . . .

A National Violence Against Women (NVAW) survey in the late 1990s did not assess cyberstalking, but it found that 8 percent of women and 2 percent of men were stalked by offline methods. The stalking definition used in the NVAW survey required a high level of victim fear. If the definition required that the victims be only somewhat or a little frightened by the behavior, then the stalking rates from that national sample rise considerably to 12 percent for women and 4 percent for men. According to a review by Lorraine Sheridan and her colleagues, the lifetime prevalence of stalking for women is 12 to 16 percent and for men is 4 to 7 percent. This means that approximately 1 in 6 women and approximately 1 in 14 men will be stalked in their lifetime. . . .

Studies have found that more women than men are stalked using offline methods, but at least one study has found that cyberstalking may affect more men than women and one study by Jerry Finn assessing cyberstalking/online harassment in a college sample found no gender differences. Finn's data collected in 2002 indicated that 58 percent of his sample had received unwanted pornography via e-mail or instant messenger, and between 10 and 15 percent of the sample reported that they had repeatedly received e-mails or instant messages that threatened, insulted, or harassed. Fourteen percent of the sample received such messages even after they told the sender to stop sending messages. Sexual minority students were more likely than heterosexual students to receive repeated threatening, insulting, or harassing e-mails from strangers or people that they barely knew. Finn hypothesized that this may be due to the increased harassment faced by gay, lesbian, bisexual, and transgendered individuals in the offline world.

Post-Intimate Stalking and Intimate Partner Violence

Stalking is most often perpetrated by current or former romantic partners. In his review, Brian Spitzberg finds that approximately 50 percent of stalking stems from prior romantic relationships, 25 percent is perpetrated by strangers, and 25 percent is perpetrated by acquaintances. Much stalking occurs after a romantic relationship ends, and the person who was rejected is typically the one to engage in stalking behavior. Keith Davis and his colleagues found that anger and jealousy after a romantic relationship dissolves are associated with post-breakup stalking. They also found that expressions of love are highly correlated with stalking, which supports the assertion that many people stalk their ex-partners in hopes of reuniting. Stalking may be referred to, in this context, as "unwanted pursuit."

Post-intimate relationship stalking seems to be more likely when a relationship has been abusive. T. K. Logan, Carl Leukefeld, and Bob Walker found that college students who had been stalked had higher rates of physical and emotional abuse within their relationship than students who had not been stalked. Jennifer Becker and Penny Leisring also found in a college sample that physical abuse within a relationship was associated with post-breakup unwanted pursuit behaviors. Mindy Mechanic, Terri Weaver, and Patricia Resick, in their study of battered women, found that dominance and isolation within a relationship were associated with stalking behaviors perpetrated against women. Jennifer Langhinrichsen-Rohling found that about 25 percent of sheltered battered women acknowledged engaging in stalking and unwanted pursuit behaviors toward their abusive partners during separations. Most of the stalking was bi-directional in nature. In other words, many of the male partners were also engaging in stalking and unwanted pursuit behaviors.

Partner violence does not necessarily end after a breakup, and stalkers have been known to engage in physical and psychological aggression toward their ex-partners. In a study by Karl Roberts, 35 percent of the college women who had been stalked were victims of violence during the stalking. T. K. Logan, Lisa Shannon, and Jennifer Cole surveyed women who had restraining orders against violent partners or ex-partners and found that the women who had been stalked by their partners or ex-partners experienced more violations of restraining orders and more severe abuse than the victimized women who had not been stalked. Stalking has been characterized as a "severe form of emotional/psychological abuse." Stalking and psychological aggression seem to have similar antecedents, such as a need for control, anxious attachment, and harsh parental discipline.

Characteristics of Stalkers

What do we know about stalkers? Most of the research examining the characteristics of stalkers has focused on those who perpetrate stalking using traditional offline methods, and few studies have focused exclusively on cyberstalkers. However, since many cyberstalkers engage in offline methods of stalking in addition to using technology to stalk their victims, the research examining offline stalkers is likely relevant. Paul Bocij asserts that almost a third of cyberstalkers use offline stalking methods in addition to using technology.

Domestic violence perpetrators and stalkers seem to share many of the same traits. A history of childhood abuse and disrupted attachment are common among stalkers and batterers. Some stalkers and batterers also appear to have borderline personality disorder traits. Borderline personality disorder is characterized by an intense fear of abandonment, impulsivity, emotional instability, and unstable interpersonal relationships. Thus, when people with borderline personality disorder traits are rejected by their intimate partners, they may have extreme difficulty handling the loss, and they may persistently and inappropriately attempt to reconnect and avoid abandonment. . . . Jealousy and a need for control are also characteristics shared by domestic violence perpetrators and stalkers.

We know very little about the characteristics of cyberstalkers in particular. The gender distribution of cyberstalking may be different than that of offline stalking; equal rates of cyberstalking seem to be found across genders, at least in college populations. Cyberstalking can be so easy to perpetrate from the comfort of home that cyberstalkers may have less psychopathology than offline stalkers. This is a hypothesis worthy of study. Paul Bocij points out that not all cyberstalkers (or offline stalkers) have psychological disorders. Stephen Morewitz hypothesizes that cyberstalkers may have higher socioeconomic status than offline stalkers, as reflected in their access to the Internet and other means for electronically mediated communication, such as cell phones and BlackBerry-like handheld devices. He points out, however, that this potential difference is likely to diminish as free e-mail and Internet access become even more widespread.

Information regarding treatment for cyberstalkers is needed. Oliver Howes discussed a case in which a 32-year-old woman was treated for compulsively sending text messages to her ex-boyfriend after he ended the relationship. She was spending four hours per day sending text messages and was treated with the antidepressant Trazodone and with behavior modification. The behavior modification component of treatment involved monitoring the patient's behavior, using relaxation methods, and scheduling time for sending messages with increased intervals between messages. The patient's compulsive texting gradually ceased. While the improvement for the woman in this case study is encouraging, it should be noted that without a control group we cannot know for certain whether improvement was due to the specific treatment utilized. Controlled trials of treatment for cyberstalkers are clearly warranted.

Effects on Victims

Offline stalking and cyberstalking can have various effects on victims ranging from mild annoyance to severe fear and psychological maladjustment. Symptoms of depression, drug use, and posttraumatic stress disorder have been found among stalking victims. . . . In Michele Pathé and Paul Mullen's clinical sample, they found that 24 percent of stalking victims experienced suicidal thoughts or attempted suicide. Kathleen Basile and her colleagues found in a nationally representative sample of the U.S. that stalking was associated with posttraumatic stress symptoms even after controlling for other types of violence perpetrated by the stalker. T. K. Logan and Jennifer Cole found stalking to be associated with anxiety symptoms over and above other forms of intimate partner violence in their sample of women who had obtained restraining orders against their violent partners. Karen Abrams and Gail Robinson suggest that women stalked by ex-partners may experience low self-esteem and guilt over their choice of romantic partners. Some victims may turn to substances as a way of coping with their victimization. Sheryl Pimlott-Kubiak and Lilia Cortina found that men and women who had been stalked had higher levels of prescription and illegal drug use than non-victims. Pathé and Mullen found that stalking victims reported increased smoking and drinking as a result of their victimization.

In addition to psychological consequences, some stalking victims also receive physical injuries. Women stalked by intimate partners or ex-partners are over four times more likely to be physically injured than women stalked by others. Over 80 percent of women who are stalked by an intimate partner have also been physically assaulted by that partner. Acquaintances, as well as intimate partners, can physically harm their stalking victims. Amy Boyer was shot and killed in 1999 by a cyberstalker, Liam Youens, who was able to locate her work address online. Boyer's former schoolmate, Youens had posted his plans to murder her online. Youens claimed he had been in love with her for years. He committed suicide right after killing her.

Many stalking victims report that they have taken precautions and have changed their routines as a result of being stalked. Some victims move and change jobs. Jayne Hitchcock bought a gun for self-protection after she was cyberstalked and her phone number and address had been posted online by the perpetrator. . . .

Preventative Measures and Steps to Take if Cyberstalked

There are various things that can be done to reduce the odds of being a victim of cyberstalking. For example, everyone should periodically conduct an Internet search to see what information about them is available online for all to see. If they find information that they would like removed, they should contact the Web master of the site where the information is located. People should use extreme caution when posting information about themselves, considering the public nature of information on the Internet. Emily Spence-Diehl argues that people should only post information that they would be comfortable having on the front page of their local newspaper. Thus, college students should utilize privacy functions on social networking Web sites like Facebook and MySpace so that they can control who has access to the material they post. They should think twice about posting any personal information on these sites. If college students do not want their ex-partner to know, for example, that they are now dating someone new, then they should refrain from posting such information or pictures with their new partner on social networking Web sites.

To avoid file corruption due to computer viruses sent by stalkers, backing up files on a scheduled basis is recommended. Computer users should also check for and regularly install updates to their operating systems to maximize security. Computer passwords and personal identification numbers (PINs) should be changed regularly, too. Bruce Arnold urges computer users to choose Internet service providers based on professionalism rather than lowest cost. He also recommends that people be cautious about including their cell phone numbers in e-mail signature files.

Once people determine that they are being stalked, there are many concrete steps they can take. Jerry Finn and Mary Banach and Sharon Miceli, Shannon Santana, and Bonnie Fisher list numerous resources that provide information and assistance to stalking victims, including the Working to Halt Online Abuse Web site, http://www.haltabuse.org. As soon as a person feels uncomfortable with the behavior of a potential stalker, sending a clear statement to the perpetrator that the behavior is unwanted is crucial. J. Reid Meloy recommends that a third party, such as an attorney, spouse, or mental health professional, contact the perpetrator once a pattern of behavior has been established. According to Meloy, the third party should alert the perpetrator that the behavior is unwanted and that the police will be contacted if the behavior continues. If a stalker continues to contact the victim after being told to stop, then the offense becomes "aggravated stalking." Avoiding further contact with the perpetrator will be critical because contact may serve to reinforce or encourage the stalking behavior.

The victim should retain and print all "cyber-evidence," such as e-mails, facsimiles, instant messages, and Web postings. If the software being used does not lend itself easily to printing the communication, then a screen capture utility should be used to document the cyberstalking behavior. Cyber-evidence will enable the victim to make a stronger case against the stalker if police and judicial involvement is warranted. However, most stalking police reports do not lead to arrests, and restraining orders are not necessarily effective; one review found they were violated 40 percent of the time and that they were thought to have intensified the stalking 20 percent of the time. Victims and their advocates should be aware that certain acts by the victim, such as filing a restraining order or threatening to contact authorities, may lead to retaliation or violence by the stalker. Bocij recommends contacting the police if one receives a threat that they believe someone will act on.

Victims should take steps to privatize any personal information about them on the Internet and should block e-mail and instant messages from perpetrators. They should consider contacting the Internet service providers used by their stalkers to request that stalkers' memberships be canceled. A complaint to the Internet service provider or re-mailer will often cause e-mail harassment or "e-mail bombing" to stop. Victims can also change their usernames, their e-mail and instant messaging addresses, and their e-mail providers. Louise Ellison suggests that women use a male or a gender neutral username. Victims can also use encryption software so that only intended recipients can read sent messages. They should also make sure that none of the security codes or accounts that they have (for example, health insurance) use their social security number as the identification number. Antivirus software and a firewall program should be utilized. . . .

Amanda Lenhart

NO

Cyberbullying and Online Teens

About one third (32%) of all teenagers who use the internet say they have been targets of a range of annoying and potentially menacing online activities—such as receiving threatening messages; having their private emails or text messages forwarded without consent; having an embarrassing picture posted without permission; or having rumors about them spread online. . . .

Depending on the circumstances, these harassing or "cyberbullying" behaviors may be truly threatening, merely annoying or relatively benign. But several patterns are clear: girls are more likely than boys to be targets; and teens who share their identities and thoughts online are more likely to be targets than are those who lead less active online lives.

Of all the online harassment asked about, the greatest number of teens told us that they had had a private communication forwarded or publicly posted without their permission. One in 6 teens (15%) told us someone had forwarded or posted communication they assumed was private. About 13% of teens told us that someone had spread a rumor about them online, and another 13% said that someone had sent them a threatening or aggressive email, IM or text message. Some 6% of online teens told us that someone had posted an embarrassing picture of them without their permission.

Yet when asked where they thought bullying happened most often to teens their age, the majority of teens, 67%, said that bullying and harassment happens more *offline than online. Less than one in three teens (29%) said that they thought that bullying was more likely to happen online, and three percent said they thought it happened both online and offline equally.*

These results come from a nationally-representative phone survey of 935 teenagers by the Pew Internet & American Life Project.

In focus groups conducted by the Project about the issue, one 16-year-old girl casually described how she and her classmates bullied a fellow student: "There's one MySpace from my school this year. There's this boy in my anatomy class who everybody hates. He's like the smart kid in class. Everybody's jealous. They all want to be smart. He always wants to work in our group and I hate it. And we started this thing, some girl in my class started this I Hate [Name] MySpace thing. So everybody in school goes on it to comment bad things about this boy."

The Gender Gap

Girls are more likely than boys to say that they have ever experienced cyberbullying—38% of online girls report being bullied, compared with 26% of online boys. Older girls in particular are more likely to report being bullied than any other age and gender group, with 41% of online girls ages 15 to 17 reporting these experiences. Teens who use social network sites like MySpace and Facebook and teens who use the internet daily are also more likely to say that they have been cyberbullied. Nearly 4 in 10 social network users (39%) have been cyberbullied in some way, compared with 22% of online teens who do not use social networks. . . .

Fewer Communications Are Private Anymore

The rumor mill speeds up.

A bit more than one in eight or 13% of teens said that someone had spread a rumor about them online. A girl in middle school told us: "I know a lot of times online someone will say something about one person and it'll spread and then the next day in school, I know there's like one of my friends, something happened online and people started saying she said something that she never said, and the next day we came into school and no one would talk to her and everyone's ignoring her. And she had no idea what was going on. Then someone sent her the whole conversation between these two people."

Girls are more likely to report someone spreading rumors about them than boys, with 16% of girls reporting rumor-spreading compared with 9% of boys. Social network users are more likely than those who do not use social networks to report that someone had spread a rumor about them (16% vs. 8%). . . .

Older Girls Receive More Online Threats

One in eight online teens (13%) reported that someone had sent them a threatening or aggressive email, instant message or text message. One fifteen-year-old boy in a focus group admitted, "I played a prank on someone but it wasn't serious. I told them I was going to come take them from their house and kill them and throw them in the woods. It's the best prank because it's like 'oh my god, I'm calling the police' and I was like 'I'm just kidding, I was just messing with you.' She got so scared though."

Older teens, particularly 15- to 17-year-old girls, are more like to report that they have received a threatening email or message. Overall, 9% of online teens ages 12–14 say they have been threatened via email, IM or text, while 16% of online teens ages 15–17 report similar harassment.

Among older girls, 19% have received threatening or aggressive email, IMs or text messages. Social network users are more likely than those who do not use social networks to report that someone had sent them a threatening or aggressive email (16% vs. 8%).

Um, I Swear That Is Not Me

Fewer teens, some 6%, reported that someone had posted an embarrassing picture of them online without their permission. Not surprisingly, given the number of photos posted on social networking websites, users of those sites are more likely to report that someone had posted embarrassing pictures of them online without their permission—9% of social network users reported this, compared with just 2% of those who do not use social networking sites. Similarly, teens who post photos themselves are more likely to report that someone has posted an embarrassing photo of them without their permission. One 17-year-old boy explained "I'm not a big fan of MySpace. Well, I got in trouble from one of them at my school. I had one and they [other friends] put a bad picture up there [on her page] and I got in a little trouble at school. . . . Some girl just put up like pictures of us on New Year's Eve and the Dean saw it."

Intense Internet Users Are Bullied More

Online teens who have created content for the internet—for instance, by authoring blogs, uploading photos, sharing artwork or helping others build websites—are more likely to report cyberbullying and harassment than their peers. Content creators are also more likely to use social networks—places to create and display and receive feedback on content creations, and social network users are also more likely to be cyberbullied. . . .

Bullying Happens More Often Offline

Two-thirds of all teens (67%) said that bullying and harassment happens more *offline* than online. Fewer than one in three teens (29%) said that they thought that bullying was more likely to happen online, and 3% said they thought it happened both online and offline equally.

Girls are a bit more likely than boys to say that bullying happens more online (33% of girls vs. 25% of boys), though overall, both boys and girls say that kids their age are more likely to be harassed offline. White teens are a bit more likely than African-American teens to think that bullying is more of a problem online—32% of white teens said bullying happens more often online, while 18% of African-American teens said the same. Teens who have online profiles are just as likely as those who do not to say that bullying happens more often offline.

Teens who have been cyberbullied are more likely than their peers who have not been bullied to say that they believe bullying happens online more than offline. However, the majority of bullied teens say that bullying is more likely to happen offline than online. More than 7 in 10 (71%) of teens who have not experienced bullying believe it happens more often offline, while 57% of teens who have been cyberbullied themselves say bullying happens more offline.

Why Do Teens Bully Online?

In our focus groups, we asked teens about online experiences they had with bullying and harassment. In some cases what we heard was that adolescent cruelty had simply moved from the school yard, the locker room, the bathroom wall and the phone onto the internet. The simplicity of being able to replicate and quickly transmit digital content makes bullying quite easy. "Just copy and paste whatever somebody says," a middle school girl explains as she describes online bullying tactics. "You have to watch what you say," counsels another middle school girl. "If that person's at their house and if you say something about them and you don't know they're there or if you think that person's your friend and you trust them and you're like, 'Oh, well, she's really being annoying,' she could copy and paste and send it to [anyone]." Another middle school girl describes how the manipulation of digital materials can be used to hurt someone. "Like I was in a fight with a girl and she printed out our conversation, changed some things that I said, and brought it into school, so I looked like a terrible person."

Some teens suggested that it is the mediated nature of the communication that contributes to bullying, insulating teens from the consequences of their actions. One high school boy responded to the question whether he had heard of cyberbullying: "I've heard of it and experienced it. People think they are a million times stronger because they can hide behind their computer monitor. Also known as 'e-thugs.' Basically I just ignored the person and went along with my own civilized business." A middle school girl described "stuff starting online for no reason."

Intolerance also sparks online bullying incidents, as a middle school girl related in a focus group. "I have this one friend and he's gay and his account got hacked and someone put all these really homophobic stuff on there and posted like a mass bulletin of like some guy with his head smashed open like run over by a car. It was really gruesome and disgusting."

Bullying has entered the digital age. The impulses behind it are the same, but the effect is magnified. In the past, the materials of bullying would have been whispered, shouted or passed around. Now, with a few clicks, a photo, video or a conversation can be shared with hundreds via email or millions through a website, online profile or blog posting.

Methodology

This report draws on two main research project methodologies—a telephone survey of teens and parents, and a series of focus group discussions with teens. The Parents & Teens 2006 Survey sponsored by the Pew Internet and American Life Project obtained telephone interviews with a nationally representative call-back sample of 935 teens age 12 to 17 years old and their parents living in continental United States telephone households. The telephone sample was pulled from previous Pew Internet Project surveys fielded in 2004, 2005, and 2006. Households with a child age 18 or younger were called back and screened to find 12- to 17-year-olds. The survey was conducted by Princeton

Survey Research Associates International. The interviews were done in English by Princeton Data Source, LLC, from October 23 to November 19, 2006. Statistical results are weighted to correct known demographic discrepancies. The margin of sampling error for the complete set of weighted data is ±3.7%. The response rate for the full survey is 46% of the previously interviewed households.

A total of 7 focus groups were conducted with youth in June 2006. Three of the groups were conducted in an East Coast city and three were conducted in a Midwestern city. One focus group was conducted online, with high schoolers and a mix of boys and girls. The other six groups were single gender, and interviewed 7th and 8th graders, 9th and 10th graders and 11th and 12th graders, one each of boys and girls for each grade group. . . .

POSTSCRIPT

Are Online Services Responsible for an Increase in Bullying and Harassment?

The selections in this issue demonstrate how new problems emerge as we move from "mass" media to more personally produced and consumed media. Can technology be an excuse for bad behavior? We have been working to understand "media literacy" for many years now, but should we also think about the need to discuss "technological literacy"?

Familiarity with immediate two-way communication forms is not likely to change in the near future, but we might expect to start seeing the impact of interactive media as we use more technology for a wide variety of purposes. The problem of online harassment and cyberbullying has become so prevalent in our society that even the FCC has begun to take a stand on identifying and defining social behaviors online (see http://www.fcc.gov/owd/understanding-harassment.html).

There are many groups available on the Internet to help parents and teachers deal with children and cyberbullying. The group "Stop Cyberbullying Now" presents information for children and teens from 7 to 17 (http://www.stopcyberbullying.org/index2.html), and the National Crime Prevention Council has sponsored a contest to involve children and teens in creating messages to raise awareness of cyberbullying (http://www.ncpc.org/newsroom/current-campaigns/cyberbullying/). The Web site Ars Technica explains the impact of the Megan Meier Cyberbullying Prevention Act (http://arstechnica.com/tech-policy/news/2009/05). The Pew Internet & American Life Project has also produced a report called "Social Isolation and New Technology," in which they report on social isolation that sometimes results from more use of social technology and social systems on the Internet (http://www.pewinternet.org/).

As the selections in this issue show, human behavior sometimes changes when technology is introduced. If we are to successfully adopt social networking and other forms of online communication, we need to continue to pay attention to the deleterious effects that may result. Only by critically examining the social use of social media can we retain positive social behaviors that are necessary for socialization and survival in a more fully technologized world.

ISSUE 18

Are People Better Informed in the Information Society?

YES: Linda Jackson, Alexander von Eye, Frank Biocca, Gretchen Barbatsis, Yong Zhao, and Hiram Fitzgerald, from "Does Home Internet Use Influence the Academic Performance of Low-Income Children?" *Developmental Psychology* (vol. 42, no. 3, 2006)

NO: Mark Bauerlein, from *The Dumbest Generation: How the Digital Age Stupefies Young Americans and Jeopardizes Our Future* (TARCHER/Penguin, 2008)

ISSUE SUMMARY

YES: Linda Jackson et al. conducted a 16-month survey of Internet use by youth age 10 to 18 in low-income homes. They found that youth who used the Internet more had higher scores on standardized tests of reading achievement and higher GPAs. This work supports the optimism surrounding the Internet as a tool to level the educational playing field.

NO: Mark Bauerlein finds the hopes for better-educated youth in the digital age to be an empty promise. Youth spend much of their leisure time in front of computer and television screens, but the information age has failed to produce a well-informed, thoughtful public. Instead we have a nation of know-nothings who don't read, follow politics, or vote—and who can't compete internationally.

Many people feel that as we move toward a more technologically oriented lifestyle, we, as a nation, and as participants in the new information society, are inevitably moving toward a better quality of life. It almost seems logical that better technology is the result of moving from more primitive forms of communicating to more sophisticated, faster, and efficient means. But an age-old question is whether the ability to communicate equals a quality communication experience. Without a doubt, messages that can be sent, retrieved, and enhanced may all appear to be technological breakthroughs and positive transactions. But there is another side to this scenario in which we must address whether an excess of information truly informs.

In this issue, we examine two selections that ask whether the Internet and other digital technologies have created a better-informed society. Jackson and her colleagues demonstrate the potential of the Internet to enhance educational outcomes for low-income children. Bauerlein is troubled by the poorly educated youth of this generation. Although they are dubbed digital natives, he argues that this is a dumb generation, unable to perform the intellectual work needed for the future of the United States. How can you reconcile these two selections? Both contain factual material. Can both be true?

Jackson et al. were involved in an extensive longitudinal study of Internet use in low-income homes. Their findings were complex, but one conclusion is inescapable: The Internet showed the potential to enhance academic achievement. The introduction to this article tells us that other studies have been equivocal. Issues for you to judge are whether this study seems valid and reliable. Are you convinced that their finding is "inescapable"? If not, what other research questions would you pose? If you are convinced that this conclusion is correct, then how could the outcome for a generation of digital natives be so poor?

The Information Highway and the Digital Age stimulated hopes for a generation able to multitask, plumb the depths of digital information, and create a sophisticated synthesis. The ability to communicate across platforms should be almost inbred, with most everyone able to capture and stream audio and video, create Web sites, post their creations to YouTube, and use sophisticated hardware and software to easily accomplish these tasks. Yet the chapter titles in Bauerlein's book are a litany of accusation: knowledge deficits, the new bibliophobes, online learning, and nonlearning are a few titles. The culprit is the digital age.

Despite the number or sources and technologies available, people are not better educated or more informed today. His statistics are frightening. If Bauerlein is correct, there is much evidence to support the idea that as time goes by the public's knowledge of basic civics and politics becomes even weaker. If this is the scenario of the future, we must question whether the information society represents a better world, or a world in which we have lost much of what we already had.

As a concluding issue to this book, these selections ask the reader to make real decisions about how they feel about new technologies and the quality of our lives. The author Neil Postman wrote about predicting what our future would be like in his book, *Amusing Ourselves to Death* (Penguin, 1985). Postman recalled earlier authors, like George Orwell, who, in 1949, wrote a futuristic book called *1984* (Harcourt, Brace), and Aldous Huxley, who, in 1932, wrote *Brave New World* (London, Chatto, & Windus). Each of these authors focused on the most common form of media available to them—print media in the form of their book—and each dealt with the future in a different way. Orwell foretold of a time in which people couldn't read because they had no books. Huxley's world envisioned a world with books, but the people chose not to read. We will conclude this volume by asking you, our readers—does a new, improved Internet help transfer and store information that helps you lead a better informed of life?

YES ↵

Linda A. Jackson et al.

Does Home Internet Use Influence the Academic Performance of Low-Income Children?

Decades of research has focused on the issue of whether using computers facilitates learning, typically measured as school performance. After reviewing dozens of studies of school learning with computer-based technology, including five meta-analytic reviews, Roschelle and colleagues came to the less-than-satisfying conclusion that the findings are inconclusive. For example, one meta-analytic review of over 500 studies (kindergarten through twelfth-grade students) found positive effects of computer tutoring applications on achievement test scores. However, other uses of the computer, such as simulations and enrichment applications, had no effects. Still other findings suggest that the benefits of computer-based instruction are clearer for mathematics and science than they are for other subjects. For example, a study by the Educational Testing Service found that using computers to engage higher-order thinking skills was related to better school performance in mathematics by fourth and eighth graders.

Roschelle et al. offered three explanations for the equivocal findings with respect to computer-based instruction and school performance. First, variability in hardware and software among schools participating in the research may explain the equivocal findings. Second, the failure of schools to accompany technology use with concurrent reforms in the other areas, such as curriculum and teacher professional development, may explain the failure to find beneficial effects of technology use on academic performance. Third, the lack of rigorous, structured longitudinal studies may explain the failure to find positive effects of computer-based instruction, as well as information technology use in general, on academic performance. Rochelle and colleagues suggest that positive effects are most likely to emerge when technology is used to support the four fundamentals of learning: active engagement, participation in groups, frequent interaction and feedback, and connections to real-world contexts.

Subrahmanyam and colleagues reviewed the research on computer use and cognitive skills, focusing on a broad array of cognitive competencies but particularly on visual intelligence skills, such as spatial skills and iconic and image representation skills. These authors conclude that computer use does contribute to cognitive skills, specifically to visual skills. For example, playing certain types of computer games, namely action games that involve rapid

From *Developmental Psychology*, 42(3), May 2006, pp. 429–434 (refs. omitted). Copyright © 2006 by American Psychological Association. Reprinted by permission via Rightslink.

movement, imagery, intense interaction, and multiple activities occurring simultaneously, improves visual intelligence skills. As the authors point out, these skills "provide 'training wheels' for computer literacy" and are "especially useful in the fields of science and technology, where proficiency in manipulating images on a screen is increasingly important." However, they also note that, "computer game playing can enhance a particular skill only if the game uses that skill and if the child's initial skill level has matured to a certain level." Moreover, ". . . much of the existing research on computer games has measured effects only immediately after playing, and thus does not address questions about the cumulative impact of interactive games on learning."

Other findings point to a relationship between technology use and academic performance, although causal relationships have been difficult to establish. Several studies show that the presence of educational resources in the home, including computers, is a strong predictor of academic success in mathematics and science. Having a home computer has been associated with higher test scores in reading, even after controlling for family income and other factors related to reading test scores. Still other findings indicate that participating in a networked community of learners improves educational outcomes for at-risk children. Some researchers have even suggested that recent nationwide increases in nonverbal intelligence test scores may be attributable to "exposure to the proliferation of imagery in electronic technology."

Overall, whether using computer-based technology contributes to children's academic performance remains uncertain. Available evidence suggests that having a home computer is linked to somewhat better academic performance, although most studies fail to control for factors that covary with having a home computer (e.g., parental income and education). The effects of computer-based school and after-school activities are unclear, although favorable effects have been observed under some circumstances (e.g., when a supportive learning environment exists; Project TELL, 1990–1997). Even more uncertain is whether using the Internet at home has positive or negative effects on academic performance, such as school grades and standardized tests of achievement. Overall, based on evidence of positive effects of using computer-based technology on academic performance, the following hypothesis was formulated:

Hypothesis 1. Greater home Internet use will be associated with better academic performance in the months that follow than will less home Internet use.

Also of interest in the HomeNetToo project was the frequency and nature of low-income children's home Internet use.[1] Numerous surveys have attempted to measure the frequency of children's Internet use—the length of time children spend online. Estimates vary widely, depending on how Internet

---

[1]A variety of motivation, affective, and cognitive antecedents and consequences of home Internet use were assessed in surveys completed at pretrial, 1 month, 3 months, 9 months, and posttrial (i.e., 16 months).

use is measured (e.g., self-report, automatically recorded), the ages of children sampled, when data were collected (i.e., year of the study), and how Internet use is defined (e.g., length of time online, frequency of use). At one extreme are estimates that children spend approximately 1 hour a day online. At the other extreme are estimates that children spend only 3 hours a week using the Internet. These findings contrast with popular opinion that America's children are spending a great deal of time online.

Other research examined the nature of children's Internet use—what they actually do when they go online. Once again, findings vary, depending on the same factors that influence estimates of the frequency of Internet use as previously discussed (e.g., ages of children sampled). Some studies find that children's primary use of the Internet is for schoolwork, specifically searching the Web for information needed for school projects. The second most common use of the Internet is to communicate with peers using e-mail, instant messaging, and chat rooms. However, the extent of children's Internet use for communication is unclear, in part, because few studies have recorded actual use (versus self-reported use) and, in part, because studies are so few.

Gross, using the diary report of upper-middle-class adolescents, found that the extent to which the Internet was used for communication was dependent on the number of acquaintances, family, and friends online. Communication was the number one use of the Internet in Gross's study, a finding that has appeared consistently in more recent studies using upper-middle-class adolescents. Less clear is whether this finding was true in 2000 for poor adolescents and whether it was or still is true of younger children. Conceivably, younger children may use the Internet more for information gathering than they do for communication.

Based on the limited research available about the frequency and nature of children's Internet use, the following hypotheses were formulated:

Hypothesis 2. Children will spend between 3 hours weekly and 1 hour daily using the Internet at home.

Hypothesis 3. The Internet will more often be used for information than for communication.

Another interest of the HomeNetToo project is the relationship between children's sociodemographic characteristics and their Internet use. Previous research on these relationships has focused almost exclusively on adults. Findings for adults indicate race and age differences in Internet use.[2] African Americans use the Internet less than do European Americans; younger adults use the Internet more than do older adults. Gender differences in Internet use, though prevalent globally, have decreased dramatically in the United States. In 1995, approximately 95% of Internet users were men and boys. By 2002, one half

---

[2]Although socioeconomic status has consistently been related to Internet use, our sample was intentionally homogeneous with regard to this factor.

of all users were woman and girls. Researchers have attributed this gender shift to the proliferation of Internet communication tools that have attracted women and girls to it. In support of this view, studies indicate that women are more likely than men are to use the Internet for communication.

Whether sociodemographic characteristics influence children's Internet use is unclear from existing research. Race differences in children's Internet use have not been examined, especially when access to the Internet is not an issue (i.e., within socioeconomic groups). Among teens, some evidence suggests that African Americans use the Internet less than do European Americans. Some additional evidence asserts that older children use the Internet more than do younger children, especially for communicating with peers. Studies of gender and children's Internet use are sparse, and findings are mixed. One study found gender parity in all Internet activities except the number of Web sites visited: boys (ages 8 to 13) visited more Web sites than did girls the same age. Another study found that, although teenage girls used the Internet less than did teenage boys, they were more likely than boys were to use e-mail (56% of the girls versus 43% of the boys). Based on existing research, the following hypotheses were formulated:

> *Hypothesis 4*. African-American children and younger children will use the Internet less than will European American children and older children, respectively.

> *Hypothesis 5*. Girls will use the Internet's communication tools (e.g., e-mail) more than will boys; boys will use the Internet's information tools (e.g., Web pages) more than will girls.

We also explored relationships among age, Internet use, and academic performance. Two questions were of particular interest. First, does age influence the nature of Internet use such that younger participants use the Internet more for information whereas older participants (i.e., adolescents) use it more for communication? Second, are the effects of Internet use on academic performance, if any, similar across the age range considered in this research (i.e., age 10 to 18 years)? Alternatively, does any evidence exist of a developmentally "sensitive" period during which Internet use has the greatest impact on academic performance?

Methods

Participants and Procedures

Participants in the HomeNetToo project were 140 children residing in a midsize urban community in the Midwestern United States. Demographic characteristics of adult participants are described elsewhere. Participants were recruited at meetings held at the children's middle school and at the Black Child and Family Institute, Lansing, MI. Requirements for participation were that the child be eligible for the federally subsidized school lunch program, that the family have a working telephone line for the previous 6 months, and that the family never had home Internet access. Participants agreed to have their Internet use automatically and continuously recorded, to complete surveys at multiple points during the project, and to participate in home visits. In exchange, the households received home computers, Internet access, and in-home technical support during the Internet recording period (i.e., 16 months). At the end of the project, participants kept their computers and were assisted in locating inexpensive Internet service.

As indicated earlier, children were primarily African American (83%), primarily boys (58%), and primarily living in single-parent households (75%) in which the median annual income was $15,000 or less (49%). Average age was 13.8 years (SD = 1.95), median age was 13 years, and modal age was 12 years. Ages ranged from 10 to 18 years, although nearly three-quarters of participants (71%) were between 12 and 14 years of age.

Measures

Internet use. Four measures of Internet use that were automatically and continuously recorded for 16 months for each participant are considered in this report.[3] The measures are time online (minutes per day), number of sessions (logins per day), number of domains visited (per day), and number of e-mails sent (per day). Some examples of domains visited by participants are http://www.anygivensunday.net (entertainment), http://www.senate.gov (government information), and http://www.kcts.org (news and current events). Internet use measures were divided into five time periods, three corresponding to survey administration points plus half-year and 1-year points. The time periods were: Time 1 (1 to 3 months), Time 2 (4 to 6 months), Time 3 (7 to 9 months), Time 4 (10 to 12 months), and Time 5 (13 to 16 months). Latent linear growth curve analysis was used to evaluate time-related changes in Internet use and academic performance.

Academic performance. Participants' grade point averages (GPAs) and scores on the Michigan Educational Assessment Program (MEAP) tests of reading and mathematics achievement were obtained directly from the local school district (with parental permission). MEAP tests are standardized tests of known (high) reliability that Michigan educators use to inform decisions regarding educational policy and expenditures. GPAs were obtained for Fall 2000 (the semester before the project began), Spring 2001 (after 6 months of project participation), Fall 2001 (after 1 year of project participation), and Spring 2002 (the semester the project ended [April 2002]). MEAP scores were obtained for 2001 (for tests taken after 5 months of project participation) and 2002 (for tests taken 1 month after the 16-month project ended).

---

[3] A total of 20 measures of Internet use were recorded for each participant.

Results

Academic Performance and Internet Use

Descriptive statistics for measures of percentile ranks on the MEAP tests of reading and mathematics achievement are presented in Table 1. *Hypothesis 1* states that greater Internet use will be associated with better academic performance in the months that follow. Several steps were taken to evaluate this hypothesis.

First, race, age, and gender differences in Internet use and academic performance were examined to determine whether any of these sociodemographic characteristics needed to be controlled in the analyses to predict academic performance from each measure of Internet use (in separate analyses). Second, stepwise regression analyses were used to predict academic performance from Internet use during the preceding time period. Third, latent linear growth curve analysis was used to model relationships between Internet use and academic performance.

Consistent with *Hypothesis 4,* African-American children and younger children used the Internet less than did European American children and older children, respectively. However, no gender differences in Internet use were noted, contrary to *Hypothesis 5.* Additional analyses indicated that African-American children had lower GPAs and standardized test scores than did European American children ($ps < .05$) but that age and gender were unrelated to academic performance. Thus only race was controlled in the analyses to predict academic performance from Internet use.

Regression analyses were used to predict GPA from Internet use during the preceding time period. . . .

Results of these analyses indicated that, after controlling for race (step 1), Internet use did not predict GPA obtained after the first 6 months of the project. However, Internet use did predict GPA obtained after 1 year of home Internet access, and at the end of the 16-month trial. More Internet sessions were associated with higher GPAs.

Table 1

Percentile Ranks on Standardized Tests of Academic Achievement

	2001			2002		
	N	Mean	SD	N	Mean	SD
Reading Comprehension	95	31.85	28.03	75	35.03	29.72
Reading Total Score	95	31.93	28.55	74	33.65	28.34
Mathematics Comprehension	80	32.45	25.69	50	33.60	23.30
Mathematics Total Score	91	29.15	24.85	73	30.53	25.82

Note. Tests were the Michigan Educational Assessment Program (MEAP) tests.

To predict performance on standardized tests of academic achievement (i.e., MEAP percentile ranks) in Spring 2001, measures of Internet use during the first 6 months of the project were used. To predict MEAP performance in Spring 2002, measures of Internet use at Time 5 were used.

Results of these regression analyses indicated that Internet use during the first 6 months of the project predicted reading comprehension and total reading scores obtained at the end of that time period. More time online was associated with higher reading comprehension and total reading scores. Similarly, Internet use during the last semester of the project (Time 5) predicted reading comprehension and total reading scores obtained at the end of that semester. More Internet sessions were associated with higher reading scores. Mathematics scores could not be predicted from Internet use, regardless of which time period and which measure of Internet use was considered.

We also examined whether academic performance predicted Internet use rather than the reverse. Support for the latter would undermine a causal role of Internet use in changes in GPA. Children's GPAs for Fall 2000 were used to predict Internet use at Time 1, GPAs for Spring 2001 were used to predict Internet use at Time 3, and GPAs for Fall 2001 were used to predict Internet use at Time 5. In none of these analyses did GPA predict subsequent Internet use. . . .

Thus results of the regression analyses indicate that children who used the Internet more subsequently had higher GPAs and higher scores on standardized tests of reading achievement than did children who used the Internet less. The reverse was not true. Children who had higher GPAs and higher standardized test scores did not subsequently use the Internet more than did children who had lower GPAs and test scores. . . .

Frequency and Nature of Children's Internet Use

According to *Hypothesis 2*, children will spend between 3 hours per week and 7 hours per week (1 hour per day) using the Internet. Averaging across the 16-month trial, HomeNetToo children spent approximately 27 minutes per day online, at the low end of the broad range predicted by *Hypothesis 2*. Children participated in 0.6 sessions per day, suggesting that they did not logon daily, and visited approximately 10 domains per day. Children sent very few e-mail messages (less than one per week). Thus, consistent with *Hypothesis 3*, HomeNetToo children were more likely to use the Internet for information gathering than they did for communication.

Sociodemographic Characteristics and Internet Use

As previously indicated, consistent with *Hypothesis 4*, African-American children and younger children used the Internet less than did European-American children and older children, respectively. Contrary to *Hypothesis 5*, no gender differences were noted in Internet use. Thus girls were no more likely than boys were to use the Internet's communication tools; boys were no more likely than girls were to use the Internet's information tools.

Age effects on Internet for communication versus information purposes were evaluated in regression analyses to predict e-mail use at each time period from participants' age (controlling for race). No effects of age were noted in any of these analyses.

Discussion

Children who used the Internet more had higher GPAs after 1 year and higher scores on standardized tests of reading achievement after 6 months than did children who used it less. Moreover, the benefits of Internet use on academic performance continued throughout the project period. Children who used the Internet more during the last 4 months of the project had higher GPAs and standardized test scores in reading than did children who used it less. Internet use had no effect on standardized test scores of mathematics achievement.

Previous research has produced equivocal findings with respect to the effects of information technology use, specifically computer use, on cognitive outcomes. At best, some evidence suggests a positive relationship between computer game playing and visual spatial skills and between owning a home computer and school performance, although the causal nature of the latter relationship has yet to be established. Whether Internet use contributes to children's academic performance has, until now, never been systematically investigated. Thus, until now, no evidence exists that using the Internet actually improves academic performance, despite optimism surrounding the Internet as a tool to level the educational playing field.

Why did Internet use enhance HomeNetToo children's academic performance, specifically, their reading performance? One possibility is that children who spent more time online were also spending more time reading compared with their unconnected peers. HomeNetToo children logged on primarily to surf the Web. Web pages are heavily text based. Thus, whether searching for information about school-related projects or searching for information about personal interests and hobbies (e.g., rock stars, movies), children who were searching the Web more were reading more, and more time spent reading may account for improved performance on standardized tests of reading and for higher GPAs, which depend heavily on reading skills. The absence of Internet use effects on mathematics performance is consistent with this view. Web pages do not typically engage mathematics skills. New research is needed to establish the mediational role of reading in the relationship between Internet use and academic performance.

Another subject for future research is whether Internet use has a similar positive impact on the academic performance of all children. Children in the HomeNetToo project were performing well below average in school, as measured by both GPAs and standardized tests scores. Possibly, the academic performance benefits of Internet use are limited to children in this performance range. Children whose academic performance is average or above average may not only fail to show similar benefits of Internet use, but may also show decrements in academic performance with more time online. Whatever the results of future research may be, our findings suggest that the implications of the "digital divide" in Internet use may be more serious than was initially believed. One possibility may be that children most likely to benefit from home Internet access—poor children whose academic performance is below average—are the very children least likely to have home Internet access. Additional research is needed to determine whether Internet use has similar, different, or no effect for middle-class and upper-middle-class children and for low-income children with average or above-average performance in school.

Children in the HomeNetToo project used the Internet approximately 30 minutes a day, at the low end of the broad range suggested by previous research. Contrary to popular beliefs, media hype, and some previous research, HomeNetToo children made scant use of the Internet's communication tools. E-mail, instant messaging, and chat room conversations were infrequent activities at the start of the project, and the number of children participating in these activities dropped dramatically by the end of the project. Indeed, after 16 months of home Internet access, only 16% of the children were sending e-mail or participating in chat, and only 25% were instant messaging.

Why did HomeNetToo children make so little use of the Internet's communication tools? One explanation is so obvious as to be easily overlooked. HomeNetToo children were poor. In all likelihood, their friends and extended family members were poor. Poor people do not typically have home Internet access. Moreover, other evidence obtained from parents indicates that children were often forbidden from participating in chat or other activities that involved contact with strangers online. Thus, with no friends and family to e-mail, and with chat activities and conversations with strangers explicitly forbidden, the fact that HomeNetToo children made so little use of the Internet's communication tools is not at all surprising.

Another explanation for children's infrequent use of the Internet's communication tools lies in cultural influences on communication preferences. The majority of the children in the HomeNetToo project were African American (83%). African-American culture is historically an "oral culture." For example, recent evidence indicates that African Americans prefer face-to-face communication to a far greater extent than do European Americans. The impersonal nature of the Internet's typical communication tools (e.g., e-mail) may have discouraged African-American children from using them. Perhaps as communication on the Internet becomes more enriched with oral and visual cues, Internet use may become more appealing to members of other cultures.

Children's sociodemographic characteristics were related to their Internet use. As in previous research, older children used the Internet more than did younger children. No evidence has been found that age influences whether the Internet was used for information or communication purposes or that age influences the benefits of Internet use to academic performance. However, unequal distribution of participants across the age range (10 to 18 years) may have obscured the finding of significant age effects (71% of participants were between 12 and 14 years of age). Nevertheless, our evidence that home Internet use benefits the academic performance of children as young as age 10 suggests that early home access for all children may be critical to leveling the educational playing field.

Extending previous research with adolescents and adults, European-American children in our research used the Internet more than did African-American children. As with age, these findings have implications for educational policy aimed at leveling the educational playing field. Although home Internet use may account for only a small portion of the variance in academic performance, race differences in home Internet use may serve to exacerbate existing race differences in academic performance.

The persistence of race differences in Internet use when access to the technology is not an issue suggests that cultural factors may be contributing to the racial digital divide. Perhaps the culture of the Internet, created primarily by European-American men, is not a welcoming culture for African-American children. Perhaps the design of Web pages, again primarily by European-American men, lacks esthetic appeal for African-American children.

Systematic research is needed to examine whether cultural characteristics and technology design interact to influence technology use and enjoyment. For example, if a preference for oral communication is responsible for race differences in Internet use observed in the HomeNetToo project and other studies, then changes in interface design that accommodate this preference may help reduce or eliminate race difference in use. As Internet technology evolves to support more multimodal, multisensory experiences, it may be better able to accommodate cultural influences on communication and other preferences.

Mark Bauerlein

→ **NO**

The Dumbest Generation: How the Digital Age Stupefies Young Americans and Jeopardizes Our Future

When writer Alexandra Robbins returned to Walt Whitman High School in Bethesda, Maryland, ten years after graduating, she discovered an awful trend. The kids were miserable. She remembers her high school years as a grind of study and homework, but lots more, too, including leisure times that allowed for "well-roundedness." Not for Whitman students circa 2005. The teens in *The Overachievers,* Robbins's chronicle of a year spent among them, have only one thing on their minds, SUCCESS, and one thing in their hearts, ANXIETY. Trapped in a mad "culture of over-achieverism," they run a frantic race to earn an A in every class, score 2350 or higher on the SATs, take piano lessons, chalk up AP courses on their transcripts, stay in shape, please their parents, volunteer for outreach programs, and, most of all, win entrance to "HYP" (Harvard-Yale-Princeton).

As graduation approaches, their résumés lengthen and sparkle, but their spirits flag and sicken. One Whitman junior, labeled by Robbins "The Stealth Overachiever," receives a fantastic 2380 (out 2400) on a PSAT test, but instead of rejoicing, he worries that the company administering the practice run "made the diagnostics easier so students would think the class was working."

Audrey, "The Perfectionist," struggles for weeks to complete her toothpick bridge, which she and her partner expect will win them a spot in the Physics Olympics. She's one of the Young Democrats, too, and she does catering jobs. Her motivation stands out, and she thinks every other student competes with her personally, so whenever she receives a graded test or paper, "she [turns] it over without looking at it and then [puts] it away, resolving not to check the grade until she [gets] home."

"AP Frank" became a Whitman legend when as a junior he managed a "seven-AP course load that had him studying every afternoon, sleeping during class, and going lunchless." When he scored 1570 on the SAT, his domineering mother screamed in dismay, and her shock subsided only when he retook it and got the perfect 1600.

Julie, "The Superstar," has five AP classes and an internship three times a week at a museum, and she runs cross-country as well. Every evening after dinner she descends to the "homework cave" until bedtime and beyond. She got "only" 1410 on the SAT, though, and she wonders where it will land her next fall.

These kids have descended into a "competitive frenzy," Robbins mourns, and the high school that should open their minds and develop their characters has become a torture zone, a "hotbed for Machiavellian strategy." They bargain and bully and suck up for better grades. They pay tutors and coaches enormous sums to raise their scores a few points and help with the admissions process. Parents hover and query, and they schedule their children down to the minute. Grade inflation only makes it worse, an A- average now a stigma, not an accomplishment. They can't relax, they can't play. It's killing them, throwing sensitive and intelligent teenagers into pathologies of guilt and despair. The professional rat race of yore—men in gray flannel suits climbing the business ladder—has filtered down into the pre-college years, and Robbins's tormented subjects reveal the consequences.

The achievement chase displaces other life questions, and the kids can't seem to escape it. When David Brooks toured Princeton and interviewed students back in 2001, he heard of joyless days and nights with no room for newspapers or politics or dating, just "one skill-enhancing activity to the next." He calls them "Organization Kids" (after the old Organization Man figure of the fifties), students who "have to schedule appointment times for chatting." They've been programmed for success, and a preschool-to-college gauntlet of standardized tests, mounting homework, motivational messages, and extracurricular tasks has rewarded or punished them at every stage. The system tabulates learning incessantly and ranks students against one another, and the students soon divine its essence: only results matter. Education writer Alfie Kohn summarizes their logical adjustment:

> Consider a school that constantly emphasizes the importance of performance! results! achievement! success! A student who has absorbed that message may find it difficult to get swept away by the process of creating a poem or trying to build a working telescope. He may be so concerned about the results that he's not at all that engaged in the activity that produces those results.

Just get the grades, they tell themselves, ace the test, study, study, study. Assignments become exercises to complete, like doing the dishes, not knowledge to acquire for the rest of their lives. The inner life fades; only the external credits count. After-school hours used to mean sports and comic books and hanging out. Now, they spell homework. As the president of the American Association of School librarians told the *Washington Post,* "When kids are in school now, the stakes are so high, and they have so much homework that it's really hard to find time for pleasure reading" (Strauss). Homework itself has become a plague, as recent titles on the subject show: *The End of Homework: How Homework Disrupts Families, Overburdens Children, and Limits Learning* (Etta Kralovec and John Buell); *The Homework Myth: Why Our Kids Get Too Much of a Bad Thing* (Alfie Kohn); and

The Case Against Homework: How Homework Is Hurting Our Children and What We Can Do About It (Sara Bennett and Nancy Kalish).

Parents, teachers, media, and the kids themselves witness the dangers, but the system presses forward. "We believe that reform in homework practices is central to a politics of family and personal liberation," Kralovec and Buell announce, but the momentum is too strong. The overachievement culture, results-obsessed parents, outcomes-based norms . . . they continue to brutalize kids and land concerned observers such as Robbins on the *Today* show. Testing goes on, homework piles up, and competition for spaces in the Ivies was stiffer in 2007 than ever before. A 2006 survey by Pew Research, for instance, found that more than half the adults in the United States (56 percent) think that parents place too little pressure on students, and only 15 percent stated "Too much."

Why?

Because something is wrong with this picture, and most people realize it. They sense what the critics do not, a fundamental error in the vignettes of hyperstudious and overworked kids that we've just seen: they don't tell the truth, not the whole truth about youth in America. For, notwithstanding the poignant tale of suburban D.C. seniors sweating over a calculus quiz, or the image of college students scheduling their friends as if they were CEOs in the middle of a workday, or the lurid complaints about homework, the actual habits of most teenagers and young adults in most schools and colleges in this country display a wholly contrasting problem, but one no less disturbing.

Consider a measure of homework time, this one not taken from a dozen kids on their uneven way to the top, but from 81,499 students. In 110 schools in 26 states—the 2006 *High School Survey of Student Engagement.* When asked how many hours they spent each week "Reading/studying for class," almost all of them, fully 90 percent, came in at a ridiculously low five hours or less, 55 percent at one hour or less. Meanwhile, 31 percent admitted to watching television or playing video games at least six hours per week, 25 percent of them logging six hours minimum surfing and chatting online.

Or check a 2004 report by the University of Michigan Institute for Social Research entitled *Changing Times of American Youth: 1981–2003,* which surveyed more than 2,000 families with children age six to 17 in the home. In 2003, homework time for 15- to 17-year-olds hit only 24 minutes on weekend days, 50 minutes on weekdays. And weekday TV time? More than twice that: one hour, 55 minutes.

Or check a report by the U.S. Department of Education entitled *NAEP 2004 Trends in Academic Progress.* Among other things, the report gathered data on study and reading time for thousands of 17-year-olds in 2004. When asked how many hours they'd spent on homework the day before, the tallies were meager. Fully 26 percent said that they didn't have any homework to do, while 13 percent admitted that they didn't do any of the homework they were supposed to. A little more than one-quarter (28 percent) spent less than an hour, and another 22 percent devoted one to two hours, leaving only 11 percent to pass the two-hour mark.

Or the 2004–05 *State of Our Nation's Youth* report by the Horatio Alger Association, in which 60 percent of teenage students logged 6 hours of homework per week or less.

The better students don't improve with time, either. In the 2006 *National Survey of Student Engagement,* a college counterpart to the *High School Survey of Student Engagement,* seniors in college logged the astonishingly low commitments to "Preparing for class." Almost one out of five (18 percent) stood at one to five hours per week, and 26 percent at six to ten hours per week. College professors estimate that a successful semester requires about 25 hours of out-of-class study per week, but only 11 percent reached that mark. These young adults have graduated from high school, entered college, declared a major, and lasted seven semesters, but their in-class and out-of-class punch cards amount to fewer hours than a part-time job.

And as for the claim that leisure time is disappearing, the Bureau of Labor Statistics issues an annual *American Time Use Survey* that asks up to 21,000 people to record their activities during the day. The categories include work and school and child care, and also leisure hours. For 2005, 15- to 24-year-olds enjoyed a full five and a half hours of free time per day, more than two hours of which they passed in front of the TV.

The findings of these and many other large surveys refute the frantic and partial renditions of youth habits and achievement that all too often make headlines and fill talk shows. Savvier observers guard against the "we're overworking the kids" alarm, people such as Jay Mathews, education reporter at the *Washington Post,* who called Robbins's book a "spreading delusion," and Tom Loveless of the Brookings Institution, whose 2003 report on homework said of the "homework is destroying childhood" argument, "Almost everything in this story is wrong." One correspondent's encounter with a dozen elite students who hunt success can be vivid and touching, but it doesn't jibe with mountains of data that tell contrary stories. The surveys, studies, tests, and testimonials reveal the opposite, that the vast majority of high school and college kids are far less accomplished and engaged, and the classroom pressures much less cumbersome, than popular versions put forth. These depressing accounts issue from government agencies with no ax to grind, from business leaders who just want competent workers, and from foundations that sympathize with the young. While they lack the human drama, they impart more reliable assessments, providing a better baseline for understanding the realities of the young American mentality and forcing us to stop upgrading the adolescent condition beyond its due.

This book is an attempt to consolidate the best and broadest research into a different profile of the rising American mind. It doesn't cover behaviors and values, only the intellect of under-30-year-olds. Their political leanings don't matter, nor do their career ambitions. The manners, music, clothing, speech, sexuality, faith, diversity, depression, criminality, drug use, moral codes, and celebrities of the young spark many books, articles, research papers, and marketing strategies centered on Generation Y (or Generation DotNet, or the Millennials), but not this one. It sticks to one thing, the intellectual condition of young Americans, and describes it with empirical evidence, recording something hard to document but nonetheless insidious happening inside their heads. The information is scattered and underanalyzed, but once collected and compared, it charts a consistent and perilous momentum downward.

It sounds pessimistic, and many people sympathetic to youth pressures may class the chapters to follow as yet another curmudgeonly riff. Older people have complained forever about the derelictions of youth, and the "old fogy" tag puts them on the defensive. Perhaps, though, it is a healthy process in the life story of humanity for older generations to berate the younger, for young and old to relate in a vigorous competitive dialectic, with the energy and optimism of youth vying against the wisdom and realism of elders in a fruitful check of one another's worst tendencies. That's another issue, however. The conclusions here stem from a variety of completed and ongoing research projects, public and private organizations, and university professors and media centers, and they represent different cultural values and varying attitudes toward youth. It is remarkable, then, that they so often reach the same general conclusions. They disclose many trends and consequences in youth experience, but the intellectual one emerges again and again. It's an outcome not as easily noticed as a carload of teens inching down the boulevard rattling store windows with the boom-boom of a hip-hop beat, and the effect runs deeper than brand-name clothing and speech patterns. It touches the core of a young person's mind, the mental storehouse from which he draws when engaging the world. And what the sources reveal, one by one, is that a paradoxical and distressing situation is upon us.

The paradox may be put this way. We have entered the Information Age, traveled the Information Superhighway, spawned a Knowledge Economy, undergone the Digital Revolution, converted manual workers into knowledge workers, and promoted a Creative Class, and we anticipate a Conceptual Age to be. However overhyped those grand social metaphors, they signify a rising premium on knowledge and communications, and everyone from *Wired* magazine to Al Gore to Thomas Friedman to the Task Force on the Future of American Innovation echoes the change. When he announced the American Competitiveness Initiative in February 2006, President Bush directly linked the fate of the U.S. economy "to generating knowledge and tools upon which new technologies are developed." In a *Washington Post* op-ed, Bill Gates asserted, "But if we are to remain competitive, we need a workforce that consists of the world's brightest minds. . . . First, we must demand strong schools so that young Americans enter the workforce with the math, science and problem-solving skills they need to succeed in the knowledge economy."

And yet, while teens and young adults have absorbed digital tools into their daily lives like no other age group, while they have grown up with more knowledge and information readily at hand, taken more classes, built their own Web sites, enjoyed more libraries, bookstores, and museums in their towns and cities . . . in sum, while the world has provided them extraordinary chances to gain knowledge and improve their reading/writing skills, not to mention offering financial incentives to do so, young Americans today are no more learned or skillful than their predecessors, no more knowledgeable, fluent, up-to-date, or inquisitive, except in the materials of youth culture. They don't know any more history or civics, economics or science, literature or current events. They read less on their own, both books and newspapers, and you would have to canvass a lot of college English instructors and employers before you found one who said that they compose better paragraphs. In fact, their technology skills fall well short of the common claim, too, especially when they must apply them to research and workplace tasks.

The world delivers facts and events and art and ideas as never before, but the young American mind hasn't opened. Young Americans' vices have diminished, one must acknowledge, as teens and young adults harbor fewer stereotypes and social prejudices. Also, they regard their parents more highly than they did 25 years ago. They volunteer in strong numbers, and rates of risky behaviors are dropping. Overall conduct trends are moving upward, leading a hard-edged commentator such as Kay Hymowitz to announce in "It's Morning After in America" (2004) that "pragmatic Americans have seen the damage that their decades-long fling with the sexual revolution and the transvaluation of traditional values wrought. And now, without giving up the real gains, they are earnestly knitting up their unraveled culture. It is a moment of tremendous promise." At *TechCentralStation.com*, James Glassman agreed enough to proclaim, "Good News! The Kids Are Alright!" Youth watchers William Strauss and Neil Howe were confident enough to subtitle their book on young Americans *The Next Great Generation* (2000).

And why shouldn't they? Teenagers and young adults mingle in a society of abundance, intellectual as well as material. American youth in the twenty-first century have benefited from a shower of money and goods, a bath of liberties and pleasing self-images, vibrant civic debates, political blogs, old books and masterpieces available online, traveling exhibitions, the History Channel, news feeds . . . and on and on. Never have opportunities for education, learning, political action, and cultural activity been greater. All the ingredients for making an informed and intelligent citizen are in place.

But it hasn't happened. Yes, young Americans are energetic, ambitious, enterprising, and good, but their talents and interests and money thrust them not into books and ideas and history and civics, but into a whole other realm and other consciousness. A different social life and a different mental life have formed among them. Technology has bred it, but the result doesn't tally with the fulsome descriptions of digital empowerment, global awareness, and virtual communities. Instead of opening young American minds to the stores of civilization and science and politics, technology has contracted their horizon to themselves, to the social scene around them. Young people have never been so intensely mindful of and present to one another, so enabled in adolescent contact. Teen images and songs, hot gossip and games, and youth-to-youth communications no longer limited by time or space wrap them up in a generational cocoon reaching all the way into their bedrooms. The autonomy has a cost: the more they attend to themselves, the less they remember the past and envision a future. They have all the advantages of modernity and democracy, but when the gifts of life lead to social joys, not intellectual labor, the minds of the young plateau at age 18. This is happening all around us. The fonts of knowledge are everywhere, but the rising generation is camped in the desert, passing stories, pictures, tunes, and texts back and forth, living off the thrill of peer attention. Meanwhile, their intellects refuse the cultural and civic inheritance that has made us what we are up to now. . . .

A healthy society needs a pipeline of intellectuals, and not just the famous ones. An abiding atmosphere of reflection and forensic should touch many more than the gifted and politically disposed students. Democracy thrives on a knowledgeable citizenry, not just an elite team of thinkers and theorists, and the broader knowledge extends among the populace the more intellectuals it will train. Democracy needs a kind of minor-league system in youth circles to create both major-league sages 20 years later and a critical mass of less accomplished but still learned individuals. Noteworthy intellectual groupings such as liberal anti-communists in the forties, Beats in the fifties, and neo-conservatives in the seventies steered the United States in certain ideological directions. History will remember them. But in every decade labors an army of lesser intellectuals—teachers, journalists, curators, librarians, bookstore managers, diplomats, pundits, amateur historians and collectors, etc., whose work rises or falls on the liberal arts knowledge they bring to it. They don't electrify the world with breakthrough notions. They create neighborhood reading programs for kids, teach eighth-graders about abolition, run county historical societies, cover city council meetings, and host author events. Few of them achieve fame, but they sustain the base forensic that keeps intellectual activity alive across the institution that train generations to come.

Apart from ideological differences and variations in prestige, greater and lesser intellectuals on the Right and Left, speaking on C-SPAN or in rural classrooms, focusing on ancient wars or on the Depression, blogging on Romantic music or on postmodern novels . . . all may unite on one premise: knowledge of history, civics, art, and philosophy promotes personal welfare and national welfare. Intellectuals may quarrel over everything else, but at bottom they believe in the public and private value of liberal education. Columbia professor John Erskine called it "the moral obligation to be intelligent" 90 years ago, and every worker in the knowledge fields agreed. In the heat of intellectual battle, though, they rarely descend to that level of principle and concord. They usually concentrate friends and enemies within the intellectual class, where that conviction goes without saying, and in formulating rejoinders for the marketplace of ideas, they forget that the marketplace itself must be sustained by something else against the forces of anti-intellectualism and anti-knowledge. Intellectuals can and should debate the best and worst books and ideas and personages, and they will scramble to affect policies in formation, but what upholds the entire activity resides beyond their circles. It grows on top of public sentiment, a widespread conviction that knowledge is as fundamental as individual freedoms. For intellectual discourse, high art, historical awareness, and liberal arts curricula to flourish, support must come from outside intellectual clusters. Laypersons, especially the young ones, must get the message: if you ignore the traditions that ground and ennoble our society, you are an incomplete person, and a negligent citizen.

This knowledge principle forms part of the democratic faith, and it survives only as long as a fair portion of the American people embraces it, not just intellectuals and experts. The production of spirited citizens requires more than meditations by academics and strategies by activists, and it transpires not only in classrooms and among advocacy groups. Learning and disputation, books and ideas, must infiltrate leisure time, too, and they should spread well beyond the cerebral cliques. This is why leisure trends among the general population are so important. They log the status of the knowledge principle, and when they focus on under-30-year-olds, they not only reveal today's fashions among the kids but also tomorrow's prospects for civic well-being.

As of 2008, the intellectual future of the United States looks dim. Not the economic future, or the technological, medical, or media future, but the future of civic understanding and liberal education. The social pressures and leisure preferences of young Americans, for all their silliness and brevity, help set the heading of the American mind, and the direction is downward. The seventies joke about college students after late-sixties militance had waned still holds.

"What do you think of student ignorance and apathy?" the interviewer asks the sophomore.
"I dunno and I don' care"—

It isn't funny anymore. The Dumbest Generation cares little for history books, civic principles, foreign affairs, comparative religions, and serious media and art, and it knows less. Careening through their formative years, they don't catch the knowledge bug, and *tradition* might as well be a foreign word. Other things monopolize their attention—the allure of screens, peer absorption, career goals. They are latter-day Rip Van Winkles, sleeping through the movements of culture and events of history, preferring the company of peers to great books and powerful ideas and momentous happenings. From their ranks will emerge few minds knowledgeable and interested enough to study, explain, and dispute the place and meaning of our nation. Adolescence is always going to be more or less anti-intellectual, of course, and learning has ever struggled against immaturity, but the battle has never proven so uphill. Youth culture and youth society, fabulously autonomized by digital technology, swamp the intellectual pockets holding on against waves of pop culture and teen mores, and the Boomer mentors have lowered the bulwarks to surmountable heights. Among the Millennials, intellectual life can't compete with social life, and if social life has no intellectual content, traditions wither and die. Books can't hold their own with screen images, and without help, high art always loses to low amusement.

The ramifications for the United States are grave. We need a steady stream of rising men and women to replenish the institution, to become strong military leaders and wise political leaders, dedicated journalists and demanding teachers, judges and muckraker scholars and critics and artists. We have the best schools to train them, but social and private environments have eroded. Some of the kids study hard for class, but what else do they learn when they're young? How do they spend the free hours of adolescence? They don't talk with their friends about books, and they don't read them when they're alone. Teachers try to impart knowledge, but students today remember only that which suits their careers or advantages their social lives. For the preparation of powerful officials, wise intellectuals, and responsible citizens, formal schooling and workplace training are not enough. Social life and leisure time play essential roles in the maturing process, and if the knowledge principle disappears, if books, artworks, historical facts, and civic debates—in a word, an intellectual forensic—vacate the scene, then the knowledge young people acquire later on never penetrates to their hearts. The forensic retreats into ever smaller cells, where nerds and bookworms nurture their loves cut off from the world.

Democracy doesn't prosper that way. If tradition survives only in the classroom, limping along in watered-down lessons, if knowledge doesn't animate the young when they're with each other and by themselves, it won't inform their thought and behavior when they're old. The latest social and leisure dispositions of the young are killing the culture, and when they turn 40 years old and realize what they failed to learn in their younger days, it will be too late.

The research compiled in the previous chapters piles gloomy fact on gloomy fact, and it's time to take it seriously. Fewer books are checked out of public libraries and more videos. More kids go to the mall and fewer to the museum. Lunchroom conversations never drift into ideology, but Web photos pass nonstop from handheld to handheld. If parents and teachers and reporters don't see it now, they're blind.

If they don't respond, they're unconscionable. It's time for over-30-year-olds of all kinds to speak out, not just social conservatives who fret over Internet pornography, or political Leftists who want to rouse the youth vote, or traditionalist educators who demand higher standards in the curriculum. Adults everywhere need to align against youth ignorance and apathy, and not fear the "old fogy" tag and recoil from the smirks of the young. The moral poles need to reverse, with the young no longer setting the pace for right conduct and cool thinking. Let's tell the truth. The Dumbest Generation will cease being dumb only when it regards adolescence as an inferior realm of petty strivings and adulthood as a realm of civic, historical, and cultural awareness that puts them in touch with the perennial ideas and struggles. The youth of America occupy a point in history like every other generation did and will, and their time will end. But the effects of their habits will outlast them, and if things do not change they will be remembered as the fortunate ones who were unworthy of the privileges they inherited. They may even be recalled as the generation that lost that great American heritage, forever.

POSTSCRIPT

Are People Better Informed in the Information Society?

It would be wonderful if we could predict the future with certainty, but unfortunately, even predictions are subject to change. It is interesting to note that virtually every new form of technology, especially media, has often been greeted with a mixed sense of optimism and pessimism. New technologies challenge us to think of new practices, new values, and new structures. Sometimes the combination of those elements suggest comfort, ease, and security—other times the threat to what we already know can be a disconcerting feeling of change, without control. We might be able to look back at the evolution of media and think that the variety of content available is great, but it would also be possible to see how our media forms have changed in negative ways too. Your parents were of the generation who knew free television and radio—when media in the airwaves was delivered to the home without a hefty cable bill. Today, unless you live in a part of the country where broadcast signals can still be received in your home, you may not have any choice in your delivery service or the charges affixed by your program provider.

One of the pleasures of science fiction is that there is usually enough evidence in any portrayal of the future that elements of the story appear to be plausible. There are many futuristic novels like *1984* and *Brave New World* which, in their day, sent chills down the spines of readers. Today's equivalent of these novels would be a film like *The Matrix*.

To read more accounts of how media and technology can and do affect the quality of our lives by facilitating changes within our major institutions—such as education, government, and through popular culture, we suggest a number of readings from a variety of viewpoints. As mentioned previously, Neil Postman's classic *Amusing Ourselves to Death* looks at the impact of television on our lives. His thesis is that even news has to be packaged to be entertaining, and the desire to be entertained stretches to other institutions as well, like schools and within our political arena. Postman's later books, *Technopoly* (Vintage, 1992) and *Building a Bridge to the 18th Century* (Alfred A. Knopf, 1999), also deal with the subtle changes we often experience, but never critically question, as we venerate science and technology and exclude very human traits such as morality and common sense.

Former Secretary of Labor Robert Reich has written a very enjoyable, readable book focusing on social change in America, with some reference to the role of media and technology. See Reich, *The Future of Success* (Alfred A. Knopf, 2001). And for more specific references to media, see John Naughton's *A Brief History of the Future: From Radio Days to Internet Years in a Lifetime* (Overlook Press, 1999).

Contributors to This Volume

EDITORS

ALISON ALEXANDER is professor of telecommunications and senior associate dean at the Grady College of Journalism and Mass Communication at the University of Georgia. She is the past editor of the *Journal of Broadcasting & Electronic Media,* and past president of the Associate for Communication Administration and the Eastern Communication Association. She received her Ph.D. in communication from Ohio State University. She is widely published in the area of media and family, audience research, and media economics.

JARICE HANSON is professor of communication at the University of Massachusetts, Amherst, and the current Verizon Chair in Telecommunications at the School of Communications and Theater, Temple University. She was the founding dean of the School of Communications at Quinnipiac University from 2001 to 2003. She received a B.A. in speech and performing arts and a B.A. in English at Northeastern Illinois University in 1976, and she received an M.A. and a Ph.D. from Northwestern University in Radio-TV-Film in 1977 and 1979, respectively. She is author or editor of 18 books and numerous articles. The most recent books include *24/7: How Cell Phones and the Internet Change the Way We Live, Work and Play* (Praeger, 2007) and *Constructing America's War Culture: Iraq, Media, and Images at Home* (co-edited with Thomas Conroy) (Lexington Books, 2007). She lives in Massachusetts with three furry creatures: Dewey, Xena, and Frank.

AUTHORS

CHRIS ANDERSON is an editor at *Wired* magazine. His most recent book is *Free: The Future of a Radical Price* (Hyperion Books, 2009).

CRAIG A. ANDERSON is a professor in the department of psychology, University of Iowa. He has written extensively on human behavior and violence.

MARK BAUERLEIN is a professor of English at Emory University. He recently served as the director, Office of Research and Analysis, at the National Endowment for the Arts. Apart from his scholarly work, he publishes in popular periodicals such as *The Wall Street Journal, The Weekly Standard,* and *The Washington Post.* His latest book, *The Dumbest Generation: How the Digital Age Stupefies Young Americans and Jeopardizes Our Future,* was published in May 2008.

GAL BECKERMAN is a reporter for *Columbia Journalism Review.* He was the New York bureau chief of the *Jerusalem Post* and has been researching and writing a history of the movement to free the Jews from the Soviet Union during the Cold War.

LISA FAGER BEDIAKO is president and cofounder of an organization called Industry Ears, a nonprofit independent organization that focuses on the impact of the media on communities of color.

ERIC BOEHLERT is a journalist who most often writes about media, politics, and pop culture. His book, *Lapdogs: How the Press Rolled Over for Bush* (Free Press, 2006), addresses how the press has been used by politicians.

ROB BOSTON is a journalist who writes about issues of the separation of church and state. His most recent book is *Why the Religious Right Is Wrong about Separation of Church and State* (Prometheus Books, 2003).

JOHN E. CALFEE is a resident scholar at the American Enterprise Institute in Washington, D.C. He is a former Federal Trade Commission economist, and he is the author of *Fear of Persuasion: A New Perspective on Advertising and Regulation* (Agora, 1997).

JAMES W. CAREY was the CBS Professor of International Journalism at Columbia University. He also served on the advisory board at the Poynter Institute for Media Studies.

KAREN E. DILL is an associate professor of psychology in the School of Social and Behavioral Sciences at Lenoir-Rhyne University in North Carolina.

SHARI L. DWORKIN is an associate professor of behavioral medicine in the Department of Psychiatry at the New York State Psychiatric Institute and Columbia University. Her research centers on how gender inequalities and privileges influence risk for HIV, and on the impact of media on body image.

PAUL FARHI is a staff writer for *The Washington Post* who has written extensively on media industries and products.

THE FIRST AMENDMENT CENTER is a project of Vanderbuilt University in Nashville, Tennessee, and Arlington, Virginia. The organization sponsors a Web site on which issues of the First Amendment are featured, including commentary and discussion items. The site can be located at http://www .firstamendmentcenter.org/.

JULIA R. FOX is an associate professor of telecommunications at Indiana University–Bloomington. Her research interests include television news coverage and how people process and remember television news messages.

HENRY A. GIROUX holds the Global TV Network Chair in English and Cultural Studies at McMaster University in Canada. A prolific author, his most recent book is *Youth in a Suspect Society: Beyond the Politics of Disposability* (Palgrave Macmillan, 2009).

DINYAR GODREJ is an editor with the *New Internationalist*. Recent books include the *No Nonsense Guide to Climate Change* (2006) and *Peace (Books to Go)* (2005), both published by New Internationalist Publications.

M. KATHERINE GRIMES teaches English at Ferrum College in Virginia and specializes in research and teaching concerning psychology and young people.

PAUL M. HIRSCH is a professor at the Kellogg School of Management at Northwestern University. He is the author of many articles on management practices and mass media organizations. His research interests include organization theory and media industries.

JOHN HOCKENBERRY is a three-time Peabody Award winner, four-time Emmy award winner, and *Dateline NBC* correspondent; his weekly public radio commentaries have been heard on *The Infinite Mind* since its first broadcast in March 1998. John has had broad experience as a journalist and commentator for more than two decades.

BARRY A. HOLLANDER is an associate professor of journalism at the University of Georgia. His research interests include the political effects of new media and the interaction of religious and political beliefs.

LINDA A. JACKSON is a professor in the Department of Psychology at Michigan State University. She has research interest in the cultural, social, and psychological factors influencing the use and consequences of information technologies.

HENRY JENKINS is the director of the comparative media studies program at MIT. He has co-authored several books, including *Democracy and the New Media* (Cambridge, MIT Press 2003).

PENNY LEISRING is an associate professor at Quinnipiac University in Hamden, Connecticut. Her work in psychology deals primarily with the prevention and reduction of aggressive behavior in adults and children.

AMANDA LENHART directs the Pew Internet & American Life Project's research on teens, children, and families.

MICHAEL P. LEVINE is the Samuel B. Cummings Jr. Professor of Psychology at Kenyon College, where he teaches and conducts research on abnormal psychology, eating disorders, body image, and the development of personality.

JEFFREY J. MACIEJEWSKI is an associate professor of advertising in the journalism and mass communication program at Creighton University. He writes about the implications of natural law for mass communication.

SARAH K. MURNEN is professor and chair of the Department of Psychology at Kenyon College. Her research focuses on gender-related issues from a feminist, sociocultural background.

HORACE NEWCOMB is director of the Peabody Awards and Lambdin Kay Professor at the Grady College of the University of Georgia. He is the editor of *Museum of Broadcast Communications Encyclopedia of Television* (Fitzroy Dearborn, 1997).

DAVID T. OZAR is a professor of philosophy and past director of the Center for Ethics and Social Justice at Loyola University of Chicago. His areas of research include health care ethics, professional ethics, normative ethics, social/political philosophy, and philosophy of law.

RHODA RABKIN is an adjunct scholar at the Enterprise Institute for Public Policy and Research.

MATTHEW ROBINSON is managing editor of *Human Events* and the author of *Mobocracy: How the Media's Obsession with Polling Twists the News, Alters Elections and Undermines Democracy.*

WADE ROUSH lives in San Francisco and is a senior editor of *Technology Review.*

CHUCK SALTER is a senior writer for the magazine *Fast Company.* The organization also sponsors an online resource, FastCompany.com.

JANIS SANCHEZ-HUCKLES is a professor at Old Dominion University and the Virginia Consortium Program in Clinical Psychology. Her research involves the power of media images and how they distort social images of the lives of people.

HERBERT I. SCHILLER was Professor Emeritus of Communication at the University of California, San Diego upon his death in 2000. He was the author of a dozen books on the media, information, and culture and a foremost proponent of the critical/cultural perspective in the United States.

MICHAEL SCHUDSON is the author of six books and editor of two others concerning the history and sociology of the American news media, advertising, popular culture, Watergate, and cultural memory.

BRIAN SCOGGINS is a Gonzaga University criminal justice graduate.

JACK G. SHAHEEN is a committed internationalist and a devoted humanist who focuses on the damage that stereotypes do to racial and ethnic images. He is a professor emeritus at Southern Illinois University and former consultant on Middle East affairs for CBS.

CLAY SHIRKY divides his time between consulting, teaching, and writing on the social and economic effects of Internet technologies. His consulting practice is focused on the rise of decentralized technologies such as peer-to-peer, Web services, and wireless networks. Mr. Shirky has written extensively about the Internet since 1996. Over the years, he has had regular columns in *Business 2.0* and *FEED;* and his writings have appeared in *The New York Times, The Wall Street Journal,* and the *Harvard Business Review.*

LEE SIEGEL is a writer who received the 2002 National Magazine Award for Reviews and Criticism. He writes essays on culture and criticism.

DON TAPSCOTT is chief executive of New Paradigm, a think tank and strategy consulting company. He also teaches at the Rotman School of Management at the University of Toronto.

SIVA VAIDHYANATHAN is an associate professor of culture and communication at New York University. He is the author of *Copyrights and Copywrongs: The Rise of Intellectual Property and How It Threatens Creativity* (NYU Press, 2001).

FAYE LINDA WACHS is currently on the faculty of behavioral sciences at California Polytechnic–Pomona. Her research focuses on women and men's body images, sport, and issues of masculinity.

GEORGIE ANN WEATHERBY is an assistant professor of sociology and criminal justice at Gonzaga University.

LANA A. WHITED is a professor of English at Ferrum College in Virginia. She is the editor of *The Ivory Tower and Harry Potter: Perspectives on a Literary Phenomenon* (University of Missouri Press, 2002).

ANTHONY D. WILLIAMS is research director at a think tank called New Paradigm, where he specializes in areas of innovation and intellectual property. He teaches at the London School of Economics.